Cyber War versus Cyber Realities

# CYBER WAR VERSUS CYBER REALITIES

## Cyber Conflict in the International System

Brandon Valeriano

*and*

Ryan C. Maness

# OXFORD
UNIVERSITY PRESS

Oxford University Press is a department of the University of
Oxford. It furthers the University's objective of excellence in research,
scholarship, and education by publishing worldwide.

Oxford    New York
Auckland    Cape Town    Dar es Salaam    Hong Kong    Karachi
Kuala Lumpur    Madrid    Melbourne    Mexico City    Nairobi
New Delhi    Shanghai    Taipei    Toronto

With offices in
Argentina    Austria    Brazil    Chile    Czech Republic    France    Greece
Guatemala    Hungary    Italy    Japan    Poland    Portugal    Singapore
South Korea    Switzerland    Thailand    Turkey    Ukraine    Vietnam

Oxford is a registered trademark of Oxford University Press
in the UK and certain other countries.

Published in the United States of America by
Oxford University Press
198 Madison Avenue, New York, NY 10016

Library of Congress Cataloging-in-Publication Data
Valeriano, Brandon.
Cyber war versus cyber realities : cyber conflict in the international system /
Brandon Valeriano, Ryan C. Maness.
pages cm
ISBN 978-0-19-020479-2 (hardback)
1. Cyberspace operations (Military science)    2. Cyberterrorism.
3. Technology and international relations.    4. Internet and international
relatins.    I. Maness, Ryan C.    II. Title.
U163.V36 2015
355.4—dc23
2014039240

9  8  7  6  5  4  3  2  1
Printed in the United States of America
on acid-free paper

*Dedicated to John Vasquez and J. David Singer*

# CONTENTS

# PREFACE

## PROJECT BEGINNINGS

We started working in the cyber security field in 2010 when Derek Reveron invited one of us to a cyber security conference at the Naval War College. There were a lot of great and important minds in the room that day, but we were struck at how little theory, evidence, and logic were applied to the question of cyber conflict.

Lots of statements were made with no facts to back them up; the prevailing assumption was that cyber was the new threat, it was proliferating, and it would change the course of interstate relations. We were skeptical, but, more important, we wanted evidence and theory, and we wanted to move past the conjecture found on the proliferating news talk shows. The time since our first encounter with cyber security has only reinforced our view that rigorous analysis is needed regarding the topic.

To that end, this is a book about evidence and the nature of international threats. We have been influenced greatly by J. David Singer and John Vasquez. Singer created the Correlates of War project at the University of Michigan, which sought to empirically categorize and collect data on the origins of war. Vasquez used this data later to produce inductive theories regarding the nature of war in the system. Their goals were to explain what we know about the world, but also to do so in a scientific fashion.

We need evidence and rigorous data to guard against the tendency many have to make grand statements with little connection to actual processes. Singer taught us about the nature of data collection, the need for building a knowledge base through comprehensive data collection. Vasquez taught us about the nature of theory, induction, and the construction of threats in the international system. More often than not, threats and displays of power politics engender a response opposite to what is intended (often concession). These moves generally provoke counter-threats, escalation, and outright conflict. It is for this reason that the era of cyber security is dangerous; it needs rigorous analysis to counter the prolif-erating cyber hype motifs. We need to understand how cyber threats are con-structed, who makes them, and the reactions to them in order to understand how to best respond to the developing arena of cyber military tactics.

Marc Maron, on his popular WTF Podcast, made an offhand remark that he does not prepare for his comedy performances. He feels that preparing is for cowards, that you need to be ready and willing to fail in your work since there is a fine line between a unique achievement and total failure. Skirting this line led him to ruin many times in his career, but it has also led him to the transcendent place he is at now. He reached the heights of his field by putting it all on the line and risking total devastation in his Podcast, a new and untested medium in 2009. Now he has one of the most popular podcasts, a TV show, and is more popular than ever on the comedy circuit.

Maron's path to success reminds us that we need to think a bit about this frame in our own work. Are we really willing to fail? Are we cowards? Do we skirt that fine line between success and ruin?

We need to push for research that might encompass what we call political science without a net. This is how we characterize this research on cyber security. One massive global destructive cyber incident could invalidate our theory of restraint and regionalism in cyberspace. Of course, one case does not disprove a theory, but it can terminally harm it. The easy path would have been to articulate a frame of the future where cyber conflict dominates the system. We could write about the notion that we will see continued and constant netwar that will change how nations interact, rise and fall, and conduct strategy. These sorts of claims are easy to make, clouded by caveats and qualifications, and the frame can successfully be employed to describe one view of the cyber world or can even be applied to research about drones, airpower, and other frames of future war.

Frames that suggest massive changes to the system are largely inaccurate. We have failed to see cyberwar really proliferate in the decades since the ubiquity of digital communications. Russia has failed to use the tactic in Ukraine and Crimea, even after using it liberally, if in a restrained manner, during the Georgia invasion of 2008 and in Estonia in 2007. The United States rejected the widespread use of cyber tactics in Iraq (2003), Afghanistan (2002), and Libya (2011). Cyber terrorists and non-state actors use the tactic, but with little actual impact. Cyber technologies have changed our daily lives, but to argue that they have and will change our foreign policy and military strategy is too easy a claim and very difficult to prove wrong when articulated with unlimited time horizons. Taking a new weapon and arguing that it will change the world is a simple case to make; taking a new weapon and suggesting it is just more of the same, like ancient espionage practices, is difficult. In fact, it is important to take this position because arguing for the coming cyber threat risks provoking escalation and conflict. The frame becomes a self-fulfilling prophecy because the idea is so simple; people believe it to be true because it seems logical. Who does not feel vulnerable when they lose Internet access and cell phone service?

It sometimes feels as if our field of international relations is becoming stagnant. Not because we are not asking big questions or are not doing policy-relevant research, but often because we do not take big risks. Defying conventional wisdom is wonderful, even liberating. We need to insert more fear in our work; otherwise, as Maron says, we are cowards.

In this book, we make strong predictions about the future, using evidence from the recent past to outline the course of cyber conflict between states. We argue here that there is restraint in cyberspace, that cyber interactions are mainly regional on the international level, and that cyber terrorism is a limited tactic that will not change the course of international interactions. We make these predictions based on a large dataset of cyber interactions, and we use this data to test our theories. Finally, we outline the course of our possible cyber future. This is a future where offensive cyber actions are taboo and, hopefully, international institutions rise up to limit the dangers this domain might pose.

## CYBER SECURITY RESEARCH

This is a crucial time for cyber security research, as the field has only just begun. We stake out a position in this debate that is counter to many that would seek to hype the cyber threat. The future is what states will make of it, but we hope that our perspective might add some much needed rationality to the field of cyber security.

We are under no illusions that we have described the entire past and future of cyber interactions. The future is in the process of being built. We can only make statements based on the evidence we have. Things are changing every day in the cyber security field; our statements here describe what we observe now. This entire effort is an early attempt to outline a path toward researching contemporary security developments with scientific standards of evidence and theory construction. As always, this project reflects our understanding of the cyber security landscape and conforms to our own intellectual biases.

We encourage others to use this work as a starting point to elaborate more on the cyber security field and how it is connected to international relations processes. There is much work to be done, and we hope others will help us move toward a greater understanding of the cyber security threat landscape.

Brandon Valeriano
April 20, 2014
In Glasgow coffee shops, on planes, and trains
Ryan C. Maness
April 20, 2014
At my desk at home, in my office, and in Chicago coffee shops

# ACKNOWLEDGMENTS

There are many people to thank. This book was a long time coming and could not have been completed without the help of many interested parties and friends.

The University of Glasgow was instrumental in providing an institutional home and a future for Valeriano. The entirety of this book was written with the generous support the institution gives for its research faculty. The added normative context of this book was also inspired by the discussions and atmosphere of the UK, in particular with Cian O'Driscoll, Laura Sjoberg, Eric Heinze, and Caron Gentry. Within the University, Chris Carmen, Eamonn Butler, Myrto Tsakatika, and other members of the staff who attended various presentations provided key comments and encouragement that helped develop this work.

Derek Reveron's invitation to the Naval War College to attend a cyberwar conference in 2010 was important in starting this research. An early version of our ideas appeared in a book chapter in his edited volume, *Cyberspace and National Security*. Without him, and the comments of those who attended those important Naval War College talks, none of this work would have been possible.

Various institutions and organizations were important in providing a venue for discussion as this work progressed. The Air War College, Naval War College, University of Denver, Massachusetts Institute of Technology, University at Albany, Whiter College, Menlo Park College, and the University of Southern California all hosted invited talks. Other institutions such as the US Department of Defense, the US State Department, the Intelligence Community, Estonia's Lennart Meri Conference, the Up with Chris Hayes show on MSNBC, Scotland Herald, NBC Chicago, and the British Broadcasting Company all provided opportunities to share our ideas. Foreign Affairs ran an early version of our data, and the blogging collective the Duck of Minerva hosted many of our ideas as they were in development, as did the Atlantic Council.

There are many cyber scholars who were important for the development of this work. Nazli Choucri, Joseph Nye, Erik Gartzke, Jon Lindsay, Thomas Rid, Derek Reveron, Heather Roff, Emmet Touhy, Jason Healey, Jacob Mauslein, James Fielder, all provided comments. Other International Relations and Political Science scholars such as Doug Gibler, Stephen Saideman, Victor Asal, Patrick James, Dennis Foster, Melissa Michelson, Konstantios Travlos, Dan

Nexon, Fred Bergerson, Cullen Hendrix, and Samuel Whitt provided important comments and feedback.

Our own students have been important for comments and intellectual development: Rob Dewar, Sam Bassett (who was with us early, coding the dataset), Lauren Pascu, Stephen Powell, Signe Norberg, and Hugh Vondracek provided feedback, coding assistance, and editing help.

The Carnegie Trust for Universities of Scotland—Small Research Grant was helpful in completing this project. The Journal of Peace Research (2014) published an early version of Chapter 4 as "The Dynamics of Cyber Conflict between Rival Antagonists, 2001–2011," Journal of Peace Research 51 (3): 347–360.

And of course, there are our friends whom would we would like to thank. Valeriano thanks Jim Frommeyer, Victor Marin, Walther Pappa Catavi, Phillip Habel, and Richard Johnson. He would also like to thank his family. Maness would like to thank his parents, who are looking down on him with pride.

In particular, we would like to thank John Vasquez, whose style and ideas permeate everything we do.

All data can be found at brandonvaleriano.com, drryanmaness.wix.com/irprof, our book webpage www.cyberconflict.com.com.

An updated version of Chapter 5 is available in a forthcoming 2015 article in Armed Forces and Society titled 'The Impact of Cyber Conflict on International Interactions'.

# Cyber War versus Cyber Realities

# CHAPTER 1

# The Contours of the Cyber Conflict World

## INTRODUCTION

This is a book about cyber conflict and the process of international cyber interactions, a critical question given the climate surrounding the nature of the shifting international security landscape. We are guided by the division between what we call *cyber hype* and threat inflation, on the one hand, and the empirical realities of cyber interactions as they actually occur in the international system, on the other. These divisions are important because they represent the two dominating perspectives in the cyber security debate. The cyber hype perspective would suggest that we are seeing a revolution in military affairs with the advent of new military technologies. The moderate perspective is guided by careful consideration of what the real dangers are, as well as the costs of the overreaction. These two sides outline the perspectives of many in the emerging cyber security field.

Our concern is that fear dominates the international system. The contention is that harm is a constant factor in international life (Machiavelli 2003; Hobbes 2009); everything is a danger to all, and all are a danger to most. It is through this prism that the international affairs community approaches each technological development and each step forward, and it does so with trepidation and weariness. Because of the hype surrounding the development of cyber weaponry, the step toward what might be called cyber international interactions is no different. With the advent of the digital age of cyber communications, this process of fear construction continues to shape dialogues in international relations as cyberspace becomes a new area of contestation in international interactions. Old paradigms focused on power politics, displays of force, and deterrence are applied to emergent tactics and technologies with little consideration of how the new tactic might result in different means and ends. We argue that these constructed reactions to threats have little purchase when examined through the prism of evidence or when judged compared to the normative implications of action. There is an advantage to bringing empirical analysis and careful theory to the cyber security debate.

The emerging fear that we seek to counter is the perspective that cyber weapons will come to dominate the system and will change how states and individuals interact.

In this book, we uncover how cyber conflict among international actors actually works by presenting an empirical account of these types of interactions since the turn of the century. We then use this data to uncover the foreign policy implications of this new domain of conflict and also examine how this type of conflict is being governed through international norms and regimes. Throughout, we develop theories of cyber conflict that seek to evaluate the nature of cyber fears and myths that dominate the debate on this ever important topic. We do not minimize the cyber security issue, but instead seek to analyze its dynamics in light of evidence, and we suggest a policy course in light of these findings.

## CYBERSPACE AND CONFLICT

Currently, the cyberspace arena is the main area of international conflict where we see the development of a fear-based process of threat construction becoming dominant. The fear associated with terrorism after September 11, 2001, has dissipated, and in many ways has been replaced with the fear of cyber conflict, cyber power, and even cyber war.[1] With the emergence of an Internet society and rising interconnectedness in an ever more globalized world, many argue that we must also fear the vulnerability that these connections bring about. Advances and new connections such as drones, satellites, and cyber operational controls can create conditions that interact to produce weaknesses in the security dynamics that are critical to state survival. Dipert (2010: 402) makes the analogy that surfing in cyberspace is like swimming in a dirty pool. The developments associated with Internet life also come with dangers that are frightening to many.

In order to provide an alternative to the fear-based discourse, we present empirical evidence about the dynamics of cyber conflict. Often realities will impose a cost on exaggerations and hyperbole. We view this process through the construction of cyber threats. The contention is that the cyber world is dangerous, and a domain where traditional security considerations will continue to play out. A recent Pew Survey indicates that 70 percent of Americans see cyber incidents from other countries as a major security threat to the United States, with this threat being second only to that from Islamic extremist groups.[2]

This fear is further deepened by hyperbolic statements from the American elite. US President Barack Obama has declared that the "cyber threat is one of the most serious economic and national security challenges we face as a nation."[3] Former US Defense Secretary Leon Panetta has gone further, stating, "So, yes, we are living in that world. I believe that it is very possible the next Pearl Harbor could be a cyber attack . . . [that] would have one hell of an impact on the United States of America. That is something we have to worry about and protect against."[4]

United States elites are not alone in constructing the cyber threat. Russian President Vladimir Putin, in response to the creation of a new battalion of cyber troops to defend Russian cyberspace, noted, "We need to be prepared to effectively combat threats in cyberspace to increase the level of protection in the appropriate infrastructure, particularly the information systems of strategic and critically important facilities."[5] The social construction of the cyber threat is therefore real; the aim of this book is to find out if these elite and public constructions are backed with facts and evidence.

First, we should define some of our terms to prepare for further engagement of our topic. This book is focused on international cyber interactions. The prefix *cyber* simply means computer or digital interactions, which are directly related to *cyberspace*, a concept we define as the networked system of microprocessors, mainframes, and basic computers that interact at the digital level. Our focus in this volume is on what we call *cyber conflict*, the use of computational technologies for malevolent and destructive purposes in order to impact, change, or modify diplomatic and military interactions among states. *Cyber war* would be an escalation of cyber conflict to include physical destruction and death. Our focus, therefore, is on cyber conflict and the manifestation of digital animosity short of and including frames of war. These terms will be unpacked in greater detail in the chapters that follow.

The idea that conflict is the foundation for cyber interactions at the interstate level is troubling. Obviously many things are dangerous, but we find that the danger inherent in the cyber system could be countered by the general restraint that might limit the worst abuses in the human condition. By countering what we assert to be an unwarranted construction of fear with reality, data, and evidence, we hope to move beyond the simple pessimistic construction of how digital interactions take place, and go further to describe the true security context of international cyber politics.

In this project we examine interactions among interstate rivals, the most contentious pairs of states in the international system. The animosity between rivals often builds for centuries, to the point where a rival state is willing to harm itself in order to harm its rival even more (Valeriano 2013). If the cyber world is truly dangerous, we would see evidence of these disruptions among rival states with devastating effect. Rivals fight the majority of wars, conflicts, and disputes (Diehl and Goertz 2000), yet the evidence presented here demonstrates that the cyber threat is restrained at this point.[6] Overstating the threat is dangerous because the response could then end up being the actual cause of more conflict. Reactions to threats must be proportional to the nature of the threat in the first place. Otherwise the threat takes on a life of its own and becomes a self-fulfilling prophecy of all-out cyber warfare.

Furthermore, there is a danger in equivocating the threat that comes from non-state cyber individuals and the threats that come from state-affiliated cyber actors not directly employed by governments. If the discourse is correct, non-state entities such as terrorist organizations or political activist groups should be actively using these malicious tactics in cyberspace in order to promote their goals of fear and awareness of their plight. If the goal is to spread fear and instability among the perceived enemies of this group, and cyber tactics are the most effective way to do this, we should see these tactics perpetrated—and perpetrated often—by these entities. This book examines how state-affiliated non-state actors use cyber power and finds that their actual capabilities to do physical harm via cyberspace are quite limited. This then leaves rogue actors as the dangerous foes in the cyber arena. While these individuals can be destructive, their power in no way compares to the resources, abilities, and capabilities of cyber power connected to traditional states.

The future is open, and thus the cyber world could become dangerous, yet the norms we see developing so far seem to limit the amount of harm in the system. If these norms hold, institutions will develop to manage the worst abuses in cyberspace, and states will focus on cyber resilience and basic defense rather than offensive technologies and digital walls. Cyberspace would therefore become a fruitful place for developments for our globalized society. This arena could be the place of digital collaboration, education, and exchanges, communicated at speeds that were never before possible. If states fall into the trap of buying into the fear-based cyber hype by developing offensive weapons under the mistaken belief that these actions will deter future incidents, cyberspace is doomed. We will then have a restricted technology that prevents the developments that are inherent in mankind's progressive nature.

Two themes dominate this analysis. The first is the goal to systematically account for international processes and the conduct of cyber security. We offer facts and evidence to help evaluate how cyber tactics have been used, will continue to be used, and will be used in the future. The world can be a dangerous place, but sometimes our reaction to threats is more detrimental than the nature of the threat. To that end, our second theme is that cyber conflict between states is rare, is restrained, and can be a tool in the domain of espionage rather than a demonstration of raw power. We analyze how states marshal cyber power, but we also place this evidence in the context of the development of strategy and doctrine. Understanding how cyber conflict actually occurs in reality is a key task in the field, and here we scope out the landscape of cyber interactions between states and state representatives. Our theory of cyber restraint depends on four processes: (1) the nature of the weapon and its reproducibility, making it a one-shot weapon of limited effectiveness; (2) the potential for blowback, given that initiating states are often weaker than the state they seek to infiltrate; (3) the natural potential of collateral damage in cyberspace since the technology is not limited to military space; and (4) the potential harm to civilians due to these considerations. Because of these concerns, restraint dominates in the cyber realm.

In the rest of this volume we will describe the contours of conflicts in cyberspace, the theories that dictate the patterns of conflict, the dynamics of interstate interactions, and the developing norms in the system. In this examination of the past, present, and future of cyber political interactions, we hope to understand the greatest development in the twenty-first century thus far; the goal is to keep fear from dominating the discourse.

## THE CHANGING SHAPE OF INTERNATIONAL RELATIONS

This project represents a view of international cyber conflict through the lens of the international relations field. The arena is mainly cyber conflict among states or directed toward states in the realm of foreign policy. The domain is clear; we cannot speak about the nature of cyber crime, but only about the nature of international interactions among states and their affiliates. There is a history and method of analyzing these events that feed directly into the nature of cyber conflict between international competitors.

To understand cyber conflict in the international relations realm, we must understand who uses the tactic, where, how, and for what ends. We therefore define cyber conflict as the use of computational technologies in cyberspace for malevolent and destructive purposes in order to impact, change, or modify diplomatic and military interactions between entities. We are speaking of cyber conflict as a foreign policy tool used by states or individuals against states.

In 2011, the US government declared that a cyber incident is similar to an act of war, punishable with conventional military means (White House 2011; Tallinn Manual 2013).[7] This is a significant step, because it allows the response to a non-physical malicious incident in cyberspace to be in the physical, kinetic form. Conflict then shifts from cyberspace to conventional forms. Rarely have we seen non-physical threats become the source of physical counter threats (Valeriano and Maness 2014). This represents a new direction in the way that threats and actions are interpreted in the international sphere.

The Department of Defense notes that "small scale technologies can have an impact disproportionate to their size; potential adversaries do not have to build expensive weapons systems to pose a significant threat to U.S. national security."[8] In 2013, a US private commission led by former US Ambassador to China John Huntsman and former Director of National Intelligence Dennis Blair went even further, suggesting that corporations would have the right to retaliate with cyber operations if other measures fail to deter cyber theft.[9] Here, the government would be removed from the process, thus allowing an international strike against an enemy by individuals and non-state actors. This is a significant and an unprecedented step in international relations, as an individual could now respond to threats from a state, rather than just receive them. Huntsman, one of the drafters of the report advocating this strategy, noted, "China is two-thirds of the intellectual property theft problem, and we are at a point where it is robbing us of innovation to bolster their own industry, at the cost of millions of jobs. We need some realistic policy options that create a real cost for this activity because Chinese leadership is sensitive to those costs."[10] As the report documents, the "realistic" policy options are cyber operations.

To prevent a cyber intrusion in the first place, the Huntsman-Blair commission argues that we must be willing and able to launch a counter-threat, and it indicates that such a reaction is the responsibility of all of society: individuals, the state, and the military.[11] This argument blurs traditional foreign policy practices, because it enfranchises the responsibility of retaliation to individual or non-state actors, and leaves the state out of the process of its traditional role in international affairs. Going even further, the US government has also started to develop automated cyber capabilities known as "Plan X."[12] This program would find the source of the incident and automatically retaliate against the cyber perpetrator without the approval or oversight of human beings. Thus this step removes the individual and decision-maker from the process of policy and operational choices. It cannot be argued that cyber operations are not causing a shift in the way foreign policy is made; our contention is that this shift might be problematic in light of evidence.

In addition to cyber decision-making processes that shift how organizations and groups respond to threats, we also see cyber actions becoming part of the normal process of threat construction in international relations. Cyber operations, cyber crime, and other forms of cyber activities directed by one state against another are now considered part of the normal range of combat and conflict (Azar 1972; Valeriano and Maness 2014). It is now acceptable to respond to an incident in one domain, cyberspace, through another domain, the physical and conventional layer; thus these responses become the norm in international relations. Although the difference between the layers can be blurred, this is still an important and critical development. Perhaps there has been no greater shift in international dynamics since the end of the Cold War. The barriers between the hypothetical and the abstract have broken down due to the fears of the costs that the cyber world imposes in the physical world. As Clark and Knake (2010: xiii) argue, "cyber war may actually increase the likelihood of the more traditional combat with explosives, bullets, and missiles." The domains have blended together and have transformed into a new potential path to conflict.

According to proponents (Clarke and Knake 2010; Carr 2010; Kello 2013) who help construct the discourse of cyber politics in this debate, international interactions are shifting due to the advent of cyber technologies. The rising fear of cyber combat and threats has brought about a perceived reorientation of military affairs. Our entry into this debate is to first examine how cyber tactics are actually used from a macro perspective, and then to examine if these potential leaps in logic are warranted given the evidence and analyses presented in this volume.

Clarke and Knake (2010: 32) frame the cyber debate as transformational, stating, "there is a credible possibility that such conflict [cyber] may have the potential to change the world military balance and thereby fundamentally alter political and economic relations." Further, even academics are making similar claims; Kello (2013: 32) declares that "[t]he cyber domain is a perfect breeding ground for political disorder and strategic instability. Six factors contribute to instrumental instability: offense dominance, attribution difficulties, technological volatility, poor strategic depth, and escalatory ambiguity. Another—the "large-N" problem—carries with it fundamental instability as well." The question we have is, what is the reality of this threat and prospect? We aim to return the debate on cyber conflict to a more nuanced approach based on empirics substantiating the actual dangers of cyber combat. While there is a real danger of cyber combat, one must remain prudent in relation to the actual threat, not the inflated threat presented by the imagination. Data and analysis allow us to make more accurate policy choices as to how to react, based on the current state of relations.

Often, cyber policy is made based on "worst case scenario" analyses. Analysts, the media, and governments ask what is the worst that can happen, and what can be done to respond to these situations. This is the issue brought up by commentators who suggest that corporations and individuals should be allowed to respond to cyber conflict through their own international actions, removing the state from the process due to the perceived extreme nature of the threat. Others point to the threat of a "Cyber Pearl Harbor," a theory that was given serious weight when mentioned by US Secretary of Defense Leon Panetta.[13] At the time of this writing, the term *cyber conflict* results in over one million hits on Google, which reveals the level of attention that it is receiving.

Basing policy and strategic advice on the worst possible case utilizes the straw man approach (Walton 1996) to design responses and capacity. Making a point based on a perceived extreme example of an event, which usually has little connection to the actual debate at hand—or, in many cases, to reality—is unhelpful. Here we demonstrate that international cyber interactions are typically benign communications that are removed from the security discourse. This is not to say that worst case analyses are never warranted; however, through our findings we assert that traditional security processes (where a threat is articulated, responded to, and then escalated by the opposing side in response to the newer threat) do not apply in the cyber domain. This then makes policy based on the worst case problematic, if not damaging, to international diplomacy. By securitizing cyberspace, there is the potential for the worst case to become the reality and the norm. To move beyond this process, we must examine how states and other international actors actually interact in cyberspace. We must examine the worst cases of abuse, the typical cases of abuse, and the normal day-to-day interactions to understand the scope of cyber interactions. Through this process we can describe, shape, and develop arguments about cyber political interactions based on reality and empirical realities, rather than hyperbole and fear.

## THE NATURE OF CYBER CONFLICT: CYBER REALITY

In this volume we present evidence that suggests that cyber incidents and disputes between states are seldom-used tactics that have not escalated to the possible doomsday propositions that many cyber security companies, pundits, and popular media outlets would have us believe.[14] We also present no evidence of cyber conflict escalating to more severe tactics anytime in the near future, although it is possible that this may happen (Valeriano and Maness 2012). In this book we explain and develop the logic for the current dynamics of cyber conflict. We also investigate the myths and suggestions brought on by what are deemed the most destructive cyber incidents that have occurred so far.

Using our explicit data collection procedures (fully explained in Chapter 4), we find that over an 11-year span, from 2001 to 2011, the dawn of the potential cyber era, rival states have undertaken 111 total cyber incidents within 45 larger cyber disputes. An incident is an isolated operation launched against a state that lasts only a matter of hours, days, or weeks, while a dispute is a longer-term operation that can contain several incidents. Only 20 out of 126 rival pairs of states have engaged in government-sanctioned and targeted cyber conflicts since 2001. We look at international rivals because they are the most conflict-prone dyads in the international system (Diehl and Goertz 2000); therefore, if cyber conflict is going to be used as a viable tactic against an enemy, it is most likely to be utilized between rivals. Furthermore, out of a severity scale from one to five, with five being the most severe, the highest recorded score for a cyber incident between rivals is three, which equates to a targeted operation on a state's national security strategy. In fact, there are only 14 examples of incidents that reach a severity ranking of three in our data. These incidents usually involve targeting military operations, such as sabotage of a nuclear weapons program or stealing stealth jet plans. This indicates that cyber conflict has remained at a low level for the past decade, and although the frequency of cyber incidents and disputes has increased over time, the severity level has remained constant and at a low level.

We also utilize our collected data (Chapter 5) to uncover the reactions that cyber conflicts provoke between states in the foreign policy realm. Surprisingly, our results demonstrate that the primary tactic evoking conflictual foreign policy responses from victimized states is the relatively benign distributed denial of service (DDoS) cyber method, which will be explained in more detail in the following chapters.[15] This is unexpected because the long-term damage done by these types of cyber incidents is minor to nonexistent. Furthermore, incidents and disputes launched by states where the goal is to attempt to change the national security strategy of the target state will also lead to negative foreign policy responses. This is not surprising because states will usually escalate tensions with a source of coercive force (Vasquez 1993).

Our data also uncover a surprising number of regional state fights over territory motivating cyber conflict. Most rival dyads that engage in cyber conflict are neighbors; thus evidence of regionalism for cyber conflict is present. This finding is counterintuitive to the nature of cyberspace, which is global and instantaneous. Some say that cyber conflict transcends boundaries and borders. As Chansoria (2012: 1) notes, "Information Warfare (IW) especially in the digital ether of cyberspace has become a realm that defies borders, challenges state boundaries, and most significantly, provides the military of a nation to realize certain political goals, allowing for a more precise form of propaganda." Yet evidence presented here demonstrates that cyber conflicts are not disconnected from the typical international conflicts over space and place.

The research also demonstrates that nearly half of all cyber incidents in our data can be coded as theft operations, in which a government is attempting to steal sensitive information from another government. This alludes to cyber conflict just being the newest form of one of the oldest professions of the civilized world: espionage. Why put your human spies at risk by sending them to your enemy's territory to steal weapons plans when it is much easier and cost effective to steal these plans in cyberspace? This process is evident in the China-US rivalry; the Chinese have stolen Lockheed Martin plans and have also hacked into the Pentagon's secure network several times.

China is by far the most active state in the use of cyber tactics as a foreign policy tool; it is the most engaged and is the main initiator of cyber conflicts. The United States ranks second, and is the most targeted state. Other states include regional rivals in East and South Asia, the Middle East, and the former Soviet Union. Overall, cyber activity does not correlate with power, technology, or resources. Put simply, these tactics are part of a larger function of active foreign policy disputes between states. Low-severity cyber conflicts will likely make up the future normal relations range of low-level contentious actions between states and their proxies.

Regionalism is found to be prominent in what is usually thought of as a global issue and a global problem. Territorial disputes can lead to disagreements among rivals, and rivals who have territorial disputes will usually be neighbors (Vasquez and Leskiw 2001). Cyber tactics are then used because they are quick, easy, and can affect the rival's populace by inflicting pain on a large area swiftly. DDoS methods can shut down government websites. Vandalism methods can send propagandist messages through the Internet and affect the psyche of the enemy population. Cyberspace is therefore a perfect forum for low-level, widespread, and sometimes psychological threats to an enemy population.

Finally, each interactive cyber unit has unique dynamics; that is, not all cyber conflict is created equal. For example, China seems to initiate cyber espionage or theft operations against states as a means to exert power, while India and Pakistan have been enmeshed in a propaganda war in cyberspace. Which states are involved with what targets, therefore, matters greatly when it comes to cyber conflict at the state level of interaction. The evidentiary context of cyber conflict is critical to the examination of how the tactic is used. Often analysts describe cyber initiators as nameless and faceless (Clarke and Knake 2010: 34; Carr 2010: 89). They often invoke the overstated and elusive attribution problem in cyberspace. Yet this is where international relations scholarship is so critical. We can know who is most likely to utilize cyber tactics against whom. Cyber incidents and their perpetrators are not mysterious given the targets. There are often real concrete issue disagreements that provide the proper context for cyber conflicts. We need to get to the root causes of conflicts in order to understand and eliminate dangerous cyber interactions.

## EXAMPLES OF CYBER CONFLICT: FLAMBÉ AND THE GREATEST INTERNET ATTACK—EVER!

Most tomes examining cyber conflict approach the subject from the most devastating and damaging cyber incidents that have occurred in recent history. Stuxnet is often the center of the analysis. Stuxnet and other such incidents, like Red October, Titan Rain, and Flame, will not be ignored in this volume; we will spend considerable time examining the myths associated with these often cited major cyber incidents. Yet, the hypothetical tale that Clarke and Knake (2010: 67) lay out is typical of the cyber hype industry and is troubling for many reasons. This is a hyperbolic worst-case scenario that presents what could be possible in cyberspace if US relations soured with a cyber power such as China or Russia.

> Several thousand Americans have already died, multiples of that number are injured and trying to get to hospitals. There is more going on, but the people who should be reporting to you can't get through. In the days ahead, cities will run out of food because of the train-system failures and jumbling of data at trucking and distribution centers. Power will not come back up because nuclear plants have gone into secure lockdown and many conventional plants have had their generators permanently damaged. High tension transmission lines on several key routes have caught fire and melted. Unable to get cash from ATMs or bank branches, some Americans will begin to loot stores. Police and emergency services will be overwhelmed. (Clark and Knake 2010: 67)

Instead of taking the extreme and using it to justify the analysis, we must do more if we are covering the true scope of cyber interactions globally. It is critical and important to describe the shape of international cyber relations by examining the typical, the average, or the common cyber conflicts, and the failures demonstrated by those who utilize cyber tactics. One of the most interesting cyber operations has been dubbed Flambé. A variant of the Flame virus, it is likely that cyber specialists utilized and repurposed the code of the Flame incident (that had plagued Iranian networks) for their own ends.[16] In May 2012, computers in the office of former French President Nicolas Sarkozy displayed evidence of malware. According to the French Press, "the attackers were able to get to the heart of French political power, harvesting the computers of close advisers of Nicolas Sarkozy and obtaining 'secret notes' and 'strategic plans.' "[17]

What is interesting is not the actual operation, but the method of the incident, as well as the weaknesses that were revealed. For one, the fact that the hackers utilized the basics of the Flame code demonstrates a typical problem with cyber weapons: once used and let out into the wild, anyone and everyone can then use them for their own ends. Weapons developed over years at vast expense can now be used by one's enemies to harm an ally. Due to this problem, is it therefore difficult to argue that major cyber weapons will not be released into cyberspace, which is public, because of how they may be used by others. In short, cyber weapons are not private and are challenging to contain, especially if the target does little to prevent the cyber incident.

Flambé is also interesting for the weaknesses it displays in the target. French policymakers were duped into accepting false Facebook "friends." These new friends then contacted members of the staff, according to their particular interest, who were then prompted to open seemingly harmless Word or PDF files that were infected with the Flame malware. This allowed hackers access to the French system, and the ability to access sensitive information.

Some might say that this demonstrates the ingenuity of the initiator, and this is true, but it also demonstrates that many successful cyber efforts can put the focus of failure in part on the target. That vital French systems were not "air gapped" and disconnected from the basic Internet, as well as Facebook, is seen as irresponsible, even shocking. That members of the staff of the French government would enter their security credentials in response to random Internet queries should be addressed, and protocols need to be adjusted or even created. There is great danger in cyberspace if such critical and responsible members of staff can be duped so easily. This suggests that we need to do a lot more than develop cyber weapons to protect a state; basic cyber hygiene or protocols on how to use one's personal computer in a secured network need to be applied.

More often than not, simple measures should be taken, for example updating software programs, providing for gaps between computer systems and the public, and giving basic training about Internet behavior to vital staff. Instead, many advocate more offensive methods, skipping past the banal and everyday types of efforts that Flambé lays bare. Flambé likely tells us much more about cyber interactions and cyber defenses than most realize. Flambé is not an outlier; most security professionals have many such stories of economic cyber conflict being successful because of the failures of the target, rather than the brilliances of the infiltrator.

Another event important for the development of views on cyber conflict occurred on March 26, 2013. The *BBC, New York Times*, and other major news organization breathlessly promoted it as the greatest cyber attack ever.[18] Elsewhere it was dubbed the DDoS incident that "almost broke the Internet" by increasing traffic so much that normal processes would not work.[19] CNN noted, "It is the biggest attack we've ever seen."[20] In reality, a dispute between an e-mail spammer, Spamhaus, and an Internet protection force, CyberBunker, got heated and spilled over into the public sphere. A rise in Internet traffic would be indicative of the greatest cyber infiltration ever, but there was no evidence of such an increase. There were no Netflix outages, as the *New York Times* suggested. Internet news website Gizmodo noted, "why are the only people willing to make any claims about the validity or scope of the incident directly involved?"[21]

The key takeaway from this incident is that the public and elites often do not understand, or care to really investigate, the nature of cyber operations as they occur. They take the word of the state or a company at face value, while doing little research. This inflates the hype surrounding the tactic of cyber operations. How would one know if this was a great cyber operation—what evidence for this event was there that supported such reporting? Instead, the news media relied on a few selective and biased quotes to support their reporting.[22]

The corresponding issue is that the debate on the nature of cyber conflict is often led by—and benefits—self-interested Internet security firms. They have an interest in the escalation of cyber fear and the creation of a cyber weapons industrial complex. Fear has been good for business, as "the global cyber security industry is expected to grow an additional $7.2 billion in the next four years, according to projections."[23] Academics, scholars, and policymakers must recognize this and come to their own conclusions as to whether or not this hype is warranted. To truly understand the nature of cyber conflict, we must be able to analyze, predict, and explain how cyber incidents do occur, why, and by whom. In skipping this step, the foreign policy community has done a disservice to the international community, as they have skipped the step of examining the problem and have gone straight to the policy advice stage of the process. It is our goal to explain the actual nature of cyber conflict in the modern world in order to return debate on the issue to a more rational and considered perspective.


## THE STAKES IN THE DEBATE AND CYBER VULNERABILITY

Some argue that cyber attacks could be considered acts of war (Stone 2012). With the increased digital connections between society, states, and individuals, some see a weakness that will be exploited through sheer probability and opportunity. McGraw (2013: 109) states "our reliance on these systems is a major factor making cyber war inevitable, even if we take into account (properly) narrow definitions of cyber war. The cyber environment is target rich and easy to attack." Rich targets are inherent in the cyber world, and therefore are said to be points of weakness for states.

There is an aspect of dependency inherent in the Internet that is frightening to some. As Waltz (1979: 144) notes, interdependence is a relationship among equals. When non-equals interact in the cybersphere, there is a notion of dependency and also vulnerability, since there is an inherent notion of inequality in the relationship. With inequality and vulnerability comes fear. This is compounded by the fact that the great majority of individuals, even policymakers and Internet technology professionals, do not even understand how the Internet works.

Few have offered measured and rational responses to the fear that actions in cyberspace and cyberpower provoke. The stakes are fairly clear; the notion is that we are vulnerable in our new digital societies. McGraw (2013) sees cyber conflict as inevitable, but the most productive response would be to build secure systems and software. Others take a more extreme response by creating systems of cyber deterrence and offensive capabilities. States may protect themselves by making available and demonstrating the capabilities of offensive cyber weapons, as the fear of retaliation and increased costs of cyber operations will deter would-be hackers once they see these weapons in operation. The danger here is with cyber escalation; by demonstrating resolve and capability, states often provoke escalatory responses from rivals and trigger the security dilemma. Furthermore, the application of deterrence in cyberspace is inherently flawed in that it takes a system developed in one domain (nuclear weapons) and applies it to a non-equivalent domain (cyber), an issue that we will dissect further in this volume.

Evidence presented in this book suggests that there is a different process happening in cyberspace. There is an operating system of norms in cyberspace that dictates how actions should be considered. This is the idea we will explore in full in Chapter 8. For now, it is sufficient to say that norms do not require external enforcement via a supranational authority, but only construction and maintenance of the current status quo, as our evidence of restraint in cyber conflict demonstrates.[24] Setting up a system of punishment and offense in the international system could be detrimental to natural connections in an ever more digitalized international society.

Difficult and complicated choices have to be made. Offensive options are easy, and defensive options are prone to failure (Dipert 2010: 385). Yet conventional offensive options are dangerous, and are apt to lead to escalation in international interactions (Leng 1993); the cyber world may be different. For now, we have seen relatively minor cyber conflicts in the system, but the fear that the future engenders might provoke irrational responses and further escalation. We can be slightly satisfied that current realities do not support the contention that cyber war is in our future, but ignoring evidence and buying into the hyperbole push us down a path where cyber conflict becomes an enduring reality.

The stakes are clear. Defensive operations often move quickly toward walls and moats that will inhibit digital collaborations and connections. Providing a path for offensive action or deterrence will likely provide a context for further escalation. The use of force to demonstrate capabilities is detrimental and counterproductive in the context of deterrence since it likely engenders further escalation. Instead of deterrence logic, what we call cyber restraint, a concept presented in Chapter 3, dominates the system for now, but what will happen in the future?

Perhaps the most insidious prospect is that speculators will seize on the fear responses that exist in society and will construct a cyber-industrial complex. This complex will both warn of the dire threats in cyberspace and unleash the worst cyber incidents that might make these fears a reality, thus creating a self-inflated and self-fulfilling prophecy. Internet security companies now give advice to government and policymakers, yet no one questions their perspective and the benefit they gain if there is a system of constructed cyber fear. To break down this prospect, we must fully understand the nature of cyber fear.

## THE NATURE OF CYBER FEAR: COUNTERING CYBER HYPE

The question of cyber conflict is predicated on the need to perceive threats in an insecure world. The idea is that we live in an anarchic world and thus are always doomed to competition and conflict (Hobbes 2009). The cyber world is no different. There is the need for some to operate under a system of perpetual fear, given these systemic considerations. Who will protect us from cyber threats?[25] Many note that the cyber world is dangerous and prone to targeting. Singer and Friedman (2014: 130) in some ways promote this type of danger inherent in our systems, noting "if the computers on robotic weapons systems are compromised, they could be 'persuaded' to do the opposite of what their owners intended. This creates a whole new type of conflict." These predictions are something we believe must be countered with evidence, theory, and analysis.

Dunn-Cavelty (2008: 1) suggests that the growing perceptions of fear among governments and policymakers only exacerbate cyber threats. "Confusion and misinformation," as Singer and Friedman (2014: 7) note, drive the fear motifs that pervade discussions about cyber interactions. These processes are propped up by worst-case scenario narratives of what could happen if cyber conflict were to reach its full potential and shut down power grids, launch intercontinental missiles, and cause a major breakdown in international order. These threat perceptions in popular discourse will then lead to policy changes, and with policy changes come lucrative cyber security contracts with governments to ensure the safety of the public. This in turn will keep the threat levels high as long as these security contracts are renewable (Dunn-Cavelty 2008). Our work supports these ideas, but more important, demonstrates empirically that the cyber threat is inflated.

Perceptions are the key; if a state operates under this system of cyber fear, offensive action is surely warranted since it is perceived to be the natural response and the most effective method of ensuring security in the digital world. Yet this is the antiquated power politics path long since discredited in world politics (Vasquez 1999). In this context, we buy into the myth that our enemies are real, and are even more dangerous if they operate under the fog of cyberspace.

The often-stated attribution problem also dominates the cyber debate. The contention is that we can never really know who is infiltrating whom (Andres 2012) because of the nature of the Internet and connections; thus the entire cyber system is to be feared. There is no natural identification for each machine. Internet protocol (IP) addresses are fluid and moving. Traffic can be rerouted at a whim. Because of this problem, many suggest that we need cyber restrictions and forensics to maintain the shape of digital interactions.

While the Internet's infrastructure may be problematic and in need of evaluation, building in more identifications and security measures to restrain interactions is unnecessary. We must move beyond the forensics model of international communications and think more about how interactions actually take place and why. If the South Korean television companies are hacked by a coordinated and well-timed piece of malware, it is almost useless—if not counterproductive—to know what country the incident physically came from. Knowing that the Internet traffic was routed from China does not solve the problem. The source of the incident, North Korea, is obvious to all who understand international politics.

The debate on cyber relations needs to move back to the basics of international politics. We need to get at the root causes of conflicts rather than restrict the nature of interactions in the first place. Few states but North Korea would have a genuine interest in a propaganda campaign against South Korea. The solution to the problem is not to punish or retaliate against North Korea, but to look toward the causes of the conflict. International cyber problems are not devoid of international affairs processes, yet we seem to assume this is so in cyber interactions because these operations are seen as occurring in a separate domain. The problem of attribution, or the impossibility of being able to locate the source of cyber incidents in the international domain, is often stated as an obstacle to understanding cyber conflict. Yet those who follow international relations developments should not be surprised that Estonia was attacked by Russia in 2007, that North Korea continued to wage cyber battles with the South, or that China seeks through digital espionage what it cannot buy on the normal security market. While cyberspace is a separate domain, it is not unconnected from the normal political domain that is the genesis of conflicts.

To move beyond the fear and hype in cyberspace, we must understand the nature of international politics and the roots of disputes in the physical world. These disputes feed directly into cyber operations. Restraint is operational now and needs to continue, and the goal of this research is to discover and disseminate how we can ensure that rationality dominates the construction of cyber fears.

Just because something can happen does not mean it will. We argue that for now and for the foreseeable future, restraint dominates in cyberspace despite the worst-case predictions of prognosticators. States generally react in the international environment in a manner conducive to their interests. Sometimes, however, the security dilemma enters the elite and public discourse and can push states toward overreaction. The fear from perceived threats, such as those in the cyber domain, may influence the foreign policy decisions made by states (Jervis 1979). While there are counter-examples of the worst practices and failures, the norm is to cooperate and participate in constructive dialogue in the system. Considerations such as collateral damage and escalation usually guard against an unleashing of damaging cyber weapons.

We find that the security dilemma has no place in these international interactions. The cyber world is nebulous; an infiltration against a military facility in this realm could bleed into the public sector. Malicious cyber incidents on infrastructure have been and will continue to be rare to nonexistent because states are restrained due to the high probability of civilian harm, the nature of the weapons (single use), and the weak payoffs if utilized (Gartzke 2013). These types of offensive cyber actions are just as unlikely as interstate nuclear or chemical weapons attacks. There is a system of normative restraint in cyber operations based on the conditions of collateral damage, plus the factors of blowback and replication.

Foreign policy tactics in the cyber world can be replicated and reproduced. Any cyber weapon used can be turned right back on its initiator. On top of this, it is likely that severe cyber operations will be bring retribution and consequences that many states are not willing to accept. We have seen many interstate conflicts since the advent of the Internet age, but the largest and only cyber operation thus far during a conventional military conflict, the 2008 Russo-Georgian skirmish, consisted of almost trivial DDoS and vandalism. Since then, Russia has even avoided using cyber weapons during the Crimean and larger Ukrainian crises of 2014. Other operations are mainly propaganda operations or occur in the realm of espionage. That the United States did not use cyber tactics against Iraq, Afghanistan, or Libya, at least as directed at the executive level, signifies that cyber tactics are typically restrained despite significant constituencies in the military that want to use the weapons. Stuxnet is the outlier, as our data demonstrate, not the norm or the harbinger of the future to come.

Cyber operations are limited in that their value is negligible, the consequences of a massive cyber incident are drastic, and the requirements to carry one out are vast. The idea of a lone cyber hacker being able to bring states to their knees is a fantastic one. Cyber operations like Stuxnet require an exceptional amount of funds, technical knowledge, luck, and on-the-ground assets for successful implementation. Massive and truly dangerous cyber operations are beyond the means of most countries. These statements are not opinions, but contentions made based on the facts at hand and the data we have collected.

We also see regionalism dominate in cyberspace. Despite the vastness and transboundary capacity of the Internet, most operations are limited to local targets connected to traditional causes of conflict, such as territorial disputes and leadership disagreements. Issues are important (Mansbach and Vasquez 1981) in world politics and in cyber politics. This is why international relations scholarship is so important in relation to the cyber question. Cyber operations are not taken devoid of their international and historical contexts. What has happened in the past will influence how future technologies are leveraged and where they are applied. The goal of this book will be to use this theoretical frame to explain the cyber conflict dynamics of rival states, as well as non-state actors willing and able to launch cyber malice.

## PLAN OF THE BOOK

Our goals are clear; we intend to return the debate on cyber conflict to some measure of rationality and thoughtful theoretical analysis, which is sorely needed in the field. By grounding our analysis in the field of international relations, we can clearly outline theories about the conduct, operation, and consequences of cyber conflict. We can also outline the normative structure of restraint in the system now, and also what a rational response to cyber fears might be during the current era. The book uncovers the realities and dynamics of state-to-state cyber conflict in the twenty-first century based on the theories we have developed to explain the evolution of cyber tactics. The realities that we uncover have implications for future policy responses to cyber questions.

Chapter 2 attempts to cover the basics of cyber conflict and cyberspace; it is the chapter on terms, ideas, and methods. Choosing the right and appropriate terms for the study of this newest branch of international relations scholarship is probably the most controversial aspect of many investigations into cyber dynamics. This chapter spells out what we deem the appropriate use of terms that define the most important aspects of cyberspace, cyber conflict, and cyber security.

What do *cyber war, cyberspace, cyber conflict, cyber attack, cyber espionage*, and *cyber terrorism* mean as terms of analysis? How do we know these examples when we see them? These are all-important terms, and their discussion deserves an entire chapter. Chapter 2 produces what we hope to be a more nuanced and less contentious list of terminology for cyber conflict processes. We also examine the cyber conflict debate and the contours of the field as it currently stands during its early phase of development.

The groundwork for the theory of this volume is laid out in Chapter 3. We develop the notion of cyber restraint, which guides this analysis through a careful examination of what cyber conflict should not be framed within, the concept of deterrence. We also disseminate and construct the terms *cyber espionage* and *cyber terrorism* to develop theories of cyber action that can engage these situations. Finally, we seek to explain the importance of regional interactions in cyberpower relationships. This chapter develops the empirical and logical relationships that we investigate for the rest of the book.

Chapter 4 outlines our comprehensive data on cyber incidents and disputes between rival states. Much discussion of the concept of cyber conflict and the changing dynamic of future security interactions is founded upon the study of what might be, or what might happen under the worst case scenario. To truly engage with the topic, we need to understand how states have used cyber tactics thus far and what we can gain from the current dynamics of cyber conflict. To that end, the chapter includes information on all cyber interactions between rival states in the last decade and delineates the patterns of cyber conflict as reflected by evidence. We find here that the actual magnitude and pace of cyber disputes among rivals do not match popular perception; only 20 of 126 active rivals have engaged in cyber conflict, and their interactions have been limited in terms of magnitude and frequency. The coming era of cyber conflict should continue to exhibit these patterns, despite the fears mentioned in the cyber discourse.

What are the foreign policy implications of cyber conflict when the tactic is used as a tool between rival states? This is the topic of Chapter 5, an often ignored query in the cyber debate. Analysts suggest that the rise of cyber security and the cyber domain of combat have led to a revolution in military affairs. The structure, content, and location of interactions on the battlefield have supposedly changed in light of this development. Few have attempted to examine just what happens when states use cyber tactics against one another. This step allows us to cut through the bluster common in the news media and from cyber security organizations. Using the dataset of cyber incidents and disputes presented in Chapter 4, we are able to measure the level of conflict and cooperation observed after a cyber incident or dispute to understand the true impact of this new tactic on foreign policy dynamics at the weekly events level. We ask four fundamental questions: Does cyber conflict raise the level of conflict interactions between states? Do states capitulate to the cyber aggressor out of fear? Or does cyber conflict have no effect on the dynamics of conflict and cooperation between states? Are there different conflict-cooperation dynamics based on the type and severity of the cyber incident or dispute? We find that only one method of cyber conflict, denial of service, affects conflict-cooperation dynamics between states. We also find that cyber incidents and disputes have statistically significant impacts on foreign policy when regional powers and dyads containing the United States are involved.

Chapter 6 looks at recent "famous" cyber conflicts that have been covered extensively in the international press. Instead of reacting to events as they happen, we take a step back and examine the true qualitative nature of these incidents to understand just what the methods, motives, and impact of the events were. Measured analysis, in form of structured and focused case studies, is used to replace the hyperbole that typically results directly after an incident. We look at Stuxnet, Shamoon, and Bronze Soldier cyber operations to investigate just what happens when a state uses cyber tactics and the impact of said uses of power.

Chapter 7 uncovers the actions of several non-state cyber engagers and finds that fear is their greatest weapon. However, this message of fear is spread through benign methods and overall low-severity-level incidents, suggesting that the impact and long-term damage on targets is very minimal to non-existent. Here we look at the Cyber Gaza campaign against Israel in 2012, the Syrian Electronic Army's campaign against the United States, and the multi-target Red October operation discovered in 2012, in an effort to understand the motivations, course, and impact of cyber operations by non-state actors.

In Chapter 8, we examine the system of rules and norms in cyberspace based on the Just War tradition. Cyber conflict is a reality, but the threat it produces does not meet popular perception. Security experts, the media, and various governments are focused on the tactic, yet we know very little about how cyber conflict is used by states and the associated norms created around the tactic. There can be justice in cyber conflict, with the goal being to avoid further harm. The main problem is that the nature of cyber weapons often makes them indiscriminate and apt to lead to collateral damage. There can be measured uses of cyber tactics, but often this is not the case given the nature of the Internet and digital society. For these reasons, a systematic normative restraint is in operation in cyberspace. How effective and lasting this system is depends on the continuing nature of the cyber taboo and potential institutional responses to the cyber conflict issue.

The true danger in cyber conflict is that one state will overuse the tactic and push other states to do the same. To this end, a system of justice in the use of cyber technologies needs to be incentivized. How do countries manage cyber relations, and how can responses to the threat be made proportional to the tactic?

The future is bright, but only if we avoid securitizing and militarizing the domain so as to meet perceptions of fear. We must also be careful when constructing and condoning cyber industrial complexes, and therefore allow the fluid nature of the Internet and digital society to have a positive impact on all, rather than becoming a source of vulnerability and conflict.

## CHAPTER 2

# Cyber Power, Cyber Weapons, and Cyber Operations

## INTRODUCTION

*As modern society leans ever more heavily on the Internet for commerce, communications and the management of its vital infrastructures, its fragility becomes an ever greater concern.*
Mark Bowden, *Los Angeles Times*, October 23, 2011

We now live in a digital era in which the speed, interconnectedness, and level of computer interaction between states and individuals is growing at an exponential rate. Choucri (2012: 13) suggests that "cyberspace has created new conditions for which there are no clear precedents." As with most new things, this new reality brings fear since the infrastructure we depend on is thought to be fragile and too complex. We depend so much on digital communications that it stands to reason that we are also vulnerable to threats that originate from this realm. As Bowden's quote makes clear, the fragility of what we most depend on is a source of vulnerability for some. Rid (2013: vii) even suggests that we are addicted to the Internet, and this is a source of concern as our habit is therefore fragile.

The fragility, addiction, and dependency we have on the Internet signals weakness for some. Weaknesses often are exploited by those who seek to gain, especially in a situation of historical enmity. Yet, these ideas are assumptions; there is a perception of fragility and of dependency that might not match the reality of the situation. If the perceived weakness and fragility become the dominant frame, there is a potential for the fear invoked to translate to the securitization notion of forthcoming conflict, exploiting this weakness. We argue throughout that the opposite might be true, that Internet and cyber interactions are more stable than most believe and therefore this domain can be a source of cooperation.

Cyberspace will become the domain of conflict only if we let the fear process take hold and dominate the discourse; the perception of fear then becomes a self-fulfilling prophecy.

The CNBC network in the United States produced a documentary on cyber warfare that documents the typical securitized discourse in this arena. Their introductory statement is a typical example of the hyperbolic statements associated with cyber conflict. "In the United States, we are Internet dependent. Our financial systems, power grids, telecommunications, water supplies, flight controls and military communications are all online—making them vulnerable to countless cyber incidents by cyber criminals. The goal could be a 10-minute blackout, a breach of national security, a stock trading glitch or the theft of millions of dollars worth of intellectual property."[1] In short, everything from our money to our water is vulnerable to infiltration. The question is to what extent these extreme warnings and fears are warranted. How vulnerable is any given country to cyber malice, and what evidence do we have for cyber conflict in the last decade? Should this fear be the basis for reorganization in military structures and doctrine?

To answer these questions, we must outline the source of the debate and the terms surrounding the usage of the key concepts in the cyber discourse before we move forward with our investigation. For our purposes, *cyber conflict* is the use of computational technologies for malevolent and destructive purposes in order to impact, change, or modify diplomatic and military interactions between states. This analysis is focused on state interactions in the realm of foreign policy. Once we understand the contours of the debate about cyberspace and national security, we can move on to predicting, explaining, and propagating cyber systems of restraint that might be more ordered responses to the threats that emanate from this domain.

## CYBER CONFLICT TERMINOLOGY

Predicting the amount, level, and context of cyber conflict is dependent on how the term is defined, framed, and engaged. One could argue (as do Lewis 2010; Rid 2013; and Gartzke 2013) that cyber war in terms of conflicts, where lives are lost, will not occur. Others say that these cyber threats and their proliferation are socially constructed and that we must be more nuanced in choosing our terms and metaphors (*cyber war, Cyber Armageddon, cyber 9/11,* etc.) so that these inflated threats do not feed into the hype, as those who take a constructivist approach argue (Nissenbaum 2005; Hansen 2011; Hansen and Nissenbaum 2009). Still others argue (Clarke and Knake 2010; Kello 2013; and Lewis 2013) that we are seeing or will see a proliferation in cyber war because digital society will be a logical extension of the security domain. This proliferation framework is problematic in that most of these incidents are actually trivial and have become a normal part of Internet based-interactions.[2] Simple probes and intrusions become classified as conflict interactions. We are now at the point where someone guessing at a Twitter password is classified by the media as a hack who has committed an act of cyber war.[3] On the other hand, defining cyberwar as the loss of life in the traditional war framework poses a high bar for the realization of the criteria, given the characteristics of cyber technologies. Middle-ground approaches taken by those such as Choucri (2012) and Dunn-Cavelty (2008) are overwhelmed by the extremes in the debate.

For us, the prefix *cyber* simply means computer or digital interactions.[4] To understand the shape of cyber interactions, we must define what we (and others) mean by cyberspace, cyber power, cyber war, and cyber conflict. Once this task is done, we can move on to predicting and explaining the domain of our analysis. So not to ascribe to either extreme, the first step is to lay out the perspectives of our question and investigation.

### What Is Cyberspace?

Most major authors on the topic of cyberspace have defined the term, but it is useful to dissect these frameworks and come to our own conclusions as to what the term means. Clarke and Knake (2010: 70) define *cyberspace* as "all of the computer networks in the world and everything they connect and control. It's not just the Internet . . . cyberspace includes the Internet plus lots of other networks of computers that are not supposed to be accessible from the Internet." Our main issue with the definition is the normative quality of it, which suggests that things that are not supposed to be accessible from the Internet are. We find this a rather distracting way of pointing out the weakness in command and control systems. If the air gap between systems is breached, or things are connected to the Internet that should not be, it is often through human means and not the fault of the system itself. In any case, this issue is more of an analysis and systems issue than a definitional issue. In addition, limiting *cyber* to computer networks is a bit narrow and restricts the integration of new cyber technologies into the paradigm. The term *microprocessor* might be more accurate.

The definition that Nye (2011) invokes is much closer to the actual content of what cyberspace is for most who utilize the term in the political context. "The cyber domain includes the Internet of networked computers but also intranets, cellular technologies, fiber-optic cables, and space-based communications. Cyberspace has a physical infrastructure layer that follows the economic laws of rival resources and the political laws of sovereign justification and control" (Nye 2011: 19). While the legal and economic aspects of cyberspace are to be investigated, the basics of the domain are clear. All computer, network, digital, cellular, fiber, and space-based forms of communications, interactions, and interconnections are what make up cyberspace.

We also must not forget the state. As Singer and Friedman (2014: 14) note, "cyberspace may be global, but it is not 'stateless' or a 'global commons,' both terms frequently used in government and media." There is very little anarchy in cyberspace because it remains the domain of states and is governed by institutions and networks, such as the Internet Corporation for Assigned Names and Numbers (ICANN).[5]

Conceptually, the layering aspect of cyberspace is important as we move forward. Nye (2010: 3) notes that the overlaps between the physical and virtual aspects of cyberspace are where the physical "follows the economic laws of rival resources and increasing marginal costs, and the political laws of sovereign jurisdiction and control." The informational layer is much more nebulous and fluid. Costs are cheap and speed is instantaneous at the information level, yet making a link with the physical layer is problematic within the frames of conflict and economics. This is where the conflict results in cyberspace. It is not at all clear that cyberspace is a separate domain from the physical. In fact, it likely relies on physical characteristics of size, quality, and distance for space and capacity.

Choucri (2012: 8) supports this notion of blended layering, noting, "we view cyberspace as a hierarchical contingent system composed of (1) the physical foundations and infrastructures that enable the cyber playing field, (2) the logical building blocks that support the physical platform and enable services, (3) the information content stored, transmitted, or transformed, and (4) the actors, entities and users with various interest who participate in this arena in various roles." All these layers, actors, roles, jurisdictions, and interactions are what make up cyberspace. These layers also tell the story of the political domain of cyberspace.

Libicki defines cyberspace with four tenets which state that the concept is "(1) replicable, (2) consists of recognized actions, such as text in English, codes understood to humans as opposed to binary code which most cannot understand, (3) tends to have persistent rules or technologies, and finally, (4) is divided between the physical layer and synthetic layer that is information and knowledge" (Libicki 2007: 4). Cyberspace is replicable, which also means that the concept is expanding and repairing at the same time. As our ability to store information increases and the speed at which information travels expands, the domains of cyberspace increase (Libicki 2007). Having recognized actions in common is important since the concept must be measurable and not be reduced to abstract quantities.

In addition to this, what cyberspace entails makes it dangerous to some. Some suggest that what cyberspace is, in and of itself, makes the act of cyber warfare possible. Clarke and Knake (2010: 73–74) note "1) The flaws in design; 2) flaws in hardware and software; and 3) the move to put more and more critical systems online." The flaws in design and hard/software are manmade, not an aspect of cyberspace as a domain. The move to put more systems online is part of the natural evolution of systems and their component parts. The flaws are physical, and are not domain specific.

We argue that the move to put more critical systems online is a natural part of the process of development, not a flaw in the system or vulnerability. The flaw comes when individuals put sensitive systems and information in locations that are accessible to an undesired audience. The flaw also comes when weak systems are put in place with vulnerabilities that can be exploited. The assumption that cyberspace in and of itself as a concept is vulnerable due to the nature of the system is an incorrect application of the idea. As we stated from the start, the fragility of the Internet is a trope and an assumption.[6] This trope relates back to the common assumption of vulnerability through interaction, not the functional assertion of stability through interaction.

The level of analysis problem in international relations is also manifesting here (Singer 1972). While the layers in cyberspace may blend, it does not automatically follow that actions in the system can affect individual states, nor should it be assumed that actions by individuals can affect the system as a whole, or states in particular. An organization or access point can be targeted, but if that happens it does not mean that the entire system in a state was vulnerable, only that part of it was. This was very clear in the Estonian case, when the entire state was put offline, not because of the dynamics of the incident, but because of the choice of the state government.

It does seem clear that cyberspace as a term is laden with political meaning and implications. For this reason, we prefer the Nye definition in that it focuses on what the term actually entails and suggests the problems that might result from it, but it places no normative judgment as to the efficacy of the cyber issues in the political sphere. Cyberspace is then the networked system of microprocessors, mainframes, and basic computers that interact in digital space. Cyberspace has physical elements because these microprocessors, mainframes, and computers are systems with a physical location. Therefore cyberspace is a physical, social-technological environment—a separate domain but one that interacts and blends with other domains or layers. It clearly is not isolated and cuts across spectrums. What happens on the physical layer of cyberspace is where we engage political questions.

## What Is Cyber Power?

Politics is about the distribution of influence. The fundamental nature of politics regards the authoritative allocation of valued things (Easton 1953: 5). Cyber politics is no different. As Choucri (2012: 9) notes, "all politics, in cyber or real arenas, involves conflict, negotiation, and bargaining over the mechanisms, institutional or otherwise, to resolve in authoritative ways the contentions over the nature of particular sets of core values." The cyber domain is no different from conventional frames of politics. It is this realm with which we are concerned. When cyber interactions occur at the international level, the age-old question of who gets what, when, where, and how becomes even more pressing as technology becomes a part of everyday life.

Just who has cyber power often relates back to questions of capabilities and resources. As Nye (2010: 3) notes, "power depends on context and cyber power depends on the resources that characterize the domain of cyberspace." Traditional powers such as the United States, China, and Russia seem to be the most dominant cyber actors because they have the resources, manpower, and money to support massive cyber operations. Demchak (2011) sees offensive cyber power as an enhancement of a powerful state's overall military capabilities, not just a stand-alone tactic. In this way, cyber power can offer the potential to expand the overall military capacity of a state.

The problem is that this construct leaves out the ability of small states such as Israel, Estonia, and North Korea to be just as relevant in the cyber world. In some ways, states can use the nature of the domain to expand influence because cyber power is cheaper to acquire than military hardware. But acquiring cyber weapons does not mean that weaker states will always use them against their stronger adversaries. Purchasing zero-day vulnerabilities and utilizing them for the state is an easier option than conventional military operations. Yet, the impact of such excursions has failed to demonstrate a true and actual change in state-to-state interactions (Valeriano and Maness 2014). Table 2.1 gives a general picture of ten states that have cyber capabilities. The selected states are the most visible in cyber conflict dialogues. Our purpose here is not to dive into the nature of cyber power, but to explore the state of the cyber landscape as it currently is composed.

*Table 2.1* OVERALL CYBER CAPABILITIES AMONG SELECTED STATES

| State | Cyber Offense | Cyber Dependence | Cyber Defense | Total Score |
|---|---|---|---|---|
| Iran | 4 | 5 | 3 | 12 |
| Great Britain | 7 | 2 | 4 | 13 |
| Estonia | 3 | 1 | 9 | 13 |
| South Korea | 6 | 4 | 4 | 14 |
| North Korea | 3 | 9 | 2 | 14 |
| Germany | 7 | 2 | 6 | 15 |
| Israel | 8 | 3 | 4 | 15 |
| United States | 10 | 2 | 5 | 17 |
| China | 8 | 4 | 5 | 17 |
| Russia | 7 | 3 | 8 | 18 |

Conceptualized and altered from: Clarke, Richard A., and Robert K. Knake. 2010. *Cyber War: The Next Threat to National Security and What to Do about It* (New York: Harper Collins).
Maness, Ryan C., and Brandon Valeriano. 2014. *New Sources of Power: Russia's Coercive Cyber and Energy Policy* (unpublished manuscript).

Table 2.1 is the presentation of our scale of state cyber capabilities. Each value is based on a scale of one to ten (Clarke and Knake 2010; Maness and Valeriano 2014: Chapter 4). Offensive capabilities measure how sophisticated a state's cyber weapons are, as well as how well trained and computer savvy their citizenry is. Cyber defense measures how protective a state is over its cyberspace. Does the state own or have control over the Internet service providers (ISPs)? Does the state have the "kill switch" that can cut off all incoming and outgoing cyber activity? Furthermore, how resilient and adaptive a state is can also establish methods of defense against potential aggressors (Demchak 2011). Cyber dependence is a reverse score: the higher the score, the less dependent a state's daily activities and infrastructure are on the Internet, and the lower the score, the more dependent (Maness and Valeriano 2014: Chapter 4). Estonia gets the lowest score because of how "plugged-in" it is to the web for important infrastructural needs such as electricity and water (Clarke and Knake 2010). Therefore, the more dependent a state is on cyber technology, the more vulnerable it is (Clarke and Knake 2010: 148).

States with proficient offensive capabilities include Israel, China, and the United States. These states have a proven track record of the most sophisticated cyber weapons to date. The United States (and possibly Israel) was responsible for the Olympic Games cyber dispute with Iran, which employed Stuxnet, Flame, Duqu, and Gauss. These forms of malware are some of the most advanced yet seen. China has been behind the most cyber espionage campaigns and has hacked into and stolen information from military networks including those of the United States, India, and Japan. It also caused foreign policy rifts between China and these targeted states (Karatzogianni 2010a). These countries' capabilities and their willingness to use them, albeit in a limited role, are why they are given the top offensive scores.

Lindsay (2013) argues that sophisticated worms such as Stuxnet enhance the power of stronger states over weaker ones. "The complexity of weaponization makes cyber offense less easy and defense more feasible than generally appreciated, and cyber options are most attractive when deterrence is intact. Stuxnet suggests that considerable social and technical uncertainties associated with cyber operations may significantly blunt their revolutionary potential" (Lindsay 2013: 365). Therefore, cyber offense gives powerful states another option in their arsenal when employing action against their weaker adversaries. An offensive strike such as Stuxnet could deter states from launching cyber operations against the United States, out of fear of retaliation in kind by similar sophisticated offensive incidents. The weaker state might be better off investing in defensive measures that protect against the offensive strike, rather than trying to match their stronger adversaries in cyberspace.

The most defensively capable cyber states include Estonia, Germany, and Russia. Estonia is the tiny Baltic country that was infiltrated by Russian hackers in the now infamous Bronze Soldier dispute of 2007. After removing a Soviet-era war memorial from the center square of Tallinn, the capital city of Estonia,

Russia responded with a series of cyber incidents that effectively shut down many Estonian public and private websites (Maness and Valeriano 2014). The aftermath of this dispute has prompted Estonia to be a leader in cyber security issues, and it is now the host of the NATO Cooperative Cyber Defense Center of Excellence. Russian hacker talent is nationalistic and savvy, and the events in Estonia seem to verify this construct (Karatzogianni 2010b). This is why Estonia gets high marks in defense. Germany has been a proponent of a strong defense ever since cyber conflict became a hot button issue and has put up more protective measures than most free societies in the world.[7] Russia's defensive score comes from the fact that the FSB (Federal'naya sluzhba bezopasnosti), the successor to the notorious Soviet-era KGB, monitors all cyber traffic coming in and out of Russia. It also requires that all foreign ISPs register and be monitored. These states are therefore more ready than most for the cyber Armageddon, if it ever comes to fruition.

Estonia is the most cyber-dependent state in the world, meaning that most daily activities, from banking to renewing one's driver's license, to military command posts, are dependent on Internet technologies (Maness and Valeriano 2014). In Chapter 6, we discuss how this tiny country was the victim of Russian cyber malice in 2007 and how it has taken steps to be part of the international process of cyber norms ever since. If these countries' networks were to be compromised, the daily lives of its citizens would be disrupted the most. This is why the 2007 dispute with Russia was given international attention. Estonians' daily lives were relatively more disrupted than most others would have been due to the digitalized nature of the state. Government and private sector networks were inoperable for days and in some cases for two weeks. This dependence can be a weakness of sorts in cyber conflict; therefore the lower the score a state gets, the more potentially damaging a cyber operation can be if fully implemented. The United States is also very cyber dependent. Its power grids, banking system, and national defense entities are reliant upon the networks of the Internet. On the other end of the spectrum for this score, North Korea gets a high score of nine because its citizenry is not dependent on the Internet for its daily concerns; the great majority probably have never even heard of the Internet. The widespread impact of a cyber operation from abroad would not be acutely felt, as it would be in Estonia or the United States.

What is compelling about cyber power is the ability of the tactic to bleed into other arenas, suggesting that it is not a new and separate domain. What happens in cyberspace does not stay in cyberspace. As Nye (2011: 19–20) notes, the use of resources in terms of sea power tends to only apply to winning naval battles, but these tactics can apply to land battles, commerce, and other arenas. Cyber power has many of the same characteristics. Weaknesses displayed in the cyber arena can influence how states interact in all areas and levels; this has an impact on trust between states and corporations.

It is also useful to remember that cyber power differs in that the indicators of the instrument vary (Sheldon 2012: 214). The connection between the physical realm and cyber realm can sometimes be tenuous; other times they are more manifest. While some cyber capabilities can apply to physical components, such an application is often the result of a weakness in the systems of the target rather than a benefit of the tactic itself. If someone is able to use a cyber technique to destroy a building or harm critical systems, it is often because of errors in operation at the receiving end, rather than the ability of the initiator to exploit weakness.

Cyber power is the ability to control and apply typical forms of control and domination of cyberspace. Cyber politics and power blur, as strong states typically have the most cyber power. What is unique about cyberspace is the ability of small states to compete on the same playing field as strong states. Of course, our entire discussion is limited by the material framework of cyber power. The material framework is appropriate given our focus on cyber conflict later in this volume, but it does leave many aspects of cyber capabilities out of the equation.

Non-material cyber power is important to considerations of how cyber relationships would be managed. As we suggest above, the more technologically capable states are, the more likely they are to have offensive cyber capabilities. Others are encouraged to explore the social forces surrounding technological innovation and how these interact with cyber power. The offensive framework is easy to deduce, but marshaling cyber power based on education, technology, and coding ability alone could make states cyber powers that cannot compete on the conventional battlefield. These developments have important ramifications for how we study cyber interactions and other topics such as repression, protest, and rebellion in the modern state.

### What Is Cyber War?

The first step in defining *cyber war* requires articulating what war actually is in the modern era. Missing this step, as Rid (2013) notes, often allows for the misapplication of what one means by war in the first place. As Clausewitz (2007: 11) wrote so long ago, "knowledge of the nature of war is essential to the management of the political intercourse." Betz and Stevens (2013) find that the mismanagement of terms by academics, the media, and policymakers can feed into the cyber hype: "We must be wary of the way in which cyber security discourse structures our thinking, channeling it into modalities that are misleading. The appropriate use of analogical reasoning should therefore be a priority for those involved for cyber security" (Betz and Stevens 2013: 148). For the cyber realm, as with all discourse suggesting political violence, we cannot discuss or engage the question of cyber war without understanding what we mean by war and how it is connected to the political discourse.

War is sustained intergroup violence that usually results in the deliberate infliction of death and injury on the opposing side. This is a key aspect of what war is. Without the violence, injury, and death, the term loses much of its meaning and implication. The field of international relations was founded to reduce the scourge of warfare (Schmidt 2002). By warfare, we mean destructive operations that seek to maim, kill, or wound physical individuals and/or to damage or destroy property.

War is also a way to make decisions regarding a difference of opinion, but often a suboptimal method (Mead 1940) of deciding who gets what in the international system. When war exists, particular types of behaviors and attitudes are appropriate, and this is no different for the cyber enterprise. Cyber war allows tactics and techniques far beyond the normal conduct of interstate relations.

Before we move on from the definition of cyber war, it is useful to remember the Correlates of War empirical definition of war, which is a military conflict waged between (or among) national entities, at least one of which is a state, which results in at least 1,000 battle deaths of military personal. This is a key point to remember, as some have noted that there is really no such thing as a cyber war if there are no battle deaths involved (Rid 2011, 2013). The fact that there could be battle deaths does not mean that there will be battle deaths, so we should remember this in our discourse about cyber war.

So just what is cyber war? Stone (2012: 7) argues that the violent effects of cyber war need not be lethal to fall under the conception of war. This contention is tenuous since modern conceptions of war need to consider the deliberate and lethal application of force for there to be a war. Anything short of this is just conflict and violence in its basic sense, not war.

Perhaps the earliest Western conception of cyber conflict comes from Arquilla and Ronfeldt (1993), who wrote on the topic of what they call *netwar* and *cyber war*. They argued, first, that cyber war would be generally fought between militaries and that netwars would be fought between non-state, paramilitary, and other irregular forces (Arquilla and Ronfeldt 1996: 275). With the advent of cyber war and netwar, they argue that conflict "will increasingly depend on and revolve around, information and communications" (Arquilla and Ronfeldt 1996: 275).

Clark and Knake (2010: 6) define cyber war "as actions by nation-states to penetrate another nation's computers or networks for the purposes of causing damage or disruption." The important thing to take away from this definition is the notion that cyber war is a conflict between states. While cyber conflict can occur between non-state entities or individuals, our focus here is on the conduct of international affairs at the interstate level.

Another aspect of Clark and Knake's (2010: xiii) conception of cyber war is that it is not some sort of "victimless, clean, new kind of war we should embrace." In fact, cyber war, if it ever does occur, is likely to be very dangerous and bloody. Infiltrating civilian space and infrastructure is likely to impact the entire range of society and cause minor nuisances at the low end, and major catastrophe at the high end. "Cyber war skips the battlefield: systems that people rely upon, from banks to air defense radars, are accessible from cyberspace and can be quickly taken over or knocked out without first defeating a country's traditional defenses" (Clarke and Knake 2010: 32). By definition, any cyber war should be bloody because it causes the loss of life, even if it skips the battlefield, so to speak. Rid (2013: 12) counters this idea by arguing that "most cyber attacks are not violent and cannot sensibly be understood as a form of violent action."

Rid's (2011: 139) modification of the notion of cyber war, such that "violence inflicted through computer code is indirect and unqualified," is important. The cyber sphere is disconnected by a layer from the physical sphere; therefore the violence is indirect. This also makes violence unqualified. Nye's (2011) definition is a bit clearer about the nature of cyber conflict and the connection to the physical layer: "A more useful definition of cyber war is hostile actions in cyberspace that have effects that amplify or are equivalent to major kinetic violence" (Nye 2011: 20–21). Stone (2012) makes a similar point in that cyber war can be seen as a factor that multiplies force, rather than an act that commits the sides to the infliction of death.

In the end, Lindsay's definition does seem the simplest and perhaps the most useful. Lindsay (2013: 372) argues that cyber warfare "employs computer network attacks as a use of force to disrupt an opponent's physical infrastructure for political gain." Certainly warfare would require the use of force, but we are not so sure that this factor is characteristic even for a small amount of cyber actions. More critically, disruption of infrastructure is just one goal of many, but the definition offered here does well to consider force, the political nature of the incident, and the objective.

In addition to definitional questions of layers and kinetic impact, cyber war also must include elements in its conception of how it operates in the real world. As Nye (2010: 22) notes, in traditional battles, the defender has the advantage due to their knowledge of the terrain and direction of attack. In the cyber world, these advantages disappear since states often do not know where the incident will come from or even if an infiltration is occurring until after the "battle" begins.

Nye (2010: 23) also notes that in cyber conflict, the government does not have the monopoly on violence. Non-state actors and individuals could play a role in cyber battles; they could start them and could escalate them. The problem with this template is that individuals often do not have the resources or capabilities to compete with national cyber teams. It is also becoming more and more likely that states will be responsible for cyber activity that originates from within their boundaries, regardless of blame or attribution, because of the nature of national control of Internet structures.

The final aspect of cyber war that we will discuss is its geographic nature. The idea is that cyber conflicts can occur anywhere and everywhere. Since cyber tactics are disconnected from physical space, the application of the new domain will be demonstrated throughout the world. As Clarke and Knake (2010: 31) discuss, "cyber war is global: in any conflict, cyber attacks rapidly go global, as covertly acquired or hacked computers and servers throughout the world are kicked into service. Many nations are quickly drawn in."

While theoretically cyber conflict can be global, we must also remember that conflict in general is not global. Despite advances in the speed of communications and transportations, the old adage that conflict is local still holds. Most wars are fought over territorial issues (Vasquez and Valeriano 2010), and the spatial dynamics of these issues mean that most conflicts are localized. Despite having capabilities that can transcend place and space, we continue to fight very local conflicts. Continent-defying ballistic missiles are rarely or never used. When global battles are fought, such as the conflicts between the United States and its allies against Afghanistan or Iraq, we still see many local contextual issues arise. It takes months to build the capacity to fight. Supplies still need to be brought in; local knowledge needs to be acquired. Advances in technology have not necessarily changed who is fighting whom and how. We will likely continue to see this traditional conception of conflict in cyber battles, despite the ideas of cyber gurus. For these reasons, we prefer to use the term *cyber conflict* throughout.

## Cyber Conflict

It does seem clear that the term *cyber war* is overwrought and descriptive of a process that has yet to occur. Rid (2011, 2013) is correct to point out that cyber war is not happening. We argue that the processes developing in cyberspace are a bit different from traditional warfare, but that *conflict* is still an apt term. Cyber conflict is a tactic, not a form of complete warfare. It is not even a separate domain. It is a tool in the arsenal of diplomacy and international interactions, just as other forms of threats, and offensive and defensive actions in the toolbox of a state's arsenal of power. As Dunn-Cavelty (2008) notes, the cyber threat thus far is inflated, but it is a popular tool for politicians, policymakers, and defense contractors in contemporary discourse. To conflate cyber war with war is epistemologically dangerous.

Nye (2011a: 21) defines cyber warfare as "hostile actions in cyberspace that have effects that amplify or are equivalent to major kinetic violence." Many others mirror the same thoughts in their definitions, such as Hersh (2010), who defines *cyber war* as the "penetration of foreign networks for the purpose of disrupting or dismantling those networks, and making them inoperable." Our concern is that in order to define *cyber conflict* in the international relations realm, we must understand who uses the tactic, where, how, and for what ends. The Nye definition focuses on violence and leaves out the method of the cyber incident. The Hersh definition focuses solely on the dismantling of networks.

The Dartmouth cyber study group defines *cyber warfare* as involving "units organized along nation-state boundaries, in offensive and defensive operations, using computers to infiltrate other computers or networks through electronic means" (Billow and Chang 2004: 3). This definition gets us closer to what we actually mean when we discuss cyber affairs in the international discourse, yet it still uses the frame of warfare. This definition is also limited to nation-states. Nation-states are the primary focus of our analysis, as we spell out later, but it should not be a definitional limitation. In addition, the offensive and defensive frame is a bit narrow and entirely leaves out the European conduct of cyber operations, which are based on resilience, a third way of cyber tactics. Finally, to focus solely on computers leaves out avenues of breaching such as mobile phones and other unapplied technologies.

We use the term *cyber conflict*, as opposed to *cyber war*, because the term is better suited for the topic at hand and is not necessarily indicative of warfare. Much like the Correlates of War project and its Militarized Interstate Dispute (MID) dataset (Ghosn, Palmer, and Bremer 2004), we conceive of cyber conflict on a continuum where lower-level operations like DDoS incidents are the simplest forms of malice and higher infrastructure infiltrations are the most devastating and severe. Cyber conflict operates on a continuum that is unlikely to include the loss of life, but this is an open empirical question that we will refrain from making judgments on as of yet. The MID project codes severity ordinally, where the least severe coding is the threat to use force, while the most severe is nuclear warfare. Nuclear warfare has not happened and is not likely to happen. It is not assumed to happen either, but it could happen. Therefore we follow this construct and suggest that the correct term is *cyber conflict*, which can include low-level operations and extremely severe operations involving death. What would be important, then, is to examine the history of cyber conflict as it occurs, in order to understand which types of cyber conflicts provoke responses and escalation. We do assume escalation from the start.

Our definition of *cyber conflict* is the use of computational technologies, defined as the use of microprocessors and other associated technologies, in cyberspace for malevolent and/or destructive purposes in order to impact, change, or modify diplomatic and military interactions between entities. Unpacking this definition more, cyber conflict must occur in cyberspace through the use of computational technologies. We do not want to be more specific as to how the tactic will be used in order to account for future developments in the technology. To say that cyber conflict can only happen on computers forgets the natural evolution of microprocessors and how we use such technologies. What must be clear is that cyber conflict remains in the realm of conflict, which is a disagreement on preferred outcomes. There is a witnessed disagreement over preferred international bargaining outcomes for all cyber combat operations. One state is a revisionist actor and wishes to change the relationship between different parties, so these actions are part of the diplomatic or military sphere focused on changing behaviors to achieve a positive outcome.

It might also be useful to be mindful of Rid's (2013: 3) suggestion that cyber conflict may be warfare in the fifth domain—the realm after land, air, sea, and space.[8] While the domain is not sacred, incidents in cyberspace can impact land, air, sea, and space (Rid 2013: 166). The domains of air, space, and sea are also not sacred, since even a space attack could impact land tactics. We must move beyond this domain-based framework, but thinking of where the tactic is focused is useful in distinguishing how it is different from other tactics and forms of warfare.

Here, we are speaking of cyber conflict as an aggressive foreign policy tactic used by states against other states.[9] Our definition is expansive and can include non-state actor cyber operations, as covered in Chapter 7, but the purpose of our investigation in this book is a bit more focused. Obviously, cyber conflict is not limited to only state-level actors, but can come from individuals, terrorist organizations, corporations, and other relevant non-state actors. Therefore there are three areas of cyber conflict, as suggested by Nye (2011b): governments, organizations, and individuals. Government cyber operations cover cyber conflict between government actors and foreign policy decision-makers. Organizational cyber conflict would typically involve organized non-state actors such as terrorist networks or groups such as Anonymous. Individual-based cyber conflict would cover rogue actions by lone operators functioning to cause crime, chaos, or general malice.

Since our work deals with the realm of foreign policy, the primary focus of this analysis is on explicit government-to-government cyber combat. There would also be a need for different sorts of theories and ideas to explain these actions because they fall beyond the normal range of state-based foreign policy interactions. An empirical study of non-state actor organizational or individual cyber conflict cannot be ignored, however, and this is why we decided to devote a chapter to these actors. In general, organization and individual cyber actions would generally focus on the functions of economic espionage, cyber crime, cyber terrorism, or general fear-invoking chaos.

## TECHNICAL ASPECTS OF CYBER CONFLICT AND CYBER WEAPONS

Before we move forward with our analysis, we must also define and describe the types of cyber weapons available to states. Few people understand the Internet, and even fewer understand the nature of cyber weapons. What tools do states have at their disposal that can do harm to their rivals? *Cyber weapons* are "computer codes that are used, or designed to be used, with the aim of threatening or causing physical, functional, or mental harm to structures, systems, or living beings" (Rid and McBurney 2012: 6).

Weapons are, as Rid (2013: 36) notes, "instruments of harm." Cyber weapons obviously vary by type, distinction, usage, and application. We delineate four basic methods (weapons) that cyber conflict initiators have at their disposal. The methods of cyber incidents and disputes we code are comprehensive according to cyber combat tactics and analysis. We begin with the simplest form of cyber weaponry—website defacements or vandalism. Operators use Structured Query Language (SQL) injection or cross-site scripting (forms of injected code) to deface or destroy victims' webpages (Carr 2010). This form of malice basically takes over the site for a few hours or days and displays text or pictures that demean or offend the victim site. For example, in 2008 Russian hackers defaced many government websites in Georgia with pictures likening President Mikheil Saakishvilli to Adolf Hitler. Although rather benign, these methods may have important psychological effects. The loss of control of a government webpage may be a relatively harmless occurrence, yet the effect of this action on the population can be multiplicative. Generally, these types of incidents have a propaganda element. They also are a form of control, suggesting to the target that they lack the capability to control their cyberspace operations, or, more important, their territorial domain.

Next on the list (although more sophisticated, arguably not more severe than vandalism) is the distributed denial of service method, or what we call simply DDoS. These operations flood particular Internet sites, servers, or routers with more requests for data than the site can respond to or process (Reveron 2012a). This method shuts down the site, thereby preventing access or usage. Government sites important to the functioning of governance are therefore disrupted until the flooding is stopped or the hackers disperse. Such methods are coordinated through *botnets*, or, more colorfully, *zombies*, a network of computers that have been forced (or willingly joined in rare occasions) to operate on the commands of remote users (Clarke and Knake 2010).

A DDoS dispute was the primary method used by Russian hackers in the 2007 Bronze Soldier dispute with Estonia. Government and important private sites were hijacked by zombie networks and effectively shut down for a number of days or even weeks. The primary impact of the defacement method is the temporary disruption of service. To solve the problem, Estonia shut off Internet traffic coming into and out of the country, effectively compounding the problem.

Intrusions, which include Trojans and trapdoors or backdoors, are the third level of methods used in cyber conflict. These are more targeted and thus can be more severe than defacements and vandalism with regard to longer-term damage. Trapdoors or Trojans are unauthorized software added to a program to allow entry into a victim's network or software program. They permit future access to a site once it has been initially intruded upon (Reveron 2012a). Intrusions need to be added to software, can remain dormant for a long time, and then propagate themselves without notice (Carr 2010). These methods are difficult to detect or repeal with firewalls or security software, as they are not malicious upon entry into a network. They only become malicious once they become operational.

The China-based Shady Rat, Ghost Net, and Titan Rain operations are examples of Trojans that have been able to intrude upon the networks of many governments and steal state secrets. These must be installed by a user and are implemented at the whim of a hacker's command (Northcutt 2007). An operator can install the malicious program at one point in time and then activate it at a later date. These programs can be inside a secure network for weeks, months, or even years before they are activated and their true destructive purposes are realized. Shady Rat or Titan Rain could have been sitting within US military networks for years before the actual theft operations were implemented.

The purpose of trapdoors (or backdoors) is to steal sensitive information from secured sites. These methods can have destructive effects on a state's national interests. The major difference between Trojans and trapdoors is that trapdoors do not need a human hacker to begin the implementation process, while Trojans do. Trapdoors can be given a pre-dated command to activate their damaging potential. A recent example of a trapdoor method is the vulnerable chips found in Boeing's 787 onboard computers in 2012.[10]

Along with some methods of intrusions, the use of infiltrations constitute an act of war, as the US Department of Defense has declared.[11] Infiltrations and intrusions are not scalar with regard to which one is more severe, but they are generally more sophisticated, more targeted, and thus more severe than defacements or denial of service weapons.[12] *Infiltration* is the term we use to categorize what is more commonly known as malware. It is different from intrusions in that different methods are used to penetrate target networks. There are five major methods of infiltrations: Logic bombs, Viruses, Worms, Packet sniffers, and Keystroke logging (Clarke and Knake 2010). These five methods are precision infiltrations that go after specific data or force computers or networks to undertake tasks that they would normally not undertake.

Advanced persistent threats (APTs) add another layer to the scope of cyber methods and can come in any of the four methods discussed above (Sanger 2012). Examples of APTs are the Stuxnet worm, the Flame virus, and the Shady Rat infiltrations. APTs are different from traditional targeted methods in that they are customized, and move more slowly to avoid detection. Their intentions usually are more malicious and advanced and almost certainly come from states, and their targets are much more specific.[13] The level of sophistication is unmatched, meaning highly covert and intentional state action is behind the malicious intent, making APTs the most likely to evoke strong, negative, and escalatory reactions from the target state if and when discovered.

There are five types of infiltrations: (1) logic bombs are programs that cause a system or network to shut down and/or erase all data within that system or network; (2) viruses are programs that need help by a hacker to propagate and can be attached to existing programs in a network or act as stand-alone programs (they generally replicate themselves with the intention of corrupting or modifying files); (3) worms are essentially the same as viruses, except they have the ability to propagate themselves; (4) packet sniffers are software designed to capture information flowing across the web; and (5) keystroke logging is the process of tracking the keys being used on a computer so that the input can be replicated in order for a hacker to infiltrate secure parts of a network (Clarke and Knake 2010: Chapter 3).

An important element of the types of cyber weapons available includes the impact of each weapon on the target. The use of weapons for psychological reasons is an important aspect of cyber conflict. The user of a cyber weapon intends to threaten or cause harm to its target (Rid and McBurney 2012). Knowing that a state possesses certain cyber capabilities could be enough to get a state to capitulate or negotiate a way out of a disagreement with its adversary.

Another important element of cyber weapons is the nature of their usage. As Dipert (2010: 391) notes, they are weapons "whose effectiveness will likely rapidly diminish." With time, each infiltration becomes less effective because the target then becomes aware of the issue and corrects the problem. Cyber conflict is thus unique in many aspects, making the applicability of the security dilemma to this domain suspect at this point in time. This aspect of cyber warfare is new and unique. Gartzke (2013: 42) calls these weapons "use and lose capabilities, since revealing the capacity to damage an enemy through the internet typically also means tipping the enemy off to vulnerabilities that can be addressed, or inflicting harm that is temporary and thus does not have a durable effect on the balance of power." Rowe (2008) adds that cyber weapons are expensive. This means that after they are utilized, they are no longer cost-effective, as they can only be used once or twice. States are thus not inclined to pour money into a cyber offensive weapon because of diminishing returns on the investment. This plays an important role in our theory of how cyber weapons are used and the nature of restraint in cyber systems.

Geers (2010) notes that cyber weapons can come in forms ranging from mere nuisances to bringing down a state's critical infrastructure. Thus, a "one size fits all" categorization is not in order. We address this concern in Chapter 4 by discussing the different dynamics of cyber conflict with different pairs of states. Geers also notes that cyber weapons can be used by states and non-state actors, are not limited to combatants, and have the potential to disrupt the lives of many people at one time. Besides the devastating effects of nuclear weapons, which have the ability to wipe out entire populations, no other type of conventional weapon has the potential reach of cyber weapons (Geers 2010: 2). If cyber weapons are utilized to their full potential, the world could be more dangerous than during a Cold War between two nuclear-armed superpowers.

Lewis (2009) asserts that cyber weapons transcend international borders and sovereignty, which can lead to fuzzy interpretations by target states and possibly war. Intruding upon a state's physical wires and networks is comparable to a military invasion. Kelsey (2008) goes further and argues that cyber weapons are more likely to violate international neutrality laws than conventional attacks and should therefore be tolerated and accepted—but only to an extent. Since they are more likely to be used and therefore are not completely preventable, some rules of the game need to be applied. A normative system of tolerance should be applied, and this is discussed more in Chapter 8. There should be some wiggle room as to when a state can and cannot initiate a cyber incident or dispute, thus according to Kelsey, Article 51 of the UN Charter does not apply in cyberspace (Kelsey 2008).[14] He states that to prevent crises from escalating after a cyber operation has been launched, there must be some tolerance as long as the cyber incident does not go too far. We disagree with this premise. Allowance of cyber conflict should not become a norm, we assert, because states could push the limits of interpretation and escalate a situation to crisis and even war. Our theory of cyber restraint addresses this in Chapter 3.

## PREDICTING CYBER CONFLICT

Many argue that cyber warfare has already begun. Clarke and Knake (2010: 31) write that "in anticipation of hostilities, nations are already preparing for the battlefield. They are hacking into each other's networks and infrastructures, laying in trapdoors and logic bombs . . . this ongoing nature of cyber war, the blurring of peace and war, adds a dangerous new dimension of instability." They add that the prospect of highly volatile crises increases under the tactic given the speed at which cyber incidents can occur (Clarke and Knake 2010: xi).[15]

Singer and Friedman (2014: 133) go so far as to suggest that cyber war will be game changing, introducing operations that were only possible in the realm of science fiction. There is little question that the Internet and digital connectivity have changed the international relations landscape. While all these ideas may be true, it does not mean that we are in an era of cyber warfare or have seen a "game changer." It is likely correct that most future conflicts will have a cyber element to them, as will all elections, campaigns, humanitarian efforts, and other sorts of international interactions, but the question of direct cyber warfare is a bit different.

*Security* as a term generally means that there are threats (real or imagined) that states, individuals, and the system face, which have an impact of interstate relations and the domestic political environment. Thus the cyber threat, although thus far not very worrisome, must be dealt with by governments nonetheless (Dunn-Cavelty 2008). States are secure only when they master all arenas, which, as Choucri (2012: 38) notes, now include cyberspace in addition to land, sea, air, and space. This suggests that insecurity comes from a fundamental weakness in any area of the overall security portfolio. Eriksson and Giacomello (2009) analyze varying levels of control of the digital domain by states, and suggest that states such as China, an autocratic state with much control over the information flowing through its bandwidth, may have an advantage over freer states if cyber war actually came to fruition. This contributes to the debate between cyber liberty and security, and will be discussed more in Chapter 8. The perception for many is that we are in a period of cyber insecurity. In order to maintain security in an insecure world, demonstrations of cyber capabilities need to be made to shore up the weak spots in state defenses. However, we find that this may not be necessary for the cyber domain.

Reveron (2012a) chronicles the history of the terms *cyber war* and *cyber warfare* going back to their first usage by the US government in 1977 and the potential for use in war during the 1991 Gulf War. He (2012a: 15) notes, "while cyber war has not yet occurred and civilians clearly dominate cyberspace, the military services have recognized the importance of cyberspace in both peace and in war." The factors, such as the relative cheapness of the technology (except for cyber offensive weapons such as Stuxnet), the rising conflicts with states such as China, and the rush by military organizations to acquire cyber technology, all suggest that cyber war is in our future.[16] The argument is that these factors are likely the fundamental drivers of cyber conflict between states.

Each factor that Reveron (2012a) notes is derived from international relations theory and scholarship. Cheap weapons technologies are more likely to be used because actors have ready access to such capabilities. The cheaper it is to acquire a weapon, the more likely it is to be used (Lorell et al. 2000). The coming conflict with China (Christensen 2006) and other similar frames of future warfare also suggest to some that cyber conflict is going to occur because it is now connected to the military sphere and future conflicts cannot leave out this aspect. Finally, the rush by military organizations to acquire technology also increases the chances that the tactic will be used. Military buildups and rapid increases in capabilities have historically been demonstrated to increase the probability of conflict (Sample 1998; Richardson 1960).

According to the cyber prognosticators, cyber weapons are no different. Rapid increases in cyber technology will make it easier, cheaper, and more likely that states will utilize these technologies because there is a reduced cost and a psychological aspect of wanting to leverage new weapons to new situations. When applied to cyber conflict, all these factors are still dubious and afflicted with conjecture. At best, they are guesses, open to empirical and theoretical investigation. It is unclear whether or not weapons technology developed in this area will be used in other arenas. Actually, due to the connection to the civilian sphere, it seems less likely that these technologies will be used. Even Clarke and Knake (2010) frequently note the difficulty in applying cyber tactics against terrorists in the banking sector. It is unclear why a state that is restricted in the real world by norms and institutions will suddenly have a free hand to act in the hypothetical-future world. This is the conjecture most writers make in this area, and it is perplexing. It is not even clear that we are in an era of cyber arms races, given that there has yet to be a study that quantifies the buildup of cyber weapons in the framing of military buildups.

Just because a weapon is available does not mean it will be used. It must be remembered that states must have a reason for conflict for operations to break out (Mansbach and Vasquez 1981). Even the worst offenders in international history had demands and revisionist claims that motivated action. The cyber world will be no different; issues will continue to matter, and weapons will be used in a clear context, not just because a state has them.

Finally, it is unclear if conflicts in expected areas will actually develop. There are vigorous debates as to whether there really will be future conflict with China. Some, like Valeriano and Vasquez (2011), argue that there is no set course for major power conflict. Certainly, there will be cyber conflicts between states already fighting, like India and Pakistan, and Russia and its former vassal states, but it is unclear if other global powers will use the technology in combat.

Choucri (2012) uses Lateral Pressure theory (see Choucri and North 1975) to develop logic for when actors will seek change in the international system. The model is based on a configuration of variables that include population, resources, and technology that will push states to expand beyond their boundaries. There needs to be a proper configuration in place to propel states toward cyber conflict.[17] This effort to articulate a clear theory of cyber action is one of the few in the field. We hope to push further in this volume.

Using a rationalist and bargaining (Bueno de Mesquita 1981; Snidal 1985; Fearon 1995; Powell 1999) framework would lead others to suggest that cyber war between states, where cyber conflict functions like war, will not occur. As Gartzke (2013: 1) notes, "put another way, advocates have yet to work out how cyber war actually accomplishes the objectives that typically sponsor terrestrial military violence. Absent logic of consequences, it is difficult to believe that cyber war will prove as devastating for world affairs and for developed nations in particular as many seem to believe."

Other strategic thinkers differ from scholars like Gartzke. Some would agree with Sheldon's (2012: 208) contention that the ability of cyber technologies to "manipulate the strategic environment" and also weaken the enemy makes cyber tactics likely to be utilized in the future. They are now part of the command "toolbox" (Sheldon 2012: 209) available to the military. As Choucri (2012: 4) notes, the physicality of cyberspace is different, allowing for disputes that transcend the constraints of geography and physical location. This addition to the military toolbox makes cyber tactics potentially unique and likely to be utilized on the international battlefield, according to some.

Clarke and Knake (2010: 30–31) take the perspective that we have not yet seen what can really be done in cyberspace. What have been exhibited so far have been primitive cyber incidents. Yet, as Reveron (2012b: 230) notes, "just because we can imagine cyber war does not mean that it can be waged." This leaves us a lot of room to theorize and engage the question of the future of cyber conflict. There are two clear extremes. In one, cyber conflict will happen and will become a regular aspect of international relations. The other extreme is that cyber conflict will not occur and will be safe in a digital future—a frame some might call *cyber skepticism*. There is a clear middle path that has yet to be developed, and we will argue this for the rest of this book. This approach can be framed as *cyber moderation*. Cyber conflict will occur, but the conflicts themselves will be trivial, will not result in a change in behavior in the target, and will largely be regional cyber incidents connected to traditional international issues at stake between states. This leads us to question the direction of the future uses of the tactic. We argue for the examination of the real sources of disagreements between states that might drive the cyber conflict we observe in the system.

To this point, studies about the impact of cyber-technologies on foreign relations are purely speculative; no one has yet examined the shape and consequences of cyber operations. Pundits and scholars have not been limited by the lack of analysis from fear-mongering and inflated threats. As Lynch (2010) puts it, "a dozen determined computer programmers can, if they find a vulnerability to exploit, threaten the United States' global logistics network, steal its operational plans, blind its intelligence capabilities, or hinder its ability to deliver weapons on target." It is quotes like these that could lead to an increase in spending on cyber defense that might be disproportionate to the threat exhibited. Rather than suggesting that the nature of combat has changed, we are interested in measuring if, how, and why it has changed. The shift toward the knowable rather than "unknown unknowns" of the cyber domain is important in scholarly discourse and could perhaps lead to a more proportional means of defense for governments involved in rivalries or on the cyber battlefield. This is an important point since deterrence is unlikely to work in the cyber arena.[18]

The next question relates to how cyber tactics are perceived by the enemy and what the foreign policy impact of such disputes could be. Cyber conflicts in the international system could potentially destroy command and control structures of the military and foreign policy apparatus, wipe out the media communications of a state, destroy financial memory and wage economic combat, target the health industry and hospitals, or wither the ability of domestic units to protect the citizenry by eliminating technology used by police. However, all these impacts are purely speculative.[19]

The real utility in cyber conflict seems to be much more muted than many pundits believe. Information and money can be stolen, confusion and chaos can ensue through the activation of computer viruses; but these outcomes fail to compare to damage done by large-scale military options or even economic sanctions. The events of 9/11 have more "shock value" than stealing secrets from the Pentagon. Since most military networks are decentralized, the installation and implementation of effective malware is a difficult if not impossible proposition. For example, the Stuxnet worm that hit the Iranian nuclear program had to be planted from the inside with traditional intelligence operatives or through an outwitted Iranian employee. Even the new advanced chip that the National Security Agency (NSA) has developed to hack into systems first has to be implanted in the system to make the transmitter work.[20] Most people overestimate a hacker's ability to carry out large-scale infiltrations; these operations are rarely successful without major failings in the security of the target.

In terms of conflict operations, the attractiveness of the target in relation to the capability used is a critical equation rarely examined. What good would a cyber conflict between rivals be if it does little physical or psychological damage to a rival state? The focus of rivalry is to punish or burn the other side (Valeriano 2013); it is unclear if cyber tactics can achieve this. Furthermore, if a cyber incident takes a long time to have an impact, and might only impact a limited number of targets that only a few leaders know about, what good is the use of the tactic? Much is made about the secret nature of cyber operations, yet the paradox is that we would then know very little about the impact of covert operations of foreign policy dynamics. The value of the tactic seems minimal when one thinks of the potential for direct attack between states. On the extreme end, a large-scale operation that might wipe out the United States' Eastern Seaboard Power Grid would be catastrophic, but it would also be punished with immense retaliation.

That restraint exists in the realm of cyber conflict is an idea few seem ready to engage. Some have begun to make this point in various forums. Rid (2011, 2013) argues that cyber war in the extreme sense that death will result has not yet occurred, and is unlikely to occur. "Cyber war has never happened in the past, it does not occur in the present, and it is highly unlikely that it will disturb our future" (Rid 2013: xiv). Likewise, Gartzke (2013) develops the logic for cyber war being utilized by states as a low-level form of conflict. We (2014) have made this point in our research on Russian foreign policy, which argues that cyber conflict is literally the least damaging and easiest option that Russia could use to retaliate against Estonia during their dust-up in 2007.

In summary, little is known about the actual impact of cyber tactics. Much speculation has been made with little connection to the realities that are discernible. The risk to the initiator in relation to the impact of cyber tactics does not make the use of cyber strategies a very optimal option in the international system. Restraint will dominate, since the costs are potentially so high, even with the inclusion of non-state actors acting as proxies. This leaves us to further outline our theory of cyber restraint and regionalism as we move to the empirical study of conflict.

We now live in a digital era in which the speed, interconnectedness, and level of interaction between states and individuals are growing at an exponential rate, a trope well established in the discourse. This new reality brings fear, as the infrastructure we depend on is thought to be fragile. Since we depend so much on digital communications, it stands to reason that we are also vulnerable to threats that originate from this realm. Everything from our money to our water is vulnerable to cyber malice.

We dispute these assumptions, and build a theory to challenge this conventional wisdom. The question is to what extent these extreme warnings and fears are warranted. How vulnerable is any given country to cyber malice, and what evidence do we have for cyber conflict in the last decade? Should this fear be the basis for reorganization in military structures and doctrine?

## WHAT IS TO BE DONE ABOUT CYBER CONFLICT?

It remains clear that there are many notions of what cyber war/conflict is, how it will evolve in the international system, and the propensity for conflict in the future, yet no scholar in the international relations field has actually attempted to both systematically account for the probability and frequency of cyber conflict (Choucri 2012: 43) or to test a theory of cyber action.

In fact, Guitton (2013) suggests that since no one has actually accounted for the usage of cyber tactics at the systemic or interstate level, there is an extreme disconnect between cyber security policies and the actual sources of cyber threats. This is a key step lost in the process. Some feel that explaining past instances of cyber conflict behavior is a pointless task, but for many it is the most critical step that seems to have been missed.

Understanding the past and current uses of cyber power can help us explain and predict future uses and responses to the tactic. Guitton's (2013) main point is that deterring future cyber threats should be focused on law enforcement mechanisms and cyber crime, rather than framing the issue as an external national security problem. We go further in this book and argue that by understanding the true nature of the cyber threat, who uses the tactic against whom, and at what level, we can make accurate statements about the future use of the tactic in the international relations sphere.

With a focus on offensive cyber operations and the inflated nature of mythical cyber threats, there seems to be a misdirected application of the technology in the policy sphere (Dunn-Cavelty 2008). Instead of a revolution in military affairs, cyber tactics just seem to have refocused the state on external threats that then escalate through the typical process of the security dilemma. In some ways, fears of cyber conflict become self-fulfilling prophecies. Dunn-Cavelty's (2008) work is instructive here, as it dissects this growing cyber threat perception in the United States and the driving engine behind it—cyber defense contracts. By focusing on the external threats, rather than the internal criminal threat that comes from cyber enterprises, we may have missed many opportunities at collaboration and institution building. There obviously needs to be a global accounting for cyber actions and plans, even those that inflate cyber fears, as Clarke and Knake (2010) agree.

The use of the European model of resilience, as Davi (2010) suggests, might be beneficial in its promotion of multilateral institutional and cooperative measures of deterrence in cyberspace. Singer and Friedman (2014: 36) define resilience as "what allows a system to endure security threats instead of critically failing. A key to resilience is accepting the inevitability of threats and even limited failures in your defenses." The EU already has an exceptional framework for cooperation and collaboration; using this institution as a steppingstone to further deepen international cyber agreements might be a beneficial path. Also, modeling cyber strategies on resilience-based methods rather than offensive methods might ameliorate the security dilemma.

There is much to learn from those who do not overstate the cyber threat. The developing foundations of cyber action at the multilateral and legal level are promising (Ferwerda, Choucri, and Madnick 2011), but are also in danger of being ignored and washed away by the military imperative that seems to have taken hold. It is likely that some combination of institutions, legal frameworks, and defensive and reliance-based strategies are important steps forward (Miller, Brickey, and Conti 2012). We hope that the examination conducted in the following chapters will make this point even more strongly.

## GUIDING THE REST OF THE INQUIRY

Rid (2013: 142) makes the interesting point that since cyber war is not taking place in the form of violence, death, and destruction, cyber conflict actually reduces the amount of overall violence between states. Activities such as espionage and subversion become more cost-effective (Rid 2013: 142), but also more benign and less risky in some senses. This is an interesting path, but no one has sought to follow it, to dissect the context of cyber conflict between states, and to examine their impact.

It could also be argued that offensive strategies are the worst path to follow in cyber technologies because they only provoke the opposing side to do likewise. Since cyber weapons are cheaper and easier to produce than conventional weapons, many states could then quickly level the playing field by building their own offensive weapons. This would suggest that the typical path of conflict preparation is not fitting for cyber operations, and it brings us back to the idea that notions of balance between offense and defense are not operational in this domain.

The point of this volume is to uncover all of the questions put forth thus far with theories, data, and analysis. First, we proceed by constructing a theory of cyber conflict, a missing development in the debate that is crucial. We then outline the dynamics of current cyber conflict between states, according to our data collection of active cyber incidents and operations between 2001 and 2011. Further, we examine the foreign policy impact of these events by looking at the level of conflict and cooperation after cyber conflict and dissecting the qualitative impact of noteworthy cyber incidents.

By understanding the dynamics of cyber conflict, we can then make accurate statements about their efficacy and impact in order to suggest policy ideals surrounding the technology. Now that we have cleared the conceptual minefield and have defined our terms, we can move forward with our investigation. The literature on cyber conflict and the terms used are very divergent, problematic, and outright confusing at times. We have endeavored to explain how cyber conflict between states should be defined and examined. The next step is to develop our own theory of cyber conflict.

Perspectives diverge. Some, like Clarke and Knake (2010), suggest that cyber conflict is in our future, while others, like Rid (2013) and Gartzke (2013), suggest that cyber war will be limited. The question we ask is different: What do we know thus far? We ask this question so that we can predict what the dynamics of cyber conflict will be in the future. Short of war, what cyber interactions have been seen, and what will these interactions tell us about the future course of cyber conflict? By understanding these questions, we can hope to develop a rational and constructive response to the actual threat that emanates from cyberspace and that contains the reactions to the realm of reality.

## CHAPTER 3

# Theories of Cyber Conflict

## Restraint, Regionalism, Espionage, and Cyber Terrorism in the Digital Era

### INTRODUCTION

In this chapter we provide a theoretical framework for the analysis and prediction of cyber conflict in the international system. For many, the goal of theory is to provide the proper framework to investigate empirical and normative ideas. This is necessary to maintain logical consistency, maximize explanatory power, and provide for predictions given a certain set of circumstances or conditions. Unfortunately, this step is often missed in the cyber security field. Research in the field should be tied to reality and evidence because the stakes are so high; there is also no room for conjecture in such a critical aspect of the security dialogue.

To this point, the discourse on cyber conflict, weapons, policy, and security clearly lacks an engagement of theory and evidence in relation to the international system. There are many questions that scholars and policymakers raise; however, there are few real deductive or inductive explorations of cyber processes by these people. Cyber strategies and analysis at this point are entirely anti-theoretical. Many misapply basic international relations concepts and ideas as they see fit. There is a sizable gap between a constructive analysis of a critical international process and the actual evaluation of cyber interactions.

New tactics sometimes require new modes of thought to deal with their implications. Instead, cyber theorists seem to be focused on either predicting a constant use of cyber tactics or misapplying deterrence logics to the study of cyber interactions. The main flaw of the entire cyber security enterprise is a complete lack of theoretical engagement beyond a few atypical examples—one of the few being Choucri's (2012) examination of cyber power and lateral pressure.

We hope to rectify this problem by laying out a theory of cyber political inter-actions based on the principle of restraint in cyberspace and the issue-based perspective of international politics. We argue that cyber options are usually removed from the toolkit of responses available to a state because massive cyber operations would escalate a conflict beyond control, would lead to unaccept-able collateral damage, and would leave the initiating side open to economic and computational retaliation. When cyber operations are used, they typically are low-scale events akin more to propaganda and espionage than warfare. This leads to cyber restraint, a form of operations derived from deterrence theory but not dependent on it. We also argue that there will be a large amount of regional inter-actions in cyberspace because these conflicts are tied to traditional reasons that states disagree, namely territorial conflicts. Understanding these perspectives will be critical in analyzing emerging cyber security threats

## CYBER POLITICS AND THE ROLE OF THEORY

Without theory, key aspects of cyber dynamics can be left unexplained, unex-plored, or ignored. What processes are at work, why are they chosen, and how are they used? What predictions can be made, and what leads to the generation of these predictions in the first place? We hope to fill this gap in this chapter. Here we seek to elucidate a theory of cyber conflict that addresses who will be the tar-gets, what methods will be used, and what level of operations will be conducted to deal with the problem in an offensive or defensive manner.

Our perspective is based on empirical realities, which constitute an important part of any analysis (Vasquez 1999). Naturally, normative implications will not be ignored, but the first goal should be to explain and predict empirical proper-ties. In this book we produce both an inductive and deductive series of logics to explain the use of cyber technologies in international relations. Based on the study of rivalry (Valeriano 2013; Diehl and Goertz 2000) and the issue-based perspective (Mansbach and Vasquez 1981), we argue here that rivalries are the main entities that will utilize cyber interactions, and they will mainly do so in a restrained manner through regional interactions characterized by other ongoing issues of high salience, such as territorial or regime status issues. As such, our main focus in this volume is on state-involved cyber interactions, as we argue that these are the main entities that have the capabilities and the resources to carry out actual cyber "war" or are the target because of their far-reaching actions. The issue-based perspective helps us solve one perplexing outcome of cyber research to this point: Why do so few states utilize the tactic, and why has it failed to impact state-to-state relations when it has been used?[1] By connecting cyber issues to the wider perspective of an issue-based system of conflict evaluation, we are able to correctly place state-based cyber issues in their rightful context, the contentious stakes between countries. By locating the main threat of cyber actions in the study of rivalry, we move beyond the oft-repeated attribution problem and locate the cyber threats in their current conflict environment, based on the information already at hand.

The question for many in the cyber security community is whether or not a system of deterrence can work in cyber operations (Kugler 2009; Goodman 2010). Scholars and pundits fall on both sides of the spectrum. Some advocate that there can be deterrence in cyberspace. They contend that the fear of retaliation can prevent potential initiators from using cyber weapons on a target (Kugler 2009). Others argue that there can never be a form of deterrence in the cyber world because these incidents can be anonymous and quickly destructive, preventing deterrence considerations from operating (Betts 2013). Others push for offensive and defensive operations, thereby ignoring deterrence.

A system of deterrence is unrealistic in cyber operations because credibility is lacking and actors cannot retaliate due to the uncontrollable nature of the weapon. We argue that restraint comes into play in this system for this reason. Cyber maneuvers to demonstrate resolve and credibility are also limited because of the potential of displayed capabilities to be replicated back on the originator, and the high likelihood of collateral damage. Also, the idea of quick and anonymous incidents is misguided and inaccurate given that most cyber interactions occur during periods of rivalry, and thus the perpetrator is often known. Deterrence processes require intense long-term planning and surveillance.

Deterrence logic in the cyber security field is problematic because often the target is responsible for the infiltration in the first place, due to its own vulnerabilities and weaknesses. This makes the process inoperable, since the first step toward a solid system of deterrence is a strong system of protection, but countries seem to be jumping first toward systems of offense rather than defense. It must be remembered that in nuclear deterrence, the target must survive the first strike to have any credible system of retaliatory capability. How is this possible when countries do not take defenses seriously, nor do they focus on any viable system of resilience?

Deterrence also fails since the norms of non-action in relation to cyber activities dominate the system, making retaliation in cyberspace or conventional military space unrealistic. Threatening cyber actions are discouraged; as evidence demonstrates, non-action becomes the new norm. How then can credibility in cyberspace ever be established? For credibility to be in operation, a key characteristic of deterrence theory, capabilities must be made known and public. This demonstration effect is nearly impossible in cyber tactics because in making your capabilities known, you also make them controlled and exposed.

Finally, deterrence is not in operation in the cyber realm because counter-threats are made. These occur not in the form of massive retaliation generally invoked in conventional deterrence logics, but in the form of marginal low-level actions that only serve to escalate the conflict further. For an action to be prevented under deterrence, the defensive threat has to be greater than the offensive threat. Despite the possibility that cyber tactics must be persuasively catastrophic, the norm in the cyber community is for cyber actions to be either based on espionage or deception, not typically the sort of actions associated with persuasive consequences preventing an action in the first place (Lindsay 2013; Gartzke 2013). Deterrence is the art of making known what you want done or not done, and enforcing this course of options through threats. In terms of cyber deterrence, the concept is utterly unworkable.

If deterrence is not at work for cyber conflict, then compellence may fit the dynamics of cyber interactions. Cioffi-Revilla (2009) notes the difference between deterrence and compellence in the context of cyber conflict, writing that "compellence is therefore about *inducing* behavior that has *not* yet manifested, whereas deterrence is about *preventing* some undesirable future behavior. Accordingly, compellence works when desirable behavior *does* occur as a result of a threat or inducement (carrots or sticks, respectively)" (126). We see neither compellence nor deterrence working in cyber conflict, as states self-restrain themselves from the overt use of the tactic. Therefore neither is prevented or induced into non-use by threats.

While cyber technologies might not apply to traditional deterrence logics, this does not mean that other forms of normative constraints on conflict fail, making an operation that seems like deterrence workable. We argue that a system of cyber restraint is in operation. Cyber operations are limited due to the nature of the tactic and the conditions that limit the engagement of targets by cyber victims or offenders. Cyber incidents can be replicated right back to the target, making the tactic risky to display. There might also be blowback in the form of retaliations directed at the attacking state's extended interests. If one state utilizes a cyber tactic, the target state could use the offense as an opportunity to target civilians on the initiating side, limiting the usefulness of the operation in the first place. Finally, the tactic is too expansive to control. It is nearly impossible to limit the amount of damage done to civilians and infrastructure if cyber capabilities are utilized.

For these reasons, a system of cyber norms are in operation that limit the amount of damage a state can inflict using cyber technologies. Thus, although states may have the capabilities to unleash weapons into cyberspace, they are restrained from doing so nearly all of the time, even during war. Surprisingly, even the most cyber-capable states in the system (United States, China, and Russia) are restrained from utilizing their most potent cyber weapons during conflict. This could mean that they prefer other tactics, but the bottom line is that cyber tactics have been used less than one would think if we are truly experiencing a period of technological revolution in military tactics. The United States did not use cyber tactics during the operation in Libya and only at a low level against individual cells in Afghanistan. There was a similar outcome with Russia against Ukraine in 2014, with little evidence of direct cyber action beyond seeking to control domestic groups within Russia. A policy outcome of cyber restraint typically ensues in these cases, and states will generally fail to take advantage of cyber capabilities, handcuffing their options out of choice. The process is much like placing an individual in a straitjacket to limit further harm. To protect others, including those in the state of interest, the initiator limits the options on the table and restrains its own ability to conduct operations. This is not deterrence in the mutually assured destruction variant, but indeed an entirely different concept that we deem *cyber restraint.*

We argue that cyber tactics tend to be utilized for regional interactions, if at all. This defies presumptive cyber logic since the tactic is removed from the physical boundaries of states and can be launched at global scale in a matter of seconds. Cyber operations should be able to be launched anywhere and anyplace in response to real or imagined threats, so why would the theory call for regional foundations?

In reality, we find the locations of cyber conflict generally confined to regional interactions. This is likely because the level of animosity needed to utilize cyber tactics generally only occurs between states who have historic conflicts rooted in territoriality and other issues that can lead to war proneness (Vasquez and Valeriano 2010). The only states that defy these patterns are the hegemonic powers that conduct global operations; otherwise, most operations will be local and connected to traditional issues that divide states.

Going further, we spell out a theory of cyber espionage and how cyber terrorism will be utilized by states. Here we define *cyber espionage* as the use of dangerous and offensive intelligence measures to steal, corrupt, or erase information in the cybersphere of interactions. What is unusual about cyber espionage is the paradox of the tactic being common, but also literally the least a state can do. When cyber actions are exhibited, they tend to be low-level espionage actions that do not rise to the level of conflict or warfare. States seem to be very measured and concentrated in their cyber espionage activities. They take action for specific reasons if there is a demonstrated weakness in a target. If a target seems to take few measures to protect the home base and its resources, the initiator will exploit the vulnerability. In the espionage realm, states seem to be doing the least they can, given that their demonstrated capabilities often far outweigh their actual expressions of activity. States will restrain themselves from unleashing the full weight of their cyber capabilities, because the damage done is not worth the costs. Simple cost-benefit analysis would suggest that this will be the course of cyber operations in the future, yet the discourse takes on a troubling and inflammatory tone, in terms of what others predict. In short, some hype the collective fears in the system for their own ends.

What we end up seeing in this domain is spycraft, not warcraft. Operations are taken to exploit a weakness in security, rather than operations taken to exploit or crush a target. Choices in the cyber realm are not made based on a need to infiltrate a target, but almost solely on the opportunity to hit a target based on its failures to secure basic protection. When the walls are down, the state will do what it can to gather information. When the walls are up, the state will be restrained and will not seek to use methods to break down the walls, because there will be consequences for these actions. China has been notorious for finding and exploiting gaps in American cyberspace defenses, but it has also sought to limit its conflictual interactions with the United States in most other realms. In this way, we see cyber espionage activities as a method to make known what can be done in relation to defense gaps, rather than a method to seek exploitation based on offensive capabilities.

Our theory of cyber espionage runs parallel with how cyber terrorism is used.[2] States will support cyber terrorists when it is easy to do so, when the target is simple to exploit, and to punch above their weight in terms of capabilities. Cyber terrorism is a method primarily used by weaker states to exploit a demonstrated weakness in the target and to create a situation of equal footing between two largely unequal powers. Yet, this is a tentative step; the state actor hides behind the non-state terrorist actor. Once again, this is almost the least a state can do with its toolbox of aggressive cyber actions.

Non-state cyber terrorism is relatively weak and benign. To reiterate, our focus here is on state-based actions, but we should make it clear that non-state actor terrorist initiatives in cyberspace are limited because of the nature of the tactic—therefore our selection of domains is warranted and critical.

Instead of being an easily utilized method of hitting an enemy, as common myths indicate, extreme cyber actions are generally only available to state-based actors because of the money, time, and skill involved to exploit cyber targets. We will dive into the reasons for the weakness of non-state/terrorist actors more fully in Chapter 7, when we examine the process of Cyber Gaza and other operations. Stuxnet is also indicative of this process, and we will explore it in more depth in Chapter 6. In the Stuxnet case, the state actors must have had massive amounts of money and technological knowledge to create, transport, and initiate the cyber weapon. They also must have had assets inside the target willing to help make the operation a success. On top of this, they had to be incredibly lucky (or unlucky, in terms of how Stuxnet was released into the wild). Paradoxically, powerful states are the only ones who can really marshal offensive cyber capabilities to commit state-sponsored cyber terrorism, but they will not utilize this step, since the action would be so costly in terms of reputation.

We develop the logic behind state-based cyber terrorism in this book. It is a method used to equalize the playing field when a state has fallen behind its target. Yet there are limits to these operations, as the consequences can be high and embarrassing for the sponsor of the individual hacking group. In this way, actions taken to exploit demonstrated weaknesses are often ignored in that they are also the fault of the target rather than a demonstration of the power for the initiator. More extreme actions are limited because the cyber offenders know there will be retribution for their actions. All these considerations combine to produce the outcome we predict in general: cyber restraint.

Our theory is social constructivist in nature (Berger and Luckmann 1967; Onuf 1989). As others, such as Dunn-Cavelty (2008), Eriksson and Giacomello (2009), and Hansen (2011), have suggested, cyber threats are socially constructed. The danger that cyber incidents can portray between rival factions can construct a very real threat that will then lead to escalated tensions between these entities (Hansen 2011). Furthermore, the public as well as corporate framing of cyber incidents as a threat, real or imagined, can lead to a change in a state's perception of the threat, which in turn would demand action, either diplomatically or militarily (Nissenbaum 2005; Eriksson and Giacomello 2009). The state would find the need to securitize itself from these cyber threats, which could spill over into more conventional responses, such as airstrikes or economic sanctions (Hansen and Nissenbaum 2009). We follow these points and agree that the nature of and response to cyber threats are socially constructed by many diverse factors, such as government messages, media talking points, and popular culture. This orientation makes us question the nature of the cyber discourse and focus on empirical observations rather than the message of such attacks.

What is also important for our project is that the initial choice to launch a cyber operation and the response to offensive operations are socially constructed by the overall situation of rivalry and its history, the system of norms in operation at the time, and the nature of fear-based responses in the attacked or threatened society. Without focusing on these factors and moving beyond the material-based form of cyber operations, we would remain trapped by the fascination of new technology. While technological developments are important, what really matters is how they are used and the responses they elicit during operations. For these reasons, our theory is grounded on the notion that responses are conditioned by engagement with reality, and this engagement is a function of the time, location, and system in operation.

Overall, the generation of theories for cyber-based state interactions is a critical step that is sorely needed at this time. Cyber security is a wide-open field in international relations. We have developed the theories presented here in a deductive and inductive fashion, and then test them according to the available data and cases. This can help us grasp the reality of modern cyber interactions. The long-term future may be very different, but for now and in the coming decades, cyber operations led by states, used through the tactic of espionage and through state-sponsored cyber terrorists, will be limited due to restraint dynamics, and generally will be restricted to regional operations connected to ongoing geopolitical struggles.

## RIVALRY AND CYBER INTERACTIONS

In this study we develop the logic for cyber interactions among interstate rivals. The benefits of examining the rivalry population, rather than interactions between all states, are clear and logical. Why focus on all possible dyads when we have exhaustive data on those states most likely to engage in crises, escalated conflicts, and wars (Diehl and Goertz 2000; Thompson 2001)? By only examining the rivalry population, and other associated examples of historic antagonism, we should be able to focus on the enemies experiencing obvious forms of cyber conflict and dismiss much of the noise and misdirection common in cyber enterprises. In some ways, this selection of domain solves the commonly referred to attribution problem in cyber relations.

The concept of rivalry brings history and a past pattern of interactions back into the study of political science, and is an important response to the rise of the data revolution in the field. To understand why wars or crises develop, one must look at the history of interactions at the military, diplomatic, social, and cultural level. Rivalry is simply defined as long-standing conflict with a persistent enemy (Diehl and Goertz 2000) or based on perceptive views of threat (Thompson 2001). For a rivalry to exist, there must be a long history of events and complicated interactions leading up to the situation. When war or limited conflict does occur, there is usually a long-standing and recent history of animosity that pushes both sides toward combat. It would therefore make sense that cyber weapons would be added to the arsenal of rival interactions and should be investigated under this context.

The next important consideration for rivalry in relation to cyber tactics is relative gains or losses. The issue positions of the states engaged in a rivalry are made in relation to the attitude of the other side (Vasquez 1993). Foreign policy perspectives during a rivalry are often not made out of strategic rationality, but out of the simple, and perhaps immature, position of denying a gain to the enemy. The phrase "to cut the nose to spite the face" comes to mind in rivalry (Valeriano 2013). Rivals are in some ways addicted to perpetual conflict because of their singular outlook of targeting the enemy. This spiraling competitive relationship can be a dangerous situation in international affairs due to the buildup of hatred and tensions over time. Cyberspace could be a fruitful battlefield for such rivals.

Another process in rivalry is what is called the normal relations range (Azar 1972), where rivals try to manage competition and engagement through low-level operations. In the process of cyber espionage, the tactic is likely utilized to manage low-level proxy battles that avoid direct confrontations and therefore manage the rivalrous relationship. South Korea and Japan seem to exhibit this behavior, as both have much animosity toward each other, yet are also close allies with the United States. An example of this is the March 2010 DDoS flooding of Japanese government sites, which marked the seventieth anniversary of a 1940 Korean resistance movement against Japanese occupation. The Japanese responded in kind with a DDoS incident of its own. Cyberspace seems to be the perfect forum for them to vent their frustrations with each other.

As most rivalry scholars note, there must be some degree of competitiveness, connection between issues, perception of the other as an enemy, and long-standing animosity, for a pair of states to be called rivals (Diehl and Goertz 2000; Thompson 2001). These issues are central for how one codes and operationalizes the term *rivalry*. There is the contention that rivals are selected by the researcher, but this is why it is advantageous that we have two different rival datasets to utilize; they help avoid the bias that is inherent in data collection. In any case, rivals are only selected into existence in that they may be the only states to selectively participate in serial crises connected to competitive issues. These are exactly the cases we wish to examine in this volume. States that act without serial competition act in a different manner from rivals, and are beyond the scope of our analysis.

There might be some obvious drawbacks with the focus on rivalry in our study of cyber interactions. Gartzke and Simon (1999) make the point that rivalry could be a hot hand—an example of a loaded deck, so to speak—that is not reflective of the true state of affairs. While this effect is possible, especially if we focus on rivals that are measured only through a certain number of disputes, it is also unlikely to impact our analysis since we do focus on states that are also considered perceptive rivals (Thompson 2001) or rivals in fact, if not in disputatiousness. The original domain of this study was restricted to rival states, but we have expanded this study to include examples of states that might be engaged in what are called cyber rivalries, like Estonia and Russia. Our focus on rivalry is purely theoretical and helps to operationalize our concepts. The use of case studies to move beyond data-based analysis should help us specify better how cyber interactions work in a manner unfettered from the rivalry framework.

The question for this analysis is what might the impact of cyber conflict be on rivalry relations? Cyber incursions are tactics used to gain an advantage either diplomatically or militarily against a target. During a rivalry, one would think all options should be on the table; war and cyber conflict then become viable foreign policy options.

Escalation to war in a rivalry typically develops after a certain number of high-tension events occur in a rivalry relationship. Interestingly, after a rivalry is born through the process of escalation, the normal relations for rivalry interactions tend to take the form of espionage, war games, brinksmanship, and economic warfare. It is in this context that rivals should display a certain degree of hesitance to use cyber tactics against their rivals due to the fear of retaliation and to manage the tense relationship. An early case study of a few rivals who engaged in cyber conflict in the post-Soviet region leads us to propose that there is a degree of restraint at work during cyber conflict between rivals (Valeriano and Maness 2012). One would expect that rivals would be the most likely to use cyber tactics, yet evidence so far suggests that they are restrained beyond all reasonable expectations and predictions.

Analyst Bruce Schneider has written exhaustively on worst-case thinking about cyber conflict. He points out that such conjecture involves imagining the worst possible outcome and then acting as if it were a certainty. "It substitutes imagination for thinking, speculation for risk analysis, and fear for reason."[3] What is interesting is that cyber rivals should be the sorts of actors who use cyber technologies the most if these worst-case prognostications are true, yet preliminary investigations tell us that this is not the case; actions tend to be reserved in cyberspace. So what dictates how rivals will interact in cyberspace?

Our theory of cyber interactions stakes out a clear position to start, and we argue that restraint and regionalism dominate. We do not hypothesize that the worst-case actions will be the result of cyber interactions, rather that the norm should follow the current pattern of limited use of cyber technologies on the foreign policy battlefield. We could theorize that rivals will use cyber conflict extensively against their enemies because it fits a pattern of interactions governed by hatred. We could then also highlight a few spectacular examples of cyber conflict. Our theory, however, is counterintuitive to this logic, and macro-evidence supports this notion. Scholarship grounded in deterrence theory is where we develop our argument about why cyber conflict is relatively absent among rivals. Instead of deterrence, we argue that restraint characterizes cyber relationships.

## FROM DETERRENCE TO RESTRAINT IN CYBER OPERATIONS

Restraint plays a critical role in the cyber realm. Unfortunately, scholars and analysts have mistakenly applied a theory of deterrence to cyber actions (Goodman 2010; Guinchard 2011). Here we examine just what a policy application of deterrence would mean in the realm of cyber conflict. How can deterrence work in the cyber discourse? What processes would need to be observed for this to work, and how can this policy application work in practice?

We argue that the use of the theoretical idea of deterrence in the cyber realm is a misapplication of deterrence theory. Lawson (2012: 2) suggests that the use of the term *deterrence* in the cyber realm could be dangerous: "the war metaphor and nuclear deterrence analogy are neither natural nor inevitable and that abandoning them would open up new possibilities for thinking more productively about the full spectrum of cyber security challenges, including the as yet unrealized possibility of cyber war." Different motives, centered on the concept of restraint, provide a more accurate reading of cyber outcomes and processes. Furthermore, restraint is the policy outcome but not necessarily a process; we need other ideas and terms to describe the policy process of states limiting responses and uses of cyber conflict in reality. The term *cyber straitjacketing* seems to be the most applicable, in that cyber powers are prevented from taking extreme cyber actions due to the confines of the technology and also to prevent self-harm.

Our main point is that we need to develop new theories of cyber interactions, in order to understand and explain the process. Applying old theories from different contexts is of limited value in the cyber discourse, as new ideas and concepts need to be brought to the forefront to explain the dynamics of cyber conflict. In this vein, we propose cyber restraint, cyber regionalism, and cyber operations as espionage, rather than predicting the frequent and ubiquitous use of cyber tactics in the international system.

## Deterrence in History and Theory

Deterrence theory has been the bedrock of US national security strategy since the beginnings of the Cold War. As Brodie (1946: 76) puts it, prior to World War II, the purpose of the military was winning wars, and after World War II, the purpose of the military establishment is to prevent wars from occurring in the first place. The consequences of conventional and unconventional conflict have escalated to the point where the goal should be the defense rather than the offense. The result was what some call *decision-making deterrence theory*, which purports that the consequences of war can be made so costly that only an irrational leader would consider war and attack as a viable option (Zagare and Kilgour 2000: 17).

Deterrence policy, based on mutually assured destruction and unilateral threats, is thought to have maintained a peaceful system for over 50 years. Derived from Schelling's (1966) analysis and suggestion that military strength can be used for coercion, deterrence theory heavily influenced post-atomic foreign policy construction. Instead of risking engagement in direct conflict, great powers developed nuclear arsenals to prevent attack and to ensure security. Jervis (1979) explains the buildup of deterrence as an extension of diplomacy, where expressions of force are communicated between sides to deter moves, rather than using overt force. States are effectively trying to avoid a conflict spiral and a never-ending situation of continuous threats by making the ultimate threat, and preventing the first steps toward conflict.

Rationality is a key component of deterrence scholarship. For many, it is a loaded term that has various meanings according to the situation. In the deterrence literature, it basically means that an actor will weigh the costs and benefits of action, determining the best path given the information at hand. Given the constraints of the system and actors, the rational actor often chooses to cooperate (Zagare and Kilgour 2000: 21). Yet this is dependent on information and access. Without information to weigh the costs and benefits of action, it is almost impossible to determine what a rational outcome might be, given a situation.

As was suggested long ago by Kahn (1960), there are two types of deterrence operations: immediate and extended. Extended deterrence refers to threats made to third parties, while immediate threats are related to the state in question. Immediate direct deterrence between two parties often fails. When states try to enhance their security position through threats, alliances, and military buildups, they often fail to provoke the reaction intended—concessions. In fact, states often provoke further conflict and more extreme threats (Vasquez 1993; Hensel and Diehl 1994) when they make moves in order to deter further violence.

For the concept to work, the threat inherent in a deterrence operation has to be very clear if the tactic is to be utilized as a policy option. As Betts (2013) notes, "the deterrent warning must be loud and clear, so the target cannot misread it." In the nuclear paradigm, it is very clear what must not be done and what the consequences of such action would be. In the conventional conflict setting, modern applications of deterrence are much more difficult in operation, since it is unclear what the response to an operation will be, and what level of punishment a state would be willing to commit to in various situations. As the hegemon, the United States has nearly unlimited power and capabilities, yet it is still challenged and attacked by enemies who know that the consequences of action will be drastic. This presents a challenge to the conduct of deterrence as a policy outcome.

As a tool of foreign policy, deterrence can be the primary way to explain and examine foreign policy interactions during the Cold War (Zagare and Kilgour 2000: 4). Moving forward, many identify the logical problems inherent in deterrence and try to push past the antiquated applications of the theory. Some, like Vasquez (1991), even suggest that deterrence was not the main reason for the long Cold War peace. The absence of territorial disputes and salient issues between the nuclear powers explains why major power wars were avoided. Others articulate new policies like Perfect Deterrence theory (Zagare and Kilgour 2000) and complex deterrence (Paul et al. 2009). Perfect Deterrence theory (Zagare and Kilgour 2000: 289) suggests that the potential initiator has to be both capable (in that the threat hurts) and credible (in that the threat can be believed). While these processes may provide a solution to the logical and empirical problems inherent in classical deterrence, these conditions are tough to fulfill in the cyber world. How would one know that a threat hurts unless a demonstration of capability is made? The paradox is that once a demonstration of capability is made, the cyber weapon is then put out into the wild for all to dissect.

Our theory of restraint in cyber conflict refers back to this original conception of extended deterrence with modifications. Clearly deterrence in its original conception—avoiding conflict through threats—does not apply to the cyber conflict paradigm, but there are aspects of the system that will continue to hold. Comprehensive restraint relates to deterrence from spectacular attacks, such as nuclear weapons and devastating Internet intrusions or infiltrations focused on power systems and health services. States are constrained from undertaking such actions, through fears of retaliation and escalation of the conflict beyond control. The logic here is that extreme measures will be prevented through the fear of extreme consequences. Our theory does not depend on notions of credible threats, rational actors, or perfect information to work, only that the initiating side understands the drawbacks to its proposed action, and therefore will choose a more restrained approach to the situation. It is through this process that we will expect to see few cyber conflicts of a severe nature in the immediate future.

## Cyber Deterrence as Concept

Moving into the cyber context, there is a healthy debate as to whether or not deterrence works in cyberspace. Kugler (2009) argues that while a deterrence system would not be perfect, it could protect the United States from being infiltrated. If the costs of a cyber incident or dispute are considered grave enough, the potential initiator will choose to not to take that step. Therefore, deterrence could be a success in the cyber realm. Goodman (2010: 102) goes much further, arguing that since deterrence works in the physical world, it must also apply to the cyber world because the cyber domain is inseparable from the physical.

This line of reasoning leads to many interesting questions and problems if deterrence is to work in cyberspace. There are many issues that cyber deterrence scholars themselves point out. For one, many cyber incidents will be too minor to provoke deterrent actions and considerations (Kugler 2009: 329). For example, Chinese intrusions on the *New York Times* network, in response to an unfavorable investigative story, would not be an issue critical enough to provoke the wrath of the United States. These actions may cause consternation, but the real question is whether they fall under the umbrella of deterrence calculations. When most cyber operations fall in such a grey area or are really espionage actions, can we expect deterrent threats to be applicable in preventing action?

The most troubling aspect of cyber deterrence is the nearly universal application of offensive methods to deter adversaries. Kugler (2009: 310) notes, "endeavoring to deter cyber attacks is a matter both of assembling the physical capabilities for defending against them and of employing offensive capabilities—cyber, diplomatic, economic, and military tools—for inflicting unacceptable damage in retaliation." Saltzman (2013) goes further, arguing that the best method of deterring cyber incidents is through offensive posturing in order to provoke an enemy into backing down. These ideas are then translated into policy, as the proposed new head of US Cyber Command argues that there needs to be an offensive element for all American military units, in order to demonstrate that there is a capability and will to respond to all cyber threats.[4] As we will explain, offensive actions are problematic in cyberspace for many reasons—the main being the unpredictable nature of cyber weapons, the high likelihood of collateral damage, and the fact that once a cyber weapon is used, it is no longer an element of power. For these reasons, and a host of others, cyber offensive actions are dangerous and will fail to provide the protection sought in traditional deterrence theory.

In fact, from a review of non-cyber deterrence dynamics, utilizing offensive weapons is neither the objective nor the norm. Weapons, especially nuclear weapons, are frequently denoted as defensive options, and employing weapons systems signifies a failure of deterrence, not a step toward deterrence. Yet, in the cyber realm, the need for offensive capabilities seems to be assumed under the umbrella of defense. More of an issue is the assumption that the offensive route is the best method to deter further aggression. This ignores decades of peace science research suggesting that countering a threat with a counter-threat and escalating the action will only provoke more escalation (Leng 1993; Hensel and Diehl 1994; Vasquez 1993).

Furthermore, we argue that many instances of cyber operations are a result of states trying to match a more powerful opponent on the foreign policy battlefield. Cyber technologies can equal the playing field, so to speak. Thus when states utilize cyber technologies, it is often a less capable state (for example, China) that is trying to catch up to a competitor through any method it can use to exploit weakness. Paradoxically, from our position, Goodman (2010: 109) makes the point that cyber deterrence can work when there is symmetry between competitors. Unfortunately, most cyber competitors are nowhere near equals, so the symmetry condition is often not met.

Another problem with cyber deterrence is the credibility issue. As Kugler (2009: 326) states the issue, the defender must "project an image of resolve, willpower, and capability." These traits may be difficult in cyberspace, where the intentions of actors are not made clear, due to the secrecy of the tactic. Even more critical, capabilities in the cyber realm are hidden, either in order to keep the taboo sacred or to prevent others from understanding research methods and advances. Deterrence in many ways requires perfect information. The offender must know the capabilities of the defender in order to understand whether an attack is worthwhile, yet this process is missing in cyberspace. There is no information at all, let alone snippets used in conventional systems to demonstrate capability. In the cyber world, demonstrating capability would mean tipping your hat and letting your methods be examined and replicated by the entire community. This is one of the major issues of cyber conflict, if used; it is a single-use weapon that no longer exploits an unknown problem. The problem or weakness is then known to all.

Perhaps overstating the attribution problem too much, Betts (2013) nonetheless does suggest that "deterrence is a weak tool in the increasingly important realm of cyberspace, where it can be extremely difficult to be absolutely sure of an attacker's identity." The attribution issue for many is a key limiting factor that makes cyber deterrence in cyberspace inoperable. Kugler (2009: 310) notes that there are many circumstances in which the cyber initiator will make its identity known or reliably inferred from information; so there is some debate as to how much attribution really matters in cyber deterrence. Goodman (2010: 128) argues that functional responsibility can be placed on cyber actors, muting the attribution problem.

Applying the actual tenets of deterrence theory, as applicable to conventional and nuclear conflict, to cyber conflict results in a much different and limited application of the concept to cyber interactions. Libicki (2009) argues that cyber deterrence would not work as well in nuclear deterrence. Our own reading of deterrence policy finds the doctrine inapplicable to cyberspace. Immediate deterrence is inoperable because threats often invoke the process of the security dilemma and escalating conflict. The concept of immediate deterrence applies to small actions undertaken to produce a change in behavior in the target. The often-observed result is a hardening of the issue position of the defender, and more extreme moves by the offender. This can be observed in cyber conflict when limited options are used in an attempt to produce a result or change in behavior. The result is the same as in the past: limited options only make the situation more intractable; therefore it is difficult to argue that immediate deterrence operates in cyberspace.[5]

On the other hand, aspects of comprehensive deterrence do endure in our cyber restraint framework. In dyads with nuclear capabilities, the probability of conflict declines (Beardsley and Azal 2009); thus we would expect the same among nuclear cyber powers. Dyads with ongoing military buildups and nuclear capabilities are less likely to escalate to war, even with rapid military expenditures (Sample 1998). Extending this concept to cyber relations would suggest that restraint does not work at the low level of cyber incidents, such as those of the DDoS variant or simple vandalism, since there is little to restrain a state from acting at such a minimal level. More comprehensive cyber incidents, on the other hand, are off the table. It is unlikely that a state would be willing to initiate a cyber incident to destroy a power network, social services facility, or government organization, such as the Department of Defense, due to the fear of retaliation.

Focusing on the intention of changing behavior is the correct application of deterrence to cyber politics. The problem is that by deterrence, most cyber scholars mean the prevention of initiating a dispute in the first place, rather than the resulting policy change. In the non-cyber deterrence literature, the key aspect of the condition was to either change behavior or induce policy stasis in the opposition through the fear of attack. The correct process of deterrence should be to make known what you want done or not done, and to back this position up by a threat in order to ensure that your preference is followed. Many suggest that deterrence in the cyber world would mean preventing a cyber incident, rather than a change in policy. This is simply what most people call defense. Focusing on the issue positions of each side and their foreign policy objectives really gets to the heart of the debate here. To utilize nuclear weapons to attack one side is a policy option for settling an issue disagreement. To utilize a massive cyber operation to destroy the power network in the opposition in the same way is a policy option to settle an issue disagreement; thus the issues at stake are critical for the debate on how cyber processes will play out in reality.

As time has passed, the purpose of deterrence has been removed from the actual policy choices and intentions of each side. In foreign policy, the goal for each side is to either protect the national or collective global interest over some value. It is under this context that restraint is likely to be the policy outcome of cyber positioning. Utilizing more advanced or harmful cyber methods will either escalate the conflict, break a taboo against the non-use of the technology, or not produce the targeted changed in behavior in the other side. Therefore, it is unlikely that states will conduct serious cyber operations against each other.[6]

Another key factor that many overlook is the need for credibility in the examination of cyber deterrence dynamics. Credibility is lacking in cyberspace. It is often unknown if the cyber initiator has the ability to make its threats operable. Demonstrating credible capability in the cyber world would give away the information as to how an incident would happen and thus would allow the defender to prepare for such a possible infiltration. Another issue results from the deniability inherent in cyber actions. While it can be clear who the offender is, often the aggressor hides behind the wall of cyber deniability. It is impossible to know the true extent of cyber possibilities without demonstrations of cyber power, which then limits deniability.

Credibility is the key condition that many deterrence scholars examine in the nuclear context. Some, like Schelling (1966), make the point that deterrence is useless unless the potential initiating side is seen as a credible threat. Will it actually go through with the threats it has made clear? In this way, deterrence becomes like a game of chicken, when the side that flinches last wins (Kahn 1960). This provides a flaw of logic for cyber deterrence that cannot be overcome. Leaders and publics will likely be unwilling to launch the ultimate cyber operation that would prevent incidents in the first place. To win a game of deterrence, the steering wheel needs to be thrown out the window, so to speak, rendering the threat credible. That this is the solution to the logical flaw makes cyber deterrence problematic overall. In order to establish capability, you must demonstrate the capabilities of your weapons; in that process you destroy the advantage, because your cyber weapons are now exposed for all to see.

At the top of the credibility issue, there is also the empirical flaw that the more credible, realistic, and escalating a threat is, the more likely it is that the defender will choose to respond, as non-action would signal weakness (Leng 1993). The most likely outcome to demonstrations of power and credibility in the international system is repetition by the opposing side, which demonstrates that deterrence has failed. This often escalates the situation, which is the outcome dreaded by all. There is evidence that this repressive process is in use when responding to terrorism. Dugan and Chenoweth (2013) demonstrate that repressive actions used to deter future terror actually provoke more instances of terror. We could see the similar process in the cyber world, as actions taken to deter future cyber events only increase the probability of their usage in the future.

It is unlikely that we will see demonstrated and severe cyber actions; therefore, there is a paradox that cannot be accounted for in cyber deterrence. Deterrence is only in operation when the threat is credible. If the threat cannot be demonstrated, then it cannot be seen as credible, and thus deterrence does not work in cyberspace. In addition, even if deterrence was to be used, it is likely that the reaction in the target would be the complete opposite of what was intended—resulting in escalation, not deterrence. There are many inherent flaws with the deterrence paradigm as it is applied to cyberspace.

Cyber deterrence is a process laden with paradoxes and contradictions. Cyber threats are toothless because taboos (Tannenwald 1999; Price 1995; Dolan 2013) prevent the display of cyber force in the first place. As Dunn-Cavelty (2008) asserts, cyber threats are only a reality based on perceptions. The reality of the threat does not meet the level of discourse surrounding the topic. Why would a state be limited in its actions if it is unsure of whether or not the opposing side is willing to carry out its threats? Overall, we find that the application of deterrence to cyber operations is limited, misapplied, and illogical in many areas. Instead, we move to a different notion of cyber interaction—the idea of restraint, rather than deterrence, in cyber operations.

## A THEORY OF CYBER RESTRAINT

The suggestion has been that cyber methods of international disputes are proliferating and expanding. Kello (2013) argues that theories and empirical assessments of cyber conflict in international relations scholarship are lacking or underdeveloped. He notes that cyber conflict and its dynamics are "expanding the range of possible harm and outcomes between the concepts of war and peace—with important consequences for national and international security" (Kello 2013: 8). We challenge these assertions on both counts: international relations scholarship is deeply engaged in the cyber debate; and the cyber threat is not proliferating to the point where the conceptions of war and peace need to be altered and reconstructed.

The operations of Stuxnet, Flame, Titan Rain, and Ghost Net are often given as examples of the increased usage of the tactic. The coming future should include and expand to the digital battlefield (Nye 2011). Each cyber incident is given a catchy name and is repeated breathlessly by the media. In reality, cyber methods appear to be empty and hollow, lacking the impact they are thought to be capable of, given the novelty of the tactic.[7] Here we elucidate a theory of cyber interactions focused on restraint as an operational process. Our ideas about cyber conflict are based on a complete theory of cyber interactions, as states learn to use cyber power as a new tactic. New tactics have a history of being enfranchised early in their life. Airpower, for example, was weaponized early in its history; nuclear weapons, however, were used against Japan, and the normative revulsion to these actions was so complete that usage again is considered unforgivable.

Innocuous cyber tactics might be part of what Azar (1972) called the normal relations range for a rivalry. They may function as methods of signaling displeasure or discord to a rival. The surprising finding in relation to conventional wisdom could be that rivals will tolerate cyber combat operations if they do not cross a line that leads directly to the massive loss of life. This is why it is so important to account for the severity of the operation in a theoretical frame. Cyber actions are expected to occur and even to be tolerated, as long as total offensive operations are not conducted. By total offensive operations, we mean direct and malicious incidents that might lead to the destruction of the energy infrastructure of a state, or incidents meant to take control of army units or facilities. These options are off the table for states, since they will lead directly to war, collateral damage, and economic retaliation, which would then escalate the conflict beyond the control of the state leadership. Actors in cyberspace will therefore be restrained in their use of cyber weapons.

As Nye (2011) notes, the vulnerabilities evident in the Internet make the tactic dangerous to utilize since a cyber method can be replicated right back against the initiator. A cyber worm can be examined and reproduced, then used to target the origin location (Farwell and Rohozinski 2011). Cyber weapons are not like conventional weapons; once used, they do not expire. Their life span can be unlimited if the code is altered in slight ways or if they escape the environment for which they were built. Stuxnet was launched in 2010, and in 2013 it was found in a Russian nuclear plant.[8]

Methods used in one cyber incident can be developed further for the next incident with little cost to the initiating side. For these reasons, cyber weapons can be more dangerous than conventional weapons, but also for these reasons, cyber weapons are less likely to be utilized. No state wants to show its hand and expose its technology to outside sources. This is the current contention with Stuxnet, as while it was a powerful cyber incident, it also was set out into the wild, and others likely will utilize the weapon for their own ends. This same problem exists for zero day exploits (security flaws that are unknown) that are used by initiators in cyberspace. These sorts of vulnerabilities cease to be weak points once they are used because the program operator now knows how the cyber method works and how to stop it. They are no longer zero day exploits since the vulnerability is usually patched at this point.

Another factor contributing to restraint is collateral damage. States are now limited in offensive actions due to functional norms of limited harm against civilians. An example of this logic can be inferred from the 2003 US invasion of Iraq or the 2011 NATO operations against Libya. In 2003, Bush administration officials worried that the effects of cyber combat would not be limited to Iraq, but would instead create worldwide financial havoc, spreading across the Middle East to Europe, and perhaps back to the United States.[9] The United States restrained itself from initiating cyber methods against its rival (Valeriano 2013) during outright war, as the potential fallout of such operations would, through complex networks of interdependence, extend to civilians. In addition, the United States failed to use cyber tactics against Libya during the operation to support the National Transition Coalition forces, due to concerns about the civilian impact.[10] Of course, there could be other reasons that the United States failed to use cyber tactics, but the evidence clearly suggests that civilian harm was the primary concern.

Globalization is a process whereby states are more interconnected than in the past. The other fact about the current age of globalization is that these connections occur at a pace that sometimes can defy typical measurement. The speed of interactions makes vulnerabilities in systems more devastating because proliferation of errors and cyber incidents can happen quickly. While many fear this development, the corresponding result—restraint—keeps these worst-case inclinations from becoming a reality.[11] States tend to be to be responsible, despite protestations of recklessness. Cyber states are no more reckless than other states.

The next form of restraint relates to the idea of collateral damage limiting cyber actions. We must also consider the role of norms in cyber interactions. Norms are shared standards of behavior. It has become increasingly clear that cyber operations are increasing, but only in terms of small-scale actions that have limited utility or damage potential. The real cyber actions that many warn against have not occurred. The longer this remains the case, the more likely it is that states will set up normative rules to govern cyber behaviors. This could include institutional restraints, international consultations, or legal standards. For now, however, we can only really observe functional restraints to cyber actions. As will be explored in more detail in Chapter 8, cyber actions are a sacred taboo that must not be violated. There remain red lines that no one has yet crossed. There is a chance they will be crossed, but for now we have observed states being limited in cyber actions.

Related to restraint, the process of conflict diffusion can also hinder efforts to utilize cyber technologies. As Fielder (2013: 2) notes, "during a cyber conflict, unregulated actions of third parties have the potential of unintentionally affecting U.S. cyber security policy, including cyber neutrality." The fear is that cyber conflicts can drag in unanticipated third parties, active external parties spoiling for an excuse to fight, or drag in parties seeking to remain removed from the conflict. The danger of cyber conflict is that it is so uncontrolled and undetermined; the consequences are often unclear, making battlefield calculations difficult. Thus, in order to keep a conflict from proliferating, parties will once again be restrained from using cyber actions.

The final process that produces cyber restraint is the notion of blowback or retaliation. A bit of a different concern from replication, blowback basically means that there will be responses to cyber actions, often conventional. There will be consequences to cyber actions, not in the form of mutually assured destruction, but in the form of conventional operations to cyber actions because of the normative red lines that states have instituted. The worst case, the hypothetical cyber Pearl Harbor, is unlikely to happen because the response would be so massive and would occur in the conventional form. We move beyond cyber considerations here and suggest that functional abilities to unleash pain will constrain actions in potential initiating parties. The United States has noted that a cyber incident could result in conventional responses if done as an act of war. This leaves us to speculate that there is fear attached to the use of cyber weapons. There is restraint in the usage of cyber methods because of the fear of a response.[12]

Our theory is dyadic in nature. Founded on specific responses to the attacker by the defender, we are relying on the willingness of the target to assure its own defense and not appeal to collective defense. Limiting taboos and ethical concerns might be global in nature, but the application is dyadic in nature. While a collective defense system for cyber threat might work in the EU context, system or regional responses fit in few other contexts. There can be no extended protection since engaging in punishment for a violation would then commit the same violation, starting the cycle.

The overall motivation is that fear will produce restraint in cyber actors. There are too many negative consequences of the use of cyber weapons, for states at least. The problem of attribution in cyber technologies has been mostly overstated in regard to foreign policy–motivated attacks. If South Korea is hacked with a computer network infiltration, it is generally simple to determine which state might be responsible. When Georgia is attacked in cyberspace in the midst of an invasion, the perpetrator is not difficult to deduce. There is no hiding in the cyber world; actions will come back to haunt offensive cyber states, and there are consequences for actions; thus we argue for the limited nature of cyber action, despite the cyber revolution hypothesis.

### Cyber Straitjackets

Our notion of restraint being in operation in the cyber world also suggests the concept of straitjacketing cyber actors. Restraint alone cannot really be used to describe the policy process a state might consider when contemplating a cyber incident. Restraint represents the outcome of the policy process; the term that outlines the process under consideration might be more accurately termed *cyber straitjacketing*.

States are straitjacketed in their ability to utilize cyber methods. In some ways, they are prevented from using the technology in order to prevent self-harm. Blowback and replication are real issues that need to be confronted in the cyber world. Any weapon used in this domain can be reproduced and directed back at the initiator. Using cyber tactics in many ways can harm the state more than it helps it. Likely the use of the technology will not produce a change in behavior of the target, but the action will be punished, and the cyber incident will become public. It is for these reasons that states will often willingly place their operatives in what might be considered constrained restriction. The consequences of using the technology at a maximum level are just too devastating.

Another way to describe straitjacketing is that states are handcuffed in the operation of cyber tactics. Extreme actions are limited, because the conduct of these technologies is ungoverned and unlimited. The full range of motion is limited, due to the nature of the tactic and the taboo associated with its usage. Whichever term is preferred, the outcome is still the same: the limitation of action. While there might be negative connotations associated with each term given their history, the reality remains—that states are likely constrained in their actions, despite protestations that the international system is governed by anarchy.

The paradox here is that no actor likes to be constrained in its policy choices. While the functional outcomes of the policy process and choices available to states are limited in the cyber realm, offensive posturing remains an option. States can threaten cyber retaliation in order to restrain a target from escalating a conflict, but the actual method of retaliation is often never in the cyber realm. When China infiltrates the United States in cyberspace, the United States utilizes diplomacy to solve the problem, rather than responding in a tit-for-tat manner. This avoids needless escalation, which could possibly get out of hand. Once again, the demonstration of responsibility of state-based actors defies conventional wisdom. States will even be prevented from using a cheap and quick tactic like cyber methods, because of the consequences of this use of the technology. When confronted with a new dynamic with immense potential, often states are prevented from utilizing the technology because of the difficulties in application, evaluation, and implementation.

## CONSIDERING CYBER REGIONALISM

Often scholars overlook the regional dynamics inherent in their analysis. This is particularly true in the cyber realm, where there is much more regionalism than one might expect. The idea that cyberspace extends beyond state boundaries, since the technology is not bound by location, is persuasive. Clark and Knake (2010: 31) write that "in any conflict, cyber attacks rapidly go global, as covertly acquired and hacked computers and servers throughout the world are kicked into service. Many nations are drawn in." Singer and Friedman (2014: 73) note, "there are no geographic limits." The idea is that cyber conflict is removed from typical local and regional concerns, due to the nature of the technology; as it is said, things quickly go global. Is this frame true? How much globalism is there is cyber conflict?

The problem with this frame is that, while the Internet is a realm of instant, global, and nebulous interactions, the machines being interacted with are always located somewhere. Mainframes, systems, and databases all have physical locations, and these locations are typically the targets of malicious cyber actors. Often, the targets of cyber operations are located in states that are the traditional enemies of the initiating state. This gives them the motive to launch a cyber dispute in the first place.

We must move beyond the notion of international interactions being random or based on pure power projection considerations. Chinese cyber incursions on US infrastructure are not about challenging global hegemony, but they are a reaction to real and concentrated issues between the two sides in the international system. Often these issues are territorial in nature. China has serious territorial disputes with its neighbors, most of whom are allies of the United States; these conflicts draw the two states toward continued animosity. Furthermore, the United States and the international community can and do restrict China's access to international technology and do not share the development of advanced weapons systems. For these reasons, it is logical that the Chinese would infiltrate the United States with cyber operations in order to secure information and protect the issue space around the considerations that are critical to Chinese security. The system does not determine action; actions are determined by the issues at stake, the regional dynamic in operation, and the nature of the target and its weaknesses.

International cyber interactions are determined by the issue that draws states into conflict. Most rival interactions in cyberspace will have a regional context connected to the issue of territorial considerations or disputes since most rivalries start due to territorial concerns (Vasquez and Leskiw 2001). These disputes may institute a culture of antagonism. Vasquez and Valeriano (2010) find that the modal category for war is territorial issues. This is even more relevant for rival states (see Valeriano 2013 for a review). To locate the source of cyber incidents and disputes, territorial considerations are often at the heart of the issue.

Other issues can determine action and must be considered, such as regime leadership (Vasquez and Henehan 2001). One state might target another with cyber operations in order to remove and discredit the leader in charge. This was the dynamic behind many of the disputes between Russia and Georgia when Georgian President Mikhail Saakishvilli's image was defiled. The tactic seemed to work in that he lost the next election. The same process can be seen in the recent Cyber Gaza incidents in which Palestinian activists targeted the leadership of the Israeli state. This condition also applies to human rights violations that dictate a state act, but in a restrained manner, because full intervention is problematic and costly. In either case, the issue at stake is likely a regional concern that reflects local political dynamics.

In defiance of the typical jargonized notion that cyber operations defy space and place considerations, we argue that most cyber operations, if they do happen, will occur within regional systems due to issue concerns that locate conflict in spatial subsystems. Varied and distant cyber operations will only be conducted against the great global powers. All other disputes will be located at the regional level, if not between neighbors, over territorial issues.

## LOW-LEVEL COMPETITION: CYBER ESPIONAGE

We theorize that many cyber actions that do occur are low-level demonstrations of capability or espionage-type probing activities. First, we suggest that cyber interactions will be colored by restraint and regionalism, but what of the lower-level operations typically observed in cyber dynamics? What explains the level of crime, break-ins, and information stealing that does occur in cyberspace, as directed by states? To explain this process, we focus on cyber espionage since cyber interactions tend to take the form of typical espionage operations.

The case of Russian cyber operations is indicative of the potential pattern of cyber intelligence operations in the future (Gvodsev 2012; Maness and Valeriano 2014). At first, Russia was an active aggressor, utilizing cyber incidents against Estonia in 2007 and Georgia in 2008. Since then, it has remained relatively silent in the course of cyber operations, even during the escalation in Ukraine over Crimea.[13] The answer to why this outcome has presented itself can likely be found through a series of norms and blowback to the original use of cyber tactics. The matter of how Russia has and will utilize cyber incidents in the future is likely to exhibit the patterns of low-level cyber espionage because Russia has been shamed in the past. Cyber espionage is defined as the use of dangerous and offensive intelligence measures in the cybersphere of interactions. As we have stated elsewhere (2014), the actions Russia has taken in the cybersphere are examples of literally the least they can do in the system. Their capabilities far outpace their actual use of their technologies. Russian demonstrations of cyber power have been minimal. States have utilized cyber espionage operations, but they have done so rarely, and their use of these tactics follows the pattern of restraint, as a state seeks to ward off such intrusions and recklessness if the target state leaves its defenses down.

We see this cyber-dominated espionage process at work in China. While the Chinese are active in cyberspace and have their own offensive cyber command, in reality they have used cyber incidents minimally, usually for espionage rather than outright cyber warfare. In response to negative articles about the premier of China, Wen Jiabao, the Chinese launched a series of denial of service incidents and phishing methods against the *New York Times* and the *Washington Post*. Some *New York Times'* employees' computers, passwords, and e-mail accounts were infiltrated. The media outlet had been the victim of these incidents for at least four months until security experts were able to finally shut down these phishing attempts. More interesting is that the *New York Times* and its security firm traced the incidents to a Chinese government operation known as Unit 61,398, which is part of the Chinese People's Liberation Army General Staff Department, an entity that has been troubling government and private networks in the United States for years.[14] While disconcerting, these cyber incidents failed to reach the extreme levels that most prognosticators suggest when they analyze cyber interactions. Instead of destroying American media operations, they have only sought to disrupt, punish, and steal information from those they feel prompted the aggression. There is a cause, a means, and a will displayed during these inter-actions, but the outcome is purely a demonstration of capabilities that fall in the category of espionage.

Beyond the theoretical gap we have outlined, there is also a gap in the litera-ture developing an explanation for why cyber espionage is used between states or state-based targets. Cyber intelligence operations are proliferating, but at a low level, mainly in the area of espionage, where the goal is to either steal, harass, or make known the ability to penetrate networks. Rid (2013: 82) suggests that most cyber activities we see are really espionage efforts. Considering this process, why then would states utilize cyber espionage operations over full-scale cyber offen-sive operations? What sort of defensive intelligence mechanisms does the United States have for thwarting or launching cyber espionage campaigns? To develop the logic behind this process, we must understand the intention of cyber opera-tors in the system.

The first connection between cyber abilities and actions is the observa-tion that states do literally the least they can do in the cybersphere. The point for a state-supported cyber operation seems to be to demonstrate capabilities, rather than destroy systems and operations—extreme incidents such as Stuxnet and Flame excluded. It is as if the initiators only want to make their existence and capabilities known. As with conventional deterrence policies, actions and responses are only effective if they are communicated to the target. China and Russia have achieved this goal in their cyber operations. They have made known their capabilities and reach, and then have chosen to go no further.

Why would this be the case? In terms of rivalry relations, empirical investi-gations by Conrad (2011) and Maoz and San-Akca (2012), in relation to a rival state's support of terrorists or non-state actor groups, argue that the advantage of covert operations and supporting these groups is deniability and the per-petuation of bait-and-bleed strategies that keep the conflict removed from the state interested in harming its rival. Cyber initiators hope that the infliction of wounds, which might be physical, psychological, or economic, will multiply and proliferate these problems to the target state. Likewise, cyber espionage could also be part of the usual process of a rivalry where the tendency is to burn a rival (Valeriano 2013: 13). By harassing a rival state, a state provokes a reaction. Sometimes this reaction can be offensive, but just as important, the reaction can be defensive. While defensive actions are generally benign, sometimes they go too far.

As Mueller (2006) has documented so well in relation to terrorism, the protection industry that sprang up around it has been more devastating than the tactic itself. By seeking secure forms of protection against cyber espionage threats, the target then overreacts, overprotects, and cuts itself off from the systems and opportunities the global information age has done so well to cre-ate. Just as business operations have been harmed by terrorism, business itself has been just as hardened by cyber operations. Certainly, companies can lose millions of dollars in order to clean malware and prevent cyber incidents, but they are just as likely to lose even more money in taking extreme actions to protect themselves in the future. These organizations spend money on software and infrastructure that have little or no probability of stopping what are termed *zero-day threats*. These threats are called zero-day because they cannot be anticipated and stopped—only reacted against once they happen. The paradox is in the amount that organizations spend to protect what they cannot possibly defend against. Singer and Friedman (2014: 163) note that this cyber protection industry is now worth $65 billion and is growing by 6–9 percent per year. The only security that can be assured in the cyber world is through measures to train staff to avoid common mistakes and to adhere to a system of norms.

The other process in cyber espionage is the tendency to try to balance against a rival. Balancing is neither peaceful nor beneficial (Morgenthau 1952: Chapters 11–13; Bremer 1992), but it does happen and will often be a goal of states engaged in a rivalry. In some ways, the idea is to achieve gains through non-conventional means because the rival state cannot hope to catch up to its competition through conventional tactics. This may be the motivation for the numerous cyber espionage campaigns and operations that China has launched against the US government and the American private sector. China cannot match America in terms of conventional military means, but it seems to have an edge on the United States in cyberspace in terms of willingness to use cyber tactics in the realm of espionage, and it has used these capabilities, much to the chagrin of the United States.

Finally, cyber espionage operations during a rivalry can be a way to place economic costs on the rival. The goal is to punish a rival by harassing and engaging its business community. China is particularly active in cyber espionage, causing large-scale economic losses in the United States and the East Asian region. The Mandiant report released in February 2013 has provoked a media and public frenzy regarding the fear and uncertainty surrounding China and its status in relation to the United States.[15] This report provides information accusing China of stealing sensitive documents and secrets pertinent to US national security. However, this report releases nothing new and presents little that Washington did not already know. The Chinese have been infiltrating American networks and stealing information in cyberspace for over a decade now. They either need to improve their cyber defenses or make clear to China that this sort of activity will not be tolerated. Thus far, they have done neither; we will explore this question more in Chapter 5.

Some theories of terrorism suggest that the tactic can be used to impact voting patterns or be a shortcut to a revolution (Conrad 2011). In terms of cyber espionage, the goal would then be to provoke domestic reactions through the fear of the cyber threat.[16] The corresponding dynamic is to provoke a rapid increase in military spending processes in order to destabilize the target state. This often backfires and leads to escalation (Sample 1998), yet it is still often the goal of cyber operations.

## CYBER PROXY BATTLES: STATE CYBER TERROR

In relation to the question of espionage, we must also investigate whether the state sponsorship of cyber terrorism is an active process in international affairs, and, if so, what produces these dynamics? Terrorism is defined, according to Sandler (2011), as the premeditated use or threat to use violence by individuals to obtain a political or social objective through the intimidation of a large audience. The key is to induce fear in the target to produce a change of behavior. There is generally a political policy motive behind terrorist threats. In the cyber realm, cyber terrorism generally equates to the use of computational technologies intended to disrupt and to wreak havoc and fear in a targeted online population in order to change a situation in a targeted entity. Cyber terrorism is real, but limited and mostly ineffective.

Our task here is to explore the combination of cyber terrorism and state-based resource support. The potential for the effective marshaling of resources in the cyber realm for terrorism really only exists when supported by a state-based actor. Non-state aligned cyber actors do not have the funds, resources, technological ability, and assets to mount effective cyber operations. Yet, states do. What is more, many hackers and other types of cyber criminals are motivated by job security in the long run. These "black hats" are often acquired by government agencies, nullifying the potential talent pool for cyber terrorists and cyber criminals, as they then become "white hats." Therefore, we must examine why a state would support cyber terrorism in the first place, given that terrorism is often ineffective and only serves to escalate conflicts.

The main reasons that a state would support cyber terrorism is to seek to equalize capabilities with a rival or to punish a rival sufficiently to produce a change in the target's behavior. Few resources are utilized when compared to the larger impact of conventional operations. Achieving equality at a cheap price might justify the support of terrorism for a rival state (Conrad 2011; Maoz and San-Akca 2012). In the cyber realm, this means that the purpose of terrorism is to effect a change in the target state at minimal cost to the initiator. It could also be that the state wants to compete, but must move the playing field to a different location in order to have an impact.

Seeking balancing outcomes is fundamental in international relations (Morgenthau 1948), yet the character of the process is misguided and misconstrued. Often it is balancing behavior that produces war and conflict (Wright 1965; Bremer 1992). Equality does not produce peace, yet the idea is that it will produce stability in international affairs (Waltz 1979) and therefore is a desired goal. States will therefore do what they can to achieve equality. One method of producing balanced outcomes in modern affairs is to use technology to quickly broach the distance between two sides. This might mean increasing military capabilities by stealing technology. It could also mean harming a rival's development process to prevent it from catching up. In some ways, a rival state will use a cyber tactic to seek equality. This misguided process will likely backfire, yet states will utilize this path, often through means of state-sponsored cyber terrorism.

It also remains for us to explore new methods of combat produced through cyber technologies. A state may utilize cyber terrorist methods in order to achieve the ends of a conventional military tactic, mostly through non-conventional means. To produce a change in the behavior of the target, it is no longer acceptable or feasible to utilize the military in a conventional manner. Cyberspace is an undefined arena, and one state could use cyber terrorist proxies to target a rival with little international consequence. We doubt that the actual use of these tactics will produce the desired ends, yet it still remains that these processes could motivate a state to engage in cyber terrorism.

It might also be that states utilize cyber terrorism to fight proxy battles. They might avoid direct conflict due to capability disparities. They cannot afford the costs of direct action, or they are unwilling to accept the consequences to their leadership dynasty if their efforts prove futile. In such a case, a state might engage in cyber terrorism in order to hide its true goals and methods. While the attribution problem is overstated in cyber politics, if proxies are used to fight cyber battles, then there is still deniability. This provides safety for a leader in choosing these less desirable options that seek to harm an enemy.

The final reason that a state may utilize cyber terrorist methods is to cause pain in its rival. Pain comes in many forms. For example, one state might impose economic costs on a rival in order to distract it from conflicts on other fronts. The bait-and-bleed strategy is often used in international affairs in order to wound the enemy and allow the initiating side time to fulfill its objectives. It might also be that cyber terrorist methods are used to impact the public will of the population in the target state. Instead of changing the behavior of a state, changing the behavior of a population might suit the initiator just as much. The effects of this process might even filter down to such processes as elections and voting. All sorts of outcomes are possible when cyber terrorism is used. That these outcomes have little chance of success is evident, yet these processes could still produce the outcome of state-sponsored cyber terrorism.

While we argue that the motives of cyber terrorism might be evident, the probability of success is doubtful and ultimately futile. Testing the motives behind cyber terrorism and the impact of the process is not the primary objective of this project, but it is important to lay out the process behind the decision-making when the choice to utilize these tactics is made. To explore the impact of cyber terrorist violence, we engage this idea more in Chapter 7 with an examination of the case of Cyber Gaza, Red October, and the Syrian Electronic Army.

## HYPOTHESES REGARDING CYBER INTERACTIONS

The goal of theory is to generally explain the past, present, and future according to a set of foundations and ideas that guide interpretation and investigations. With theory there must come predictions. In examining deterrence, we first deconstructed the process, but then also reconstructed a system of restraint in order to aide our predictive explanations. For some, this is the true purpose of theory. In our view, in order to progress we must specify what ideas and inclinations will guide the rest of this inquiry and under what conditions our theory might be falsified. The goal is to both move knowledge further along the path, but also to specify the path taken.

Restraint of cyber interactions due to the conditions of collateral damage, blowback, replication, and non-vital issues at stake in some cyber conflicts suggests that cyber interactions in the modern system will be limited to very few states, even among rival populations. One would expect rivals—where all sorts of negative interactions are on the table—to be the main group of states to utilize cyber technologies on the foreign policy battlefield. There is a paradox in that most cyber conflict is likely to occur between rivals, yet we have seen little conflict between cyber rivals overall so far (Valeriano and Maness 2012).

Once unpacked, it becomes all the more clear that the coming era of cyber power is overstated and is likely to be noted for the non-use of devastating technologies rather than the increased frequency. Restraint in cyberspace means that there will be limited examples of cyber conflict between states, despite the general tone of the debate, which assumes that cyber conflict is part of the developing range of options for states. This leads us to our first hypothesis.

*H1: Due to restraint dynamics, the observed rate and number of cyber operations between rivals are likely to be minimal.*

Cyber interactions will be minimal according to observed tendencies. It must be remembered that we are not predicting a complete absence of cyber operations, but a limited occurrence of the technology in light of the constraints on its usage. We argue that the non-usage of cyber operations might be a developing norm and taboo. This would suggest that it might be useful to look at norm cascades and locate the usage of developing technologies of war in this context. In the process of a norm cascade, entrepreneurs develop an idea, and this idea then spreads to over one-third of the population, which marks a tipping point when the idea becomes part of the normal process of interactions (Finnemore and Sikkink 1998: 901). We follow this path and assert a cyber usage norm tipping point, suggesting that if fewer than one-third of highly active and contentious rivals utilize cyber operations, then the technology has not proliferated and will not at this time. It is even more stark if we remember that rivals are a sample of an entire population, so the real one-third bar should be on all states; but for our purposes, observing fewer than 33 percent of the rival population engaging in the usage of cyber events would be clear evidence that even the most contentious states do not use cyber technology in foreign affairs.

Following hypothesis one, we also argue that cyber operations will be limited in severity when they do occur. States are restrained from using the technology in the first place, but this prior hypothesis does not predict the complete non-use of the technology, just that the technology will be used at a low rate. The follow-up question is how severe will the cyber tactics that do occur be? In Chapter 4 we spell out our severity scale and an explanation for the levels of cyber violence in an elaborate way.

Being especially mindful of the constraint of collateral damage, we should see evidence that the cyber operations and incidents that do occur will be relatively low-level operations to exploit obvious weaknesses. We equate this process not so much with the will of the offender, but the flaws in the target. If a state infiltrates another state in cyberspace, it is often due to the obvious weaknesses in the target's defenses. Libicki (2009) makes the point that cyber disputes happen because systems have flaws. Cyber offensive operations are dangerous and could lead to conventional escalation, but more pressing is the need for coordinated efforts to shore up the defense around critical systems and technologies. Flaws and weaknesses in systems and software must be the first step to prevent cyber operations. For now, the outcome is that flaws in the system will lead to low-level cyber actions. Much more severe incidents will be prevented because of the consequences of such incidents and the fact that such weaknesses are likely to be sealed up in the target state.

Rivals have the means and the motive to infiltrate states in cyberspace, yet they generally fail to do so, even with demonstrated weaknesses in the targets. When they do, they do not escalate the conflict by using drastic methods that lead to the loss of life. The idea of a cyber Pearl Harbor is a constructed threat generated by artificial fears. The goal should be to never present the opportunity for a Pearl Harbor–level incident to occur in the first place.[17]

Due to the threat of retaliation and the ready possibility of actual direct combat if cyber incidents are utilized, cyber operations will be limited in the international sphere. When cyber incidents are exhibited, offensive states will choose tactics that are easily hidden and free of direct responsibility. To reiterate, the damage done will be limited and mainly will be focused on low-level operations that result in minimal impacts. These hypotheses fly directly counter to popular wisdom on the persuasiveness of cyber combat.

*H2: When cyber operations and incidents do occur, they will be of minimal impact and severity due to restraint dynamics.*

In addition to the restraint limitations on the free hand of cyber conflict, we also hypothesize that cyber relations will take a regional tone. The most dangerous enemies will be local. Examples are replete: Russia and Georgia, Pakistan and India, Israel and Iran. We should see these dynamics at work for cyber rivals. While the suggestion is that wars and conflict can now be inflicted in far-off places toward far-off locations, the reality is likely much different. Since there is restraint at work for cyber conflict, those dyads that do conduct full-scale cyber operations will likely be local rivals due to the salience and immediacy of the rivalry. This is especially true for the territorial conflicts connected to many ongoing rivalries (Valeriano 2013). Rivalries spring up directly from territorial issues and displays of power; in this context, we should see many of the cyber conflicts that do occur located in regional rivalries dominated by territorial issues.

Further, states that aim to exert influence in a particular region may also turn to cyber tactics. Low-level cyber incidents constitute a relatively unimportant matter to other states. Small aggressions indicate states expanding their standing and power through these interactions. It is a form of control, or operating as a "big brother." States hoping to rise in a regional power hierarchy are likely to leverage any form of capability—not necessarily to exert force on others, but to prevent neighbors from checking their expansion. States striving for regional strength in relation to their neighboring rivals, such as China, Israel, and India, are the likely cyber conflict culprits. Regional dynamics lead us to hypothesize that states will use cyber capabilities on neighbors, not global rivals.

> H3: Cyber operations and incidents that do occur will likely be limited to regional interactions due to a connection to territorial conflicts.

Power and the display of power are a key concern in international affairs. The importance of the factor is often overstated, yet the observation basically holds that states believe power is important and therefore they do what they can to display their capabilities. When one rival is far behind the capabilities of another, it stands to reason that it will do whatever is possible to create a system of equality. The idea is that equality and balancing will create peace (Waltz 1979). While this is clearly untrue and misguided (Bremer 1992), it still motivates international behavior.

Related to our earlier hypotheses, we argue that a system of cyber norms has been created that regulates the non-usage of cyber activities at a massive and severe scale. How then are we to explain lower-level cyber operations? Many take the form of simple espionage, often termed the second oldest profession in the world. States utilize espionage techniques where possible because they represent simple steps to tackle and manage an international problem. It is under this context that we will observe cyber espionage operations.

> H4: Due to international constraints and norms, rival states will use cyber espionage in order to manage low-level competition between two actors, but this competition will be minimal and will represent the normal relations range of rival interactions.

It is in this context that we will observe states using cyber technologies in the realm of espionage and terrorism in order to catch up to their more powerful rivals. These mechanisms motivate the behavior that some find abhorrent. The likely result is more conflict and disagreements, yet the idea still dictates how states will operate. To catch up to an enemy, covert cyber operations will be utilized.

*H5: Due to power imbalances, less powerful rival states will use cyber espionage and cyber terrorism as tactics to perceptively bridge the power gap with the more powerful state.*

The motivation for this behavior is not purely a response to power balances, but also in order to create havoc and harm a rival state. In many ways, cyber operations are the least a state can do and the safest option for a rival state. While attribution is clear, there is still deniability in cyber operations, which gives states a free hand to utilize low-level cyber operations to counter a foe and cause it harm. It is under this context that espionage and cyber terrorism operations will be conducted. The problem is that these tactics can work and provoke rapid spending increases in cyber security, escalating the conflict overall.

Going further, it would be expected that relations between rival states will sour after a cyber incident and dispute. Even though we expect that these cyber operations will be at low levels overall, governments will not react well to invasion of cyberspace, networks, and websites by other governments. When cyber conflicts do happen, the reaction in the target state should raise the level of conflict, especially in the rivalry population.

This is the topic of Chapter 5. Using events data, we measure our cyber incident and dispute variables against the weekly conflict-cooperation scores between the 20 rival pairs of states that have engaged in cyber conflict from 2001 to 2011. This leads to the sixth hypothesis of this volume, which predicts an escalation of conflict when cyber operations do occur.

*H6: Cyber incidents and disputes will lead to negative foreign policy responses at the state-to-state level.*

We would also expect that major powers, because of their high profile, would be more prone to negative reactions if their networks are infiltrated. It is important for major powers to not lose face and to seem vigilant when their interests are violated. Therefore, when a major power is contained in one of the 20 dyads we analyze due to evidence of cyber conflict, we expect that relations will worsen due to the high-profile nature of the cyber operations.

*H7: Cyber incidents and disputes will lead to negative foreign policy responses when a major power is targeted.*

Furthermore, because of the intimacy of the rivalry, we expect relations between regional rivals to especially sour after a cyber incident or dispute is used as a foreign policy tool. Based on our expectation of cyber conflict at the regional level, it is prudent to test the relationship at the regional level in the events data form.

*H8: Cyber incidents and disputes between regional rivals will lead to negative foreign policy responses.*

When examining cyber reactions, intent clearly matters. We have to be able to distinguish between incidents that might be termed demonstration incidents as opposed to the more typical espionage-type actions. Due to the publicity surrounding them, we expect DDoS methods to be used most often by states and their affiliates to demonstrate the ability to harm a rival. Since they are low-level impact cyber incidents, yet they affect the daily lives of populations, there will often be a negative response to DDoS actions; they are difficult to ignore when compared to espionage actions.

Seeking to use cyber actions to change behavior in a target is also a critical negative step that is likely to invoke escalatory reactions. Coercion in cyberspace rarely works, and when states attempt these methods they only provoke a negative response in the target. The hope is that motivating a change in behavior of the target through punishing cyber methods will help it fall into line with the intent of the offender, but more often than not it only provokes a cycle of escalation and the security dilemma.

*H9: Intending to motivate a change in behavior through demonstration cyber incidents, such as DDoS methods, is likely to provoke a negative foreign policy response.*

## CONCLUSION

Theory is a critical part of political analysis. International cyber operations are political in that they are based on the demonstration of power around issue spaces or international concerns. The goal in this chapter has been to develop a theory of cyber interactions. What might predict their occurrence, targets, and level of severity in cyber conflict between states or as directed by states?

We have decided to focus our analysis on interstate rival interactions since these are the states most likely to experience and utilize cyber methods against their foes. They have the motive, means, and will to infiltrate historic enemies over real issues of contestation. It makes sense theoretically, historically, and empirically to focus on rivals as the unit of analysis.

Rivals infiltrate enemies in cyberspace for a variety of reasons, most of which are associated with territorial disputes. Other forms of cyber escalation are associated with issues of regime control, often connected to differences in policy. Few cyber operations are associated with demonstrations of power and achieving equality with a more powerful enemy, but these motives do play a role. All disputes are connected to salient issues at stake, making the use of the tactic logical and fitting in many cases.

The corresponding logic here is that while rivals will use cyber operations against each other, the level of the cyber incident will be minimal and infrequent. Rivals learn to manage their relations with each other. There are periods of tension, escalation, and war, but by and large the modal outcome is tense cooperation rather than outright violence. Due to the dynamics of restraint, cyber powers will be limited in their use of cyber operations because of the consequences of such actions. Large-scale and devastating incidents will lead to retaliation and international condemnation. Reputation (Crescenzi 2007) concerns are important in international affairs, and the gains of a cyber operation are often not worth the risk of degrading the reputation of the initiating state. Cyber actions will degrade the standing of states because most states refrain from using the technology in the realm of foreign policy.

Restraint dynamics straitjacket cyber states into constrained action in order to protect themselves from self-harm. Collateral damage on a civilian population will be punished with conventional means. Unleashing a virus on a command and control operation might seem like a logical and beneficial operation, but it renders a worm ready for dissection and replication right back to the offender. This leads to blowback, which can come in the cyber form but also occurs through conventional means.

We argue that advanced cyber operations are a taboo not to be broken. They unleash consequences disproportionate to the benefits of launching cyber disputes. Simple cost-benefit analysis would dictate that cyber operations are going to be limited and constrained as the norms surrounding the issue make the use of the tactic a sacred violation. Targeting civilians is no longer allowed in the international system with the decline in the notion of sovereignty. Lower-level operations against the military are often unsuccessful as the target is protected and knows it will be the focus of action. Failure to protect the target is often the main reason for an infiltration in the first place. If an army is out in the open, exposed to the elements including aerial attack, bombardment, and attacks from the higher ground, do we blame the tactics used against them or the failures in leadership inherent in the target? Cyber operations are real and proliferating. Yet, they are mainly lower-level operations utilized to expose some real weakness in the target rather than a demonstration of the power of the initiating side.

The next chapter investigates the dynamics of cyber operations and incidents by collecting and examining a dataset of the tactics used in a concentrated time period, which might be called the dawn of cyber power.

## CHAPTER 4

# The Dynamics of Cyber Conflict Between Rival Antagonists

The main concern we have is that the cyber security debate is focused too much on what could happen, and that it should instead transition toward examining what has happened and developments as they occur. The danger lies in focusing too much on the fear of infiltration, rather than concentrating efforts against actual and demonstrated threats. Preliminary qualitative analysis suggests that while there is evidence for a plethora of cyber disputes among post-Soviet states, they rarely take the form of serious disruptions to the national security of a state (Valeriano and Maness 2012). In addition, there is little evidence for cyber conflict among actual rivals. In reality, it seems that cyber conflict mimics the dynamics of espionage or economic combat, and is not a form of war at all, since zero deaths result from the actions (Rid 2011). Most operations are taken by private citizens to achieve economic gain or for political expression rather than military gain. Operations taken for military gain rarely pay off in the form of the "significant damage" that the US government warns and strategizes against.

In this chapter we quantify the number of cyber disputes and incidents experienced by international states in the realm of foreign policy, particularly historical antagonists, and we examine the scope, length, and damage inflicted by cyber disputes among rival states (Klein et al. 2006) from 2001 to 2011. Our data demonstrate that 20 rival dyads out of 126 engaged in cyber conflict during this time period. About one-half of these rivals experienced only one dispute during this time period. The average number of cyber incidents among rivals who participated in such behavior is three incidents. The US-Chinese dyad has experienced by far the most cyber conflicts, with 23 observed cyber incidents within five overall cyber disputes.

As will be demonstrated (in Chapter 7), even though there were 111 observed cyber incidents within 45 cyber disputes among 20 rivals, the intensity, duration, and level of cyber utilization remain low compared to the dire warnings of the media. We hope that this research can return the debate on cyber conflict to a more nuanced examination of the threat. Others should be able to use our data to come to their own conclusions. While there is a real danger of cyber combat and cyber disputes, one must remain prudent in relation to the actual threat—not the inflated threat presented by the imagination. Protection of the state against external threats is of the utmost importance, but when does the promotion of the threat impede the policy process? Next we will review our theory of cyber restraint and regionalism as we move to the empirical study of cyber conflict.

## CYBER CONFLICT: RIVALRY, RESTRAINT, AND REGIONALISM

It would be useful to summarize our theory of rivalry interactions in cyberspace before we proceed with our analysis. In terms of conflict operations, the attractiveness of the target in relation to the capability used is a critical equation that is rarely examined. What good would a cyber conflict between rivals be if it does little physical and psychological damage to a rival state? Much is made about the secret nature of cyber operations, yet we know very little about the impact of basic operations on foreign policy dynamics. The value of the tactic seems minimal when one thinks of the potential devastation that can arise from direct attacks between states. At the extreme end, a large-scale operation that might wipe out the United States' Eastern Seaboard Power Grid would be catastrophic, but it would likely be punished with immense retaliation and is thus not a realistic option short of total war. We are then left with minor incidents that are basically speculative ones, with few operations resulting in considerable damage.

Restraint exists in the realm of cyber conflict, and we have covered this issue in Chapter 3. Rid (2011, 2013) argues that cyberwar in the extreme sense that death will result has not yet occurred, and is unlikely to occur. Likewise, Gartzke (2013) develops the logic for cyberwar being utilized by states as a low-level form of conflict. We (2013) concluded, in an examination of Russian foreign policy, that cyber conflict was literally the least and the easiest option Russia could have used to infiltrate Estonia during their dust-up in 2007. We also contend that cyber interactions will take a regional tone in that rivals typically are constricted to regional interactions.

Little is known about the actual impact of cyber tactics. Much speculation has been made with little connection to the realities on the ground. In short, the risk to the initiator in relation to the impact of cyber tactics does not make the use of cyber strategies a very useful option in the international system. This is especially true in the context of the rivalry where the competition is often known and the attribution issue in cyber conflict is minimized because the enemies are obvious.

Restraint plays a critical role in the cyber realm. Derived from Schelling's analysis that military strength can be used as coercion, deterrence theory has heavily influenced post-atomic foreign policy (Schelling 1966). Instead of risking engagement in direct conflict, great powers developed nuclear arsenals to prevent attack from other states. Jervis explains this buildup for deterrence as an extension of diplomacy, where expressions of force are communicated between sides to deter moves rather than using overt force (Jervis 1979, 1989). States are effectively trying to avoid a conflict spiral and a never-ending situation of continuous threats by making severe threats.

Comprehensive restraint relates to deterrence from spectacular attacks such as nuclear weapons or devastating Internet operations focused at power systems and health services. States are restrained from such action through fears of retaliation and escalation of the conflict beyond control, even during rivalries.

Low-level cyber tactics might be part of what Azar (1972) calls the normal relations range for a rivalry. The surprising finding in relation to conventional wisdom could be that rivals will tolerate cyber combat operations if they do not cross a line that leads directly to the massive loss of life. Cyber conflict is expected to occur and is even tolerated as long as total offensive operations are not conducted. By total offensive operations, we mean direct cyber incidents that might lead to the destruction of the energy infrastructure of a state, or infiltrations meant to take control of army units or facilities. These options are off the table for rivals since they will lead directly to war, collateral damage, and economic retaliation. As Nye (2011a) notes, the vulnerabilities evident on the Internet make the tactic dangerous to use because a cyber incident can be easily replicated and sent back to the initiator in kind.

The other factor contributing to restraint is collateral damage. States are now limited in offensive actions due to function norms of limited harm against civilians. An example of this logic can be inferred from the 2003 US invasion of Iraq or the 2011 operations against Libya. In 2003, Bush administration officials worried that the effects of cyber combat would not be limited to Iraq but would instead create worldwide financial havoc, spreading across the Middle East to Europe and perhaps to the United States.[1] The United States was restrained from launching cyber operations against its rival during outright war. The potential fallout of such operations through the complex networks of interdependence would extend to civilians. There simply was not enough time to plan operations that would restrict the damage done to military targets. Economic and civilian harm are devastating to interdependent networks, and thus these moves should be avoided. In addition, the United States failed to use cyber tactics against Libya during the operation to support the National Transition Coalition forces due to concerns about the civilian impact.[2] Introduced in Chapter 3, there are two hypotheses in relation to cyber conflict.

*H1: Due to restraint dynamics, the observed rate and number of cyber operations between rivals are likely to be minimal.*

*H2: When cyber operations and incidents do occur, they will be of minimal impact and severity due to restraint dynamics.*

Due to the threat of retaliation, potential harm to civilians or economic enterprise, and the ready possibility of actual direct combat if cyber tactics are utilized, cyber operations will be limited in the international sphere. What a minimal rate of cyber disputes might be will vary according to individual perceptions. We feel that a rate of one dispute per year would be average, and more than one a year between rivals would be extreme, given that this rate is extreme for militarized disputes between even the most disputatious rivals. When cyber disputes are exhibited, offensive states will choose tactics that are easily hidden and free of direct responsibility. The damage done and intensity will be limited and mainly focused on low-level operations. These hypotheses fly directly counter to popular and academic wisdom on the pervasiveness of cyber combat (Libicki 2007; Stone 2012; Kello 2013; Lewis 2013).

In addition to the restraint limitations, in Chapter 3 we also hypothesize that cyber relations will take a regional tone. While the suggestion is that cyber actions and conflict can happen anywhere instantly, impacting targets in far-off locations, the empirics presented in this chapter may tell a different story. As restraint is the expected dynamic in cyber conflict, those pairs of states that will engage in cyber malice will be local rivals because the issues of disagreement will be more salient and immediate.

Exerting influence regionally may be an aim of a particular state, which may lead it to use cyber tactics in order to gain this influence. The goal will be to signal intent to a target. These methods are a form of control, and states looking to gain in a regional power hierarchy will use any capability, including its cyber abilities, to achieve these gains. Therefore, as presented in Chapter 3, regional dynamics lead us to hypothesize that states will use cyber capabilities on neighbors, not global rivals.

*H3: Cyber incidents and disputes that do occur will likely be limited to regional interactions.*

Finally, another process in rivalry is what is called the normal relations range (Azar 1972), where rivals try to manage competition and engagement through level operations. In the process of cyber espionage, the tactic is likely utilized to manage low-level proxy battles that avoid direct confrontations. South Korea and Japan seem to exhibit this behavior, as they have much animosity toward each other yet are also close allies with the United States.

*H4: Due to international constraints and norms, rival states will use cyber espionage in order to manage low-level competition between two actors but this competition will be minimal and will represent the normal relations range of rival interactions.*

Another process in cyber espionage is attempting to balance against a more powerful rival. Balancing neither normalizes relations between states nor does it allow for the more powerful state to capitulate (Morgenthau 1952; Bremer 1992; Levy and Thompson 2010). China cannot match the United States militarily, so it steals its military secrets and technology through cyber espionage tactics in order to bring parity with the American military.

*H5: Due to power imbalances, less powerful rival states will use cyber espionage and cyber terrorism as tactics to perceptively bridge the power gap with the more powerful state.*

## METHODOLOGY FOR THE ANALYSIS OF CYBER CONFLICT

Our goal was to create an exhaustive open source database of all cyber incidents and disputes between countries. The result is called the Dyadic Cyber Incident and Dispute Dataset (DCID). Presented and utilized here is version 1.0 of the data, released as Valeriano and Maness (2014).

We coded the data for this project by searching the archives of news stories in the *Google News* search engine and also combing through reports, books, and testimonies of cyber incidents. The US government may have a ready archive of cyber threats and disputes, but if they do, it is not available to the public. Instead we relied on our own comprehensive and focused search and archive investigations.

The question remains: was our search comprehensive enough? If a cyber dispute is evident in the public discourse, it likely had enough impact to alter the dynamics of interstate relations, which is what we seek to explore. We are confident that we have included in our data the most significant and the great majority of cyber actions that were capable of damaging relations between states. There are enough incentives for various actors to publicize their capabilities and defense abilities, so the great majority of cyber operations are largely known in the public sphere.

Some operations may remain hidden because they point to a specific weakness that the attacker or security firm may also have. We argue that eventually the truth comes out. Many cyber operations committed in the last decade are public knowledge. Generally a source will clue a reporter in to the activity and then it will be picked up by various media sources. Even Stuxnet and Flame were revealed to the media, leading to calls for investigations on the nature of the leaks; thus it is difficult for a cyber dispute to remain secret for more than a year due to the nature of the news media and Internet.[3] Since security network officers are engaged in a practice of making the potential threat known, there is little interest in hiding cyber operations. In addition, the military structures throughout the world are interested in promoting the need to build infrastructure (the cyber industrial complex) to combat cyber actions. Therefore they also have little incentive to hide cyber operations.

Finally, Internet security firms regularly release reports to demonstrate their ability to repel or combat cyber intrusions in order to gather clients. Corporations such as McAfee, Kaspersky, and Symantec have been very helpful in detailing cyber operations, but of course their information is viewed through a country- and corporate-specific lens. While states may have an interest in keeping cyber incidents secret, the interest in these security organizations and security examiners in general is to publicize these events in order to trumpet their ability to catch and neutralize these events. While there are cyber operations in the domain of espionage on occasion, these actions remain a different sort. Since the advent of the hacker community, the ethos has always been to make those violated aware of breeches, rather than hiding these breeches. The status and recognition that come with high-profile disputes (even at the state level) encourage this ethos of publicity (although anonymous or hidden behind aliases).

In the end, it must also be remembered that all prognosticators in the cyber debate are working with limited and selective information to some extent. This effort is a sample of reality, as are all empirical investigations. Instead of being deterred in this daunting task of data collection, we move forward, aware that our efforts represent only what is publicly known. We believe that this effort represents a significant and comprehensive snapshot of known cyber events from 2001 to 2011. It is the most comprehensive source of data and has been vetted by many investigators since 2011. We do not rely on media reports alone, although these reports can help make us aware of events. On balance, network security reports and cyber security reports seem to have been the most helpful in identifying incidents.

The bigger issue, in our estimation, is not finding cyber incidents and disputes, but rather figuring out when they begin or end. As Singer and Friedman (2014: 121) note, "knowing when a cyberwar begins or ends, however, might be more challenging than defining it." There are cases in our data that have no clear end date; they may still be ongoing. There obviously are cases in our data that also have inaccurate beginning dates because while cyber security firms have been forthcoming about finding cyber incidents, they might be less forthcoming on the start of each incident. They may wish to produce impressive statistics about the recognition and termination of an active cyber bug. Stuxnet and Red October are examples of cyber incidents that occasionally show up in networks to this day.

We have instituted a year lag time for reporting of events and stopped our data collection in 2011 in order to ensure enough time and distance for extensive analysis of all incidents and disputes. We concede in advance that it is possible we "missed" important cyber disputes due to the secrecy of the event and tactic.[4] This dataset is active and will be maintained, but we are confident that at this point we have a quite exhaustive database of cyber disputes and incidents.[5]

Attribution of cyber disputes can be a problematic issue. One of the advantages of the cyber method is deniability. In our dataset, states that use information warfare must be fairly explicit and evident. For some cases, attribution is easy; for example, India and Pakistan have been immersed in "tit for tat" cyber incidents for some time, and it is fairly clear that actions in this arena are state sponsored. Likewise, Russia appears to have coordinated its dispute against Georgia and has not denied its part in this operation. If the attribution of a dispute is in serious doubt, we have not coded it as a state-based action. For inclusion, either the state must have admitted its part in the cyber conflict, or security reports from the target states or cyber security companies must have confirmed the culprit's involvement. Anonymous hackers and operatives working either on their own initiative or through "off the books" enterprises have not been coded. The database parameters are based on the history of relations, the intent of the tactic, the likelihood of government complacency, and code disputes from this perspective.

The terminology for our data on cyber operations is important to note, and is presented in Chapter 2, yet will be briefly reiterated here. For individual cyber conflicts, we use the phrase *cyber incident*. Incidents such as Shady Rat include thousands of intrusions, but accounting for every single intrusion an individual operation has made is impossible and unwieldy. Therefore, Shady Rat and other multiple-intrusive incidents are coded as just one incident per dyad, as long as the goals and perpetrators remain stable and the event occurred within a limited time frame. Each cyber incident is a directed network strike by one state against another.

For operations containing a number of incidents that are part of an overall cyber campaign we use the term *cyber disputes*. Cyber disputes may contain only one incident or dozens. Furthermore, the initiator of the dispute or incident must be from a government or government affiliate in order for an operation to be included in our dataset. Targets may be non-state actors if they are important to a state's national security. Lockheed Martin, Mitsubishi, and Boeing are examples of non-state targets relevant to the national security of a state. Explanations of the type and severity of incidents and disputes for our data analysis are explained in Tables 4.1 and 4.2.[6]

The types of cyber incidents and disputes we have coded are comprehensive according to cyber combat tactics and analysis.[7] Chapter 2 details these methods in depth, yet a quick review is warranted here. The simplest methods are website defacements or vandalism. Hackers use SQL injection or cross-site scripting (forms of injected code) to deface or destroy victims' webpages. We code these methods as "1." The distributed denial of service (DDoS) method, or what we call simple "defacement," is labeled with "2." DDoS operations flood particular Internet sites, servers, or routers with more requests for data than the site can respond to or process, and they effectively shut down the site, thus preventing access or usage. Intrusions, which include Trojans, Trapdoors, or Backdoors, are

**Table 4.1** CYBER METHODS FOR INCIDENTS AND DISPUTES

| Type of Dispute | Examples | Explanation |
| --- | --- | --- |
| **1. Vandalism** | Website defacements | SQL injection or cross-scripting to deface websites |
| **2. Denial of Service** | DDoS (distributed denial of service) | Botnets used to effectively shut down websites with high traffic |
| **3. Intrusion** | Trapdoors or Trojans, Backdoors | Remotely injected software for intrusions and thefts |
| **4. Infiltrations** | Logic bombs, worms, viruses, packet sniffers, keystroke logging | Different methods are used to penetrate target networks. Can be either remotely used or physically installed |
| **5. APTs** | Advanced persistent threats | Precise, sophisticated methods that have specific targets. Move slowly to avoid detection, can be vandalism, DDoS, intrusions, or infiltrations |
| **6. Vandalism and Denial of Service** | Cyber disputes | Combined incidents of vandalism and DDoS |
| **7. Intrusions and Infiltrations** | Cyber disputes | Combined incidents of intrusions and infiltrations |

**Table 4.2** SEVERITY SCALE OF CYBER OPERATIONS

| Severity Type of Dispute | Explanation | Examples |
| --- | --- | --- |
| **Type 1** | Minimal damage | State Department website down, probing intrusions |
| **Type 2** | Targeted attack on critical infrastructure or military | Financial sector attack, DoD hacked |
| **Type 3** | Dramatic effect on a country's specific strategy | Stuxnet, Jet plans stolen |
| **Type 4** | Dramatic effect on a country | Power grid knocked out, stock market collapse |
| **Type 5** | Escalated dramatic effect on a country | Catastrophic effects on country as a direct result of cyber operation |

coded as "3." Trapdoors or Trojans are unauthorized software added to a program to allow entry into a victim's network or software program to permit future access to a site once it has been initially breached. Intrusions need to be added to software, can remain dormant for a long time, and then propagate themselves without notice. These methods are difficult to detect or repeal with firewalls or security software, as they are not malicious upon entry into a network. They only become malicious once they become operational (see Table 4.3).

Along with some methods of intrusions, infiltrations are the method states can consider an act of war, as the US Department of Defense has declared. They are different from intrusions in that different methods are used to penetrate target networks. Since there are five major methods of infiltrations, we coded them as such: 4.1 (Logic bombs), 4.2 (Viruses), 4.3 (Worms), 4.4 (Packet sniffers), and 4.5 (Keystroke logging). These five methods are precision infiltrations that go after specific data or force computers or networks to undertake tasks that they would normally not undertake.

Advanced persistent threats (APTs) add another layer to the scope of cyber methods and can come in any of the four methods discussed above (Sanger 2012). Examples of APTs are the Stuxnet worm, the Flame virus, and the Shady Rat infiltrations. According to the cyber security firm Symantec, APTs are different from traditional targeted methods in that they are customized, they move more slowly to avoid detection, their intentions usually are more malicious and advanced and almost certainly come from states, and their targets are much more specific.[8] The level of sophistication is unmatched; there are highly covert and intentional actions behind the operations.

As mentioned previously, our analysis is confined to rivals because they are the most disputatious members of the international system. We also focus on government to government interactions. Non-state actors are only included in this analysis if they are considered part of a state's national security apparatus. Furthermore, non-state actors may only be targets, not initiators. State-sanctioned cyber conflict must originate from a state. We code these targets as follows: a "1" is coded if the target is non-state (Google, Boeing), "2" if the target is government but non-military (State Department, Treasury Department), and "3" if the target is government and military (Pentagon, NORAD). We also code what we call the

---

**Table 4.3** CODING FOR CYBER INCIDENTS

---

Interaction Type

1  Nuisance (probing, disruption, chaos)

2  Defensive operation (Cisco Raider, Buckshot Yankee)

3  Offensive strike (Ghost Net, Stuxnet)

---

Target Type

1  Private/non-state but important to national security (financial sector, power grid, defense contractor)

2  Government non-military (State Department, government websites)

3  Government military (Defense of Department, Cyber Command, Strategic Command)

---

## Table 4.4 CODING FOR CYBER DISPUTES

### Interaction Type

1 Nuisance

2 Defensive operation

3 Offensive strike

4 Nuisance and defensive

5 Nuisance and offensive

6 Defensive and offensive

7 Nuisance, defensive, and offensive

### Target Type

1 Private/non-state

2 Government non-military

3 Government military

4 Private and government non-military

5 Private and government military

6 Government non-military and military

7 Private, government non-military and military

### Objectives for Initiators

1 Disruption (take down websites, disrupt online activities)

2 Theft (steal sensitive information)

3 Change in behavior (abandon nuclear program, withdraw troops)

objective of the initiator into three broad categories: a "1" is coded if the objective is basic disruption of a state's day-to-day activities; "2" if the objective is to steal sensitive information, plans, or secrets from the target state; and "3" if the initiator is attempting to alter the state's behavior. An example of the latter objective is the US-Israel cyber dispute with Iran, as the overall objective of this operation is to deter Iran from continuing its nuclear program. Codes for multiple targets or multiple objectives in cyber disputes are presented in Table 4.4. Cyber activity in the realm of crime, economic sabotage, and general chaos by such groups as Anonymous are beyond the scope of this analysis. We focus on rivals based on spatial consistency (same actors), duration, militarized nature of competition, and linked issues (Klein et al. 2006: 335); or by perception (Thompson 2001).[9] There are 126 active and ongoing dyadic interstate rivals from 2001 to 2011.[10]

## CYBER DYNAMICS

The full summary of our data is reported in Table 4.5. Here we list who uses cyber tactics against whom, the number of cyber incidents and cyber disputes a state

**Table 4.5** SUMMARY OF CYBER DISPUTES AMONG RIVAL STATES (2001–2011)

| Rival A (number initiated) | Rival B (number initiated) | Cyber Incidents | Cyber Disputes | Most Severe Dispute | Highest Method Type | Highest Objective | Highest Target Type |
|---|---|---|---|---|---|---|---|
| China (20) | US (3) | 23 | 5 | 3 | 6 | 2 | 7 |
| Pakistan (7) | India (6) | 13 | 3 | 3 | 4 | 2 | 3 |
| North Korea (10) | South Korea (1) | 11 | 3 | 2 | 6 | 1 | 6 |
| Israel (7) | Iran (4) | 11 | 2 | 3 | 6 | 3 | 5 |
| China (7) | Japan (0) | 7 | 7 | 3 | 4 | 2 | 3 |
| South Korea (4) | Japan (3) | 7 | 5 | 2 | 3 | 2 | 4 |
| US (6) | Iran (1) | 7 | 2 | 3 | 6 | 3 | 5 |
| China (5) | Taiwan (0) | 5 | 2 | 2 | 3 | 2 | 2 |
| China (4) | India (0) | 4 | 1 | 3 | 6 | 2 | 6 |
| Russia (3) | Georgia (1) | 4 | 1 | 1 | 5 | 3 | 4 |
| Russia (4) | Estonia (0) | 4 | 1 | 2 | 2 | 1 | 2 |
| Russia (3) | US (0) | 3 | 3 | 3 | 4 | 1 | 3 |
| North Korea (3) | US (0) | 3 | 1 | 1 | 5 | 1 | 2 |
| China (2) | Vietnam (0) | 2 | 2 | 2 | 4 | 2 | 2 |
| Lebanon (1) | Israel (1) | 2 | 2 | 1 | 4 | 1 | 2 |
| North Korea (1) | Japan (0) | 1 | 1 | 1 | 2 | 1 | 2 |
| India (1) | Bangladesh (0) | 1 | 1 | 1 | 3 | 3 | 2 |
| Syria (1) | US (0) | 1 | 1 | 1 | 1 | 1 | 2 |
| Kuwait (1) | Iraq (0) | 1 | 1 | 2 | 4 | 1 | 2 |
| China (1) | Philippines (0) | 1 | 1 | 2 | 3 | 2 | 2 |

111 cyber incidents, 45 cyber disputes

Average cyber incident severity: 1.65; average cyber dispute severity: 1.71 (out of 5)

13 enduring, 4 proto, 3 strategic rivals engage in cyber disputes

20 out of 126 rival dyads (15.9%) engage in cyber disputes

has been involved in, the highest severity type of a dispute, the highest method used by the state, the highest target type the state has used, and the highest objective of the initiating state. Our list is comprehensive and represents all publicly acknowledged or clearly attributable cyber incidents and disputes between rival states from the years 2001 to 2011. [11]

The most immediate point that can be made about these results is that very few states actually fight cyber battles.[12] Only 16 percent of all rivals engage in cyber conflict. In total, we have recorded 111 cyber incidents and 45 disputes over the 11-year period of relations between the 20 rivals.

The next question relates to the strength and power of each incident and dispute. The severity levels of these incidents and disputes are also, on average, at a very low level. The average severity level for cyber incidents is 1.65 and for disputes is 1.71. These numbers lie between the least severe to second least severe scores. This means that most cyber conflicts between rival states tend to be mere nuisances, disruptions, and benign. This is surprising, considering the awareness of the issue in the media and the military. It is also perplexing considering that these states are active rivals that often have public military disputes with one another; in fact, engaging in militarized disputes is a necessary condition of rivalry, yet we fail to demonstrate many cyber disputes. Perhaps the cyber threat is over-inflated in relation to its actual impact.

Table 4.6 shows which methods are used for the initiating states' objectives in international cyber conflict. The objectives of the initiators for cyber disputes are at an overall low to average severity level, with disruptions at an average of 1.39, espionage at 2.39, and attempts to change state behavior at 2. Advanced

**Table 4.6** AVERAGE SEVERITY FOR DISPUTE INITIATOR OBJECTIVES AND CYBER METHODS USED

| Dispute Initiator Objective | Average Dispute Severity Score | Methods Utilized | Average Incident Severity Score | Number of Incidents |
|---|---|---|---|---|
| **Disruptions** | 1.39 | Vandalism | 1.01 | 20 |
| | | DDoS | 1.06 | 18 |
| | | Intrusions | 1.00 | 6 |
| | | Infiltrations | 1.85 | 14 |
| **Espionage** | 2.39 | Intrusions | 1.91 | 20 |
| | | Infiltrations | 2.29 | 14 |
| | | APTs | 2.09 | 11 |
| **Change in Behavior** | 2.00 | Vandalism | 1.00 | 2 |
| | | DDoS | 1.00 | 3 |
| | | Intrusions | 3.00 | 2 |
| | | Infiltrations | 2.67 | 9 |
| | | APTs | 2.73 | 11 |

persistent threats (APTs) are the most severe methods, with an average score of 2.09 for espionage objectives and 2.73 for behavioral change objectives. Infiltrations are the second most severe, with an average of 1.85 for disruptions, 2.29 for espionage, and 2.67 for coercion. Intrusions are used primarily for espionage campaigns and are a favorite method of the Chinese, but have also been used as disruptions. For these methods we recorded an average severity score of 1.00, 1.85, and 3.00, respectively. DDoS methods register with less severe scores, at 1.06 for disruptions and 1.00 for behavioral change. Finally, vandalism records scores of 1.01 for disruptions and 1.00 when used as a tool of propaganda in attempts to change the policies of states. What is significant here is that none of these methods is above the severity level of three; thus our data show that cyber conflict is being waged at a manageable and overall low level.

We expect to find a minimal number of incidents, defined as one attack per year for each rivalry dyad. Our analysis demonstrates that only four dyads experience more than 10 incidents, and only three dyads experience more than five disputes during the 11-year time frame, suggesting that the rate of cyber incidents is low for the total 126 rivalry dyads in our sample. Table 4.7 lists the frequent offenders of cyber combat.[13] The United States and China are at the far end of the scale, with several cyber rivalry dyads (six for China, five for the United States), while the other states have few consistent dyadic cyber interactions. The United States and China also have been engaged in 56 cyber incidents and 25 cyber disputes during the duration of our dataset examination. Many of these incidents and disputes are with each other, with China being the initiator most of the time.

The Chinese are the most active initiator (41 incidents) of all the countries that engage in cyber conflict. This may be interpreted as China being a major cyber aggressor, and this interpretation may be part of the upswing in perceived severity and fear of cyber conflict that has infiltrated popular media outlets. However,

*Table 4.7* TOP 10 STATES BY NUMBER OF RIVAL CYBER DYADS

| State | Number of Cyber Dyads | Total Cyber Incidents | Total Cyber Disputes |
|---|---|---|---|
| **China** | 6 | 41 | 29 |
| **United States** | 5 | 36 | 12 |
| **India** | 3 | 18 | 5 |
| **Japan** | 3 | 15 | 13 |
| **North Korea** | 3 | 15 | 5 |
| **Russia** | 3 | 11 | 5 |
| **South Korea** | 2 | 18 | 8 |
| **Iran** | 2 | 18 | 4 |
| **Israel** | 2 | 12 | 4 |
| **Pakistan** | 1 | 13 | 3 |

the majority of cyber incidents and disputes that China has initiated during the time period analyzed are theft operations. As hypothesized in Chapter 3, China engages in cyber espionage because it is the least it can do without outright provocation of its more powerful competitor, the United States. China is a rising power not only in East Asia, but globally. It must be wary of its power projection with Japan, South Korea, and Taiwan regionally and with the United States globally. It seems that it has found its outlet in cyberspace, as the data presented here show that China is by far the most active user of cyber tactics among the world's rivals. More on the reactions to cyber incidents and disputes from the target states of China will be discussed in the next chapter.

Table 4.8 shows all incidents and operations that can be identified as cyber espionage campaigns, where the initiator's objective is to steal sensitive information from the target government or private sector essential to national security. Twenty-seven of the 111 cyber incidents (24 percent) are cyber espionage

***Table 4.8*** PUBLICLY KNOWN CYBER ESPIONAGE INCIDENTS
AND OPERATIONS

| Initiator | Target | Name | Start | End | Attribution | Severity |
|---|---|---|---|---|---|---|
| **China** | **Japan** | **Hack and extort** | **12/27/2007** | **6/1/2008** | **0** | **2** |
| | | Hack and extort | 12/27/2007 | 6/1/2008 | 0 | 2 |
| | | **Earthquake hack** | **3/11/2010** | **3/14/2010** | **0** | **2** |
| | | Earthquake hack | 3/11/2010 | 3/14/2010 | 0 | 2 |
| | | **Mitsubishi hack** | **09/01/2011** | **11/4/2011** | **1** | **3** |
| | | Mitsubishi hack | 09/01/2011 | 11/4/2011 | 1 | 3 |
| **China** | **Vietnam** | **Shady RAT** | **8/1/2006** | **1/1/2010** | **0** | **2** |
| | | Shady RAT | 8/1/2006 | 1/1/2010 | 0 | 2 |
| | | **Vietnam hack** | **7/3/2011** | **7/6/2011** | **0** | **2** |
| | | Vietnam hack | 7/3/2011 | 7/6/2011 | 0 | 2 |
| **South Korea** | **Japan** | **Earthquake hack** | **3/11/2011** | **3/14/2010** | **0** | **2** |
| | | Earthquake hack | 3/11/2011 | 3/14/2010 | 0 | 2 |
| **China** | **Philippines** | **Philippines hack** | **3/28/2009** | **3/30/2009** | **0** | **2** |
| | | Philippines hack | 3/28/2009 | 3/30/2009 | 0 | 2 |
| **China** | **United States** | **Espionage operations** | **1/1/2003** | **Ongoing** | **3** | **3** |
| | | Titan Rain | 1/1/2003 | 4/1/2006 | 1 | 2 |
| | | Shady RAT | 8/1/2006 | 1/1/2010 | 0 | 2 |
| | | State Dept theft | 1/1/2006 | 7/7/2006 | 1 | 2 |
| | | Ghost Net | 5/27/2007 | 8/1/2009 | 1 | 2 |
| | | 2008 Campaign hack | 8/1/2008 | 8/04/2008 | 1 | 1 |

(*Continued*)

*Table 4.8* (CONTINUED)

| Initiator | Target | Name | Start | End | Attribution | Severity |
|---|---|---|---|---|---|---|
| | | Night Dragon | 11/1/2009 | 2/11/2011 | 1 | 2 |
| | | Commerce theft | 11/1/2009 | 11/5/2009 | 1 | 2 |
| | | Pentagon Raid | 3/1/2011 | 3/10/2011 | 0 | 3 |
| | | F-35 plans stolen | 3/39/2009 | 4/1/2009 | 1 | 3 |
| | | White House theft | 11/7/2011 | 11/8/2011 | 1 | 2 |
| | | Senator Nelson theft | 3/1/2009 | 3/1/2009 | 1 | 1 |
| | | Byzantine series | 10/30/2008 | 6/30/2011 | 1 | 2 |
| | | **Aurora** | **6/1/2009** | **1/1/2010** | **1** | **2** |
| | | Google hacked and info stolen | 6/1/2009 | 1/1/2010 | 1 | 2 |
| **United States** | **China** | **Response to espionage** | **2/29/2006** | **5/6/2010** | **2** | **2** |
| | | Cisco Raider | 2/29/2006 | 5/6/2010 | 2 | 3 |
| | | Buckshot Yankee | 4/29/2010 | 5/1/2010 | 2 | 1 |
| | | Shotgiant | 3/10/2010 | Ongoing | 1 | 2 |
| **China** | **Taiwan** | **Espionage operations** | **8/1/2006** | **1/1/2010** | **1** | **2** |
| | | Shady RAT | 8/1/2006 | 1/1/2010 | 0 | 2 |
| | | Ghost Net | 5/27/2007 | 8/1/2009 | 1 | 2 |
| **North Korea** | **South Korea** | **Government theft** | **6/1/2008** | **7/9/2009** | **0** | **2** |
| | | Military official failure | 6/1/2008 | 9/2/2008 | 0 | 2 |
| | | Government theft | 9/8/2008 | 9/8/2008 | 0 | 1 |
| | | Government shut down | 7/6/2009 | 7/9/2009 | 0 | 2 |
| **China** | **India** | **Espionage operations** | **8/1/2006** | **4/7/2010** | **3** | **3** |
| | | Sensitive military information stolen | 40,272 | 4/7/2010 | 1 | 3 |
| | | Prime Minister's office hacked and info stolen | 12/15/2009 | 12/15/2009 | 1 | 2 |
| | | Shady RAT | 8/1/2006 | 1/1/2010 | 0 | 2 |
| | | Ghost Net | 5/27/2007 | 8/1/2009 | 1 | 2 |
| **India** | **Pakistan** | **South Asian Cyber Espionage** | **2/1/2013** | **7/2/2013** | **0** | **3** |

(*Continued*)

**Table 4.8** (CONTINUED)

| Initiator | Target | Name | Start | End | Attribution | Severity |
|-----------|--------|------|-------|-----|-------------|----------|
| | | Telenor Pakistan incident | 3/17/2013 | 3/17/2013 | 0 | 2 |
| | | Tranchlulas incident | 2/1/2013 | 7/2/2013 | 0 | 3 |

The boldfaced are cyber disputes; non-boldfaced are cyber incidents.
Attribution is whether or not a government acknowledged involvement in the cyber espionage: 0 = no comment, 1 = denial, 2 = acknowledgment, 3 = multiple attribution for operations. Severity is based on an ascending scale, with 1 being benign attacks and 5 being the most severe.

incidents. Thirteen of the 45 cyber disputes (27 percent) in our data are cyber espionage campaigns. China is the most active cyber espionage state in our list of rival states engaged in cyber conflict. An espionage incident at the highest severity level recorded, that of "3," is the Chinese theft of Lockheed-Martin's F-35 jet plans. The effects of these infiltrations have yet to be seen, but China has quickly been demonstrating the development of American-style weapons systems. China is using its abilities in cyberspace to harass its more powerful competitor, the United States, and regional competitor, India. China uses its cyber abilities to counter US power as well as to provoke the United States into increasing defense spending due to perceived insecurity. China is also perhaps doing the same thing to India, to keep it down.

As indicated in Table 4.8, China is the most active in the use of cyber espionage as a foreign policy tactic. Many of these cyber espionage operations are directed toward regional targets. Perhaps the purpose is to project China's regional prowess in East Asia—to let its rivals, most notably Japan and Taiwan, know that it is the regional hegemon. Another possibility is that this is as far as China can go with these displays of power, as these states are aligned and allied with the United States.

Quite the opposite is found with the next most active state in cyberspace, the United States. The United States is generally not the initiator of cyber conflict, and is usually a target of its enemies.[14] We find evidence of great restraint from the American foreign policy regime, as previous research (Maness and Valeriano 2014) has found the United States to be the most offensively capable state in cyberspace. The United States is the creator of some of the most sophisticated infiltrations in the world, but has used its grand capabilities sparingly. Stuxnet has perhaps been the most sophisticated worm to be launched willingly against another state (toward Iran, and others by mistake), yet it seems that unless a state is blatantly defying international rules and trying to develop nuclear weapons technology, a rival of the United States will not suffer the great capabilities of the global hegemon. The next chapter covers American cyber restraint when infiltrated by China in more detail.

Table 4.9 identifies the most severe cyber disputes uncovered in our investigation. The most immediate piece of information gathered from this table is that the severity of cyber disputes has been moderate to low in relation to the attention the event has gathered in the media. There have been no events that led to massive damage of critical infrastructure. In addition, there have been no disputes that resulted in the loss of lives.

The most significant cyber disputes are ones that either severely damage states' strategic plans or are attempts to steal sensitive state and military secrets. Stuxnet, Flame, Gauss, and Duqu are all incidents that were part of the larger "Olympic Games" nuclear program dispute that was launched against Iran in order to discourage the Iranians from continuing their nuclear program. This is the only significant cyber dispute to have attempted to alter a state's behavior. We found similar incidents to be scarce in our data, which indicates that cyber tactics are usually only

### Table 4.9 MOST SEVERE CYBER DISPUTES

| Name of Dispute, Date | Rival | Severity | Target Type | Initiator Objective | Description |
|---|---|---|---|---|---|
| "Olympic Games" Iran Nuclear Program strikes, 6/1/2009– Present | US-Iran, Israel-Iran | 3 | 5 | 3 | Flame, Stuxnet, Duqu, and Gauss attacks disrupt Iran's nuclear program |
| Chinese theft operations on US and US response, 1/1/2003– Present | US-China | 3 | 7 | 2 | Titan Rain, Cisco Raider, Pentagon Raid, F-35 plans, Shady Rat, Ghost Net, Byzantine |
| US Power Grid hack, 8/24/09– 8/25/09 | US-Russia | 3 | 1 | 1 | Russia suspected of hacking US power grid |
| Mitsubishi hack, 9/1/2011– 11/4/2011 | China-Japan | 3 | 1 | 2 | Japanese defense firm Mitsubishi hacked, information stolen |
| Chinese theft operations on India, 8/1/2006– Present | China-India | 3 | 3 | 2 | Sensitive military information stolen |

used to steal from or cause minor disruptions to an enemy. The Chinese theft of the F-35 plans is a good example from the years-long Chinese theft operations against the United States. While traumatic to the country and military establishment, these events are by no means critical in terms of severity or impact. Stuxnet and Flame may have set back the Iranian nuclear weapons program, yet most estimates suggest that the recovery time was a few months to three years (Sanger 2012). While the Chinese may have stolen advanced jet plans, they have yet to develop the capabilities necessary to replicate American technology at a level capable of supplying its troops with steady weaponry, particularly jet engines. Far more devastation would result from the potential Chinese theft of stealth helicopter technology in relation to the Bin Laden assassination raid in 2011 and the capture in 2001 of signals from an intelligence plane (the Hainan Island incident).

The other three most severe cyber disputes in our database occurred between the United States and Russia, China and Japan, and China and India. The Russian hack of the US Eastern Seaboard Power Grid is ranked as one of the most severe because a hacker could have shut down power for one-third of the US population, which would have led to a geopolitical disaster between the Cold War foes. All sources of this infiltration have pointed to Russia; therefore it is now difficult for the Russians to deny their part. A blackout in the Eastern United States would result in a nadir of relations between the two countries not seen since the Cuban Missile Crisis. It seems that the Russians merely wanted the Americans to know what they were capable of in cyberspace. The reason the China-Japan and China-India cyber disputes made the top five is the fact that China launched these disputes with the intention of stealing military secrets from their rivals. Espionage on the military could escalate tensions between rivals more quickly, as will be discussed in the next chapter.

One important observation from the analysis of this data is that there has only been one cyber dispute that accompanied a conventional armed conflict. Several vandalism and DDoS incidents disrupted government and telecommunications companies in the tiny state of Georgia during its five-day conflict with Russia. These incidents were not part of any military strategy; rather, they were propagandist messages and disruptive measures utilized to instill fear and confusion in the Georgian government and population. As noted in Chapter 2, Russia is one of the most cyber-capable states on the globe; therefore Russian restraint, even during a military campaign, is evident given the lack of severity of their incidents. Thus no state has opted to open the Pandora's box of escalated cyber conflict during conventional military campaigns. Opportunities are replete: the Iraq War of 2003, the NATO Libya campaign, and possibly Syria, if international intervention is ever initiated, are all examples. We have observed evidence for cyber restraint even among the most capable states in the international system.

It is important to note that the burden for all these events can fall squarely on the defender. If the Pentagon's research partners are going to be targeted, one must prevent these highly sensitivity plans from being located in accessible locations in the first place. It is likely that such an incident or dispute will not be a simple intrusion, but rather a phishing attempt that was surprisingly successful.[15] Stuxnet, while moderately devastating, was conducted by a conventional infiltration of Iranian systems by a spy or unwilling accomplice. These failures fall squarely at the lack of defense in the target, and should not be blamed on the tactic. The most interesting example of this is the recent Flambé dispute waged against France. Reportedly, computers in the president's office were targeted.[16] The intrusion was perpetuated through a fake Facebook account. A few office members accepted the friendship requests, and then clicked on links from the fake account.

Again, our data are a retrospective account of cyber actions by states from 2001 to 2011. Prospects for escalation of cyber conflict in the future are possible; however, enough time has passed that we do not see many cyber incidents going beyond our severity score of 3. Russia, a country that is not the greatest example of cyber restraint, refrained from using severe cyber methods against Ukraine in 2014 during the Crimea crisis. Stuxnet remains the most sophisticated cyber incident, and, as we will show in Chapter 6, the blowback to that event has been severe. Healey (2013) selectively traces cyber malice back to 1986 and finds a similar lack of severity in cyber actions. Incidents such as the Morris Worm (1988) and Cuckoo's Egg (1989) were at the same level as most vandalism and DDoS campaigns, and would be coded with a severity score of 2. Therefore, our data find that while the number of disputes and incidents are proliferating, the severity remains stable at the lower thresholds. Furthermore, the fact that more states and organizations are switching to digital technology only raises the chances of a cyber incident of a high severity, yet evidence continues to accumulate that cyber powers act with restraint. Through time, more cyber actions will occur, but our prediction of low severity rates constrained by restraint dynamics will likely continue to hold.

## CYBER REGIONALISM

Regionalism clearly plays a role in cyber conflict. Figure 4.1 maps cyber incidents in the Middle East. Blast radii mark the location and level of the incident, while the arrows show their source. The vast majority of cyber incidents occur in regional rivalries. Israel and Iran's cyber conflicts continue with their push for regional dominance. Those who discovered the Shamoon incident on Saudi Arabia point the blame at Iran, as relations between the two are souring. Cyber conflict in the Middle East, therefore, has the potential to escalate. Shamoon will be analyzed in detail in Chapter 6.

Cyber conflict also tends to exist in dyads with a major regional power, such as China, Israel, and India. Figure 4.2 maps cyber incidents in East Asia. China

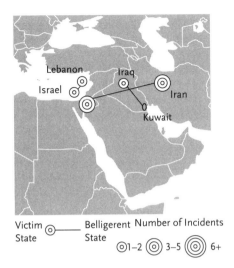

**Figure 4.1**
Cyber Conflict in the Middle East

**Figure 4.2**
East Asian Cyber Incidents

frequently infiltrates its neighbors, including unidirectional cyber tactics on Philippines, Vietnam, and Taiwan. The triad of North Korea, South Korea, and Japan show a continued conflict online. The states engaging in cyber conflict expand their power in non-traditional theaters. The tactics are enough to get rivals' attention, but do not create enough havoc to warrant a militarized response. This fails to falsify our hypothesis on cyber espionage, as most of China's rivals in East Asia are under the US military umbrella of protection; therefore provocation of these rivals in a conventional military fashion could provoke an escalatory response from the United States. Furthermore, when it comes to confronting the United States itself, it seems that China can best demonstrate its rising power in a managed and non-escalatory fashion in cyberspace. More on this phenomenon is discussed in the next chapter.

South Asia provides another theater for cyber conflict. Figure 4.3 maps South Asian cyber conflict. The India-Pakistan dyad features continued cyber conflict, with both sides perpetrating defacements. India and Pakistan, which share one of the most heated rivalries in recent times, have not escalated their conflictual relations in cyberspace. The cyber conflict for this dyad seems to be limited to a propaganda battle, although our latest data show that espionage campaigns between the rivals may be developing. When India and Pakistan wish to confront each other, they will use a more conventional tactic. Military grandstanding or diplomatic threats seem to be the primary tactics in this rivalry. India also exerts its

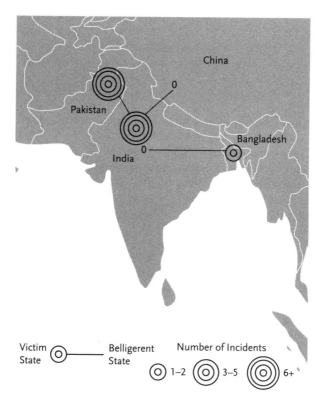

**Figure 4.3**
South Asian Cyber Incidents

cyber strength on neighboring Bangladesh without response. One-way incidents like this (and from China above) suggest that target states have a fear of retaliation or lack capabilities.

Further support for our regional hypothesis is summarized in Table 4.10. Here we list all rivals involved in cyber conflict. As indicated, 15 of our 20 cyber rivals are also regional rivals. Regional rivals are pairs of states that are in close proximity to each other, and have territorial disputes or policy disputes over the region in question. Furthermore, 93 percent (14 of 15) of these cyber rivals were either involved in a territorial issue or dispute, or both, prior to the cyber incidents. For territorial issues, we combed Huth and Allee's (2009) dataset to connect their territorial claims data to ongoing cyber disputes and incidents. We

*Table 4.10* CYBER RIVALS AND TERRITORIAL ISSUES/DISPUTES

| Rival A | Rival B | Same Region? | Huth Territorial Issue? | COW Territorial MID? |
|---------|---------|--------------|-------------------------|----------------------|
| China | India | Y | Y | Y |
| China | Japan | Y | Y | Y |
| China | Taiwan | Y | Y | Y |
| China | Vietnam | Y | Y | Y |
| China | Philippines | Y | Y | Y |
| North Korea | South Korea | Y | Y | Y |
| North Korea | Japan | Y | Y | Y |
| South Korea | Japan | Y | Y | Y |
| India | Pakistan | Y | Y | Y |
| India | Bangladesh | Y | Y | Y |
| Israel | Iran | Y | N | Y |
| Israel | Lebanon | Y | Y | Y |
| Iraq | Kuwait | Y | Y | Y |
| Russia | Georgia | Y | Y | Y |
| Russia | Estonia | Y | Y | N |
| US | China | N | N | Y |
| US | Russia | N | N | N |
| US | North Korea | N | N | Y |
| US | Syria | N | N | N |
| US | Iran | N | N | N |

75 percent (15 of 20) of cyber rivals are regional rivals

93 percent (14 of 15) of regional cyber rivals have territorial issues

93 percent (14 of 15) of regional cyber rivals have territorial MIDs

40 percent (2 of 5) of non-regional cyber rivals have territorial MIDs

0 percent (0 of 5) of non-regional cyber rivals have territorial issues

*Source:* Huth and Allee (2009); Ghosn, Palmer, and Bremer (2004).

found that only Israel and Iran did not have a territorial issue pressing prior to a cyber incident.

We also looked at territorial militarized disputes to connect our cyber incidents to militarized territorial responses. For territorial militarized interstate disputes (MIDs) we sifted through the Correlates of War (COW) dataset and found that only Russia and Estonia have not escalated tensions to a militarized level, where mobilization of troops, naval vessels, or air forces would occur (Ghosn et al. 2004).[17]

Cyber conflict has roots in more conventional forms of territorial disagreements; these disagreements raise tensions to a certain level where states will act, both conventionally and in the cyber realm. Territorial disputes are directly connected to the increased probability of a militarized dispute and war (Vasquez and Henehan 2001; Senese and Vasquez 2008; Vasquez and Valeriano 2010). For regional rivals, cyber conflict is found to be in its proper context, part of the normal relations range of rival interactions (Azar 1972). Most cyber disputes are regional in context, and the great majority of these cases involve ongoing issues that extend beyond the cyber world.

The only exception to cyber conflict's regional tendency is cyber conflict involving the United States, which has a vested military and economic interest in all of the non-regional cyber rivalry dyads. All five non-regional rivals involve the United States, with only two of the five having a territorial dispute, both of which involve territorial disputes with third parties. One dispute is with China, where the United States defended the territorial integrity of Taiwan, and the other involved North Korea over its perpetual territorial dispute with South Korea.

The United States is the global hegemon, and it is also one of the most "plugged-in" of all states, making it an attractive target to cyber initiators. In the cyber world, the United States and China are outliers. It is not surprising that the global cyber interests of the United States and China defy the normal territorial dynamics of most cyber interactions that involve rivals. Hypothesis three could be modified to state that minor powers will operate at the regional level, but major powers operate at the global level. The danger is clearly that these operations will shape international norms and will make cyber operations permissible.

## CYBER STATE-TERRORISM

In our data, there is also very little evidence of state-supported or sponsored groups utilizing cyber terrorism. In total, we have six incidents listed in Table 4.11. The incidents that are listed are very low in severity and impact, all scoring a one. All cyber state-terrorist incidents were defacements and hit government non-military networks. The Lebanon-Israel and Iran-Israel incidents occurred in response to the border clashes between Hezbollah and the Israeli military and also in response

**Table 4.11** TERRORIST GROUP INVOLVEMENT IN CYBER INCIDENTS BETWEEN STATES

| Name of Incident, Date | Rival | Severity | Target Type | Initiator Objective | Description |
|---|---|---|---|---|---|
| **Cyber Jihad (Hezbollah sponsored)** 1/1/2001–8/1/2001 | **Lebanon-Israel** | 1 | 2 | 1 | Various attacks by various countries warded off by Israel |
| **Electronic Jihad** 9/1/2000–9/1/2000 | **Iran-Israel** | 1 | 2 | 1 | Electronic jihad, Islamist rhetoric on Israeli sites |
| **Cyber Jihad** 8/1/2001–8/1/2001 | **Iran-Israel** | 1 | 2 | 1 | Cyber Jihad, widespread DDoS attacks |
| **Lebanese action hack** 10/27/2006–10/27/2006 | **Iran-Israel** | 1 | 2 | 1 | Response to Israeli-Lebanese conflict |
| **Operation Cast Lead Retaliation** | **Iran-Israel** | 1 | 2 | 1 | Operation Cast Lead Retaliation, disruption of Israeli websites |
| **ICID defacement** 10/11/2011–10/11/2011 | **Pakistan-India** | 1 | 2 | 1 | India's Criminal Investigation Dept hacked by Muslim party from Pakistan protesting violence in Kashmir |

to Israeli policy in the Palestinian regions, where Hezbollah defaced Israeli websites in response to settlement expansion or airstrikes in Gaza. These incidents were all propaganda attempts, and Israeli websites were back online in a matter of hours. The lone Pakistan-India cyber state-terrorist incident involved a Pakistani Muslim fundamentalist party hacking India's Criminal Investigation Department in response to the ongoing violence in the disputed region of Kashmir. This propagandized vandalism incident was swiftly contained.

One of the main goals of terrorists and the operations that they carry out against states is to instill fear in the population and create a shock value that, in the end, will change a state's policy toward a certain sect of society or that state's foreign policy. Cyber tactics do not have the same shock value in comparison to suicide bombings in a public square or the hijacking of aircraft. Furthermore, as large amounts of funding are needed to pull off the more complicated and malicious cyber incidents, terrorists and the states that fund their operations are better off funding the more conventional and more eye-opening terrorist tactics that have been seen in recent times in Mumbai, New York, and Moscow. Therefore, cyber state-terrorism is something that is not going to be a part of many terrorist networks' arsenal any time soon. We will examine this topic more in Chapter 7.

## CYBER SPILLOVER

Our concept of cyber spillover is defined as cyber conflict that seeps and bleeds into the traditional arena of militarized and foreign policy conflict. While it is dubious to claim that the cyber domain is disconnected from the physical domain given that cyber technology has to be housed somewhere, it is also true that there are very few incidents of cyber actions causing physical damage (the only case being Stuxnet). Our question is not about the transition from cyber to physical, but about when cyber disagreements lead directly to conventional foreign policy disputes between states, thus altering how international interactions work.

The claim is that the cyber era is different and that we will see drastically new dynamics evident in the international discourse. If true, we would often see cyber conflicts and events transition from the digital realm to the normal international realm. We decided to examine the empirical veracity of these claims. The data demonstrate a bit of a different story. We find that only three of these incidents, the Russia-Georgia incident during the 2008 five-day conventional conflict, the East China Sea Dispute between Japan and China in 2010, and the US-Syria incident in 2011 during the genesis period of the now bloody Syrian civil war are connected to further international tensions under what we might consider a militarized interstate dispute (MID), or a use, display, or threat of force (using the newly released MID 4.0 data). Only one incident actually preceded a militarized interstate dispute. This took place in 2008, with perhaps the most well-known case of cyber actions during a militarized campaign. It involved the series of defacements and DDoS incidents that Russia conducted against Georgia during the August 2008 five-day conflict (see Table 4.12). However, the claim that these cyber actions led directly to this military campaign is dubious at best.[18] The militarized campaign did not need the preceding cyber incident to succeed, and the primary purpose of the cyber portion of the Russian campaign was to instill fear and confusion within the Georgian government and people. The cyber dispute in and of itself did not cause the conventional conflict.

In the two other militarized disputes involving cyber activity, the cyber incidents did not precede the militarized ones; therefore there is only shaky evidence for cyber spillover becoming part of relations among rivals. One incident involved Japan and China and their continuing rivalry over territorial concerns in the East China Sea. We found that when a cyber incident seeps into the conventional international affairs battlefield, the reason is likely that the disputes are connected to salient territorial issues.

The other incident in Table 4.13 occurred between the United States and Syria. On that occasion, the Syrian government, in reaction to US Ambassador to Syria John Ford's visit to the besieged city of Hama at the beginning of the bloody civil war, initiated a short series of anti-American defacements of the US State Department's official webpage. What followed was an escalation of violence in the city, initiated by Syrian government forces against rebel combatants and civilians in that city.

There are obvious caveats in these sparse findings. One might be that we have only seen the beginnings of cyber conflict; therefore we cannot make claims about the future of cyber conflict and spillover. While the future of cyber conflict is developing, we do have quite a bit of evidence of how cyber actors interact. Between our data and the fact that no real evidence of cyber spillover to the present date has occurred, we have a wide range of information available for predictions and evaluations of the proposition.

It is also the case that future uses of a technology are often dictated by how it is used early in its development. We often see this with technological developments—what is acceptable is determined early in the life of a technology.

**Table 4.12** RUSSIA-GEORGIA 2008: THE CASE OF CYBER SPILLOVER

| Dyad (Initiator First) | Name | Date of Cyber Incident | Date of Militarized Incident | Type | Target Type | Description |
|---|---|---|---|---|---|---|
| Russia-Georgia | Before the Gunfire | 4/20/2008– 8/16/2008 | 8/7/2008– 8/12/2008 | DDoS | Govt, non-military | Russia infiltrates Georgian networks |

*Source:* Correlates of War (COW) MID4 Dataset: http://www.correlatesofwar.org/COW2%20Data/MIDs/ MID40.html

**Table 4.13** CYBER-INCIDENTS ACCOMPANIED BY MILITARIZED DISPUTES

| Dyad (Initiator First) | Name | Date of Cyber Incident | Date of Militarized Incident | Type | Target Type | Description |
|---|---|---|---|---|---|---|
| China–Japan | East China Sea Dispute | 9/14/2010–9/17/2010 | 9/7/2010–present | DDoS | Govt, non-military | Chinese DDoS escalates naval tensions over the territorial disputes |
| Syria–US | Hama Visit | 7/9/2011–7/9/2011 | 7/3/2011–8/4/2011 | Defacement | Govt, non-military | Ambassador Ford's visit to Hama provokes defacement by Syria of the US State Department website. |

*Source:* Correlates of War (COW) MID4 Dataset: http://www.correlatesofwar.org/COW2%20Data/MIDs/MID40.html.

Take, for example, nuclear weapons. They were used early in their life cycle and the critical reaction was so immediate that a norm against the technology developed. On the other hand, other technologies, like machine guns, tanks, and ballistic missiles, were deployed and used widely at early stages of their development.

We shall see what the cyber future brings, but so far our work has demonstrated that states have been restrained in the use of cyber technology. Here we have demonstrated that states are mostly restrained from transitioning a cyber threat to a physical threat. This calls into question the cyber revolution hypothesis, or the idea that cyber conflict will change how interactions take place. If anything, cyber conflict seems to reinforce typical international patterns, rather than becoming a pathway for new patterns.

## ASSESSMENT

According to popular conception, we should be in the middle of the cyber conflict era now. As of the writing of this chapter, searching for the term "massive cyber attack" results in 13,500,000 hits on Google. Pundits make it seem as if the state's enemies are active now, preparing to unleash cyber Armageddon. Yet, even considering our past investigations and theory, we were shocked to find little actual evidence of cyber conflict in the modern era. Instead, we observed the absence of incidents by cyber forces even during conventional armed conflict. Rather than observing a new way of warfare, we found much of the same, regional low-level conflicts and incidents connected to territorial claims. In fact, only 20 of the 126 rival dyads engage in cyber conflict—a rate of about 15.8 percent, which is well below the suggested tipping rate of 33 percent mentioned in Chapter 3. In comparison, the incidence of cyber conflict pales in comparison to that of transnational terrorist attacks, or terrorism that involves persons from two or more states.[19] Only the Asian states of Japan, South Korea, Taiwan, and Vietnam have been victim to more cyber incidents than transnational terrorist attacks. All in all, there have been 590 times as many terrorist attacks as cyber incidents, according to our sample.[20]

Why then are there so few rivals engaging in cyber warfare? Furthermore, why are the incidents and disputes limited to mostly defacements or denial of service when it seems that cyber capabilities could inflict more damage on their adversaries? Based on our analysis, we find that our notion of restraint is a better explanation of cyber interactions than any conception of continuous or escalating cyber conflict. This issue will be further discussed in Chapter 8 as we develop this theme and argue that cyber operations represent taboos yet unbroken.

The real cyber threats may come from ambitious individuals and malicious hackers, not states or international actors. An important point for our argument is that states will not risk war with their cyber capabilities because there are clear consequences to any use of these technologies. States are not reckless, but terrorists and other cyber activists might not be so restrained. The interesting result of the process is that while cyber terrorists will likely proliferate, their ability to do damage will be limited due to the massive resources and conventional intelligence methods needed to make an operation like Stuxnet successful, a question that we explore in Chapter 7.[21] Stuxnet and Flame could be the harbingers of the future, but in reality the initiators of each incident were aided by a collusion of discrete events. With a will to initiate cyber malice, there must also come a way to do so. With such a high burden of luck and ability, it will be rare to see such important disputes continue in the future.

The cyber incidents of Red October and Flame represent the typical outcome of cyber conflict.[22] They are massive cyber operations, but have to date been used for information extraction and espionage purposes. Cyber conflict will be part of the future, but these events will only be as devastating as the target allows them to be since the potential initiator is restrained by logic, norms, and fear of retaliation. Restraint is clearly in operation for cyber conflict. Constraints can keep an actor from doing something it would usually do if left to its own devices. A rival will not blatantly infiltrate its adversary's infrastructure or secret government databases because that state may perceive the incident as it would a physical attack and respond with an equally devastating cyber incident or even with conventional military forces. As the United States has made clear, cyber incidents are considered acts of war, and it is likely that these states are not willing to escalate the rivalry to a critical and dangerous level through cyber threats and actions. The fear of collateral damage remains high for many actors, and this simple limitation may prevent persistent cyber conflict from becoming a reality. Another fear is cyber blowback, as noted by Farwell and Rohozinski (2011), in that tactics could be replicated and targeted back toward the offender.

The range of relations in the realm of cyberspace has yet to be determined, but it does seem clear that rivals operate as rivals should. They are able to manage their tensions in such a way as to forestall violence yet prolong tensions for long periods of time. Therefore, states have yet to employ widespread damage via cyberspace out of fear of the unknown. They fear the escalation of the rivalry in the absence of a critical event like a territorial invasion. Malicious and damaging cyber tactics seem not to be the norm. Even Russia has pushed for treaties among the international community that would set up norms of cyber action among states. The European Union has also promoted this idea; however, the United States is skeptical about signing on to such agreements (Clarke and Knake 2010). The best hope in reducing the possibility of cyber incidents in the future comes from strong institutions capable of managing and restricting cyber-based disputes.

The cyber-industrial complex has been a prominent force in this process (Dunn-Cavelty 2008). By operating on an active level in the industry, it makes the suggestion that it can protect against these threats; in all likelihood, the problem is that the target is vulnerable rather than that the initiator is so powerful. If networks are insecure, if individuals continue to respond to phishing attempts and lack the basic common sense necessary in cyber interactions, they will continue to fall prey to cyber incidents and disputes. Their utilization only makes the never-ending cycle of cyber operations go round. The cyber-industrial complex is complicit in the nature of this cycle, if not the direct cause.

In what is termed cyber espionage, the goal should really be to harden targets, teaching proficient cyber practices so that individuals do not fall prey to cyber incidents, and to think of rational responses to cyber threats, not the irrational and exaggerated responses we have seen quite often in the digital industry and by some governments.

State-based cyber espionage is literally the least a state can do. It chooses to take on these operations because they are easy and cost-free in that the aggressor can deny perpetration of the incidents. They are forms of harassment in a rivalry, but, as with most forms of harassment, the tactics used are relatively benign, cumulative, and serve as nuisances rather than patterns.

Cyber espionage is to be expected. The espionage industry is one of the oldest professions in this world, and it is not going away. States will use whatever tactics they can to achieve political ends. But throughout the course of history, the impact of cyber espionage has been relatively minor, and major successes can generally be attributed to errors in the target rather than the prowess of the aggressor itself.

Similarly, cyber state-terrorism is unlikely to proliferate into something dangerous any time soon. States concerned about terrorism should remain vigilant and deter terrorism in conventional domains; but the cyber domain is something that does not give terrorist cells the punch they need to get their points across to governments. Often, these organizations do not have the means or capacity to harm states.

Cyber disputes may not spread the same level of fear that a conventional physical attack may provoke. Therefore, an airstrike, naval blockade, or all-out invasion is more likely to win a diplomatic or military engagement than a botnet that shuts down the State Department for a day or prevents an ATM from dispensing money for 48 hours. Cyber conflicts, although potentially lethal, do not have the same "punch" as a physical attack. For now, we have taken a big step forward in returning the debate on cyber tactics to some measure of reality.

## CONCLUSIONS

We do not doubt that cyber incidents and disputes will increase in the future and will demonstrate a real national security threat to the state. The question we pose is how serious the threat is. Is it something we should use to promote a reorientation of security strategies? The answer is clearly a resounding no, at least in terms of interstate interactions. There is little evidence that cyber incidents and disputes are as serious as pundits make them out to be. It is not the purpose of this chapter to ponder the "what-ifs" of cyber conflict; rather, we have analyzed as best we could what has already happened and have constructed realistic future expectations from our findings.

Many states continue to debate what is commonly known as the "kill switch" legislation, or other sorts of Internet restrictions in the name of cyber security. The purpose of these proposed types of laws would be to give the state the power to shut down the Internet in the event of a severe cyber incident. We believe that this could be detrimental to commerce, privacy, and personal freedom. What is more constructive, we believe, is to create an international institution that mitigates conflict in cyberspace and sets up certain "cyber norms" of behavior, a theme we will explore more fully in Chapter 8. Energies could be then diverted to stopping cyber threats from terrorists and other non-state actors.

While states should remain vigilant and protective of their interests, there is a point when actions taken in protection of the state actually damage the state. The reduction in commerce, educational and collaborative exchanges, and knowledge is not worth the gains seen through excessive cyber protection strategies. As Mueller (2006: 1) notes in relation to terrorism, "this process has then led to wasteful, even self-parodic expenditures and policy overreactions, ones that not only very often do more harm and cost more money than anything the terrorists have accomplished, but play into their hands." The relationship between cyber conflict and threats is much the same; perhaps we are witnessing the beginning of an overblown reaction to a minor threat.

In the end, the target is almost as much at fault at the offender. A state can only steal what it allows to be stolen in the cyber world. Cybercrime is not persuasive in its ability to control weapons systems, technologies, and research unless the target allows for this unrestricted access across networks. Vigilance is important, but that is not the point of the creation of cyber commands and talk of an Internet "kill switch."

The data we have presented here illustrate that cyber disputes are rare. When they do happen, the impact tends to be minimal. Only 20 of 126 possible ongoing rivals engage in cyber combat. Of these rival interactions, most fall on the lower end in terms of quantity. In terms of quality, there are very few severe incidents and disputes, according to our classification system. While the future may bring a period of unrestricted cyber conflict, it is clear that this has not yet occurred—and, in our view, such conflict is unlikely to transpire.

Scholars in the future should remain vigilant and monitor actual cyber incidents. Moderation is called for, but this can only be done with real evidence to reduce the hysterical fears that profiteers will place on the cyber world. The future is bright for cyber relations, but only if we allow natural connections to be made to speed the process of globalization and interconnectedness, rather than inward thinking and defensive reactions to technological developments. We now move forward and use the dataset presented in this chapter to examine the impact of cyber conflict on foreign policy interactions.

## CHAPTER 5

# The Impact of Cyber Actions

*Cyber Events and the Conflict-Cooperation Nexus*

## INTRODUCTION

The March–April 2007 cyber dispute initiated by Russian hackers against Estonia created an uproarious stir in the international press. The Estonian government had decided to move a Soviet World War II–era memorial known as the "Bronze Soldier of Tallinn" from the city's central square to another location. The Russian government, taking advantage of nationalist fervor, responded to the move with outrage and shamed the Estonians. This was followed by a series of DDoS and vandalism cyber incidents that shut down and defaced government and private sector websites and caused disruptions in the daily lives of Estonian citizens (Maness and Valeriano 2014). The Western press shamed the Russians for such a brash reaction to a relatively minor move by the Estonian government.[1] More important, the cyber dispute between Russia and Estonia introduced the world to the supposed possible dangers and threats in cyberspace. Yet beyond the media hype, what was the actual foreign policy response from Estonia to Russia after this breach in the digital realm? Few have endeavored to investigate the consequences of these actions; thus the goal of this chapter is to move beyond the rhetoric.

Some have dubbed cyber conflicts "cool wars."[2] It is said that these conflicts reflect the changing dynamics of state-to-state interactions in the post–Cold War world. States are not willing or able to interact in an outright violent manner, but must restrain their actions below typical thresholds of conflict, thereby making these conflicts neither cold nor hot, but cool. They are cool conflicts because of the technology featured in the interactions. The argument is that the structure, content, and location of interactions on the foreign policy battlefield have supposedly changed in light of these developments.

In the rush to note the changing face of the battlefield, few scholars have actually examined the impact of cyber conflict and "cool" technologies on foreign policy dynamics. Instead, most studies are of a hyperbolic nature that suggests the wide-ranging impact of cyber conflict on daily social and military life. Here we attempt to counter the hype to examine exactly what happens between countries when cyber conflict is utilized as a foreign policy choice. This chapter is one of the first viable attempts to quantify the impact of cyber actions. Our goals are modest, and we hope to lay out the debate for the future. We hope to motivate the community to explore the empirical impact of cyber actions that connect to the reality of the context rather than the speculation rampant in the discourse.

The previous chapter noted that while cyber conflict is proliferating, the severity level of incidents and disputes remains minimal when compared to capabilities and worst-case scenarios dreamed up. Using the dataset of cyber incidents and disputes that we have outlined previously, we measure the level of conflict and cooperation observed after a cyber incident and dispute to understand the true impact of this new tactic on foreign policy dynamics. Three fundamental questions are asked: Does cyber conflict raise the level of conflict interactions between states? Do states capitulate to the cyber aggressor out of fear? Are there different conflict-cooperation dynamics based on the type and severity of the cyber incident or dispute?

We find that only one method of cyber tactics, less harmful than most types—denial of service (DDoS)—affects conflict-cooperation dynamics between states. The effect is negative, which means that these methods sour relations between pairs of states when they are utilized as a foreign policy tool. We also find that regional powers and dyads containing the United States have important conflict-cooperation effects when cyber incidents and disputes are involved. The latter effects are all negative, except for one pair of states: the United States and China. When China uses cyber conflict directed toward the United States, the United States will respond with diplomacy and will try to improve relations with the rising power.

These results challenge the conventional wisdom proposed by pundits. While we rely on statistical significance often, this method for some is problematic (Ziliak and McCloskey 2008). Statistical significance is a useful indicator that our evidence is not random. Otherwise we would have no confidence that our results can hold given the variations in the data. With these results in mind, we hope to push the examination of cyber conflict from speculation to reality. How do states react to cyber conflicts, and what might this mean for the future?

## RESPONSES TO CYBER CONFLICT BY RIVAL STATES

This chapter focuses on the impact of cyber events on the conflict and cooperation dynamics between rival states. Do cyber incidents influence and lead to more conflictual relations? Do cyber incidents defy conventions and lead to positive sanctions rather than negative sanctions? We cannot really answer these questions until one takes a macro view of the situation and examines the entire picture of cyber interactions through time.

In general, it would be thought that during a rivalry, a situation of constant and historic animosity, a state will do all it can to harm the other side. In some instances it will do almost anything, even harm itself, if the other side is hurt more (Valeriano 2013). Rivals participate in zero sum games of status. If a rival state uses a cyber operation to harm its enemy, the likely response will be characterized by further conflictual relations. Therefore, we argue that cyber incidents and disputes would most likely lead to an escalation of hostility between rivals. While our prior investigations have suggested that the tactic will be used at a minimal rate (Chapter 4), we would also argue that when these tactics are used the consequences are likely evident and negative.

States are restrained for many reasons. Restraint dominates because of fears of blowback, the normative taboo against civilian harm, and the problem that, once used, a cyber weapon is rendered usable by others. Blowback is important because cyber weapons are easily reproducible, or the reaction to such weapons could be conventional, violating the goal of deception that dominates most cyber actions. Norms and taboos are critical because cyber weapons are not controllable and manageable, as the makers of Stuxnet found when it escaped into civilian sectors. Finally, the utility of a cyber weapon is limited because one use makes it unlikely that it will be useful in future settings. Most cyber weapons exploit zero-day threats; once a weapon is used, the zero-day vulnerability is gone.

*H6: Cyber incidents and disputes will lead to negative foreign policy responses at the state-to-state level.*

During interactions among major powers, responses to cyber events will be escalated further due to the context of the interaction. Major powers cannot afford to be slighted by other states, or worse, by minor powers trying to punch above their weight. Major powers usually have more at stake in the international system, including their reputation and status. If breached in the cyber realm, a major power will respond coercively to save face. In this case, we should see significant responses if cyber interactions are as significant as the media and pundits make them out to be. There are limits to these responses, as governed by restraint considerations, but we would still argue that a major power is more likely to respond than a minor power.

*H7: Cyber incidents and disputes will lead to negative foreign policy responses when a major power is targeted.*

This is not to suggest that minor powers do not have a stake in the cyber debate. As we mentioned previously, small states have an incentive to utilize cyber power to catch up to major powers and exploit their weaknesses. The difference here is that the credibility and reputational calculations are different for small states. The perception of the capabilities of a large state decreases when it does not respond to international challenges, while minor powers have a freer hand to respond to threats or to ignore them if they so choose. This might be disastrous for internal politics within a small state, but the issue for us here is the relationship between states at the international realm.

The response to interactions at the regional level should also be particularly acute and devastating. The previous chapter demonstrated that, despite the notion that cyber interactions are boundless in cyberspace, they tend to be located in regional contexts. Rivals cannot afford to let regional competitors engage in harassing behavior without an appropriate response. Therefore, regional actors are increasingly likely to respond to cyber incidents with conflictual interactions. This should also be particularly true since most regional rivals contain territorial disputes, and these disputes are particularly dangerous for escalation and cooperative relations (Vasquez 1993).

*H8: Cyber incidents and disputes between regional rivals will lead to negative foreign policy responses.*

Understanding the intent of a cyber action is an important task of this investigation. We argue that cyber actors will likely be restrained in their cyber interactions, and this trend will only be muted when regional rivals interact. Another factor that might lead to negative foreign policy interactions is the nature of the cyber incident or dispute. Coercive behavior in cyberspace typically fails to achieve the desired ends. When Russia infiltrated Estonia in 2007, the reaction by Estonia was not to move closer to the Russian sphere of influence, but to fully commit to the West. When a state tries to use cyber tactics to change behavior, the targeted state will likely respond in a negative fashion.

In addition to coercion, spectacularly public cyber incidents or disputes using methods that are tough to conceal from a population, such as DDoS methods, are also likely to engender a response. A targeted state cannot afford to look weak and fail to respond to actions that seek to make a demonstration of capability. Other cyber tactics, such as espionage and nuisances, are less likely to provoke reactions because they can be concealed and the targeted state will be unlikely to wish to pursue escalatory reactions given the potential for cyber escalation.

*H9: Intending to motivate a change in behavior through demonstration cyber incidents, such as DDoS methods, is likely to provoke a negative foreign policy response.*

In order to test our hypotheses, we must utilize an events history research design comparing the impact of cyber actions to the level of conflict and cooperation between states. This is the only feasible way to understand the impact of cyber incidents and disputes on the foreign policy dynamics between states.

## THE EVENTS DATA METHOD AND HISTORY

Events-based data methodology was once the past and now seems to be the future of analysis in international politics. Events data measure any interaction, from the smallest diplomatic exchange to the invasion of a country, between two states over time. The advantage is that it allows an analysis in weekly or monthly units, painting a more finely detailed picture of the totality of relations between entities. Data is compiled by combing media sources and coding them into the appropriate categories. McClelland (1983) suggests that scholars of international relations have two basic occupations: the development of a theory of human interaction about political matters, and development of a theory of politics as values, that is, goals, preferences, and objectives. Contemporary datasets only look at specific problems (war and disputes) and de-emphasize the search for general theories of international behavior.

Events data were intended to measure the conflict and cooperation relationship between states. Due to technological limitations, human coding error, and source choices, the use of these events datasets fell out of usage after the early 1980s. Advances in variable coding has been much improved over the years, as nominal and ordinal variables, which cannot be used to measure intensity of interactions, are being replaced by interval measures in order to capture these intensity levels of dyadic interactions. However, as other datasets have an expansive temporal domain and are widely used, these datasets have become the norm in the field and events data research designs have been marginalized. Here we find the use of an events data methodology appropriate and necessary to investigate cyber interactions.

The two most well-known events datasets are the Conflict and Peace Data Bank (COPDAB) and World Events Interaction Survey (WEIS). McClelland is the originator of the WEIS events dataset, and this set covers a small time period (1966–1978), uses only the *New York Times* as a source, and has 63 nominal categories, which have no numeric value. This stands in contrast to COPDAB's 15 ordinal categories, which have significant order but cannot be used in any arithmetic-like operations. Azar's COPDAB is an exhaustive events data set that covers January 1, 1948, to December 31, 1978. It has nearly 500,000 events recorded from over 70 sources. There are 15 ordinal categories ranked from war to states merging. Azar (1972: 185) describes an event as any overt input and/or output of the type "who does what to and/or with whom and when," which may have ramifications for the behavior of an international actor or actors. Operationally, an event is any overt input and/or output of the mentioned type (Azar 1972) that may have ramifications for the behavior of an international actor or actors and which is recorded at least once in any publicly available source.

Events data has been used more frequently in recent years by scholars due to the work of Goldstein (1992). He argues that the WEIS coding scheme is more useful, and if the variables are translated into an interval scale, the dynamics of conflict and cooperation could be measured more accurately. Goldstein creates a conflict-cooperation scale out of the 63 nominal events in WEIS. As COPDAB's coding ended with 1978, over the years it has been used more sparsely. WEIS has been continued into the 1980s, and the fact that WEIS has 63 event types as well as verb-based actions, listed in Figure 5.1, means that WEIS interval level coding could help us uncover some useful relationships in the cyber realm. Goldstein

| | |
|---|---|
| −10.0 | Military attack; clash; assault |
| −9.2 | Seize position or possessions |
| −8.7 | Nonmilitary destruction/injury |
| −8.3 | Non-injury destructive action |
| −7.6 | Armed force mobilization, exercise, display; military buildup |
| −7.0 | Break diplomatic relations |
| −7.0 | Threat with force specified |
| −6.9 | Ultimatum; threat with negative sanction and time limit |
| −5.8 | Threat with specific negative nonmilitary sanction |
| −5.6 | Reduce or cut off aid or assistance; act to punish/deprive |
| −5.2 | Nonmilitary demonstration, walk out on |
| −5.0 | Order person or personnel out of country |
| −4.9 | Expel organization or group |
| −4.9 | Issue order or command, insist, demand compliance |
| −4.4 | Threat without specific negative sanction stated |
| −4.4 | Detain or arrest person(s) |
| −4.1 | Reduce routine international activity; recall officials |
| −4.0 | Refuse; oppose; refuse to allow |
| −4.0 | Turn down proposal; reject protest, demand, threat |
| −3.8 | Halt negotiation |
| −3.4 | Denounce; denigrate; abuse |
| −3.0 | Give warning |
| −2.4 | Issue formal complaint or protest |
| −2.2 | Charge; criticize; blame; disapprove |
| −2.2 | Cancel or postpone planned event |
| −1.9 | Make complaint (not formal) |
| −1.1 | Grant asylum |
| −1.1 | Deny an attributed policy, action, role or position |
| −0.9 | Deny an accusation |

| | |
|---|---|
| −0.2 | Comment on situation |
| −0.1 | Urge or suggest action or policy |
| −0.1 | Explicit decline to comment |
| −0.1 | Request action; call for |
| 0.0 | Explain or state policy; state future position |
| 0.1 | Ask for information |
| 0.6 | Surrender, yield to order, submit to arrest |
| 0.6 | Yield position; retreat; evacuate |
| 1.0 | Meet with; send note |
| 1.2 | Entreat; plead; appeal to; beg |
| 1.5 | Offer proposal |
| 1.8 | Express regret; apologize |
| 1.9 | Visit; go to |
| 1.9 | Release and/or return persons or property |
| 2.0 | Admit wrongdoing; apologize, retract statement |
| 2.5 | Give state invitation |
| 2.8 | Assure; reassure |
| 2.8 | Receive visit; host |
| 2.9 | Suspend sanctions; end punishment; call truce |
| 3.0 | Agree to future action or procedure, to meet or to negotiate |
| 3.4 | Ask for policy assistance |
| 3.4 | Ask for material assistance |
| 3.4 | Praise, hail, applaud, extend condolences |
| 3.6 | Endorse other's policy or position; give verbal support |
| 4.5 | Promise other future support |
| 4.5 | Promise own policy support |
| 5.2 | Promise material support |
| 5.4 | Grant privilege; diplomatic recognition; de facto relations |
| 6.5 | Give other assistance |
| 6.5 | Make substantive agreement |
| 7.4 | Extend economic aid; give, buy, sell, loan, borrow |
| 8.3 | Extend military assistance |

**Figure 5.1**
Goldstein's (1992) Interval Conflict-Cooperation Scale
*Source:* Goldstein (1992): 376–377

uses a −10 to 10 intensity scale with decimals to measure the intensity of individual events. The −10 score indicates the most conflictual relationship between a pair of states, which is a military attack; 10 is the most cooperative relationship, which is state merger. Goldstein's work and his scale is now used in contemporary events datasets, such as Schrodt's (1993) Kansas Events Dataset (KEDS) and King and Lowe's (2003) Integrated Data for Events Analysis (IDEA), which are machine assisted and use a variety of worldwide news sources.

In the past, due to technological limitations, collecting events data required legions of graduate students who were subject to fatigue and human error. However, Schrodt and his KEDS dataset introduced academia to the machine-assisted coding system that allowed for less error and significantly reduced the costs of data collection. KEDS is one of the prototypes of machine-assisted events data that continued WEIS's coding system, but only looks at the Middle East. King and Lowe's (2003) IDEA project is globally comprehensive, and the future success of events datasets lies with this approach.

King and Lowe's (2003) IDEA uses *Reuters* and the Virtual Reader's Associates (VRA) computer software. This software combs data from the *Reuters* newswire, which utilizes sources from all around the world. Ten million events were recorded between 1990 and 2004, making it a much bigger dataset than its predecessors. IDEA also reduces bias produced by WEIS, which relies only on the *New York Times,* and the concentrated Middle East bias of COPDAB. Scholars now have a reliable events data source that can uncover the conflict and cooperation interactions with less uncertainty about the bias of the dataset. IDEA also translates these variables into intervals by utilizing Goldstein's (1992) interval scale so that scholars can study interactions among states. We can now use events datasets such as IDEA to study not only the conflict dynamics of rivals, but the cooperation among them as well. Bringing cooperation into the equation will allow scholars to measure rivalry intensity and will lead policymakers into more informed decisions on how to interact with their adversaries. It is with this new confidence that we move forward with our analysis.

It must be noted that we did not choose the new and controversial Global Database of Events, Language, and Tone (GDELT), but the more reputable Virtual Readers Associates (VRA) to custom-build our conflict-cooperation outcomes that are our dependent variables for this analysis. We are not interested in the events themselves, but the most stable research question of positive and negative sentiment between countries at the aggregate level. Events data might be unable to capture an accurate account of protests, or cyber incidents for that matter, but it can capture conflict and cooperation, which is needed to measure reactions from states after a cyber incident or dispute. Since no scholar has uncovered the foreign policy dynamics of cyber actions between states, it is pertinent to this study to include both conflict and cooperation scores in order to be able to test for significance for both simultaneously.

Following the work of others, we create an events dataset that compiles conflict-cooperation scores between dyads that also use cyber tactics as a foreign policy tool from the years 2001 to 2011. Scores from this dataset, in the style of Goldstein's scale, serve as the dependent variable of our analysis. Our independent variables, presented in the previous chapter, cover all cyber conflict among rival states, and it is with these measures that we can uncover the impact of cyber incidents and disputes on the foreign policy relations between states.

For a complete description of the research design of this chapter, see the methods appendix that follows at the end of the book.

## DATA ANALYSIS

Table 5.1 presents the findings of the random effects model for cyber incidents. The labeled columns in the table are the explanatory variables run against our dependent variable for each separate random effects panel regression. The labeled rows include the conflict-cooperation dependent variable as well as the effects of the two control variables utilized, with each explanatory variable labeled in the column. All 95 percent confidence intervals are represented in the accompanying figures (Figure 5.2) as error bars to show the range of conflict and cooperation between rival states, as well as which factors are statistically significant. Overall,

***Table 5.1*** CONFLICT-COOPERATION EFFECTS OF CYBER INCIDENTS BY INTERACTION TYPE

|  | Cyber Incident | Nuisance | Defense | Offense | Private | Govt. Non-military | Govt. Military |
|---|---|---|---|---|---|---|---|
| **Conflict-Cooperation (DV)** | 0.264 | −3.512 | 1.424 | 0.469 | 1.815 | 0.679 | −1.047 |
| **Major Power** | 1.246 | 1.202 | 1.246 | 1.227 | 1.287 | 1.255 | 1.179 |
| **Same Region** | −1.743 | −1.781 | −1.728 | −1.742 | −1.741 | −1.728 | −1.845 |

N = 13,449

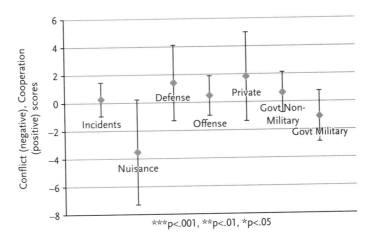

***p<.001, **p<.01, *p<.05

**Figure 5.2**
Range of Conflict-Cooperation at 95 percent Confidence Level: Cyber Incidents

cyber incidents, their types, and the nature of their targets do not have statistically significant effects on foreign policy interactions if examined according to interaction types. As cyber incidents captured by our data are overall of a low severity level, these findings are not surprising. Rivals are still using other foreign policy tactics besides cyber incidents to harm each other, but it seems clear that cyber conflict has yet to significantly affect foreign policy interactions on the balance.

Table 5.2 and Figure 5.3 show the random effects results of the different methods of cyber conflict that states have used against each other from 2001 to 2011. Again, cyber methods for incidents do not have statistically significant effects on foreign policy interactions, except for one particular method. Interestingly, distributed denial of service (DDoS) methods have statistically significant negative effects on conflict cooperation dynamics between rival states. This is surprising due to the low level of severity, as well as the usually short durations of denial of service methods. So why are there negative reactions by rival states for DDoS methods, which are low-level foreign policy tactics?

*Table 5.2* CONFLICT-COOPERATION EFFECTS OF CYBER METHODS

|  | Vandalism | DDoS | Intrusion | Infiltration | APT |
|---|---|---|---|---|---|
| Conflict-Cooperation (DV) | 0.951 | −11.456*** | 0.492 | 0.706 | 0.597 |
| Major Power | 1.315 | 1.285 | 1.233 | 1.230 | 1.237 |
| Same Region | −1.804 | −1.690 | −1.760 | −1.734 | −1.717 |

***p< 0.001
N = 13,449

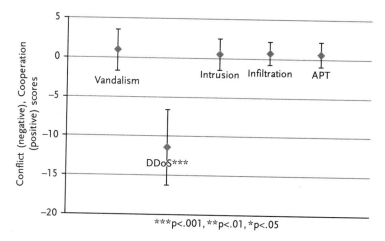

***p<.001, **p<.01, *p<.05

**Figure 5.3**
Range of Conflict-Cooperation at 95 percent Confidence Level: Cyber Methods (Incidents)

The outcomes of DDoS methods may be the reason behind the negative foreign policy responses from target states. The main goal for states that launch DDoS incidents is to shut down websites and cause havoc, which can effectively disrupt the daily lives of many people. This disruption may be trivial, yet it is still a nuisance. When a bank website is shut down, thousands of customers cannot conduct online transactions. When a government website is not working, citizens cannot access the government services they are seeking. Yet, even though the actual effect of these methods is trivial, they are important, as they amplify fears. DDoS methods, therefore, have a psychological effect on many people, which leads to conflictual responses by the targeted state. Although rather benign in terms of long-term damage, denial of service methods evokes strong and negative reactions.

Governments have publicized more severe methods of action, such as intrusions and infiltrations. However, since these methods are targeted and only affect a limited number of actors, rather than the population as a whole, they do not evoke the same responses from governments. Holsti (1992) and Colaresi (2005) find evidence for how the will of the people can sometimes drive foreign policy for states and evoke certain responses when wronged by an adversary. These findings can also explain why DDoS methods prompt governments to respond.

Table 5.3 and Figure 5.4 display the random effects results of cyber incidents coded for the intentions of the initiators as well as severity levels. The effects of these coded explanatory variables are insignificant, except when the initiator's intent is to change the behavior of the target state. Attempting to force a state to do something it otherwise would not do in a coercive manner will usually evoke a negative response (Maness and Valeriano 2014). Whether the tactic is diplomatic, military, or even in cyberspace, states do not like being told what to do, or how to conduct their foreign policy. One can see this type of resistance in Syria, where Bashir al Assad's resistance to international pressure to abdicate his rule has only hardened his attempts to hold on to power.

**Table 5.3** CONFLICT-COOPERATION EFFECTS OF INITIATOR INTENTIONS AND SEVERITY

|  | Disruption | Theft | Behavior Change | Severity 1 | Severity 2 | Severity 3 |
|---|---|---|---|---|---|---|
| **Conflict-Cooperation (DV)** | 0.652 | 1.046 | −4.229*** | −0.940 | 0.903 | 0.457 |
| **Major Power** | 1.347 | 1.400 | 1.171 | 1.085 | 1.341 | 1.214 |
| **Same Region** | −1.809 | −1.589 | −1.853 | −1.719 | −1.662 | −1.763 |

***p < 0.001
N = 13,449

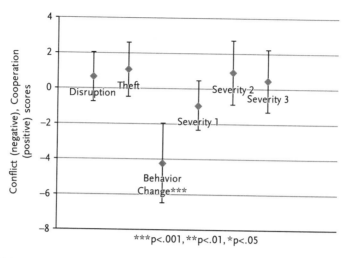

**Figure 5.4**
Range of Conflict-Cooperation at 95 percent Confidence Level: Initiator Intentions (Incidents)

Next we discuss the effects of cyber incidents using the fixed effects panel data method, which uncovers the individual directed dyadic effects of cyber incidents on foreign policy interactions. Table 5.4 and Figure 5.5 show the results of our fixed effects method and shows that overall cyber incidents, as well as major powers in a dyad, do not have any statistically significant effects on foreign policy interactions. However, the regional variable produces negative and statistically significant results. Regional rivals engage in low-level cyber incidents to exert power without escalating into more complicated and dangerous conflicts. As discussed in Chapter 4 (see Table 4.9), most cyber conflict is fought between regional rivals, usually within the context of some other, territorial-related dispute. Territorial issues are usually the most dispute-prone issues in the system, and cyber conflict is a new, low-level proxy realm for regional rivals to vent their frustrations with each other (Vasquez 1993). Cyber incidents are a way to burn the other side, using "botnets" instead of bullets (Valeriano and Maness 2012).

Table 5.4 also lists the separate effects of each directed dyad in the analysis. The country listed first in the table is the target of the cyber incident, and thus the dependent variable is the conflict-cooperation score for the directed dyad where the target responds to the incursion upon it in cyberspace the following week.[3] Most interesting for the findings in this controlled-group analysis are the statistically significant responses from the United States when it is the victim of a cyber incident. With the exception of China, the United States responds negatively and coercively to all of its rivals if it is the victim of cyber conflict. When the United States is the victim of cyber conflict originating from China, this evokes cooperative responses

## Table 5.4 CONFLICT-COOPERATION EFFECTS OF CYBER INCIDENTS WITH DYADIC DUMMIES

|  | Conflict Cooperation (DV) |
|---|---|
| **Cyber Incident (IV)** | 0.145 |
| **Major Power** | −0.110 |
| **Same Region** | −8.704** |
| **US-Iran (Directed Dyads)** | −10.159*** |
| **US-Syria** | −10.686*** |
| **US-China** | 3.229** |
| **US–N. Korea** | −4.703*** |
| **US-Russia** | −2.689** |
| **Iran-US** | −9.070*** |
| **Syria-US** | −6.712*** |
| **China-US** | 0.329 |
| **N. Korea–US** | −6.438*** |
| **Russia-Georgia** | 1.140 |
| **Estonia-Russia** | 2.667 |
| **Georgia-Russia** | 0.455 |
| **Iran-Israel** | −0.690 |
| **Iraq-Kuwait** | 1.959 |
| **Lebanon-Israel** | −6.082 |
| **Israel-Iran** | 0.053 |
| **Israel-Lebanon** | −15.125*** |
| **Kuwait-Iraq** | 3.115 |
| **China-Taiwan** | 4.039 |
| **China-Japan** | 3.737 |
| **China-India** | −3.341* |
| **China-Vietnam** | 4.298 |
| **China-Philippines** | 2.921 |
| **Taiwan-China** | 4.399 |
| **N. Korea–S. Korea** | 1.384 |
| **N. Korea–Japan** | 3.633 |
| **S. Korea–Japan** | 4.359 |
| **Japan-China** | 6.222* |
| **Japan–N. Korea** | 3.471 |
| **Japan–S. Korea** | 6.313* |
| **India-China** | −3.996** |
| **India-Pakistan** | 3.369 |
| **India-Bangladesh** | 1.356 |

*(Continued)*

**Table 5.4** (CONTINUED)

|  | Conflict Cooperation (DV) |
| --- | --- |
| **Pakistan-India** | 3.659 |
| **Bangladesh-India** | 3.378 |
| **Vietnam-China** | 2.483 |
| **Philippines-China** | 2.788 |

***p< 0.001, **p< 0.01, *p< 0.05
N = 13,449
Dyads Dropped: Russia-US, Russia-Estonia

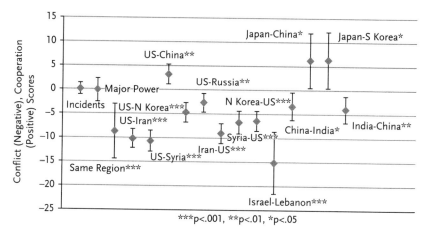

***p<.001, **p<.01, *p<.05

**Figure 5.5**
Range of Conflict-Cooperation at 95 percent Confidence Level: Directed Dyads (Incidents)

from the US foreign policy regime. This seems counterintuitive due to all of the publicly negative reports from cyber-security firms about Chinese aggression in cyberspace. We will explore this finding in detail in the next section.

Rivals of the United States also react negatively to US incursions in cyberspace. Syria, North Korea, and Iran all evoke negative and statistically significant foreign policy responses when their networks are breached. The most famous incidents in this cluster of dyads are the ones inflicted on Iran by the United States and Israel and include Flame (2009), Stuxnet (2010), Duqu (2011), and Gauss (2011). Interestingly, it seems that most of the blame for these incidents falls on the United States within Iran, as the conflict-cooperation effects of Israeli incursions do not show an impact.

The last groups of dyads that have statistically significant reactions to cyber incidents are regional. Israel-Lebanon, China-India, and India-China all produce negative foreign policy reactions to cyber incidents. One state, Japan, reacts to cyber incidents with more cooperative interactions with their regional rivals. When South Korea and China send the botnets to Japan, the Japanese governments will respond with an olive branch. It seems that Japan does not want to escalate cyber conflict with its growing East Asian competitors. Next we analyze the effects of cyber disputes, usually the lengthier and potentially more severe form of cyber conflict.

Table 5.5 and Figure 5.6 show that cyber disputes and their various types do not have statistical significance and thus do not have a clear effect on foreign policy interactions. Our random effects model shows that globally and cumulatively, cyber disputes are at a relatively low level and do not evoke the reactions expected from other forms of malicious acts propagated by rivals. If cyber disputes do not effectively burn the other side for rivals, how effective a tool is cyber conflict?

Table 5.6 and Figure 5.7 show the random effects results for the different targets that cyber disputes can potentially hit. Interestingly, only cyber disputes that target a combination of private and government non-military networks evoke a negative and statistically significant response from rival states. Disputes such as

**Table 5.5** CONFLICT-COOPERATION EFFECTS OF CYBER DISPUTES

| | Cyber Dispute | Nuisance | Defense | Offense | Nuisance-Defense | Nuisance-Offense | Defense-Offense | Nuisance-Defense-Offense |
|---|---|---|---|---|---|---|---|---|
| **Conflict-Cooperation (DV)** | −0.089 | −0.898 | Dropped | 0.371 | 1.1290 | 1.390 | Dropped | 1.991 |
| **Major Power** | 1.260 | 1.197 | 1.230 | 1.223 | 1.246 | 1.040 | 1.230 | 1.367 |
| **Same Region** | −1.762 | −1.767 | −1.777 | −1.780 | −1.801 | −1.801 | −1.777 | −1.516 |

N = 13,449
The Defense and Defense-Offense dispute types are dropped from the analysis due to lack of variance.

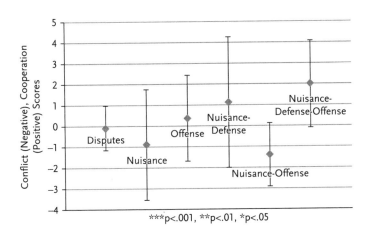

**Figure 5.6**
Range of Conflict-Cooperation at 95 percent Confidence Level: Cyber Disputes

**Table 5.6** CONFLICT-COOPERATION EFFECTS OF CYBER DISPUTES TARGETS

| | Private | Govt. Non-military | Govt. Military | Private-Govt. NM | Private-Govt. M | Govt. NM-Govt.-M | Private-Govt. NM-Govt. M |
|---|---|---|---|---|---|---|---|
| **Conflict-Cooperation (DV)** | 1.560 | 1.364 | −0.168 | −12.285*** | Dropped | −1.488 | 1.991 |
| **Major Power** | 1.200** | 1.322 | 1.221 | 0.627 | 1.230 | 1.122 | 1.367 |
| **Same Region** | −0.130 | −1.929 | −1.784 | −1.956 | −1.777 | −1.862 | −1.515 |

***p< 0.001, **p< 0.01
N = 13,449

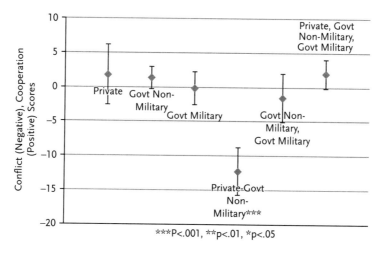

**Figure 5.7**
Range of Conflict-Cooperation at 95 percent Confidence Level: Cyber Dispute Targets

these include the 2007 Russian cyber campaign with Estonia and the propagandist exchanges between North and South Korea. Many private and government non-military targets are victims of the denial of service method, which is the method that was found to evoke negative foreign policy responses for cyber incidents. These could be the explanations behind this particular target-type of cyber dispute. Major powers whose private networks are targeted also have negative statistical significance. This is because many of these private networks have close ties to many government officials, and when these entities are hit, they demand a response from their home governments.

Table 5.7 and Figure 5.8 show that cyber disputes that involve both vandalism and DDoS methods are found to have negative statistical significance, which correlates with the finding for cyber incidents that shows negative statistical

**Table 5.7** CONFLICT-COOPERATION EFFECTS OF CYBER METHODS
FOR DISPUTES

|  | Vandalism/DDoS | Intrusion/Infiltration |
|---|---|---|
| **Conflict-Cooperation (DV)** | −2.876** | 0.369 |
| **Major Power** | −0.972 | 1.281 |
| **Same Region** | −1.797 | −1.713 |

**p< 0.01
N = 13,449

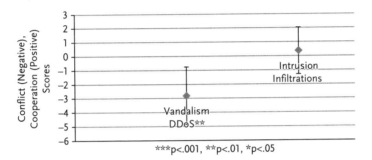

***p<.001, **p<.01, *p<.05

**Figure 5.8**
Range of Conflict-Cooperation at 95 percent Confidence Level: Cyber Methods (Disputes)

significance for DDoS methods. The widespread effects, in that these types of disputes can potentially affect a large number of people's lives, are the reasons that these disputes propagate negative responses from rivals. The psychological effects of not being able to access networks for a number of hours, days, or weeks can become frustrating and can force a government to respond to the initiating state.

Table 5.8 and Figure 5.9 show the results of our fixed effects model for cyber disputes that allows for dyadic dummies. Cyber disputes are used regionally and evoke conflictual relations after a dispute has been used. Furthermore, the same dyads found to have significance for cyber incidents are the same ones that have significance for disputes. With the exception of responses to China, the United States responds negatively to all of its rivals when it is the victim of a cyber dispute. After the Chinese infiltrated American networks for a prolonged period of time, the United States responded with more diplomatic and cooperative responses. Syria, North Korea, and Iran respond to US incursions in cyberspace with deteriorating foreign relations. For the Israeli-Lebanese, Chinese-Indian, and Indian-Chinese dyad, the target state responds to low-level disputes with escalating tensions. Finally, Japan responds to cyber disputes from its rivals with more positive diplomacy.

**Table 5.8** CONFLICT-COOPERATION EFFECTS OF CYBER
DISPUTES WITH DYADIC DUMMIES

| | Conflict Cooperation (DV) |
|---|---|
| **Cyber Dispute (IV)** | −0.373 |
| **Major Power** | −0.197 |
| **Same Region** | −8.709** |
| **US-Iran (Directed Dyads)** | −10.155*** |
| **US-Syria** | −10.690*** |
| **US-China** | 3.639*** |
| **US–N. Korea** | −4.636*** |
| **US-Russia** | −2.693** |
| **Iran-US** | −8.853*** |
| **Syria-US** | −6.717*** |
| **China-US** | 0.502 |
| **N. Korea–US** | −6.443*** |
| **Russia-Georgia** | 1.166 |
| **Estonia-Russia** | 2.689 |
| **Georgia-Russia** | 0.488 |
| **Iran-Israel** | −0.342 |
| **Iraq-Kuwait** | 1.877 |
| **Lebanon-Israel** | −6.152 |
| **Israel-Iran** | 0.175 |
| **Israel-Lebanon** | −15.177*** |
| **Kuwait-Iraq** | 3.029 |
| **China-Taiwan** | 4.039 |
| **China-Japan** | 3.737 |
| **China-India** | −3.346* |
| **China-Vietnam** | 4.298 |
| **China-Philippines** | 2.921 |
| **Taiwan-China** | 4.778 |
| **N. Korea–S. Korea** | 1.300 |
| **N. Korea–Japan** | 3.633 |
| **S. Korea-Japan** | 4.365 |
| **Japan-China** | 6.273* |
| **Japan–N. Korea** | 3.473 |
| **Japan–S. Korea** | 6.319* |
| **India-China** | −3.827** |
| **India-Pakistan** | 3.611 |
| **India-Bangladesh** | 1.269 |
| **Pakistan-India** | 3.900 |
| **Bangladesh-India** | 3.294 |
| **Vietnam-China** | 2.589 |
| **Philippines-China** | 2.792 |

***p< 0.001, **p< 0.01, *p< 0.05
N = 13,449
Dyads Dropped: Russia-US, Russia-Estonia

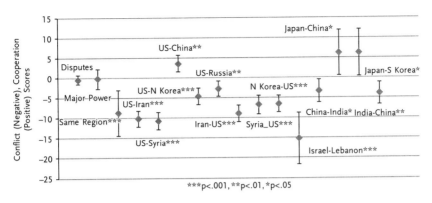

**Figure 5.9**
Range of Conflict-Cooperation at 95 percent Confidence Level: Directed Dyads (Disputes)

## ASSESSMENT

Overall, we demonstrate that most cyber incidents and disputes have no impact on general state-to-state relations at the aggregate level, and therefore our first hypothesis is falsified to this point. Only certain types of incidents, DDoS, have specific and negative repercussions in states. This is likely because DDoS events are so public and have collateral damage impacts in the daily lives of the citizens in the targeted states. Looking at intentions, we find that only incidents that intend to change the behavior in the target have dramatic and negative impacts on the conflict and cooperation levels between states.

DDoS methods in cyberspace, above all, have a psychological as well as a widespread effect on society. These methods cannot inflict the amount of lasting damage of which intrusions and infiltrations are capable; however, they are the only methods that evoke negative responses from their victims. Examples of DDoS incidents include the ones launched against Estonia and Georgia by Russia in 2007 and 2008, respectively; the 2009 Fourth of July denial of service incidents against the United States and South Korea by North Korea; and most incidents between South Korea and Japan over the 11years in our analysis. We assert that because these types of cyber tactics infiltrate the public domain, grievances toward the government for disruption of daily life are widespread, and the foreign policy apparatuses for states are forced to respond in an assertive manner. If this method is the only one to evoke a response between states, how dangerous is the current state of conflict in cyberspace? States seem to know the line, and they rarely cross it.

Incidents launched by states whose main intention is to coerce the target state to change its policy or behavior also evoke significant and negative reactions. Stuxnet, Flame, and Duqu in the Olympic Games dispute between the United States and Iran, as well as Israel and Iran, are examples of these types of disputes.

India's warning to Bangladesh to get its terrorist problem under control in March 2010 is another. These types of disputes seem to be launched when the level of relations between rivals is already sour. At the time of India's initiation, it was still reeling from the 2008 Mumbai terrorist attacks, later traced to Islamist fundamentalist groups in Pakistan. Surely the Indian government did not want the same type of carnage originating from Bangladesh. That a stern warning was given in cyberspace is an interesting foreign policy choice and signals a change in tactics by the initiating side.

Looking at regional interactions and specific dyads in the sample, disputes at the regional level tend to have a negative impact on cooperation levels. Therefore our third hypothesis fails to be falsified. These disputes generally engender negative feelings and repercussions. The interactions between many regional actors are characterized by negative levels of cooperation after the dispute. The main outlier here is China when Japan tends to respond positively to Chinese cyber disputes.

The most active region of cyber conflict is East Asia. The Chinese are the most active propagators in cyberspace, and they have initiated cyber incidents with every rival in the Far East region, including Japan, Vietnam, Taiwan, and the Philippines. All of these states are involved in territorial disputes with one another, mainly over uninhabited islands that allow for access to shipping lanes or untapped natural resources. We expect territorial disputes to be more serious, as they are the most conflict-prone types of disputes (Vasquez 1993) and the most likely type to result in war (Vasquez and Valeriano 2010).

The Japan–South Korea, Japan–North Korea, and South Korea–North Korea pairs of states have also used cyber conflict as a tool against each other in the region. Why would East Asia be a more permissive region when it comes to using cyber tools as a means of foreign policy? This region has long been carefully watched by America's military apparatus, with bases in South Korea, Japan, and the Philippines. China, the rising power in the region, wants to project its new status to its main Asian competitors and those aligned with the United States. China needs an outlet, and military grandstanding, with the possibility of escalation involving the Americans, is something that the Chinese do not want to deal with at the moment. China seems to be good at infiltrating foreign networks, and this seems to be the "least" they can do for power projection. The tactic has become contagious, which makes East Asia the busiest region for cyber conflict between states.

The countries of South Asia, which include the India-Pakistani and India-Bangladeshi rivals, are also engaged in regional cyber conflict. However, these remain at a low level, and the majority of these interactions are propagandist defacement exchanges. The India-Pakistani rivalry has been one of the most intense in the last 20 years, with crises, terrorism, and unsettled territorial disputes plaguing their relations, with much animosity directed toward each other. In a region where aggressive and coercive foreign policy is expected, the level of cyber conflict is at its lowest in both method and severity.

The region that sees bloodshed and conflict almost daily, the Middle East, is also a region where cyber conflict is utilized, albeit at a relatively low severity level. This is the region where the infamous Stuxnet was launched. Assuming that Israel's involvement in these incidents remains minimal, the only regional cyber conflicts that remain will be between rivals of the Middle East (Israel-Iran, Israel-Lebanon, Iraq-Kuwait). Even with these heated enemies, most of the incidents consist of defacements and denial of service methods. These do the least amount of actual damage in cyberspace when compared to the more destructive intrusions and infiltrations. Cyber conflict, although evoking negative foreign policy responses in the Middle East, remains at a low level in this bloody region. An important reason for this low-level of cyber conflict may be that many territorial disputes in the region have been settled (Huth 2009). Regional cyber conflict is present and significant; however, the actual damage done to states because of it remains miniscule.

The only non-regional dyads that react in a negative and statistically significant manner are those involving the global hegemon, the United States. These statistically significant findings, along with those involving China, support our second hypothesis. When major powers are involved in cyber conflict, generally negative foreign policy responses are the result. American policymakers are especially sensitive to their country being the victim of a cyber incident or dispute. In general, therefore, relations between states are not affected by cyber conflict, with the only difference being the United States. It tends to respond negatively to cyber threats and escalates the feelings of animosity in a dyad, while other states generally do not react this way.

Much attention has been given to cyber conflict in the American press recently, however, when looking at the results in Tables 5.4 and 5.8; it seems that the United States is the state that reacts the most in a conflictual manner after one of its private or government networks is infiltrated. Incidents or disputes from Iran, Syria, Russia, or North Korea on American cyberspace are met with a negative response and, at the very least, diplomatic escalation. When America returns the favor with a cyber operation on these states (except Russia, where the Americans have not initiated), these targets respond in kind with negative diplomatic action. According to Leng (2000), this tit-for-tat escalation may lead to a foreign policy crisis, which can also lead down the path to war. Leng (2000: 241) has found that there are four basic parameters of reciprocity when coercive actions are used between states: fight, resistance, standoff, and put-down. It seems that currently the United States and its cyber rivals are utilizing a standoff method of diplomatic management. Standoff occurs when there is high reciprocity in the interactions of the two states but relatively low escalation. These cyber disputes are being effectively managed; yet if the severity and scope of these disputes increase, the probability of the management of these disagreements could lead to either resistance or even fight tactics.

Another reason for caution in the United States' and its rivals' negative responses to cyber incidents and disputes can be demonstrated by the findings of Wallensteen (1984). The United States is the global hegemon, which means that states may duplicate or follow the foreign policy of the superpower. The global hegemon can set the norms and rules of international relations that allow for either a permissive or restrictive normative order (Wallensteen 1984). For example, the US invasion of Iraq in 2003 opened the door for other countries to justify their military actions in the following years. If the United States wants to mitigate cyber conflict in the future, as its foreign policy officials say they do, then the United States must choose a different course of action after it is infiltrated in cyberspace. The way they interact with China could serve as a good example and is explored in the next section.

## THE US-CHINA CYBER DYNAMIC

The only exception to a negative American foreign policy response after being compromised in cyberspace is when China is the source of cyber aggression. The United States seems to appease the Chinese with more cooperative and friendly diplomacy after being the victim, usually after the theft of information, of Chinese cyber operations. This is a good example of Leng's (2000) put-down strategy for target states, where coercive tactics are met with more accommodative strategies. A put-down strategy is when there is disagreement in which the composite scores for both escalation and reciprocity are relatively low. One side employs coercive tactics, but the other responds with a more accommodative mix of behaviors so that the disagreement does not reach a high level of escalation.

We assert that China intrudes upon the United States frequently because it is often easy to do so, as the United States has had issues with protecting its sensitive and national security networks. Here, China has both the will and the means to infiltrate the United States due to weaknesses in its defensive lines. Clarke and Knake (2010: 63) even imply that China seems to want to be caught, noting, "there seems to be a consensus that China gets more attention because, intentionally or otherwise, it has often left a trail of bread crumbs that can be followed back to Tiananmen Square." Cyber security is a clear task of the US government, but it is questionable if this extends beyond defense operations.

Inkster (2013) notes that China steals from the United States because the United States has the intellectual property to steal. The awesome spectacle that was the US military machine in Iraq in 2003 had many in China, particularly the People's Liberation Army (PLA), realizing that they needed to play catch-up in a quick yet substantial way (Inkster 2013). China has therefore employed its skill in stealing intellectual property from the United States and its defense contractors to fulfill this perceived need (Inkster 2013). Western intelligence agencies

(US National Intelligence Council, Australian Office of National Assessments, UK Joint Intelligence Committee) see the PLA as the primary actor for Chinese espionage; however, "any analysis of the role of Intelligence in China's policy community will inevitably come up against the obstacle that the workings of that community have been, and remain, opaque, and that this is particularly true when it comes to intelligence. In terms of formal structures, China has no central machinery for assessing intelligence and putting out analyses" (Inkster 2013: 54). Therefore, China is good at stealing American intellectual property, but has yet to find a productive way of assessing and utilizing the gathered intelligence to this point.

Why the cordial response to China by American diplomats after US cyberspace is infiltrated by Chinese hackers? To understand this unorthodox dynamic, we delve deeper into the US-China cyber dyad. Cyber conflict can see its roots within this dyad, as China is the first initiator of cyber conflict in our 2001–2011 dataset, and it is the most active cyber dyad in our sample, with 21 recorded cyber incidents and five disputes. Furthermore, most incidents originate from China, with 19 of the 21 incidents coming from the rising power, and only two from the status quo superpower. These two were defensive measures against ongoing Chinese infiltrations. Almost all of these Chinese incidents are either sophisticated intrusion or infiltrations, and are successful attempts to steal sensitive information, plans, or secrets either from the US government or private American entities pertinent to national security.

Examples of these Chinese theft incidents in American cyberspace include Shady Rat, Ghost Net, the Pentagon Raid, the Byzantine Series, and the F-35 jet plan theft from aircraft maker Lockheed Martin. No other state has stolen from American networks with such sophistication, reach, and frequency. Shady Rat was a multistate intrusion that stole sensitive information and secrets from many governments, and lasted for about three and one half years. It began in August 2006 and ended in the beginning days of 2010. Seventy-one parties across the globe were intruded upon, with 49 of these being networks based in the United States (India, Taiwan, Canada, Germany, the UK, Denmark, Switzerland, Japan, and the United Nations are among the other victims) in both government and the private sector.[4] This incident was a massive theft operation that stole intellectual property, government secrets, and information not intended to be released to the public. Yet, the US government reacted to this massive and long-term theft with diplomacy and indifference to the Chinese government.

Ghost Net lasted from around May 2007 until late August 2009 and infiltrated 103 governments, with the United States again being the most targeted state. This intrusion accessed networks from e-mail phishing attempts and, once inside, could turn on web cameras and microphones, recording the conversations of high-level government officials.[5] Conversations among State Department, Defense Department, and even White House officials could have been compromised, exposing high-level state secrets and policies to the government in Beijing. The US government responded to the Chinese with kind words and attempts to bridge the gap in relations.

The March 2011 Pentagon Raid was a very public and very troubling keystroke logging infiltration traced back to China, which stole over 24,000 sensitive files during the week-long incident. Deputy Defense Secretary William J. Lynn III noted that "[a] great deal of it concerns our most sensitive systems, including aircraft avionics, surveillance technologies, satellite communications systems and network security protocols."[6] This time, the American military network was deliberately and overtly breached and the massive theft operation successfully stole from the world's most sophisticated military command center. This infiltration evoked outrage from American pundits and press outlets, yet not from the US foreign policy regime. A cumulative positive Goldstein score of 31.60 is recorded for the week following the Pentagon Raid cyber incident, which was also public knowledge at the time.

The Byzantine Series was a far-reaching incident on the private sector that compromised nearly 760 companies worldwide; it lasted from October 2008 until June 2011, when it was finally sufficiently blocked. The majority of these companies were American, many that are pertinent to US national security interests.[7] The iBahn corporation is an Internet service provider that provides broadband services to the Marriott Hotel chain and others, and allowed the Byzantine hackers to access confidential e-mails from millions of executives with the compromised ISP.[8] This also enabled the hackers to move from e-mails to the actual networks of the corporations, further expanding the scope and breadth of the cyber incident from China. Yet once again, the response to this blatant violation of cyberspace was met positively by American policymakers. In late June 2011, when the incident had ceased, positive cumulative Goldstein scores of 10.60 and 16.60 are observed.

The most severe cyber incident between the United States and China, which is also in our top five list of most severe cyber incidents in our 2001–2011 sample presented in the previous chapter (Table 4.7), is the theft of the F-35 jet plans from Lockheed-Martin in March–April 2009. Considered an advanced persistent threat (APT), this incident's primary motive was to find and steal the plans to one of the best American fighter jets made by the military contractor.[9] APTs are the most sophisticated of all cyber methods and are able to either intrude or infiltrate surgically and methodically, signaling that Lockheed-Martin's F-35 plans and schematics were the intended targets. Such a precise and intentional theft of US national security secrets would surely have sparked outrage from the Obama administration or the State Department. However, a cumulative positive weekly Goldstein score of 38 is recorded for the week following the theft. This finding returns us to the question asked at the beginning of this section: Why the cordial responses from the American foreign policy regime after an intrusion or infiltration in cyberspace?

There are many reasons that US foreign policymakers have decided to respond to Chinese cyber incidents and disputes in a diplomatic and positive manner. The American trade deficit, balance of payment deficit, and huge Chinese holdings of American debt could all be reasons that the United States may have reservations about escalating relations with China over these theft operations in cyberspace. Yet, this explanation fails in that the Chinese are just as dependent on the United States as the United States is on China. The popular perception that China is catching up to the United States economically and militarily—and thus the United States does not want to upset the future hegemon—could be another reason that the United States responds diplomatically. However, this explanation fails in the face of evidence that the Chinese are not approaching equality with the United States (Beckley 2012). What is unique about the US-China cyber dyad? How can this uniqueness be interpreted?

The first aspect of the US-China cyber dyad that is unique is that it contains the world's two most powerful countries. Major powers have a lot at stake in the international system, and relations between them must be handled delicately and sometimes in a way counterintuitive to public perceptions. Another major power dyad, the Japanese-Chinese pair of states, has similar dynamics to the US-China dyad. Japan reacts to Chinese cyber incidents and disputes with positive and diplomatic foreign policy responses; therefore there may be something unique to major power cyber conflict that is not apparent in major-minor or minor-minor dyads. However, the only other major power dyad in our sample is the US-Russia dyad, where we find no significance in foreign policy responses to cyber conflict. Therefore, although major power pairs of states are the only ones to evoke diplomatic rather than coercive or escalatory responses, it is too early to make any concrete inferences as to the dynamics of cyber conflict among the world's elites.

Another aspect making the US-China cyber dyad unique is that most of the incidents and disputes are theft operations. There are only a few incidents that were intended to be disruptions; by and large, China's intent in American cyberspace is to steal information and secrets. There is not another dyad in our sample that contains such an extensive and sophisticated string of cyber incidents intent on stealing from America's book of secrets. Covered in Chapter 3, what the Chinese are doing is a very old tactic on a new playing field that is cyberspace: spying. Our theory of cyber espionage states that perceived power imbalances may lead the less powerful states to use spying techniques to bridge this perceived gap. Because cyber espionage is less risky and less costly than attempting to match the conventional US military machine, China uses this tactic to show the Americans that it is a force to be reckoned with in cyberspace. This indirect confrontation with American power seems to be working, as is evident in America's positive responses to Chinese cyber espionage.

A final unique aspect of the US-China cyber dyad is that the United States may be deliberately restraining itself from reacting with coercion to China, as escalation with China could open the Pandora's box of cyber conflict or could be the next 9/11 moment that former Defense Secretary Leon Panetta has warned about. Evidence for this assertion can also be flushed out from our data. The US-China cyber dyad is lopsided, with China responsible for 19 cyber incidents and the United States being the culprit in two. The two incidents that the United States has launched against China, Cisco Raider and Buckshot Yankee, were defensive measures to protect American networks from ongoing Chinese cyber intrusions and infiltrations. There is evidence of great restraint from the United States, as it has not employed a tit-for-tat strategy with China in cyberspace that could lead to a foreign policy crisis and escalation. The negative reactions to other states by the US foreign policy regime happen because they can be controlled, they consist of DDoS incidents which evoke negative reactions from most dyads, and they are in the long run less harmful and damaging. Chinese theft operations are deliberate and could escalate tensions with the rising power if handled the wrong way.

An added consideration is that the United States needs China to push North Korea and other powers to behave in the international system. So while cyber intrusions may be costly, the United States may be willing to pay the price of not escalating tensions in exchange for considerations in other issue areas. Often the United States is pushed to assert human rights concerns against China, but, as in cyberspace, it fails to do so because of the complex considerations in play in this dyad.

In the end, what could the United States do to respond to Chinese provocations? The United States is straitjacketed in terms of its responses due to the complicated nature of international politics, but also in relation to the specific nature of cyber conflicts. It cannot display like-mannered cyber tactics because that would degrade its own capabilities by showing its hand. Furthermore, if the United States responded to China in kind with similar cyber tactics, it would be in the interests of China to expose these incidents to reciprocate some of the blowback it has been receiving from the international community for its espionage campaigns as of late. The United States cannot escalate the situation further because there are more pressing interests that it must protect. There are limited options for states to pursue in this realm, which might be a surprising finding given that cyber conflict is such a new and fresh domain. But new domains cannot simply move beyond the constraints and nuances of past international interactions. There is a manner and style at which countries must respond to such threats, even if they are new. The relationship between China and the United States in cyberspace demonstrates the limitations and also the possibilities of cyber conflict.

A summit between China and the United States in June 2013 was uneventful in terms of resolving debates about cyber activity. The press built up the issue before the event, but the states managed no grand agreement during the meetings and politely sidestepped the issue, focusing on positive diplomacy rather than threats.[10] In short, the United States has chosen restraint and diplomacy with China as to not further tensions in cyberspace. The next step is inviting China into a multilateral and international forum for cyber restraint and cyber norms in the anarchic fifth domain in cyberspace. More on this topic is covered in Chapter 7.

The three most powerful cyber states, the United States, Russia, and China, have been in talks regarding norms in cyberspace (Maness and Valeriano 2014). This is where the more cooperative scores between the United States and China are most likely being generated. However, since 2011, relations between the United States and Russia are now at an all-time low, and domestic actions by the US Congress and Department of Justice have led to the indictment of five People's Liberation Army (PLA) members with charges of espionage and theft.[11] The progress made on the development of cyber norms as well as the cordial responses from the United States when the victim of Chinese cyber malice, therefore, may be a thing of the past.

## CONCLUSION

Following the work of Chapter 4, we have found that cyber conflict is pretty much the least a state can do to challenge a rival. By and large, most cyber incidents are allowed to occur with few repercussions. In fact, cyber exchanges between great powers like the United States and China actually result in positive relations rather than further degenerative interactions. The reason for this is likely because cyber incidents fall below the normal range of operations. They generally are silent and focused incidents meant to not upset the delicate balance of relations, even between competing rival states. When China initiates cyber incidents against the United States, the United States responds diplomatically without further cyber operations. The future could be different, but for now, powers have learned to manage relationships, even during constant and harmful cyber operations. We believe that the United States is restraining itself from reacting in a negative manner with China so as not to escalate cyber conflict to the doomsday levels that many pundits and academics say is inevitable. We also believe that the United States is trying to work with China to be part of a leadership forum of states to mitigate cyber escalation and establish cyber rules and norms.

The trend that defies these patterns is DDoS methods. This is likely because DDoS are the most public of cyber methods and hold such psychological weight that governments are forced to respond when infiltrated in cyberspace. While being low on the severity scale, they are like fireworks that go off in the night. In a digitally connected society, everyone sees them, and the state may then be forced to react. The good thing is that these reactions fall short of the level of war and outright conventional violence. If these methods are not managed in the future, they could lead to further devastating countermeasures.

For now, states seem to be happy to respond with protests and then turn the other cheek.

Incidents that also evoke negative foreign policy responses are ones that attempt to change state behavior. These include the Stuxnet and Flame incidents that are part of the Olympic Games dispute between the US-Israel and Iran. Like all forms of diplomatic coercion, states do not like being told what to do by others, especially when the coercion is a matter of national security to the target state. Iran's motives to achieve weapons-grade uranium enrichment are, in its eyes, to protect itself. Any state trying to alter this goal will be met with escalatory and coercive tit-for-tat behavior. According to Leng (2000), this is the diplomatic behavior that can escalate into military action. Part of the rulebook for cyber rules and norms, therefore, would be to abolish these types of coercive cyber incidents and disputes. Thus far, these types of cyber operations have been limited, but allowing them to become part of a state's foreign policy arsenal could lead to escalation and actual cyberwar, where casualties become a real possibility.

The 2007 cyber dispute between Russia and Estonia brought the issue of cyberwar to the forefront of international relations discussions in governments, media, and academia. However, the dispute that started it all did not evoke any significant response from the target state, Estonia, to the initiator, Russia. What it did accomplish is to begin the talks on what to do about the possible escalation of cyber conflict for the future. We intended to flush out how cyber conflict is used, handled, and reacted to by governments. Some interesting and very diverging findings have been found between different states. Not all cyber conflict is created equal, but now we can move forward with a case study of some of the most public and feared cyber incidents thus far. This is the topic of the next chapter.

# CHAPTER 6

# Stuxnet, Shamoon, and Bronze Soldier

*The Impact and Responses to Cyber Operations*

## INTRODUCTION

Throughout this volume we have made the case that cyber conflicts thus far are over-hyped and that states practice a large degree of restraint in using them. We find that the rate of conflict is not indicative of a revolution in military affairs, but rather is a continuation of espionage and nuisances otherwise common in international affairs. The next question is, if we take a closer look at the process, content, and meaning of what might be known as the prominent cyber conflicts, then what more do we learn? Do our quantitative conclusions hold up in the context of what might be called the outliers, or the black swans of the cyber security discourse? We need to support our data investigations with the story of cyber conflicts in order to reinforce the points asserted in previous chapters.

Here we demonstrate that even the most popular and well-known cyber incidents are not changing the shape of the battlefield; they are a new technology, like any other that we have seen in the past. Throughout history, militaries and governments have adapted to and utilized new technologies in the battlefield as well as for diplomacy, but rarely have they changed the shape of international affairs. It seems that cyber conflict falls into this category in that the technology alone by no means changes the shape of relationships. We go even further with our weekly events-based data investigation to suggest that, by and large, the response to cyber incidents, when they do happen, does not indicate that governments are disturbed or severely troubled by the incidents (see Chapter 5). Some tactics provoke reactions, but mainly cyber actions have been assimilated as a normal process of international life, a claim widely divergent from the tone of the general cyber security debate.

To make these sweeping claims, we have relied on data and statistics to paint a macro picture of cyber relationships. While this step is critically important and has been missing in the field, we still need to bolster our arguments with in-depth examinations of cyber actions that have happened in the past. In this chapter we focus on critical cyber actions that have in some ways altered the shape of the cyber discourse and, in some cases, are responsible for the cyber hype pundits whose declarations the media seem to buy into so readily. These events have shaped the discourse, but here we seek to understand the nature of the cyber actions, long after they have happened, in order to paint a complete picture of how cyber tactics are used.

## CYBER MYTH BREAKING

In many ways, this chapter is about myth breaking rather than myth making. Few truly understand the cyber conflicts that have occurred in the past. Even more critical, many seem to have rushed to make judgments before the full facts were presented, creating a picture of cyber conflict that does not correspond with reality. Rid notes that cyber sabotage has never happened to a US system, at least since 2000.[1] The question, then, is why do we have this result? Despite all the hype, proliferation of capabilities, and ubiquity of insecure cyber systems, we have seen restraint operating in the international system. As we argue, this system of restraint developed due to fears of retaliation, norms, the unique nature of cyber tactics, and the real possibly of censure and punishment by international institutions.

We argue that most cyber actions are tied to a clear international context of relationships, characterized by rivalry and regionalism. Despite evidence to the contrary, it seems persuasive for some that cyber conflict is a new reality and that this reality will have a significant impact on the style and context of conflicts in the future. The US Intelligence Assessment of 2013 goes so far as to note, "the growing use of cyber capabilities to achieve strategic goals is also outpacing the development of a shared understanding of norms of behavior, increasing the chances for miscalculations and misunderstandings that could lead to unintended escalation."[2] The US intelligence community ranks the cyber threat higher than the threat from terrorism, or from rogue nuclear powers.

This idea—of damaging cyber incidents and disputes changing the shape of international interactions—is problematic at the surface, but what if we critically analyze the actions, consequences, and accounts after the operations happened? It is important that we take a step back and examine the evidence after it is in, not during the course of the conflicts. It would therefore be useful to engage with the cyber operations that have happened, how they came about, and what they can tell us about cyber tactics and the applicability of our theory. Our aim is to return the dialogue to a considered and measured application of cyber action in the modern international system, devoid of worst-case scenarios and hyperbole.

## MAJOR CYBER INCIDENTS AND THE IMPACT
## OF THE CYBER DEBATE

In this chapter we focus on what many consider the major cyber incidents from the years 2000 to 2013. These are the incidents that have shaped the debate on cyber conflict; they have dictated perceptions about the domain of conflict in modern memory. We do not use general social science sampling methods here, since the goal is to support our large-N statistical work and to not make inferences. The purpose here is to explain the process of cyber conflict in relation to our theories and data. In that way, we seek to use the structured and focused case study method advocated by George and Bennett (2005), which could support our general theory and ideas. This investigation is focused on a series of cyber conflicts and structured around a set of common questions. The questions asked for all cases are the following:

1. How did the cyber incident come about?
2. What was the foreign policy and international relations context of the action?
3. What was the impact of the incident on the target?
4. What was the reaction to the incident by the target?

For our cases, we have selected two of the most popular and well-known cyber incidents in the public discourse: the Bronze Soldier in Estonia and Stuxnet in Iran. We also include one of the least understood cyber incidents to have occurred to this date: Shamoon in Saudi Arabia. These were reported early, but the media did not update the public about the course of events after they happened, and mainly failed to discuss their consequences after the initial hype. Here, we seek to provide a comprehensive account of the context of these cyber actions, the consequences of the use of these tactics, and a focus on the reaction to the incident in the target. These are all neglected topics, and we provide essential evaluations of these conflicts after they occurred, given that enough time has passed to properly analyze the events. Some (Farwell and Rohozinski 2011; Lindsay 2013; Bronk and Tikk-Ringas 2013) have covered and examined these cases in isolation, but our analysis differs in that it focuses on connections to our large-N investigations that seek to cover many different incidents under one theoretical umbrella. Here we have collected comprehensive accounts of the incidents after they have occurred, using first- and secondhand accounts of the events, and avoiding, for the most part, a reliance on reactionary news accounts that appeared shortly after the events.

We first focus on the Estonian Bronze Solider incident, presented by some as the first true "cyber war."[3] This incident was a concentrated action by Russian elements seeking to punish Estonia for its actions against a Russian nationalist symbol. Here the context is important, and is often avoided in discussion. We also find that the nature of the incident was often overstated. Now that time has passed, we are able to place the action in its proper context.

Next we move to the possibly most famous and often overstated cyber incident in modern memory, Stuxnet. In this case, the United States and Israel sought to infiltrate Iran's nuclear capabilities in order to prevent the state from advancing its nuclear agenda and to forestall the need for a conventional attack, a strategy pushed by some of the more hard-line elements within these polities. Once again, the context of the action is important in understanding why it happened in the first place. We also seek to disentangle myth from reality with regard to this incident. Evidence suggests that it was not the devastating new method of warfare that many make cyber actions out to be. Stuxnet was in reality a successful incident because of the fear it instilled in other powerful states, rather than in the actual damage it caused to Iran. This is an important effect, but it needs to be placed in its proper context when the issue is discussed, since some would seek to blow the implications of the event out of proportion and overstate the destructive impact of technology.[4]

We then move to Shamoon since the incident includes what the possible response from Iran to Stuxnet might have been. This action is also important because the hype with which the event was greeted in the cyber community needs to be judged in relation to the damage done. Shamoon was seen as another example of a new way of warfare, both conventional and economic. Yet we see that the impact was not as dramatic as was initially thought. Taking a step back and investigating these events in their proper context gives us the ability to not rush to snap judgments about operations such as this and to consider their impact properly.

Methodologically and theoretically, we follow our prior chapters and build on our theory of cyber interactions. The hypotheses that are particularly relevant to this chapter are H2, H3, H5, and H6 (all explained and elaborated in Chapter 3). The other hypotheses in our study are not directly related to this chapter, but some can be applied to particular aspects of this investigation. Here we focus on these four hypotheses due to the nature of the predictions they raise and their direct applicability to the cases examined here.

*H2: When cyber operations and incidents do occur, they will be of minimal impact and severity due to restraint dynamics.*

H2 is relevant in that it directly engages the main task of this chapter: to examine the impact and severity of the cyber tactics. While we can get at this question through macro-level data, a more fine-tuned approach is helpful in investigating the severity, as well as the impact, of cyber tactics. Delineating the mode of the incident, the progress of the incident, and its specific impact can only really occur through a case study framework.

*H3: Cyber operations and incidents that do occur will likely be limited to regional interactions due to a connection to territorial conflicts.*

Through H3 we can investigate the regional context of these cyber events. While we are clear that most cyber actions have a regional domain, we cannot be very explicit about this process without case investigations. Most cyber conflicts are not global, but instead reflect regional concerns. This is the process that plays out in the initiation of Stuxnet, Shamoon, and the Bronze Soldier since the consequences and motivations for action can generally be delineated through the case study framework.

*H5: Due to power imbalances, less powerful rival states will use cyber espionage and cyber terrorism as tactics to perceptively bridge the power gap with the more powerful state.*

Empirically, we never really investigate if power imbalances are common to the dyadic context of the initiation of cyber conflicts, as we set out to do with H5 since this would require a reconstruction of the dyadic power data, plus the construction of cyber power indicators. Here we can be clear about the disparities in power between the initiating side and the target, if there are any. We can also locate this process as potentially critical in the decision to choose cyber tactics for two of our cases: the more powerful Russia versus the weaker Estonia (Bronze Soldier) and the more powerful United States versus Iran (Stuxnet). The implication here is that power disparities can motivate action but typically in a manner opposite to that predicted (small versus big); it is unclear if cyber actions actually equalize the playing field and achieve the desired ends.

*H6: Cyber incidents and disputes will lead to negative foreign policy responses at the state-to-state level.*

Finally, we can examine H6 in much more depth here. We ask if cyber conflict raises the level of conflictual foreign reactions when and after cyber incidents occur. We cover this question through our macro events investigation in Chapter 5, but here we can be clear and use leadership and public statements to measure the reaction to these events and how they have played out through time.

It should be stated from the onset that we cannot directly test any hypothesis through the case study methods that are employed here. We can only speak to the hypotheses as they apply to the cases under investigation here. Since these incidents are selected by the researcher, the findings may not be generalizable, a limitation for all case studies. Even with this caveat, we do believe that the findings in this chapter are typical for cyber actions, and we would likely find the same results for every "major" cyber action of the last 10 years. In many ways, the purpose of this chapter is to both educate and explain the impact of cyber actions that have taken place in recent years.

## ESTONIA AND THE BRONZE SOLDIER: THE DAWN OF THE CONTEMPORARY CYBER AGE

For many, the Bronze Soldier series of cyber incidents was the first of its kind, the first true *cyber war*. We would argue that this framing goes a bit far and is an incorrect use of the term *war*. However, it is true that this was a significant cyber incident and deserves coverage if we are to evaluate the true impact of cyber conflict. The main reason that this incident is so important is because of the scale of the operation—it seems that the events reign superior in people's memories and have taken on a life of their own in the cyber discourse. For this reason, some regard this as the first true cyber conflict between two states.

Nevertheless, there is a push against this idea throughout the literature. Hansen and Nissenbaum (2009: 1170) note that the discussion relating to Estonia does not meet reality; this was not a war in cyberspace but more likely an exercise in harassment. Unfortunately, their prediction that this event would fade from memory did not come to pass, and the event is still spoken of as a devastating incident. The Estonia event goes a long way toward describing what many feel is the worst of cyber conflict because of the operation's scale and impact on civilians. As we will discuss, in some ways the scale of the operation was a result of Estonian overreaction rather than deliberate intent by the Russians.

From our perspective, this conflict represents the banality and the trivial nature of cyber conflict as it is inflated in popular perceptions. The conflict is more about what could have occurred rather than what actually happened, given that the Estonian preemptive termination of Internet links was a protective measure. In the end, Russia was shamed for its action and Estonia is now known as a center for cyber security research and a key hub in NATO. However, first we must understand what actually happened and why this event has become so prominent.

### How Did the Cyber Incident Come About?

By April 2007, Estonia had joined NATO. Three years prior, it had joined the European Union. These events signaled to Russia that Estonia had left its political orbit permanently by becoming a full-fledged member of the institutions and structures of the West.

The Estonian government therefore began a process of removing Soviet-era idolatry, where remnants and symbols of its Soviet past were to be eradicated. Part of this process was the removal of a Soviet-era grave marker in the capital city's main square, known as the "Bronze Soldier of Tallinn." This monument was a memorial of the Soviet Union's triumph over Nazism during World War II, representing a very proud and nationalistic moment for ethnic Russians still living in Estonia. This statue's removal, and its placement in a more remote location (itself a compromise initiated by the president to prevent its destruction), caused widespread outrage in Russia. Seventy-one percent of Russians said that they were outraged by the Estonian move, with only seven percent being indifferent, and only one percent supporting the move.[5] Most Estonians did not share this sense of pride and nationalism, as they saw the Soviet expulsion of the Germans in 1944 as a trade of one despotic overlord for another. For Estonians, 51 percent of the population saw the move of the monument as the right move, 23 percent of those polled saw it as the wrong move, and 27 percent said that they did not care one way or another.[6]

The response from Russia surprised many, as it initiated a very large, sophisticated, and widespread cyber dispute on April 27, 2007. DDoS methods and vandalism slammed the websites of the Estonian government and private sector. These incidents lasted for about two weeks, until around May 10. During this time, bank websites were unusable, cash machines were inaccessible, and credit cards were not accepted at many retail outlets. Furthermore, the Estonian government could not function at its full potential during this flurry of Russo-originating cyber incidents. Most government services, such as employment applications and library book renewals, are conducted online in Estonia, one of the most online plugged-in countries in the world (Clarke and Knake 2010). Estonian citizens could also not post on Facebook or respond to their e-mail.[7] Some refer to this incident as the "Bronze Solider Attack" because the action was motivated by Estonia's relocation of the Russian statue. It was the most sophisticated cyber operation to have occurred at the time.[8] International condemnation was widespread, especially from the West.[9] For us, the key questions are the following: What was the context? What was the reaction? And what were the consequences?

## What Was the Foreign Policy and International Relations Context of the Action?

The main purpose of the 2007 incident was to punish Estonia for its perceived disrespect of Russian history, culture, and identity in the removal of an important Soviet-era symbol. The clear context in this situation was an ongoing situation of historical animosity between the two sides, going back centuries. Although not considered enduring rivals in the Diehl and Goertz (2000) typology because there have been few direct militarized disputes, there is a clear situation of mutual animosity.

The Bronze Soldier dispute began when Estonia did what many states of the former Soviet Union had been doing since 1991, which is shedding their Soviet past. This need to move forward for Estonia was especially acute. It and two other Baltic States, Latvia and Lithuania, were annexed into the Soviet Union when the Red Army expelled the Nazis from the three states on their march to Berlin during World War II. These Baltic peoples did not see Soviet annexation as liberation, but rather as trading one oppressive regime for another. The bronze statue marked where Soviet soldier's remains were laid to rest and was therefore a symbol of Soviet occupation and repression to most Estonians. There was popular support for moving this grave marker to a more remote location. In March 2007 a popular mandate was added to the election ballot, and the people decided that the monument should be moved.

Estonia has a sizable 7 percent minority of ethnic Russians left over from Soviet times, and these people saw the Bronze Soldier move as disrespectful—almost sacrilegious. Their protests in Tallinn eventually erupted into riots in late April 2007. These riots lasted about two days and ended in the death of one ethnic Russian (Semjonov 2007). The Estonian government then decided to remove the statue, stone monument, and remains immediately, placing them in the Cemetery of the Estonian Defense Forces outside Tallinn. With this move, the series of cyber incidents originating from Russia began.

Some argue that when a state offends Russia's national identity as a great power, it can expect coercive retaliation from Moscow (Feklyunina 2008). We (2014) have demonstrated elsewhere that Russia is not hesitant to use power politics tactics in post-Soviet space. The fact that Russia reacted—perhaps overreacted—in a power politics fashion to this Estonian action is therefore not surprising. What is surprising is that Russia chose cyber action as the retaliation medium. Russia has used diplomatic bullying, energy supply coercion, and even military mobilization against the states of the former Soviet Union; but its use of power politics in cyberspace was not only a first for Russia, it introduced the world to the possible dangers of escalated cyber conflict (Maness and Valeriano 2014).

Paradoxically, we see evidence of restraint from Russia. Going back to Chapter 2, we noted that Russia is the most cyber-capable state in the international system. Perceiving the removal of the Tallinn memorial as a slight to the honor of the Russian state and people, Russia was heavily offended by the act. Russia could have implemented more severe cyber tactics, such as knocking out Estonia's power grid or launching a virus that would shut down hospital generators and put the lives of many in danger. However, the fact that it only used low-level vandalism and DDoS methods suggests that Russia limited its response. Although the lives of many Estonians were inconvenienced, life went back to normal after the cyber dispute had ceased. In fact, many of the worst impacts of the disputes were self-imposed by Estonia, in order to protect the state from further incursions.

## What Was the Impact of the Incident on the Target?

The Bronze Soldier cyber dispute shut down various Estonian government and private sector networks for about two weeks. No single network was inoperable for the entire two weeks, but the barrage of vandalism and DDoS methods were active for that duration. Estonia, considered to be one of the most Internet-dependent countries in the world, felt the effects of the Russian retaliation more than most countries would have, given the same situation. The result was a monetary loss of about $750 million in business and government revenues, but the country slowly recovered as the incidents were blocked and contained (Maness and Valeriano 2014). Government could not conduct normal business on the Internet, as many citizens could not access government services such as license renewal or voter registration. Commerce suffered, as credit card machines would not work; in addition, many ATMs were down, so many Estonian citizens could not access their money to buy goods and services.

Overall, we question the popular discourse surrounding this action. It is not at all clear that the incident had much of an impact beyond self-inflicted wounds by the Estonians. They choose to cut off Internet access in response to the actions. This step was a key part of the process.

Also, the dispute might not have been a surprise, as Healey (2013: 70) recounts that the real surprise was that NATO officials did not react seriously to the warnings. Bill Woodcock recounts from his time in Estonia during the dispute, "as the sensors were brought back online, the traffic graphs recalibrated, making the previous days traffic look like a fault line along the bottom of the graph, compared to the vertical spike of the attack. . . . Although this was a very large attack relative to Estonia, it was not a very large attack relative to the Internet as a whole" (Healey 2013: 79–80). It is noted that the size and scale of the DDoS incidents were not that massive; with the Healey (2013: 70) volume noting that larger DDoS incidents (not directed by countries) are often at a scale ten times larger than this incident. The question is what is the impact of all these actions?

As Rid (2013: 6–7) notes, "the only long-term consequence of the incident was that the Estonian government succeeded in getting NATO to establish a permanent agency in Tallinn, the Cooperative Cyber Defense Centre of Excellence." While this is incorrect in that the defense center was already established prior to the dispute, Estonia used the Russian incursion as a reason to make the center much more important and critical to NATO. Estonian President Toomas Ives did make the event a "cause célèbre" (Healey 2013: 71).

There is also the issue of third-party considerations. Here NATO is involved, invoking the real possibility that Estonia could have enacted the collective self-defense clause in Article 5 and dragged other NATO states into the conflict, causing a real spillover into the conventional foreign policy space.

Fielder (2013) notes that when targets receive third-party assistance, chances of an incident succeeding decrease. So while the fear was that escalation would drag in all the NATO parties, the reality is a bit more mixed in that the collective security cooperation of NATO as an institution could help protect Estonia and prevent the conflict from escalating in the cyber realm. Perhaps fears of contagion are purely theoretical given that support in shoring up defenses is likely the first step before escalation. Indeed, in hindsight, perhaps Estonia overreacted in response to these incidents by Russia, but with no precedent as to how to react, it is not surprising; this form of malicious activity had never been so public or so widespread.

### What Was the Target's Reaction to the Incident?

The psychological impact of the incident on Estonia was noticeable, and it made Estonians feel vulnerable. Sixty-five percent of all Estonians deem cyber incidents to be the greatest threat to their country, with 60 percent noting that marine pollution is the next greatest threat, while 55 percent see foreign intervention as a threat to Estonian sovereignty.[10] Yet these are only feelings and perceptions; the reality was much different. The dispute did little to cripple Estonia in any real sense. Nothing was lost or damaged beyond time and a sense of security. In some ways, this incident demonstrates the nature of cyber conflict and why it leads to a perception of weakness rather than any demonstration thereof. Estonia was still protected by NATO. There was really no danger of a conventional conflict with Russia. Terminating all Internet connections might have been an extreme reaction to the situation, but certainly the Estonians cannot be faulted for taking the necessary precautions to avoid further damage.

The real impact of the action would be felt much later in the future, demonstrating why proper distance between an incident and an evaluation of its impact is important. Seven years on, Estonia is now recognized the world over as the leader in cyber security and a proponent of cyber norms of behavior. Tallinn is the host city, now five years in a row at the time of this writing, of the International Conference of Cyber Conflict.[11] These conferences and discussions have prompted the adoption of rules for states in cyberspace and have resulted in the *Tallinn Manual*. This manual and Estonia's part in this cyber forum are discussed in more detail in Chapter 8.

It is important to note that Estonia, with the backing of its NATO allies, could have pushed for retaliatory responses and engaged Russia in a tit-for-tat escalatory cyber dispute that might have turned into a more physical confrontation between Russia and the West, much like Berlin in 1961 or Cuba in 1962. However, instead of using power politics in kind against Russia, Estonia took the high road and used the cyber defense center in Tallinn to call for a world forum to discuss how it was victimized by Russia in cyberspace.

Russia, on the other hand, was shamed. They were recognized as the rule-breaker in this occasion. The US House of Representatives even passed a resolution condemning the protests by ethnic Russians in Estonia as well as Russia's malicious use of cyber tactics against a victimized state that respects the rule of law.[12] This shame did not have a clear immediate impact, and Russia would use cyber capabilities one more time in 2008 to effect. The lack of action against Ukraine in 2014 might be taken as a sign that Russia was eventually forced into a policy of restraint.

There is some debate over how much control Russia had over its hackers and thus how culpable the state was in this action. Given that Russia infiltrated the United States in 1998 under what is called the Moonlight Maze incident (see Healey 2013: 152–163), it is not so surprising that Russia would engage in such an action after Estonia wounded Russia's honor. It is likely that Russia at least had enough power to stop the intrusions and was aware of the actions. It is more likely that the actions were directed by the state. There is little doubt that this is the case because the incidents needed the organization of many highly skilled operatives, working in coordination and with a clear motive. Russian cyberspace and its traffic are heavily monitored by the FSB, the secret police that is the successor to its more famous Soviet-era KGB. Therefore, these highly sophisticated methods used against Estonia surely got the attention of the FSB monitors, even if they did not originate from the secret organization (Gvodsev 2012). *The Guardian* at the time reported, "the attacks have been pouring in from all over the world, but Estonian officials and computer security experts say that, particularly in the early phase, some attackers were identified by their internet addresses—many of which were Russian, and some of which were from Russian state institutions. . . . Estonian officials say that one of the masterminds of the cyber-campaign, identified from his online name, is connected to the Russian security service."[13] Healey (2013: 67) notes that Russia has a history of encouraging and coordinating its patriotic hackers, especially evidenced in this case.

That the targets were hit with surgical precision indicates state involvement. The main targets of the two-week-long barrage included the Estonian presidency and parliament, nearly all of Estonia's government ministries, its political parties' websites, the main Estonian news organizations, as well as the big banks and telecommunications companies.[14] The incidents began almost in unison and ended at about the same time. To say that this was the work of amateur Russian nationalist hackers overestimates their capacity to act in coordination. The scope, precision, and organization of the Bronze Soldier dispute support the contention that this operation could only have been accomplished with government resources.

Due to the clear evidence that the dispute was directed by Russia, Estonia reacted strongly by pulling the plug, so to speak. Some might argue that they did this too strongly, but faced with the military and cyber power of Russia as a direct threat on this occasion, such actions can be seen as prudent. What is imprudent is to extend the reaction by Estonia and its self-inflicted wounds to make statements about the impact of cyber actions. The impact here was widespread because of the Estonian response, not because the dispute was so effective at first. The fear that the incidents would continue and escalate, an unknown at the time, makes Estonia's reaction at the time not that surprising.

### Lessons

The surprises here include the muted nature of the dispute by such a vast cyber power and the fact that the Estonian side caused self-inflicted wounds. While comprehensive, the Russian initiation was simply a widespread nuisance. There was no destruction, death, or widespread blackouts. That Russia has this capability is clear, but they did not use it. Their actions were restrained in this case.

Estonia's actions were not so restrained, but given the context, this is not perplexing. Faced with such an angry power while witnessing a massive and widespread cyber action, Estonia chose to cut its Internet access and thus multiplied the effect of the dispute. The lesson here should be that many cyber wounds are self-inflicted. Either security was too lax in the first place, or the overreaction to the incident created a spiraling effect that cascaded throughout the system.

The other lesson that can be drawn is the connection between cyber actions and conventional international rivalry dynamics. Although Russian use of cyber tactics has been limited, especially since it is considered the most cyber-capable state in the world (Maness and Valeriano 2014), it has still used the tactic when a perceived threat has been present, particularly in post-Soviet space. Russia also used cyber tactics against Georgia in 2008 during a five-day armed conflict with that state. This has been the first and to this point only use of cyber tactics in tandem with a conventional military campaign. Although these series of cyber incidents were similar to the ones used against Estonia, that is, low-level vandalism and DDoS incidents, and did not play a part in the overall military strategy of the Russian incursion, the cyber dispute with Georgia set a precedent for the use of cyber tactics during a conventional military campaign. This is troubling because now cyber conflict can be blurred with conventional conflict and can lead to the perpetuation and escalation of hype that we warn against in this book. Another cyber incident that has been feeding the hype is the infamous Stuxnet worm that infiltrated Iran's nuclear program. It is this cyber incident to which we now turn.

## STUXNET: FROM THE DIGITAL TO PHYSICAL

Many speak of Stuxnet as the dawning of the cyber war era, with an emphasis on the "war" part of the equation. As Lindsay (2013: 366) notes, the case works "as a proof of concept, it appears to support claims that ubiquitous digital technologies create a potent new form of warfare." Some go even further and argue that this was the true demonstration of cyber capabilities. Kerr et al. (2010: 6) quote Udo Helmbrecht, the executive director of the European Network and Information Security Agency (ENISA) at length, noting that "Stuxnet is really a paradigm shift, as Stuxnet is a new class and dimension of malware . . . one of the first organized, well prepared attacks against major industrial resources. This has tremendous effect on how to protect national (critical infrastructure) in the future." Computer security expert Mikko Hypponen goes even further by connecting Stuxnet to the Manhattan Project, stating that scientists have lost their innocence through this incident (Lardinois 2013).

Stepping a bit back from the hyperbole, the Stuxnet operation shows how cyber could transform international interactions, as it showed that digital threats can now have a demonstrated physical impact. Before the incident, such a transition was purely hypothetical; after Stuxnet, the danger is real. Lindsay (2013) suggests that Stuxnet points to the hypothesis that cyber offensive capabilities can be used by the weak to hit the strong. It could also be argued that Stuxnet is proof of cyber operations being "less expensive, less deadly, less destructive, and less risky to their perpetrators" (Denning 2012: 676). This implies some sort of moral choice in favor of using cyber weapons over conventional attacks. There is the clear possibly that cyber is a better way to conduct an intervention given that the likelihood of death is remote. Questions of morality and ethics will be addressed in full in Chapter 8.

The intention of the action surrounding Stuxnet was clear—cripple, destroy, or delay Iran's nuclear production facilities in order to forestall the need for a conventional attack. In this manner, President Obama (Sanger 2012a: Chapter 8) embraced the action as a peaceful alternative to direct conventional attack, an action for which he had no desire after the wars in Afghanistan and Iraq. The cyber option seems like a sensible option given the dire nature of the Iranian threat, as some see it. Dire threats, for some, require new weapons and techniques in order to achieve the required ends.

We will refrain from offering conjecture about the need or utility of removing Iran's nuclear capabilities; this is beyond the scope of this analysis. What is clear is that the issue was obviously critical to the United States and Israel, plus various states in the Middle East who feared that the added capabilities in Iranian hands could embolden their actions. For these states, there was urgency in action, which led to the use of cyber weapons.

The questions we have to engage in this chapter are the following: How much of an impact did this weapon have? What were the consequences for the relationship between the target and the initiator? And what general lessons can we take away from this case? The obvious desire to move swiftly and alter the status quo is to be weighed against the effectiveness of the operation. In foreign policy analysis, the ends need to be connected to the means (Vasquez 1995). Here we question the effectiveness of the means in achieving their desired ends.

## What Was the Foreign Policy and International Relations Context of the Action?

Prior to the Iraq War in 2003, American officials made much of what they termed a "decade of defiance" by Saddam Hussein.[15] It was thought that Hussein was pursuing weapons of mass destruction and therefore had to be stopped. Unfortunately for the American officials who pushed for war, no weapons of mass destruction were ever found, and it was discovered that Saddam's nuclear program had long been dormant.

The tricky issue with the war in Iraq is that perhaps the target had been chosen incorrectly (or guided by rivalry concerns, as Valeriano [2013] argues). If the goal of the Iraq War was really to stop a nation from trying to build up a nuclear weapons program in the Middle East, perhaps the target should have been Iran. The situation in Iran at the time was dominated by the debate over the nuclear weapons program. Some argued that nuclear weapons are useful and actually a step toward a safer world, while others maintained that proliferation had to be stopped at all costs (Sagan and Waltz 1995).

Prior to the Stuxnet weapon, the United Nations passed resolutions in 2006 and 2008 demanding that Iran suspend its nuclear enrichment activities. The 2006 UN Security Council (UNSC) Resolution 1737 included an embargo of all trade with Iran that encompassed any products or services involved in nuclear and ballistic missile programs, a ban on the export to or import from Iran of any arms procurement material, and a travel ban on top-level Iranian officials thought to be associated with the program.[16] UNSC Resolution 1803 in 2008 affirmed this travel ban, froze Iran's assets, and enforced all measures in the 2006 resolution. These moves were made in large part due to the fact that the International Atomic Energy Agency (IAEA) was never able to rule out an ongoing nuclear weapons program in Iran, pushing some urgency into action for those most threatened.

The urgent need, at least as the Israelis (and also Saudi Arabia) saw the situation, was to remove or degrade Iran's nuclear capabilities. This pushed the United States to authorize extreme measures to stop the program. Being hesitant to launch another combat operation, no matter how limited, Obama did not seriously consider that option due to the fatigue of the American public regarding constant warfare.

Even if they did launch an operation, it was unclear if conventional air strikes would wound the program enough to set it back, and there was the added consideration of Iran's support for terrorist organizations. These groups could be unleashed to retaliate in the region, in Israel, and in the United States. The goal then "was to convince the Israelis that there was a smarter, more elegant way to deal with the Iranian nuclear problem than launching an airstrike that could quickly escalate into another Middle East war, one that would send oil prices soaring and could involve all the most volatile players in the region" (Sanger 2012a: 190).

The Natanz plant became the focus. There was a clear target and a history of Israel using conventional attacks on it to eliminate nuclear weapons facilities. Faced with this request to launch a conventional strike, the United States felt the cyber option, a program started under George W. Bush in 2006, was the best option to achieve the desired results with minimal international relations fallout.

Lindsay (2013: 379) recounted, "Natanz has two underground production halls with enough total room for fifty thousand centrifuges; by mid-2009 the Iranians had installed about eight thousand centrifuges in one hall." This location was an obvious target, and the option of utilizing cyber weapons was on the table.

Thus the cyber option appeared to offer minimal effort but maximum gain. With this decision came the development of Olympic Games, the American program to infiltrate Iran with cyber technologies. It was a large operation with the goal to significantly destroy or significantly degrade Iran's nuclear production capabilities.

As Rid (2013: 45) notes, "the resources and investment that went into Stuxnet could only be mustered by a 'cyber superpower.'" The scale of the operation was so large that it could have only been launched by a few powers, and all fingers pointed to the United States, with its interest in delaying Iran's nuclear production to forestall a conventional action by Israel. Multiple sources have since confirmed that the operation was launched by the United States, likely with the assistance of Israel.


## How Did the Cyber Incident Come About?

The Stuxnet operation had all the hallmarks of a traditional sabotage espionage enterprise. It required a high level of technical ability, planning, capabilities, funding, ground assets, and luck. All these traits combined together to produce an operation that surpasses all other cyber actions taken to date.

The scale and scope of the operation demonstrated that it was a tool of the strong; few states could have pulled off such an operation given the details required. The perpetrator had to develop a timed and precise set of computer code for an old industrial controller, overcome an air gap, make it appear as if the centrifuges were running as normal, and have the bug report back to the controller, all without direct access. Sanger (2012a: 193) calls this the beacon that would map Iranian operations.

The development of Stuxnet began under the Olympic Games program in 2006, directed first by George W. Bush's administration and continued by Obama's administration. The total cost of the operation was at least $300 million, if not more.[17] The Natanz plant was operated by a Siemens Simatic Step 7 controller (Lindsay 2013: 380) that could be exploited through zero-day flaws. Lindsay (2013: 382) notes that four zero-day bugs had to be exploited, plus a host of other flaws that likely were not security patched.

As part of the process, the malware had to be injected into the Natanz plant, overcoming the air gap—likely through human intelligence means. Either someone got into the plant, an unknowing accomplice was compromised, or a double agent was used. Once all this was done, the malware had to replicate itself within the plant and spread to critical operations. To accomplish this end, there was probably a Stuxnet beta that reported the contours of the system and exploited it before the final virus was injected.

Since the goal of the operation was to destroy or damage centrifuge operations, the most stealthy way to do this would have been to cause industrial destruction through mechanical means. In that way, sabotage would not be automatically assumed, and Iran might slow down its production further by looking for faults in its system, missing the software alterations. As Sanger (2012a: 188) recounted through interviews, "the thinking was that the Iranians would blame bad parts, or bad engineering, or just incompetence."

The Stuxnet worm had to speed up and then speed down the centrifuges, as speed would eventually cause their destruction through wear and tear. Stuxnet did not destroy centrifuges overnight, but it likely was a two-month long operation. Since there was a significant amount of time required—monitors had to demonstrate that everything was in working order, so it appeared as if the centrifuges were acting normally—another layer of subterfuge was required in this operation. By masking the activities of the centrifuges, Stuxnet was eventually able to destroy the systems through chronic fatigue (Lindsay 2013: 384).

The operation was so complicated and detailed that there could be no assurance that the plan would work unless it was tested prior to the injection of the software. This is where luck came into the operation to make it successful. "To engineer the ICS payload, developers would need access to IR-1 centrifuges, SIMETIC software, and the peripherals installed at Natanz, all set up in a mocked-up plant in order to test and debut their code, and to rehearse the attack" (Lindsay 2013: 387). The United States intercepted Libya-bound P-1 centrifuges in Italy, making it possible to develop a mock-up system. "Soon the military and intelligence officials overseeing Olympic Games managed to borrow a few centrifuges for what they delicately termed 'destructive testing'" (Sanger 2012a: 197).

The plan was developed, tested, and finally inserted into Iranian systems. It was not an easy operation, dwarfing the complexity of anything attempted before or since. The full software probably was injected into Iranian systems sometime around October to November 2009, given that the software was designed to work to destroy centrifuges for a few months before discovery. In February 2010, Iran took close to 1,000 centrifuges offline. In mid-June, a Belarusian company named VirusBlokAda discovered the malware when it had proliferated into civilian systems (Healey 2013: 217). The remaining question is, even though the plan worked, what was the exact impact?

## What Was the Impact of the Incident on the Target?

Healey (2013: 212) notes that "Stuxnet represented a quantum leap in complexity and audacity in cyber conflict." While spectacular, innovative, and invasive, it is unclear exactly what impact Stuxnet had, based on the quick-take accounts that came out right after the discovery of Stuxnet by the public. The question of impact is critical because the cyber revolution hypothesis (Lindsay 2013: 370) suggests that weaker powers can utilize cyber technologies to gain an advantage. We would have to question this hypothesis, if even a great power cannot leverage cyber technologies to its advantage against a weaker power. After spending millions and working across multiple agencies, were the United States and its allies able to degrade Iran's nuclear capabilities through cyber means? If they failed to have an impact, what hope does a poorly funded and supported state have in achieving its goals through cyber actions?

Answers to these questions vary according to the source. Those who have an obvious interest in inflating the dangers that come from the cyber arena are the most inflammatory. Others are more measured in their application of the discussion, especially as there is distance between the event and a reconsideration of Iran's capabilities. While our perspective is skeptical, it is bolstered by evidence that supports our claims that cyber operations do not occur at a rapid clip, nor does the severity of incidents appear to be escalating in light of evidence. The case of Stuxnet demonstrates an outlier in terms of severity; the impact is not quite what is seems without a deeper investigation.

First, take the evaluations that emphasized the changing nature of conflict in light of the new cyber weapon. Early reports focused on the delay that the damage caused and that "large sections" of the plant were made idle for a number of months after the incident (Albright et al. 2011: 4). Stuxnet was seen as a success in achieving the main goal of delaying the Iranian nuclear program.

Sanger (2012b: 205) notes that 984 centrifuges ultimately were stopped, either through damage or burnout, which according to the IAEA was one-fifth of the plant's capability at the time. Recovery time was estimated in months to repair the damaged centrifuges. Removing one-fifth of the centrifuges at the Natanz plant can be seen as significant or trivial, depending on how one views such things. The real question is how much damage the incident did to the overall ability of Iran to produce enriched uranium and thus a nuclear weapon.

Extreme reactions are the norm in the cyber community. For example, as Barzashka (2013: 49) notes, Kaspersky Labs suggested that Stuxnet knocked Iran off track by five years or more. Some still say it was three to four years.[18]

Other estimates actually say that the malware helped Iran's nuclear ambitions and sped the program's enrichment attempts, putting it ahead of schedule.[19]

The intelligence community, as Sanger (2012b: 206) recounts, estimated the damage at one to two years. To be fair, they do state that most of the delay in production resulted from Iranian defensive actions in anticipation of more Stuxnet-like incidents rather than direct damage. The IAEA notes that Stuxnet did not delay Iran's production at all since they just sped up the workload on other centrifuges (Sanger 2012b: 206).

The Iranians claim that the incident resulted in no real damage (Barzashka 2013: 48), an account backed up by more recent sources. For example, Barzashka (2013: 48) argues that "Stuxnet was not very effective from the start." She further notes that "unclassified evidence of the worm's impact on uranium enrichment at Natanz is circumstantial and inconclusive."

This perspective does beg the question of whether the information provided by Iran serves to demonstrate their capacity to defy the West. One cannot be dismissive of this motive, but it also is not a self-serving strategy if the goal was really to convince the international community not to strike the country and to argue compliance with the IAEA. In any case, between the second and third wave of the Stuxnet worm, Iran increased the number of operational centrifuges—it did not decrease them (Barzashka 2013: 52). This points to the main evidence that Stuxnet had no real impact, whether or not certain centrifuges were actually damaged, and that "enrichment capacity in the Natanz plant grew in relation to previous years" (Barzashka 2013: 49). While this increase results from the increase of centrifuges in response to the lost capacity, it still remains that the event's impact was minimal at best and might have actually spurred the plant to increase capacity in response to the incident.

Lindsay (2013: 390) makes a similar conclusion, noting, "yet the same data shows that the rate of LEU production at Natanz increased from about 80 kg/month to about 120 kg/month during Stuxnet's infiltration window from mid-2009 to mid-2010. At best, Stuxnet thus produced only a temporary slow-down in the enrichment rate itself." Also, by infiltrating the plant early with cyber methods, future attacks are made impossible since this avenue is now most likely cut off due to the infamous nature of the event.

It is not even clear if the damage caused by Stuxnet would not have happened by chance given that there was a 10 percent error rate in the IR-1 centrifuges as reported by the IAEA, and Stuxnet damaged 11.5 percent of the total at the time (Lindsay 2013: 391). A random interval experiment might have proven to be much more destructive than Stuxnet.

Since the cyber nature of the incident became apparent so quickly, Iran was able to diagnose and deal with the problem effectively and swiftly.[20] Albright et al. (2011: 4) note that "without knowing the cause was malware, Iran would have struggled to understand this failure and likely would have lost valuable time worrying about more failures." That they were able to avoid this entire dissection of the program is an advantage of a cyber method for a target. Yet cyber methods also appear to be clear and evident, making their secrecy in source or method a dubious proposition. A cyber action could be silent, deadly, and stealthy, but this is only conjecture at this point. It is at least clear that the intention of the Stuxnet worm was meant to be masked, but it quickly became public knowledge because cyber actions typically have unintended consequences, including bleeding into the public domain.

Lindsay (2013) does state that the beacon portion of Stuxnet, scoping out the Iranian networks, was infinitely more successful than the actual incident. This suggests that translating a cyber action from espionage and surveillance to physical damage is difficult, if not ineffective. Physical damage is possible, but often this part of the plan is quickly discovered, making the operation almost moot. We should also note that Stuxnet did infect over 100,000 hosts in 155 countries when the worm escaped into the wild (Healey 2013: 218). Since the malware was designed to infect command systems, the software did little to civilian systems.

Also, it is unclear if Iran even really intends to produce nuclear weapons, or seeks to create the capability to produce a weapon should it require it in the future. This seems to be the actual policy decision of Iran, and it is unlikely that it was influenced by any cyber operation. Theoretically, if the goal was to demonstrate capability but not produce an actual weapon, harming facilities like centrifuges that can simply be replaced proves to have limited impact on Iranian goals. It should also be remembered that the Iranian P-1 was deemed inadequate by the Pakistanis and the North Koreans, so their destruction might have been a step that pushed Iran to move past old and outdated technology. Sanger (2012a: 188) calls them the "Ford Pintos of the nuclear world, subject to random explosion."

### What Was the Reaction to the Incident by the Target?

Stuxnet may have been a significant incident in that it gave America's allies confidence to continue to try the diplomatic path. That there has been no conventional attack on Iran to this day suggests that Stuxnet was effective from the foreign policy objectives standpoint. Stuxnet might have convinced the players at that stage to take a path that would prevent outright war. The problem with this frame is that Iran has not abandoned its nuclear production goals, and Israel still threatens its enemies often. Recent conciliatory moves by Iran appear to be motivated by a change in leadership rather than coercive actions.

It is wholly unclear if the Stuxnet worm actually had a significant impact on Iran. It is just as likely that the fear of further incidents spurred the Iranians to shore up their own defense and closed the cyber avenue as a method of harming Iranian nuclear efforts in the future. The IAEA also noted that international sanctions were having just as much of an effect on Iran as Stuxnet itself (Barzashka 2013: 50).

We also cannot rule out Russian help in Iran maintaining and exceeding its nuclear estimates, surpassing any backsliding that Stuxnet may have caused. The ongoing rivalry with the United States pushes Russia to continue to needle the United States where it can, which has resulted in Iranian support (Maness and Valeriano 2014).

After reviewing the case, Lindsay (2013: 369) concludes that "Stuxnet can be interpreted to support the opposite conclusions: cyber capabilities can marginally enhance the power of stronger actors over weaker actors, the complexity of weaponization makes cyber offense less easy and cyber defense more feasible than generally appreciated." For Lindsay (2013), the cyber revolution hypothesis fails a basic surface validity test. We need to examine future uses of cyber power, but as we will argue in Chapter 8, it does seem that a norm of non-action in the cyber realm is developing.

Since the operation was largely a failure in method, control, and impact, it is questionable if major powers will resort to cyber operations in the future. Sanger (2012a: 207) notes that "the United States lost a bit of the moral high ground when it comes to warning the world of the dangers of cyberattacks." On top of the cost and the limited impact, we have the complication of the mixed message that Stuxnet creates if the United States and other powers wish to limit the proliferation of cyber weapons; if a state seeks nuclear weapons, it had best complete the operation quickly before opposing powers intervene.

There is also the possibility of future retaliation, or something similar to the Shamoon incident (Albright et al. 2011). Bronk and Tikk-Ringas (2013: 84) suggest that Stuxnet was the motivation for Iran to develop its own offensive capabilities, leading to reports of a new threat from Iran's digital hackers.[21] This is the cyber incident we will focus on in the next section of this chapter.


## SHAMOON

Shamoon was an incident focused on the Saudi Arabian oil producer Saudi Aramco. It is not completely clear who perpetuated the incident, but all evidence points to Iran. The goals were simple: strike the enemy and try to cripple its production capabilities in order to raise the price of oil for the remaining producers, generating more revenue for states other than Saudi Arabia. This tactic would mostly benefit Iran due to an ongoing embargo affecting its ability to sell oil. The other goal was likely to retaliate for Stuxnet. Since infiltrating American facilities is so difficult, hitting Saudi Arabia, the proxy ally of the United States, would do just as well in this case.

With these goals in mind, it does not take long to point the finger at Iran, given that they have been rivals with Saudi Arabia since 1979, fighting over mainly

Islamic-based disputes for regional hegemony in the Middle East (Iran is Shiite revolutionary while Saudi Arabia is conservative Sunni), and considering Iran's fairly extensive cyber capabilities (Devine 2009).[22] Shamoon was simply the tool of a weak state attempting to damage a rival and harm, by proxy, its large state sponsor and greatest consumer of oil, the United States.

Despite hyperbolic media statements, the impact of the incident was limited to nonexistent. The media reported that 30,000 computers were destroyed, but in reality, only the boot sectors on the hard drives were destroyed, a massive but fixable problem. Replacing the hard drives of 30,000 computers likely was a lot of work for the IT staff of Saudi Aramco and harmed their digital connectivity; regardless of these consequences, the action did not demonstrate the devastating power of cyber tactics. Shamoon further supports the contention that cyber actions are difficult to accomplish, often minor in effect, and massive in perceptions given the digital nature of society. Anything more by Iran would have unleashed drastic consequences; therefore, their actions in this case were muted.

### How Did the Cyber Incident Come About?

Shamoon was launched on August 15, 2012, against the Saudi Aramco oil corporation with 30,000 computers "destroyed."[23] Aramco controls what is likely the world's largest privately owned share of oil. It was a very evident and juicy target in the cyber world since it has massive stakes of production and reserves, but also because it is not directly part of an operational government organization and thus vulnerable to external breach. Saudi Arabia notoriously had failed to coordinate a cyber protection strategy for core industries (Bronk and Tikk-Ringas 2013).

One of the reasons we have chosen to examine this particular incident is because of the nature of the dialogues surrounding it. The goal is not to make extrapolations about the changing nature of cyber conflict, but to examine the actual impact of the operation and what may have precipitated the action. The media's reaction to the incident was nothing short of hyperbolic and exaggerated. Quotes from the news stories on the cyber incident claimed that "these attacks were the most devastating to ever hit the private sector," "Shamoon computer virus attack marks new height in international cyber conflict," and "55,000 computers destroyed [by Shamoon]."[24] These quotes only demonstrate the continued hype and bluster surrounding cyber actions.

### What Was the Foreign Policy and International Relations Context of the Action?

As Bronk and Tikk-Ringas (2013) note, the regional context of the incident cannot be ignored. The Middle East is one of the most conflict-prone and rivalrous regions of the world, with 11 interstate wars since 1945, ranking second in terms of regions and warfare (after Asia at 14). It can therefore be considered the most war-prone region per capita (Sarkees and Waylon 2010). There are 34 ongoing rivalries in the region (Klein, Diehl, and Goertz 2006). It is probable that global economic factors relating to the oil economy played a role in the incident, as the stability in the region dictated that prices were dropping by 2012.

The real change was the European extension of sanctions and economic restrictions against Iran. Before, Europe had continued to purchase Iranian oil, but after 2012 this practice largely ended, with immense complications for Iran given that they now had decidedly fewer customers, but also less available hard currency, especially of the Euro variety, given currency controls placed by the United States. Therefore, Iran could not sell its oil to its various customers, while Saudi Arabia gained more customers, greater revenues, and stable access to currency. This caused envy in the region.

Also, we cannot forget that Iran had just been victimized by a foreign power with cyber technology in the form of the Stuxnet virus. If the United States could launch a cyber incident, why could not Iran? While Stuxnet had little physical impact on Iran's production of nuclear materials, the barriers it opened in terms of tactics were sure to be exploited somewhere; Saudi Arabia seemed to be just the place.

As with the Stuxnet incident, the regional nature of the dispute was important. This supports our claims in Chapter 4 that cyber conflicts have a regional tone. With Shamoon, we see Iran infiltrating Saudi Arabia, and not retaliating directly against the United States. The motives were both retribution for the Stuxnet worm and to improve the price of oil in Iran. This dispute did not happen without a regional context and an ongoing rivalry between Iran and Saudi Arabia, in addition to a rivalry between Iran and the United States.

### What Was the Impact of the Incident on the Target?

US Secretary of Defense Leon Panetta remarked that "the Shamoon virus that attacked the Saudi Arabia's state oil company, Aramco, was probably the most destructive attack the business sector has seen to date."[25] It is unlikely that the Aramco incident was the most devastating, impactful, or financially turbulent incident seen to date, but it was likely the most destructive in terms of physical damage, and therefore it represents an outlier in terms of cyber actions.

The damage done by Shamoon varies according to the source. Generally, it is accepted that 30,000 hard drives were overwritten, but not destroyed (Bronk and Tikk-Ringas 2013: 17). The idea that a computer can be destroyed remotely is basically the stuff of science fiction, or a James Bond movie. It is possible that a central processing unit (CPU) could be over-clocked and the computer could then burn out, but there are usually safety measures that would shut down a system before it overheats. To use the term "destroyed," as most news sources at the time did, buys into the notion that destruction of the physical is a possibility from the cyber realm. Nonetheless, destruction is only possible in quite limited instances and situations, and is quite complex to accomplish, as the Stuxnet case demonstrated.

Since the damage done was inflicted on Aramco's internal network, it is likely that the virus (dubbed as W32.Disttrack by Symantec) was released internally (Bronk and Tikk-Ringas 2013: 17), either by an external operative or by an internal member compromised and turned to do the bidding of Iran's enemies. The risks from cyber conflict generally come from internal failings rather than external goals. The Aramco network was vulnerable, and this vulnerability led to the incident, but to achieve this end someone had to be on the inside first.

Aramco was up and running again by August 26, a delay of over 10 days but likely affected by the caution one would take in resuming operations after such a new and comprehensive infiltration. While 30,000 computer hard drives were compromised, the question is how much damage was really done beyond the basic hard drive? What about damage to the information and resources connected to the systems? Certainly the cost of replacing the hard drives, lost operations time, hiring of outside and internal operatives to clean systems, and reputational effects reached into the millions, perhaps billions of dollars, yet this is still a drop in the bucket for a company like Aramco, which is worth $1.2 trillion and has daily operating revenues of $1 billion.[26]

Again we must ask, what was the actual impact of the action? "Although the Shamoon virus impacting the critical energy sector destroyed virtual records, these were restored without widespread destruction or physical injury" (Yannakogeros 2013). Since there was no destruction or injury, it is questionable to suggest that Shamoon was a devastating incident. The US National Intelligence Threat Assessment notes that Shamoon "rendered more than 30,000 computers on Aramco's business network unusable. The attack did not impair production capabilities."[27] This is an interesting conclusion in that the report comes from those focused on promoting the cyber threat above the terrorist threat. That Shamoon did not impair production is an implication seemingly missed by most analysts.

Bronk and Tikk-Ringas (2013: 20) stress that there is no evidence the incident affected the industrial control systems that in turn compromised drilling and refinery operations. Drilling data were lost (Bronk and Tikk-Ringas 2013: 20), but it is unclear how much information was lost and why this happened. If information was deleted and lost forever, it was perhaps more an internal than an external fault. Similar to the way in which a student who has lost a paper to a computer error but did not back up the file externally can be blamed for the failure, Aramco might be in much the same way responsible for their lost data. They should have, and likely do now have, the ability to remotely save important data in multiple locations to prevent such failures in the future. As Dehlawi and

Abokhodair (2013: 1) note, "an unprepared Aramco, was the victim of a cyber incident that 'wiped' 30,000 computers, and forced Aramco employees to disable several of its internal networks for weeks." Aramco was unprepared, but their lack of preparation was not devastating and is unlikely to be repeated again.

Perhaps the greatest impact of the Shamoon incident was not so much the lost data and operations, but the positive computer traits learned by other organizations after the incident. Corporations with such important data remits are no longer likely to fail to back up data in spots where it is vulnerable. The possibility of remotely wiping hard drives is likely gone now, at least until another zero-day exploit is found, making Shamoon a one-off weapon unlikely to be replicated because the targets now know where the vulnerability lies. There is the possibility that more is to come, but at the time of this writing we have gone two years without a similar incident.

Bronk and Tikk-Ringas (2013: 23) note, "it is difficult to conclude that Iran had nothing to do with the Shamoon incident." It fits their profile in that they often use proxies for attacks, which was reportedly the Arab Youth Group, as reported by Carr.[28] By acting in this manner, Iran made it unlikely that any similar infiltration would be as successful.

### What Was the Reaction to the Incident by the Target?

Almost no impact can be detected in this case on the Saudi Arabian side. Computers are not static targets; the systems on them, the data stored on them, are no longer isolated and fragile. While the incident might have destroyed the hard drive boot sectors of many computers, the computers themselves were not destroyed. The impact of the incident was, once again, more of a demonstration of possible worst case fears rather than a demonstration of power.

Since the impact was minimal, Saudi Arabia has not reacted in any significant manner. The United States is the one that mainly went on the offensive, with Secretary of Defense Leon Panetta giving time to the press to make it clear that the United States knew where the incidents were coming from and that it reserves the right to retaliate against such incursions in the future. It is likely not a coincidence that Iran seems to be moving toward reconciliation with the West given that this incident failed to have any impact on the situation.

This action does point to some interesting considerations in relation to deterrence theory. As we spelled out in Chapter 3, there are two main modes of deterrence, direct and extended (Kahn 1960). In this framework, extended deterrence guards against incursions on an ally, whereas direct deterrence forestalls immediate direct actions. In this case, the action was an example of the failure of extended deterrence. It might be that Iran decided to not directly provoke the United States, but this also means it was perfectly willing to infiltrate its ally. While it could be argued that deterrence worked in some sense since the United

States was not infiltrated, it still remains a deterrence failure, suggesting that the framework is of little use if protecting an ally is an important consideration.

Going back to the cyber revolution hypothesis (Lindsay 2013), there is no evidence of a cyber revolution here. A weak power, relative to the United States, did not utilize cyber to directly hit the United States since that would have been too difficult a prospect. Instead, it targeted an ally, and in its targeting, it only sought to destroy the hard drives of a series of computers. This is hardly the most devastating incident that can be brought to bear. While such an incident would be devastating to a college student finishing a term paper the night before it is due, multinational corporations are not so vulnerable. Their systems are redundant and resilient. There is little need for retaliation since the incident was so minimal in impact; ignoring the action entirely would probably be more upsetting for the initiator, and that was the path that was chosen.

## ASSESSMENT OF THE CASES

The three main events examined herein have many commonalities, but one clear thing in common—they have all been over-exaggerated by the media, some cyber scholars, and pundits. If anything, these three admitted outliers of cyber incidents demonstrate the limited nature of cyber conflict. The Estonia dispute was successful more because of the reaction of the target than any special abilities in the DDoS method to effect change. Since then, Estonia has moved closer to Europe. Stuxnet was largely uneventful, even though it did commit physical destruction for the first time. If anything, Stuxnet helped the Iranians speed up production by implementing centrifuges to replace the damaged ones. Stuxnet also cut off this avenue of infiltration for the future, barring innovations. Finally, Shamoon never "destroyed" 30,000 computers but only wiped out the boot sectors in 30,000 hard drives. There was no discernible loss of data or productivity, despite the internal network being shut down for protection. It is telling that the three major cyber incidents in the last decade fail to stand up to scrutiny and demonstrate no new impact on the international situation or real implications for strategy.

It also seems clear that these operations were not as simple and quick as depicted by conventional wisdom. Each incident developed over a period of years and likely cost millions of dollars, especially Stuxnet. While providing an option beyond physical coercion, cyber coercion does not appear to be very effective. Estonia drifted even closer to the West and is now tightly integrated into NATO. Iran's nuclear program never really slowed down. They appear ready to make a comprehensive deal with the United States, probably because of the effectiveness of sanctions in denying customers from Europe and because of leadership change within the state, rather than cyber coercion. Shamoon did not lead to any real re-evaluation of the relationship between Saudi Arabia, Iran, and the United

States. If anything, Iran wasted its chance to harm a rival's production facilities given the overall failure of Shamoon.

We see little impact of the purported major cyber actions in terms of achieving strategic objections and little impact on the target. This once more reaffirms our two main hypotheses, cyber restraint and regionalism. Cyber technology is generally a tool to help deal with regional conflicts, as can be seen with Stuxnet's cooperation between Israel and the United States in order to forestall a push for conventional attack by Israel. In Shamoon, Iran responded to Stuxnet through cyber means instead of through terrorist prox- ies. Finally, Estonia seems to represent the least Russia could have done in this case since their ability to express power is greater than what was accomplished through DDoS methods. While positive in that these instances of coercion avoided the loss of life, they also were failures and do not represent a new way of exercising foreign policy.

## CONCLUSION

Sanger (2012a: 200) ends his evaluation of Stuxnet by noting that, even though it largely failed, "in the hands of others, it could become a weapon of mass destruc- tion." The cyber discourse is filled with these sorts of quotes, suggesting that things could be much worse and will get that way. The problem with this frame is that it took a confluence of events involving the Libyans and Israelis to make Stuxnet work, not to mention years of planning and millions of dollars. The weapon could not be developed by others, given the nature of Stuxnet. To sug- gest that others could do worse is a fallacy that assumes others could develop and implement a similar tactic. Since Stuxnet was a failure for the United States when it really mattered, would it work for another state under similar circumstances? Could it really become that weapon of mass destruction given the limitations of the method, the extensive planning involved, and the restraint demanded of civilized states?

It does seem clear that the chaos in the target is a desired effect, and some- times results from cyber actions. This clearly happened in Estonia when the state took their entire system offline to prevent further incidents. Iran likely went through a period of reflection after the centrifuge failures connected to Stuxnet, going so far as to never trust their system's read-outs and having operatives in their plant report back with visual confirmations and phone calls (Lindsay 2013). Aramco will now quickly back up all drilling data in multiple locations, as should any business or critical system. Fear is an important result, but sometimes it pro- vokes the opposite of the intended objective. Fear put Estonia closer to Europe, fear shored up any industrial vulnerability in Aramco, and fear made it less likely that any external inspector would ever have access to Iran's nuclear plants—and also made it improbable that the double agents would be able to do their work.

Quite often, the effect of a cyber action is unintended. It is difficult to predict what the target will do when it encounters new methods and technologies. In these cases, the opposite occurred. Estonia continued to integrate with the West, Iran continued to enrich uranium, and Saudi Arabia continued to support the embargo against Iranian oil. If cyber conflict is used as a tool of the weak and the strong to achieve some sort of political and military ends, it has absolutely failed to this point.

Our focus on state-directed cyber actions does leave some questions unanswered about the dynamics of non-state actors in the cyber world. For state-based actors, unintended consequences are dangerous and could lead to governmental charges for wrongdoing. This restrains government-based cyber incidents. Each cyber action was carefully planned, even though the outcomes were not as expected. Can we expect to see the same for non-state actor cyber cases? This will be the question of the next chapter.

## CHAPTER 7

# Cyber Conflict and Non-State Actors

## Weapons of Fear

### INTRODUCTION

Thus far in this volume we have concentrated on state-to-state dynamics of international cyber conflict. We have suggested and found little reason to discount the idea that states are largely restrained from escalating cyber conflict beyond the most basic level of tested interactions because of such frames as blowback, fear of collateral damage, and the one-strike nature of a cyber weapon. An unanswered question is what would stop or restrain a non-state actor from committing cyber crime, cyber espionage, or cyber terrorism against a state? Since these individuals or groups are not accountable to any sort of normative or punishment dynamics, what is stopping them from unleashing the full weight of their cyber capabilities? This chapter looks at three of the most sophisticated cyber incidents unleashed against states by non-state actors—Cyber Gaza, the Syrian Electronic Army, and Red October—to investigate the question.

In August 2013, it was discovered that Syrian President Bashar al Assad's regime had used chemical weapons on rebel forces as well as civilians in the bloody civil war that has taken nearly 140,000 lives in three years.[1] The international response to breaking this coveted international norm was widespread (Price 2013), and US President Barack Obama countered these actions with a threat to use precision military strikes to punish Assad and his regime. These threats led to a counter-threat by the Syrian Electronic Army, a well-known "hacktivist" group that has infiltrated networks of countries who denounce the Assad regime in any way, including calls for Assad to step down, announcing or implementing financial or diplomatic support for the rebel groups, or threats to intervene militarily in what is perceived as an internal conflict where the international community has no jurisdiction. The most prominent target of this cyber incident was the webpage of the highly circulated *New York Times*, where the Syrian Electronic Army used phishing techniques to coax an employee into opening a well-disguised e-mail. Once access was granted through this low-level method, the group was able to control the domain-directing service for a time. The *New York Times'* domain name was hijacked, and any user logging onto the organization's website was redirected to a domain controlled by the Syrian Electronic Army, where they were bombarded by pro-Assad and anti-American propaganda.

The Syrian Electronic Army account is a telling example of the capabilities of several well-organized, non-state cyber hacktivist groups. We need to understand what the Syrian Electronic Army hoped to accomplish, its methods, and more important, its limitations. This and other cases diverge greatly from our investigations so far because these operations were launched not by state-based entities but by non-state actors or terrorists. The need to include these cases in our account of cyber conflict is clear; the target was the conventional international state unit.

This chapter dissects how non-state actors utilize cyber capabilities and the impact of their actions. We find here that temporary chaos is their greatest weapon since the impact of their tactics is minimal when compared to the capabilities of states in cyberspace. The fear that chaos creates is important, yet evidence suggests that this is the full extent of the power of non-state actors in the cyber world. Hypothesis five of this volume is tested in this chapter with non-state actors, who do not have the capabilities to combat their adversaries on the conventional military battlefield, and use cyber tactics in their attempts to hurt their more powerful adversaries. Therefore, due to power imbalances, less powerful non-state actors will use cyber espionage and cyber terrorism as a tactic to perceptively bridge the power gap with the more powerful state adversaries. Their tactics spread through benign methods and overall represent low-severity threats. We find that non-state actors fail to achieve their goals in cyberspace. This limitation points to the larger inability of cyber tactics to change the dynamics of international affairs.

The goal of this chapter is to explain the process of cyber conflict in relation to our theories and data, with the actions of non-state perpetrators as our focus. We use the structured and focused case study method (Bennett and George 2005). This investigation is focused on a series of cyber conflicts and is structured around a set of common questions. For our cases, we have selected three of the most popular and well-known cyber incidents in the public discourse. We also include one of the least understood cyber incidents that has occurred to this date. Non-state actor groups utilize a variety of methods, such as spear phishing, vandalism, DDoS, and intrusions. As in the case of Red October, sometimes these non-state hackers have the capabilities to enact a sophisticated intrusion or infiltration; however, the impact on the target, as well as the severity of the method, remains low.

We examine Cyber Gaza because the operation was initially met with awe, suggesting that it was the greatest, most crippling event in the cyber system to date.[2] In the context of a conventional ground operation in Gaza by Israel, cyber operatives responded with an enormous number of directed incidents on Israeli networks. While this was possibly indicative of a new type of warfare for unequal powers, such as Palestine when challenging Israel, the incidents were largely unsuccessful. This demonstrates that the cyber method is not the critical tactic that might level the playing field. Cyber tactics could become more important in the future, but so far we have seen a limited use of the tactic, and when it is used, it tends to be unsuccessful.

The Syrian Electronic Army is examined because it is a well-organized entity that supports the actions and policies of the Syrian government. At the time of this writing, the bloody Syrian war continues, and the Assad government has been accused of numerous human rights violations, as well as breaking international taboos by using chemical weapons on its own people. The Syrian Electronic Army is supportive of this government and its actions in cyberspace. Many of the diplomatic and foreign policy actions from states that are critical of the Syrian government are met with a retaliatory response by the Syrian Electronic Army, which usually targets major media outlets, such as the *New York Times* in the United States and the *Guardian* in the United Kingdom. Its major tactic is spreading pro-Assad propaganda messages in order to stir up public opinion in the Western states. Furthermore, it has also been suggested that the exploits launched by the Syrian Electronic Army are actually the work of the Iranian Cyber Army (whose sophistication is growing every day), which could be waiting for the right moment to strike Western networks as a retaliatory response to the Stuxnet worm that crippled Iran's nuclear program.[3] However, victimized media outlets have not censored themselves in reaction to these actions, and thus these organizations' behavior remains unchanged.

The last case we examine is Red October, an espionage campaign that used intrusion methods to steal sensitive information. Due to its wide scope of targets as well as its sophistication, it is believed that this was an espionage campaign of both Russian and Chinese origins. The goals were not the normal motif of non-state actors, as theft or harassment of the enemy was the major task of this campaign. The operation was also highly contagious in that it was able to infiltrate numerous networks through its transfer by flash drives and e-mails. Overall, the operation was able to steal sensitive information from many governments and private organizations worldwide. Red October is therefore a salient cyber incident that will have to be unpacked in this chapter. While its scope was massive, its impact has been close to nonexistent.

As with the previous chapter, our goal in this chapter is to critically assess these non-state-based cyber operations and the malice they released into cyberspace. The aim of this chapter is to explain the process and motives behind the actions of these non-state actors and the cyber conflict they created, and to connect them to our theories and data. The structured, focused, comparison of different case studies in this chapter is centered on the four questions asked in the previous chapter:

1. How did the cyber incident come about?
2. What was the foreign policy and international relations context of the action?
3. What was the impact of the incident on the target?
4. What was the reaction to the incident by the target?

## CYBER GAZA

In November 2012, Israel ramped up its military campaign and naval blockade of the Gaza Strip, directing its anger toward Hamas. A series of cyber incidents started concurrently, with the objective of infiltrating Israeli government networks in retribution. For some, it had the potential to change how non-state actors respond to actions initiated by powerful states.[4] A revolt by the anti-Israeli, pro-Palestinian cyber community began in response to actions by Israel and other developments, such as former President Morsi's anti-Semitic decrees in Egypt, including the call to "nurse our children and our grandchildren on hatred [of Jews]" and the description of Jews as "these bloodsuckers who attack Palestinians, these warmongerers, the descendants of apes and pigs."[5]

Cyber Gaza, otherwise known as #OpGaza, #OpSyria, and #OpEgypt on Twitter, generated news, interest, and concern; the question that remains is whether it had a noticeable impact on the conduct of state-based operations. What might be called the Cyber Arab Spring was not making an impact on the populations of these countries involved in civil upheaval. Actions taken in cyberspace against Israel amounted to a protest to its actions in the Gaza Strip in November 2012.

Cyber protest actions are not new; the well-known international hacktivist group Anonymous has been using cyber actions against Israel on and off for years.[6] What is different is how focused and reactive these new incidents are; it was almost as if these incidents had been prepared months, if not years, in advance, and the perpetrators were waiting for the right moment to unleash them.[7] The website Mashable reported that the cyber battle between Israel and Gaza continued long after a ceasefire on November 21, 2012, was agreed upon.[8] Clearly there was wide discontent with Israel's actions, including a naval blockade, the 18 airstrikes launched throughout the month of November, and Israel's amassing of troops on the Gaza border for a ground invasion during that tense month. This escalating crisis provoked a reactionary response in cyberspace from pro-Palestinian cyber groups. A new battleground was formed in the cyber domain, and this has reinforced the widespread idea that the battles of the future will be fought in cyberspace.

The cyber incidents by non-state cyber groups have flooded Israel, but have not done real apparent damage to the state of Israel. The typical routines of the Israeli government and the Israel Defense Forces (IDF) have not changed. The cyber operations launched against Israel only provoked a counteroffensive from Israel, and their operatives have gone right back at the pro-Gaza cyber community, sometimes with devastating effects.

### How Did the Cyber Incident Come About?

Examination of these operations is useless without discussion of the wider context of the dispute between Israel and its enemies after 2011. All of these cyber incidents launched by anti-Israeli cyber groups signal a continuation of the Arab Spring in its cyber form. The Arab Spring was a turning point in the struggle against corrupt, authoritarian governments in this part of the world, which began in 2011. The Middle East and North Africa were filled with grass-roots and spontaneous demonstrations, and these individual social movements coalesced to produce leadership turnover, as in Tunisia and Egypt. By 2012 the movement had lost momentum and its spread had been met with violent crackdowns and even civil war. Once hailed a transformative movement across the world against those in power and the status quo, including the Occupy movement in the United States, it quickly devolved from nonviolent protest to full-scale civil war to provoke transitions, a tactic that is not as effective as nonviolence (Chenoweth and Stephan 2011). After Egypt's successful ouster of President Hosni Mubarak, status quo governments in the Middle East and North Africa began to crack down on popular uprisings with more rigor, using violent means. Activists against these regimes then took to cyberspace to show their anger with their situations in these countries, and Cyber Gaza was the culmination of reactions to the violence used on the peoples of this troubled region. Government actions in Yemen, Libya, and Syria are examples of the repression that led to the popular uprisings of the Arab Spring—from the streets to the Internet.

The government in Yemen repressed its uprisings and has yet to form a government satisfactory to the opposition. Although the 33-year reign of President Ali Abdullah Saleh ended as a result of the uprisings, the country is still teetering on failed-state status; as Al Qaeda's insurgent presence there is on the rise, the north of the country is in the hands of the Zaida Shia rebels, a secessionist movement plagues the south, and malnutrition and poverty are still widespread.[9] There are plans to draft a new constitution and form a new government, but deep divides among the government and the various opposition groups make Yemen's status as a reformed country far from certain as of early 2014.

The situation in Libya was far worse, as the dictator Gaddafi resisted until the end. Libya's movement developed into a civil war that was settled when the rebels formed an effective fighting force and the international community joined the conflict. Muammar Gaddafi's four-decade reign ended in a dramatic firefight that left the leader dead from gunshot wounds. Today the country is plagued with instability, violence, and uneven development. The nearly 300 revolutionary militias have yet to disarm and still control many parts of Libya's territory. The interim government is also accused of corruption and lack of transparency.[10] The future of Libya, therefore, is uncertain.

Syria's situation is the most dire, and it seems that an end to the quagmire there is nowhere in sight, as civil war still rages. The use of chemical weapons on civilians and the blowback from these actions did not result in international intervention. The rebel groups in the country are beginning to lose ground, and it appears that the Assad regime will end up staying in power. However, hope has not faded for those wanting reform in the Arab world; a new tactic has been utilized to continue the struggle, and this is how Cyber Gaza began. Due to the failures of the conventional protests in Yemen, Libya, and Syria, it seems that a popular uprising in Gaza would surely fail and would be met with further Israeli military force; cyberspace is therefore the forum to vent frustration with the current situation in the contested region.

## What Was the Foreign Policy and International Relations Context of the Action?

Hamas, a Palestinian political group that is labeled by many governments around the world as a terrorist organization, has controlled the autonomous region of the Gaza Strip in Israel since 2007, when it gained political power from the Fatah Party, its more moderate Palestinian rival. The group has strong ties with Iran, a state that Israel views with great concern because of its pursuit of nuclear weapons. Ever since Hamas's political takeover of Gaza, it has been hoped that the group would shed its more militant tactics and would seek reconciliation with Fatah, as well as pursue a policy of mutual existence with the Israeli government. However, this has not occurred thus far, and military skirmishes between Hamas in Gaza and Israel continue to this day (Masters 2012).

In June 2008, Egypt brokered a deal between Hamas and the Israeli government in which the group promised to stop firing rockets into Israel if the Israeli government promised to allow limited trade in and out of the Gaza Strip. However, the cross-border rocket attacks continued, as Hamas felt that it did not get enough out of the deal, and the brokered peace deal began to fall apart. For three years occasional violence between the two sides was the norm, and this escalated on November 14, 2012, when Ahmed al-Ja'abari, head of Hamas's military operations, was killed by a targeted Israeli airstrike.[11]

Israel claims that these airstrikes were in retaliation for Hamas's increased rocket attacks into Israeli proper, and that the move was in self-defense and for the protection of Israeli citizens. Furthermore, on November 15, 2012, Israeli Prime Minister Benjamin Netanyahu accused Hamas of "committing a double war crime. They fire at Israeli civilians, and they hide behind Palestinian civilians."[12] The next day, on November 16, the Israeli cabinet approved the mobilization of 75,000 reservists as the Israel Defense Forces began preparing for a possible invasion of Gaza if Hamas continued its rocket attacks. On November 18 Hamas called for an end to the long naval blockade that Israel had imposed on Gaza since the organization's control of the region. On November 19, UN Secretary General Ban Ki-Moon traveled to Egypt to broker a cessation to the escalation. US Secretary of State Hillary Clinton followed on November 20 with a trip to Israel to do the same. A cease-fire was agreed to and commenced the next day, on November 21. During this crisis, the Cyber Gaza campaign was launched with numerous attempts at infiltrating Israeli networks.[13]

A Turkish ship thought to be carrying Hamas militants was also boarded in international waters, causing a strain in relations between Israel and Turkey. Israel was willing to stand its ground and see the conflict through, no matter what the cost. It seemed that Israel was going to invade and overrun the Gaza Strip and occupy the territory until Hamas had been eradicated. Hamas's only defensive conventional weapons against superior Israeli military strength were the short-range rockets that it continued to fire into Israeli territory; the number of these rockets launched into Israeli territory during this skirmish numbered over 500.[14] Facing invasion, it seemed that the only other outlet to even the playing field with the superior Israeli military was in the cyber domain, and therein lies evidence to support hypothesis five.

### What Was the Impact of the Incident on the Target?

The response to Israel's incursion into Gaza was indeed swift and massive. To date, there have been an estimated 663 Israeli affiliated websites defaced and 87 pages deleted.[15] Yet we must remain cautious, as a *Global Post* report notes: "officials in Israel said that there have been up to 44 million cyber attacks on government websites since the beginning of the military campaign in Gaza."[16] The initial wave of incidents was prevented, with the exception of two incidents on the Israeli Philippine Embassy and an Israeli private defense contractor. A second wave, launched by the group Anonymous, succeeded in defacement and shutdowns of various networks, including that of the Bank of Jerusalem.[17] Some Israeli.gov sites went down the weekend of December 8–9, 2012, but were restored by the following Monday. Other defaced webpages included the Facebook page and Twitter account of the Vice Prime Minister of Israel (see Figure 7.1). Thousands

**Figure 7.1**
Defaced Facebook Page of Israeli Vice Prime Minister Silvan Shalom
*Source:* http://thenextweb.com/insider/2012/11/21/hackers-deface-israeli-vice-pms-facebook-twitter-youtube-blog-and-claim-to-have-gmail-access/#!zmEaP.

of website passwords were released, but it is unclear how much of an impact these actions had since passwords can be changed or recovered.

The impact on the multiple targets in Israel, therefore, was minimal. Any networks that were infiltrated by a Cyber Gaza hacker were restored within a matter of minutes, hours, or days. Most of the attempts were successfully contained or deflected by Israel's cyber defenses. It was the peace agreement on November 21, brokered by the UN, the United States, and Egypt, that stopped the violence—not the actions of the hackers involved in the Cyber Gaza campaign. Diplomatic solutions were the answer to brokering peace, but the cyber actions used during this campaign did little to nothing in deciding the outcome of the dispute in November 2012. Most of these attempted breaches were blocked by Israeli cyber security, and those that did slip by were low-level defacement or denial of service methods that lasted mere minutes to hours. Therefore, although the breadth and scope of the Cyber Gaza campaign was impressive, the actual impact on the target, the Israeli government and military networks, was quite minimal.

## What was the Reaction to the Incident by the Target?

It is evident that the actions against Israel did not have their desired intent. Noting this failure, the goal should not be for those who pushed for the Cyber Gaza operation to try harder to make an impact on Israel. The battlefield in the decades-long Israeli-Palestinian conflict has changed, but we question the impact of this change. Strikes by one side only provoke continued strikes and escalation. Actions provoke counter-reactions. The continued Gaza cyber conflict will only provoke Israel to marshal its own cyber defenses, create a system of cyber offense, and further limit the rights of Palestinians. We must rethink how conflict is utilized in the modern world, and it is clear that the cyber path is not the solution. Some feel that the brunt of cyber operations will not be felt by those intended, but by the innocent and the bystanders, much as Baldwin (1985) notes with regard to economic sanctions.

The continuation of the Gaza War in the cyber realm is a new development, but what has really changed? The cyber battlefield is not a conventional arena of conflict, but a battle of a different sort. It represents the wider propaganda battle on each side. Each side makes moves to try to influence the other side, to force one to back down, and to provoke fear in the civilian population. These are cyber information battles in which the IDF (@idfspokesperson) fights with tweets and memes against website deletions by the Palestinian side. Cyber Gaza only demonstrates that the coming era of cyber conflict will not be one in which rivals fight to win in conventional terms, but in order to win the hearts and minds of a global audience.

In other regional disputes, the same outcome of relatively low-impact use of cyber tactics can be found. The territorial disputes over various islands in the East and South China Seas between China, Japan, the Philippines, Taiwan, and South Korea have been supplemented with numerous actions in cyberspace. These countries are all long-standing rivals where the probability of escalation is high; yet the use of cyber tactics between these historical enemies remains benign and akin to shouting matches, with no demonstrable impact. DeRouen and Bercovitch (2008) apply this logic to internal rivals, or factions within a state; the perpetual conflict between Israel and the Palestinians has reached the point of an enduring rivalry relationship.

While the Gaza cyber conflict demonstrates that the domain of conflict has shifted, we remain skeptical about the overall change to warfare, foreign policy, and the basic functions of civilian protest. Direct and proxy conflict continues to rage. Anonymous and the Iranian Cyber Army have joined the battle for influence, respect, and position in the conflict between Palestine and Israel. Our finding is that the foreign policy dynamics have not changed with the spread of the dispute to the cyber realm. While the continuing Gaza cyber conflict is troubling for many reasons, it is not an indication of a devastating tactic that has shaped the opinions and tactics of those engaged in conflict. These incidents are typical in that website defacements and other relatively benign forms of cyber malice, such as denial of service methods, are used every day, devoid of the context of civil unrest. Neither side has seen an obvious change in behavior or capabilities due to the cyber incidents. The number of incidents may have been dramatic, but the impact surely was not. We see the same dynamics in our next case, that of the Syrian Electronic Army; while a major nuisance for many Western media outlets, nothing beyond propagandist messages or denial of service methods deterred the targets of this group from continuing business as usual shortly after the incidents.

## THE SYRIAN ELECTRONIC ARMY

The pro-Baathist, pro-Bashar al Assad hacktivist group that calls itself the Syrian Electronic Army has been infiltrating the networks of Western media outlets since 2011. With no known direct ties to the Syrian government, this entity acts on its behalf when it interprets Western foreign policy moves as hostile or counter to Syria's national interests. In fact, US intelligence officials believe that this group is actually Iranian in origin.[18] Most of the targets are various media websites of the United States and Great Britain, such as the *New York Times*, the *Washington Post, Forbes, The Guardian*, Microsoft, and the social media outlet Twitter. It is usually the Twitter feeds of these organizations that are hijacked, where false reports are posted for several hours. Incidents from this group were first uncovered in April 2011, when it launched a series of vandalism campaigns on the social networking site Facebook.[19] The Syrian Electronic Army then launched its website shortly thereafter in May, where it officially announced that it was not part of the Assad regime group with a political purpose.[20] Assad himself has publicly confirmed that he has no involvement with the organization, although he has praised its efforts in cyberspace on behalf of his government, calling it a "real army in a virtual reality."[21] (See Figure 7.2 for the logo of this pro-Assad hacktivist organization.)

The most notable incidents that caused a public stir and government response were when the Syrian Electronic Army hijacked the *New York Times* website and

**Figure 7.2**
Official Logo of the Syrian Electronic Army
*Source:* http://www.theverge.com/2013/5/24/4363140/syrian-electronic-army-hackers.

the Associated Press's Twitter account. The two incidents will be discussed in further detail in this section. These and other notable incidents by this organization are documented in Table 7.1. At first, the Syrian Electronic Army's main method was the use of vandalism tactics, where Western targets were bombarded with pro-Assad propaganda.[22] It has continued with these methods and been successful in accessing preferred targets with spear phishing infiltrations,

*Table 7.1* SYRIAN ELECTRONIC ARMY CYBER INCIDENTS

| Date of Report | Target | Summary |
|---|---|---|
| 9/9/2012 | *Al Jazeera* | This news organization's Twitter feed, taken over by the Syrian EA, reports that an assassination attempt on Qatar's prime minister had been made. |
| 2/26/2013 | *Agence France-Presse* (**AFP**) | The French media organization's photo department's Twitter feed is hacked, where pro-Assad and anti-Obama images are posted. |
| 4/16/2013 | **NPR** | Several Twitter accounts of this organization are vandalized, where the message "Syrian Electronic Army Was Here" was posted. |
| 4/20/2013 | **CBS** | Twitter feeds for this organization are compromised, and the Syrian EA posts false stories, including evidence that the CIA has been arming Al Qaeda terrorists in Syria. |
| 4/23/2013 | **Associated Press** | The organization's Twitter feed is hijacked, where explosions at the White House resulting in the injury of President Barack Obama are reported, causing a dip in the stock market for several minutes. |
| 4/29/2013 | *The Guardian* | The news organization's website is compromised and a number of false stories are posted for a few hours. |
| 5/6/2013 | *The Onion* | The satirical website's Twitter feed is hijacked and real grievances are posted for a time, confusing readers of the usually joke-filled feed. |
| 5/17/2013 | *Financial Times* | This organization's Twitter feed is hijacked and false reports are posted for a few hours. |
| 5/26/2013 | **Sky Broadcasting Group** | The British media group's Twitter account is compromised, which also led to fear that the apps of the broadcaster had also been infiltrated. |
| 7/22/2013 | **Tango** | Messaging service has millions of e-mails and phone numbers stolen, many of which are thought to contain the names of Syrian rebels, and the Syrian EA announces that it will be handing over the information to the Syrian government. |
| 7/29/2013 | **Reuters** | The Twitter account of the news service is hacked, where a series of anti-American, anti-Turkey, and anti-Lebanon satirical cartoons are posted. |

*(Continued)*

*Table 7.1* (CONTINUED)

| Date of Report | Target | Summary |
|---|---|---|
| 8/15/2013 | *The Washington Post* | Syrian EA hijacks an article recommendation service used by American media websites. All recommended articles for the *Post* read "Hacked by SEA." |
| 8/27/2013 | Twitter | Twitter's DNS servers accessed by the Syrian EA, and therefore able to be controlled, posting false messages on various high-profile accounts. |
| 8/27/2013 | *New York Times* | The *Times'* DNS is infiltrated and then shut down by DDoS flooding and is inaccessible for hours. |
| 9/2/2013 | U.S. Marines | With the threat of the Marines possibly striking Syria over the chemical weapons accusation, the Syrian EA hacks the Marine recruiting site, where it posted a message reading "Obama is a traitor who wants to put your lives in danger to rescue al-Qaeda insurgents." |
| 10/28/2013 | Barack Obama | The US President's Twitter account is hacked where a link that was supposed to direct followers to a climate change article was redirected to a pro-Assad propaganda video. |
| 1/11/2014 | Skype | Skype's Twitter and Microsoft blog are hacked, warning users to stop using Microsoft e-mail services. |
| 1/15/2014 | Microsoft | Small number of employee e-mail accounts are accessed. |
| 1/20/2014 | Microsoft | Syrian EA hacks and defaces Microsoft Office's blog. |
| 1/25/2014 | Microsoft | Documents "associated with law enforcement inquiries" were stolen when the Syrian EA infiltrated employee e-mail accounts. |
| 2/15/2014 | *Forbes* Magazine | Syrian EA publishes a database saying it contains the login credentials for one million users of Forbes.com. |

*Source:* http://www.theverge.com/2014/1/27/5350744/syrian-electronic-army-sea-hacks.

whereby employees of targeted organizations are sent enticing messages. When opened, a virus is then installed that downloads passwords and other sensitive information. Once accessed, these networks are hit with vandalism methods. As with many non-state cyber campaigners, this organization's main motive is to get these Western countries to change their policies and perceptions of the conflict in Syria. This is done through a domain where the capabilities are more even—cyberspace.

In this chapter we analyze two cyber incidents for which the Syrian Electronic Army has claimed responsibility: the April 23, 2013, takeover of the Associated Press's Twitter account and the August 27, 2013, defacement of the *New York Times* website. These two incidents received much attention for these high-profile infiltrations, one of which affected the New York Stock exchange; the other was able to penetrate a domain registrar thought to be impervious to the pro-Assad hacktivist organization. These incidents were also very timely, as each one was released at the same time the Israeli and then US intelligence services accused the Syrian government of using chemical weapons. The message to the West from the Syrian Electronic Army was clear: stay out of the affairs of a sovereign Middle East state dealing with its own internal affairs.

### How Did the Cyber Incidents Come About?

On April 23, 2013, the Syrian Electronic Army's hijacking of the Associated Press's Twitter account allowed it to send out a false message that read, "Breaking, Two Explosions in the White House and Barack Obama is injured."[23] This was believed for a time, especially on Wall Street, where the stock market plunged 100 points in a matter of seconds until it was confirmed as "bogus."[24] What was most telling about the tweet being false was the fact that the word "Explosion" was capitalized and the president's first name was used in the message. This is uncharacteristic of journalistic reporting on the Twitter site, where the AP has a grammatical protocol when posting tweets.[25] As no other news agencies were reporting this story, the fear generated out of the hacktivist group's activity with the AP was quickly subdued. Figure 7.3 illustrates the minute-by-minute effect on the Standard & Poor's 500 Index for the New York Stock Exchange numbers when this false news was reported on AP's Twitter site.

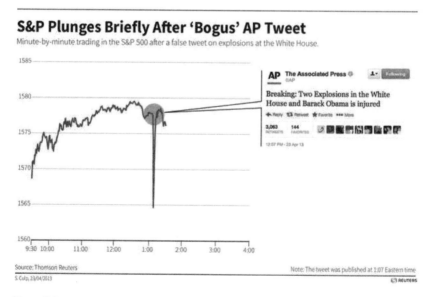

**Figure 7.3**
Associated Press False Tweet by the Syrian Electronic Army and the S & P Reaction
*Source:* Reuters 2013. http://uk.reuters.com/article/2013/04/23/uk-usa-whitehouse-ap-idUKBRE93M12Q20130423.

Later in 2013, on August 27, the website of the *New York Times* was hijacked, and its domain was redirected to one controlled by the Syrian Electronic Army. When users accessed the website during the hijacking, they would be redirected to an IP address controlled by the Syrian group, where they would be bombarded by pro-Assad, anti-Western propaganda.[26] No harm was done to any individual hard drive of anyone accessing the *New York Times*; only the paper's server was affected. In fact, users savvy enough to know the *Times'* direct IP address could access the paper with no interference from the Syrian Electronic Army.

This was not the first time the *New York Times* has been the victim of cyber malice; incidents originating from China had victimized the organization earlier in 2013, when it published a story that painted Chinese Prime Minister Wen Jiabao in a negative light. The February 2013 Mandiant Report stirred up relations between China and the United States when it accused the Chinese government of waging numerous cyber campaigns that stole government secrets and intellectual property; media website disruptions also evoked concerned reactions from American elites and the public.[27]

The Syrian Electronic Army is a reactionary group supportive of the Assad regime and his continuation as the authority in that country. This is why some suspect the group to actually be Iranian.[28] The cyber group only acts when the West does, usually when Syria's policy actions are condemned by Western leaders or media outlets. There have been plenty of these condemnations as the Syrian civil war, in which over 140,000 people have died since 2011, continues.[29]

## What Was the Foreign Policy and International Relations Context of the Actions?

When the AP Twitter account was hijacked, the Syrian Electronic Army was responding to Israel's accusation of the Assad regime using chemical weapons on the opposition forces. Although the United States' official position over the accusation by its ally was neutral, as it did not confirm or deny the use of chemical weapons by the Assad regime, the Syrian Electronic Army acted to warn the West not to take the actions seriously or threaten intervention in the civil conflict. As with many non-state cyber hacking groups, the group used craftily disguised spear phishing e-mails. Employees of the AP were coaxed into opening e-mails that granted the Syrian Electronic Army access to the news organization's Twitter account. It only takes one e-mail to be opened for this access to be granted. This happened, and it allowed for the false reporting of the White House incident, which also hurt the AP Twitter feed's credibility.

Five months later, the spear phishing success by the Syrian Electronic Army on the *New York Times* was also due to human error, when an employee opened the disguised hacktivist group's e-mail. This time, the US government acknowledged the Assad regime's use of chemical weapons on the opposition forces and civilians and publicly condemned it for this breach of international norms and law. President Barack Obama announced the possibility of military strikes on government targets, and the Syrian Electronic Army was quick to respond to these threats by hacking American media outlets. Along with the *Times*, the *Washington Post*, Twitter, and even the US Marines recruiting sites were hit with vandalism that flooded the sites with pro-Assad, anti-American propaganda. Although these incidents are troubling, the fact that this was all the group could do, when the very existence of the regime they supported was being threatened with airstrikes by the world's preeminent military power, shows that phishing followed by defacement and vandalism is perhaps all that this entirely pro-Assad group is capable of doing. If this is the case, simple training of employees of potential Syrian Electronic Army targets is all that is needed to defend against future incidents.

Demoralizing propaganda is a typical part of relations between adversaries, especially during times of war or threat of war. What the Syrian Electronic Army is doing is nothing new; only the tactic of conflict between unevenly matched adversaries has changed. Guerrilla warfare, terrorist actions, covert operations, and spy missions have all been used by weaker adversaries in times of threat. Today this is being implemented through cyberspace. The reactions to the malicious activity by the Syrian Electronic Army have perhaps received more attention than they should have, but the very nature of the targets allowed for more publicity. Yet the actual impact of the successful endeavors of this organization has been quite limited.

## What Was the Impact of the Incident on the Target?

Marc Frons, chief information officer of the *New York Times*, gave an analogy that put the August 27 incident in perspective relative to earlier incidents of 2013, such as the AP hack: "In terms of the sophistication of the attack, this is a big deal. It's sort of like breaking into the local savings and loan versus breaking into Fort Knox. A domain registrar should have extremely tight security because they are holding the security to hundreds if not thousands of Web sites."[30] In this analogy, the Syrian Electronic Army was able to get into Fort Knox through the local savings and loan. However, we see little difference in the methods used by the Syrian Electronic Army in these two cases. It is true that a domain registrar should have tighter security than a Twitter account, but it is obvious that it did not. This group infiltrated both networks the same way: spear phishing e-mails were opened by unsuspecting employees, and the Syrian Electronic Army was able to hijack both networks. The group was then able to control the networks for a time, posting false messages, flooding them with denial of service campaigns, or spreading propaganda on the sites. The major impact of these incidents was that it caused disarray among the loyal readers of these two media outlets, announced their presence, and caused a stir among the security personnel of the organizations, who believed that their networks were secure from such low-level cyber incidents. All in all, the impact of the Syrian Electronic Army's activities in cyberspace was quite benign. As hypothesis five predicts, a less powerful non-state entity used cyber tactics in an attempt to level the playing field with its more powerful adversary.

When the Syrian Electronic Army is successful, the government and population hear all about it, and the policy prescription for these kinds of actions is to increase cyber security. Companies such as Symantec and McAfee are then called in to set up firewalls against the code written from the previous Syrian Electronic Army hack(s). However, the firewalls are specific and are not programmed to combat a new code that the group may innovate, bringing the issue of cyber security back full circle. Preventing groups like the Syrian Electronic Army from infiltrating the secure networks that are important to our everyday lives and our national security is easier than one may think.

## What Was the Reaction to the Incident by the Target?

As with most state-based and non-state campaigns, the primary reaction to international cyber hacking incidents, whether they are nuisances, espionage, or coercive foreign policy moves, is to overreact. Organizations feel secure when they hire cyber security firms to increase their firewalls and guarantee protection against spear phishing methods. After the AP Twitter hijacking, the world-renowned news organization simply shut down its Twitter account. The *New York Times* was protected by the highly regarded security firm MelbourneIT. One cyber security expert explains why the infiltration of the *Times*' network was so troubling: "If Melbourne is vulnerable to phishing, and observers worry that any DNS-dependent service could be similarly vulnerable, including email routing. One solution suggested by MelbourneIT is the rarely used 'registry lock' service, which prohibits any automated changes to the DNS registry. Registrars rarely grant registry locks because of the logistical burden involved, but after this week's hacks, they may become more common."[31] This means higher costs for more security with no guarantee that they will be protected from new methods derived by groups like the Syrian Electronic Army. These groups are able to adapt and adjust to even the most highly regarded security firms, suggesting either that both networks are powerless against these groups, or that the answer to protection against these low-severity incidents is easier and less costly than one may think with proper cyber hygiene. It could also be that cyber security firms really are not capable of defending their clients' interests.

David Sanger, national security expert and regular writer for the *Times*, has discussed using the massive power of the American cyber arsenal on Syria to disrupt conventional missions carried out by Assad's troops in its bloody civil war.[32]

As conventional action has been tabled for now, these cyber tactics are cheaper, more covert, and easier to implement. However, this would only open the cyber "Pandora's box" that we have warned against throughout this volume, and the 9/11 moment that former Defense Secretary Leon Panetta warned against would be of the United States' own making. Furthermore, it is apparent that this group has the expertise to clear media outlets' firewalls with ease and to enact deface-ment and DDoS low-level damage to these organizations. If the United States does deploy its cyber abilities and interferes with Assad's war, and if the Syrian Electronic Army is from Iran, then the escalation of this group's activities rises to a level not seen before. Again, the best policy for the US government is to restrain itself, and to encourage its media outlets to do the same after a low-level incident by a non-state hacker such as the Syrian Electronic Army. Before discussing what these targets can do to protect themselves against non-state actors, we will look at a very sophisticated espionage campaign launched by a non-state actor, com-monly dubbed Red October.

## RED OCTOBER

The Red October operation is an example of a sophisticated cyber incident whose primary motive was not to deter or demonstrate action by more powerful adver-saries per se, but an espionage campaign where profit was the main motive. It was a targeted cyber incident that remained undetected for a few years. It caused government disruptions in multiple states and is known to have infiltrated important sectors. These sectors include, but are not exclusive to, government non-military (embassies), government military (aerospace, defense depart-ments), the energy sector (oil and gas, nuclear), trade and commerce (stock mar-kets, banks, investment firms), and research institutions (universities and think tanks).[33] Discovered by Kaspersky Labs in January 2013, this incident uses spear phishing as its primary method, which gives it access to a network, and then uses Trapdoor methods to steal information; the method is therefore classified as an intrusion according to our coding process presented in Chapter 4. Furthermore, Red October was an act of cyber espionage via an advanced persistent threat method, and it infiltrated these multiple secure networks. Figure 7.4 gives an overview of Red October's widespread reach and scope.

The primary targets of the Red October incident were governments, busi-nesses, and organizations of the West. The virus spread into other regions and networks, yet the primary targets were those in Europe and the United States. It is therefore suspected that the perpetrators were of non-Western origin, with many cyber security experts pointing the blame at either Russian or Chinese groups.[34] Forensic evidence shows that the codes used to infiltrate the targeted networks have both Russian and Chinese characteristics, but it has also been said that these types of characteristics could have been utilized to throw off the

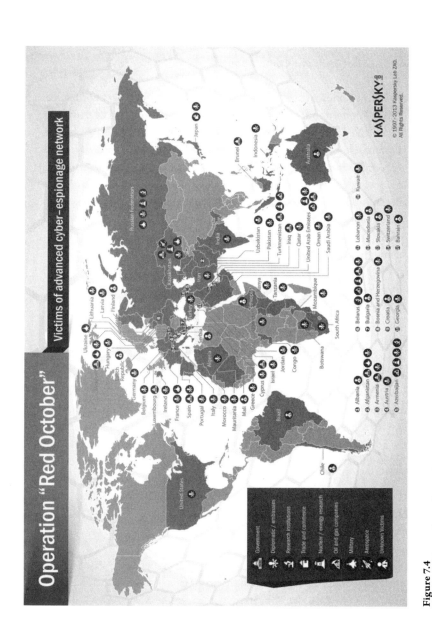

**Figure 7.4**

Victims of the Red October Cyber Espionage Incident

*Source:* http://www.kaspersky.com/about/news/virus/2013/Kaspersky_Lab_Identifies_Operation_Red_October_an_Advanced_Cyber_Espionage_Campaign_Targeting_Diplomatic_and_Government_Institutions_Worldwide.

trail to the actual individual or group who perpetrated the incident.[35] While it is clear that the primary motive was to steal top-secret information, it remains to be seen whether or not this information will be sold to the highest bidder, most likely a state.

### How Did the Cyber Incident Come About?

Unlike the two previous cases presented in this chapter, it seems that Red October did not come about because of a specific international event. However, the nature of the targets and the information that was stolen, which was mainly Western, show that the hackers may have had an anti-Western motive. According to Egan, the speculation was that the primary motive for launching Red October was because the perpetrators were suffering economic hardships, as the skills they possessed have no demand from employers in the economy of their home country.[36] People with these skills, who are able to write code and infiltrate networks, are usually highly paid and work within the confines of a state's national security apparatus, or work for a private cyber security firm. Those who live in countries with a surplus of this talent, without enough of these high-paying jobs to go around, therefore, will turn to cyber crime for a quick payday.

Forensics uncovered by Kaspersky Labs point to two locations as the genesis of the incident. With both Russian and Chinese codes in the spear phishing incident, it is more than likely that Red October originated from one of these two countries. "The attackers have Russian-speaking origins due to the number of Russian and Chinese words used in the coding. . . . Experts say this is significant as it is not known to have been used in any software other than that created by Russian programmers."[37] This would suggest that Red October came from Russia, but it would not be beyond reason to see Chinese coders working in Russian to obscure their origins.

### What Was the Foreign Policy and International Relations Context of the Action?

Red October's origins are most likely from a non-state perpetrator. Yet many have pointed their fingers at Russia, and Russia controls its networks with fierce determination. A 2013 law gave the FSB, the successor to the Soviet-era KGB, more control over the surveillance of all Russian Internet service providers (ISPs).[38] Therefore, if Red October did originate from Russia, it is more than likely that the Russian government knew about it. Furthermore, the fact that the primary targets have been the networks of the European Union and NATO shows that the initiators' loyalties lie not with the West, but with a country or region that does not have ideal relations with Europe or the United States. However, as Lardinois (2013) points out, "all of the clues pointing to Russia could simply be red herrings planted by the offenders to throw off investigators. Although the attackers appear to be Russian speakers, to get their malware onto systems they have been using some exploits—against Microsoft Excel and Word—that were created by Chinese hackers and have been used in other previous attacks that targeted Tibetan activists and military and energy-sector victims in Asia."[39]

Spear phishing is not a very sophisticated method of infiltrating a network; however, it has been used successfully to infiltrate supposedly tightly secured and high-profile networks. It is a particular favorite of non-state hackers. Red October was even able to steal information from flash drives that were plugged into network computers; therefore it was able to spread very quickly. Red October's reach could only become so widespread because the people working within the networks of NATO, the EU, the European Parliament, and the European Commission carelessly opened the e-mails containing the virus. The success of this incident was based partly on the craftiness of the e-mail sent out by the hackers, as well as the naiveté of the employees of the targets, who were not properly trained to avoid suspect e-mails when plugged in to an organization with highly sensitive security information.

### What Was the Impact of the Incident on the Target?

Red October infiltrated secure networks, mainly Western networks at diplomatic, governmental, and scientific research organizations, and gathered data and information from mobile devices, computer systems, and network equipment.[40] There have been hundreds of victims, and the equivalent of thousands of pages of sensitive intelligence and national security information have been stolen. The major impact of Red October has been a reality check as to how insecure the presumed secure networks really are. Since the discovery of the virus in 2013, the majority of Red October's activity has been contained or blocked from the infiltrated networks, and has, for the most part, disappeared from cyberspace at the time of this writing. This points to flaws in the cyber security framework; once a method becomes known, it then is easy to prevent its occurrence again.

The primary impact of the Red October incident on the variety of targets it infiltrated was the loss of sensitive information or the theft of intellectual property rights. The incident hit government and private sector targets alike, and the amount of property that the perpetrators of this incident stole is still being calculated. The Acid Cryptofiler, a well-known online storage service, which was believed to be a secure way of storing information and protecting it from potential hackers, was infiltrated. The ability to protect the customers of this cryptofiler has now come into question. This storage service is used to protect the networks of the EU and NATO, and these organizations were the hardest hit in terms of theft. The portability of the virus, as it was able to jump from flash drives into other networks, also allowed it to become widespread and global, infecting not only Western networks, but those of countries on every continent. In the end, Red October did what most non-state-originating cyber incidents have done: instill fear in the governments and private sectors of many of the most advanced countries in the world.

### What Was the Reaction to the Incident by the Target?

The question of reactions still remains. Retaliation by any victim country or network, either conventional or cyber, has not happened, since it is unclear who exactly directed the action. Nor would one expect a reaction to a theft operation such as this. What has happened since its discovery is the realization of the vulnerability of the networks used by many countries, corporations, and international organizations. Should they buy more expensive software and cryptofilers with no guarantee of network security, or should they initiate more modest and cost-effective security training programs for their employees? We assert that the latter is the more effective strategy. Cyber perpetrators are resilient, and many networks have redundancies. Cyber security firms will sell software that is designed to protect against the infiltration of high-profile organizations such as the EU and NATO. However, as these threats demonstrate, hackers adjust and employ new codes and methods that are able to circumvent the new security measures, and the process happens all over again.

Rather than blaming the hackers for the breach and installing more security software, leaving these organizations just as vulnerable as before the cyber incident, Egan discusses another path. He notes, "This is much less about the software itself and more about all these organizations, who really should know better, that apparently do not have any policy to record when they are losing important information. There should also certainly be a policy in place that says staff is not allowed to click links or download word documents."[41] What is apparent is that many organizations do not have the proper human security protocols in place. Constantin goes further and recommends even simpler methods in regard to cyber defense: "The delivery method here is 'spear phishing,' or targeted phishing. It relies on human error, so the most important thing is to inform and educate staff members. There should also be a policy about sharing sensitive data. Certain types of file should simply not be allowed to leave the network, and emails should be scanned for information that shouldn't be allowed to leave the building."[42] Therefore, in addition to enacting rules as to what and what not to open in e-mails, the employees of these organizations need to be properly trained in looking out for the telltale signs of possibly disguised e-mails with malicious intent.

As with Cyber Gaza and the Syrian Electronic Army, Red October instilled fear within governments and private organizations, even if this was not the primary objective. The theft of top secret and national security-level information left these organizations feeling vulnerable. Vulnerability may lead to overreactions and the employment of cyber security firms, who can only sell protection against known threats. Any unknown threats are still left open to infiltration or theft, and the cycle of fear and overreaction will continue.

Cyber hygiene is about more than taking away access to mainframes or hard drives, not taking classified work home, or the prohibition of the use of flash drives in the workplace. Although this will reduce the probability of infiltration by hackers such as those involved in Cyber Gaza, the Syrian Electronic Army, or Red October, the proper training of the human capital of these organizations is paramount to reducing the success of these hacktivist groups or individuals. As Singer and Friedman (2014: 64) suggest, "if a network has any kind of sensitive information in it, all users need to be regularly certified in cybersecurity basics." Cyber hacktivist and cyber criminals are very savvy and can adapt to most cyber security software programs that protect against their previous successes. They are able to adapt; and they are able to adapt quickly. The question that remains is if we, as social scientists, see cyber hygiene as the answer, then why are these organizations slow to heed to our advice? The answer to this question lies in polls of experts in different niches of the cyber security debate.

The size of the impact on society is determined by the perception of threat and impact on the target. Here we examine opinions about the cyber security threat according to perceptions among policymakers, academics, and cyber security experts in order to understand how the threat emanating from the cyber security realm is constructed in the public discourse. Each constituency has its own view on the issue, and how these views manifest is critical to perceptions about the wider societal threat coming from cyberspace.

One group examined is the experts from the cyber security industry. In January 2012, technological experts from around the globe were surveyed by McAfee and the Security and Defense Agenda (SDA) about the issue of cyber conflict. Fifty-seven percent of these practitioners believe that states are currently engaged in a cyber "arms race"—the general idea being that capabilities and the threat from this issue area are increasing at all levels. Forty-three percent believe that the worst-case scenario, damage and disruption to a state's critical infrastructure, is the most likely. A further 45 percent believe that cyber security is just as pressing an issue as border security, according to the McAfee report.[43] The report then notes that "diplomats need to start addressing this issue with more urgency," with the help of cyber security experts (the subjects of the survey). Why would the majority of cyber security practitioners argue for such expensive, expansive, and urgent measures?

The second group, from the world of academia and policy, was examined through a survey run by William and Mary University in collaboration with Notre Dame University. A sample of academics from US universities was asked, "What are the top foreign policy problems facing the United States?" They were pitted against practitioners within the US government who work within the national security apparatus.[44] Academics deemed cyber security the least pressing foreign policy problem, with only 8 percent suggesting it is a top problem. This falls right behind the fear of oil reliance (12 percent) and global poverty (12 percent). Policymakers rank cyber security nearly as low as academics. Seventeen percent see it as a foreign policy problem, right above the issue of climate change (8 percent), global poverty (3 percent), and oil reliance (4 percent). Though the experts with the most to gain monetarily predict a doomsday scenario, the experts who look at cyber conflict from a different perspective are not quite ready to see the proliferation of the cyber industrial complex.

The real question is what does the public think about these actions? All the above polls survey the cyber security community, elites, and academics, but no one has surveyed the average citizen. Pollsters should be directed to investigate the impact of these cyber incidents on the average citizen's daily life and perceptions of the conflict. Cyber Gaza, #OpEgypt, the activities of the Syrian Electronic Army, and Red October are incidents ripe for examination.

The analyses of the three cases in this chapter have shown that the impacts on the targets of these non-state groups have been minimal. What can be said is that although these breaches of network security are troubling, they could have been prevented, or the success rates of the infiltrations could have been reduced. Spear phishing methods rely on human error, and the human elements must be made aware of the dangers of opening suspect e-mails, especially that by clicking links or opening attachments in these e-mails the entire network or domain of their organizations could be compromised by the hacktivists of Cyber Gaza, the Syrian Electronic Army, or those responsible for the Red October campaign. Non-state actors in cyberspace use the fifth domain in an attempt to level the playing field with their more powerful adversaries; however, they do so with little to no effect on changing the policies of these states.

## CONCLUSION

A telling aspect of the cyber domain is the fact that not many people are aware of the actual threats posed by these cyber infiltrations and the simple cyber hygiene procedures that can reduce the probability of secure networks from being infiltrated. The majority of the public use McAfee, Symantec, or Kaspersky as their personal computer's protection software, and when these companies publish reports about the dire need for more cyber security protocols and increased and expensive firewall protection, we will most certainly trust their opinions. There is plenty of money to be made on the protection of this twenty-first-century phenomenon, and the more successes these hackers have in infiltrating the networks of various governments and publics, the more money there is to be made from this fear of the unknown future. There is less money to be made on teaching proper cyber hygiene.

A consistent line of argument that we have made is that cyber powers are restrained from using cyber capabilities due to blowback dynamics, the fear of collateral damage, and the concern that cyber incidents will lead to escalation.[45] That leaves cyber terrorists and hackers as the dangerous parties in the cyber world since they do not operate under the same restraints. Yet, it seems clear that their capabilities are limited in that they can do little to impact a nation-state with its considerable resources and systems designed for resiliency. There is little that can be done to deter a non-state actor from initiating, since there often is no clear actor to hold responsible. However, the effectiveness of the tools of non-state actors to impact important national security targets is limited.

Cyber security firms propose that governments, corporations, and other private organizations continue to hire them to protect networks from these future incidents. However, these protective measures are only as good as the last infiltration by these rogue cyber groups. They are programmed to protect against what is already known, and these malicious non-state cyber groups are able to adapt and infiltrate again under new methods. The feedback loop continues, where money is essentially thrown at the problem and the problem is not solved. Better logistics and human training, however, will be more effective. If human error within the victimized networks is the main source of the problem, then this is the problem that must be focused on and corrected.

Overall, we argue that the impact of cyber actions has so far been minimal. Even the oft-repeated fear of cyber terrorism is muted once we dive into the real dynamics of these incidents. Most cyber actions seem toothless. This is a very positive result of our analysis, but what next? The goal should be to enfranchise these findings into a system of permanent norms that govern how cyber technology is used in the foreign policy domain. The next chapter will explore the norms, ethics, and legal reactions and framework of the problem of cyber security.

## CHAPTER 8

# Cyber Rules

*Encouraging a System of Justice and Proportionality*

*in Cyber Operations*

## INTRODUCTION

In 2013, China advocated a system of cyber rules in response to accusations of cyber operations originating from within the state. Chinese Foreign Minister Yang Jiechi noted that "China, a frequent target of cyber attacks, supports international regulations under the United Nations to keep the internet peaceful, free and secure. . . . The international community is closely connected through the Internet, therefore cyberspace needs rules and cooperation, not war."[1] Around the same time, the United States echoed the same concern when National Security Advisor Tom Donilon noted that dialogue is needed "to define acceptable norms of behavior in cyberspace."[2] While it is difficult to take both China and the United States at their word for this statement, given the plethora of evidence that they are the most active cyber states in the system, the issue of cyber rules is clearly one of the most pressing considerations in the system (Valeriano and Maness 2012).[3] What remains unclear is what sort of system of rules and norms needs to be institutionalized. How can this process even work given the lack of institutions, laws, and state jurisdiction over global cyber communications?

A perplexing finding in the cyber realm is the lack of serious demonstrated incidents and disputes among interstate competitors (Chapter 4), despite the worst-case scenarios promoted in the media. When operations are exhibited, they tend to be relatively low-level operations or probes, rather than full-scale cyber incidents with destructive purposes. Guitton (2013) notes that the rhetoric and spending on cyber projects do not match up with the demonstrated threat from the issue area, and our work advocates a similar outlook, backed by empirical evidence. The question we ask is how these findings can be propagated further to establish a normative system of governance in the cyber realm. Given the obvious need for cyber rules and the relative lack of cyber activity between states, how can these two points of information combine into a system of guidance?

As the concept of a "Just War" is related to restraint and proportionality in combat, what may be called justice in cyber combat would relate to the normative policy of restraint and proportionality in cyber operations in order to limit damage to civilians and critical, non-military systems. The concept of justice in cyberspace is likely the most promising avenue to explore to locate a system of cyber rules. This development is important in that it seeks to acknowledge the moral importance of consequences of action (Fixdal and Smith 1998: 287), a critical element left out of the cyber conflict debate.

In this chapter we seek to understand the current normative unpinning of cyber conflict and also extend these considerations from incubating ideas, or emerging norms, into action or rules. Understanding the nature of the cyber threat not only raises more questions about its relative non-use by states, but also the possible potential of a future dependency of the tactic in interstate relations. Cyber threats and actions are in some ways literally the least that a state can do in the international system, and in many ways these operations are similar to drone operations.

Cyber operations can be relatively cheap technologies to utilize, and the public reaction to these tactics is negligible when compared to direct attacks or economic sanctions, as we demonstrated in Chapter 5. Therefore, how can these tactics be further minimized in the international system given these issues? How can the use of cyber tactics become entrenched as taboo in order to keep the tactic from proliferating in the future? Here we shift from an empirical investigation to a normative investigation given our findings throughout this volume.

Cyber offensive operations are dangerous technologies in that the potential for societal damage is great. Even in developing societies, the Internet and other associated forms of connectivity have become ubiquitous. The goal would be to push current observations of the limited usage of the tactic to a standard policy outcome. To this end we will examine the shape of the Just War tradition and its application to cyber conflict norms. The notion of cyber conflict as taboo will be developed in order to establish a set of normative best practices for states to follow during the course of cyber operations in the future.

This work is not an ethical reflection on cyber conflict or a direct application of the Just War ideals. Rather than utilizing the Just War tradition to be critical about the use of the technology in the past, we will use the tradition to advocate a system of guidelines, as opposed to a system of moral guidance. The hope is that we might be able to help prevent the potential horrors of cyber conflict and keep the worst-case scenarios in the realm of imagination, rather than reality, by considering the normative implications of such actions.

As covered throughout this volume, one reason that cyber interactions occur is because of vulnerabilities in the target. When the information sought is open for all to access through relatively easy and cheap techniques, the danger of cyber operations becomes pressing. This process also notes that cyber operations that do occur generally fall within the domain of espionage and other forms of spycraft, rather than war processes. Cyber operations to achieve a change in behavior rarely occur, but demonstrations of power and propaganda are frequent occurrences.

Cyber capabilities are a method of balancing against great powers. In some ways, cyber capabilities can equal the playing field and allow states like China and Russia to compete with the United States on equal footing. This idea is unrealistic: awakening the cyber capabilities of giants like the United States and the EU will only make the system more unequal, not more balanced. Nevertheless, this process does have implications for a system of justice in cyber conflict, as we will discuss. Asymmetries in the capabilities of cyber states can create opportunities to exploit vulnerabilities. Given that the impact of cyber operations has been fairly minimal and does not match the hype and hysteria in the media and from government officials, what is really at stake in this debate? Seldom used or not, cyber operations are a fact of international foreign policy interactions. They have not changed the shape of these interactions, but now they do play a role in everyday international considerations.

The *New York Times* reported, "a major cyberattack on the United States could cripple the country's infrastructure and economy, and . . . such attacks now pose the most dangerous immediate threat to the United States, even more pressing than an attack by global terrorist networks."[4] While empirics do not match this rhetoric, the statement was still made in the major US daily newspaper, and it was taken as a fact. What do these feelings about cyber conflict say about the actual process of cyber operations?

In the face of growing concerns about foreign cyber intrusions, the United States has made it very clear that it will respond with offensive cyber tactics of its own. The head of US Cyber command, General Keith Alexander, recently noted, "I would like to be clear that this team, this defend-the-nation team, is not a defensive team. This is an offensive team that the Defense Department would use to defend the nation if it were attacked in cyberspace. Thirteen of the teams that we're creating are for that mission alone."[5] While considering the offense, the United States also tries to make it clear that its main concern is defense.

The key consideration here is the ubiquity of the Internet and how much societies depend on communications for interaction, commerce, and information. Due to the nature of societal and Internet dependency, the cyber realm has been securitized (Hansen and Nissenbaum 2009: 1157), if not hypersecuritized. As the US Director of Intelligence James Clapper (2013: 1) notes, "We are in a major transformation because our critical infrastructures, economy, personal lives, and even basic understanding of—and interaction with—the world are becoming more intertwined with digital technologies and the Internet." With these developments comes the need to institute a set of standards of behavior (Clapper 2013: 1).

Without a sort of guidance provided by best practices in cyberspace, the community is open to control by the first adopters of the technology (Dunn-Cavelty 2008). The ones who used the tactic early are the ones that can set the norms. As mentioned before, many of the states focused on cyber tactics are utilizing the technology in the hope of leveling the playing field in terms of military power. Relative to material goods like tanks, ships, and missiles, cyber technologies are thought to be cheap and easy to attain.

There remains no global system of governance on the Internet and cyber community. The community of states can run the networks but cannot police and govern them in the instance of criminal and violent activities. The resulting question, then, is whether international law can work in cyberspace. This is unclear and is likely answered in the negative.[6] While many have made efforts to delineate a system of legality for cyber actions, much like in the domain of terrorism, these efforts seem to justify state-based actions after they happen. Or as Dipert (2010: 395) notes, international law does not even apply. Schmitt (2013: 5) supports this view by writing, "it is sometimes difficult to definitively conclude that any cyber-specific customary international law norm exists."

The related issue is that the laws of war remain more permissive than the morality of war and the language of the Just War tradition (Eberle 2012). We do have the Tallinn Manual (Schmitt 2013: 75) as a guide (its Rule 20 argues that international law applies to cyberspace), but the manual is really just a set of suggestions framed as rules to guide cyber behavior. While helpful, it is often contradictory, confusing, and it is not grounded in empirical social science.[7]

As mentioned in Chapter 6, one of the first prominent cyber conflicts was launched between Russia and Estonia. In 2007 the Estonian government removed the Soviet-era Bronze Soldier World War II monument from the central square of the capital of Tallinn. Russian "cyber patriots" responded in kind with a two-week barrage of cyber incidents that shut down government and private websites and networks. Many Estonians were unable to withdraw money at ATMs or access government services; this was painful, since Estonia is a cyber-dependent country. However, the overall effects of this dispute in cyberspace did not do much lasting damage, and the Estonians looked to the international forum for help. The result of this conflict was the international shaming of Russia, with Estonia being held up as the paradigm for restraint in cyber activities.

Since then, Estonia has taken the lead in the cyber realm to facilitate the communication of ideas and ideals best suited to limiting the worst practices in the cyber realm. It has been the host of the NATO-sponsored International Conference on Cyber Conflict five times since the 2007 dispute. Estonia often hosts international conferences on the dynamics of cyber conflict, and the NATO Cooperative Cyber Defense Center of Excellence is in Tallinn. Estonia survived a massive cyber invasion and has managed to thrive in the industry since. Yet we still need to move toward outlining a system of practices and norms.

What cyber norms and governance have been created? Norm cascades (Finnemore and Sikkink 1998) and the example of Estonia are important here. Norm cascades happen when there is a tipping point where most states normalize the expected behavior in the international system, and cyber norms should be no different. The states that will push for cyber norms are those that likely have been abused by the practice in the past. As noted, even the United States and China have called for systems of normative guidance. The central motivation for many of these actions is to avoid harm to civilians and critical infrastructure.

As norms are transmitted and become accepted by both early adopters and other interested parties, this system of cyber governance can be transformed into a community that believes in the ideal of the fair use of cyber tactics, or what can be called *just cyber war*. Based on early formulations by Augustine and Thomas Aquinas, the idea of Just War considers notions such as proportionality, limiting damage done to civilians, and the use of tactics as a last resort to create a community beholden to ideas of justice and restraint.

This chapter analyzes the nature of justice in cyber operations to predict and stimulate notions of justice during cyber warfare. The potential for harm is great through the use of cyber tactics. Limiting damage and allowing for the tactic to be used against appropriate actors that do not include civilians and civil projects is an important task of the cyber community. Generally, ethical considerations come about after an incident or dispute activates a state's moral responsibility (Bulley 2010: 446). The goal here is to not wait for a major cyber incident to display destructive intent but to limit the actions before they occur. A system of justice in cyber operations can be created based on the Just War tradition and the current set of norms and taboos in operation. We need more than rules; we need guidelines that consider both the ethical, moral, and strategic uses of the technology in the future.

## THE JUST WAR DEBATE

The Just War tradition considers the moral application of force and its limitations. We call it a tradition in that it is not a clear theory that leads to predictions and hypotheses, but more accurately is a set of moral guidelines for action or a set of prescriptions utilized to be critical of past and current uses of force. In this occasion, cyber conflict is considered an act of force, even if it is unconventional. Cyber conflict is not necessarily an act of war, but it can be seen as such.

The basics of the Just War tradition are outlined as the following: "1) to protect the innocent from unjust attack, 2) to restore the rights wrongfully denied, 3) to reestablish an order necessary for decent human existence" (Potter 1973: 8). In short, violence is justified when it is done on behalf of a public good in order to restore rather than destroy. Conflict should be waged under the right intentions so that the just cause motive is not used a pretext for personal aggrandizement in the form of territory or resources (Heinze and Steele 2009: 5).

Augustine of Hippo is the forebear of the tradition for many. His consideration was the application of self-defense and force, given the word of God. He thought self-defense was beyond the scope of justice, as he would rather suffer death than inflict harm (Potter 1973: 9). When an innocent enters the equation, it is then therefore acceptable to defend the innocents as charity, and then one may be justified in inflicting violence. If an innocent is harmed, the evil done requires a penalty that might include force, given the moral choices made bare by the situation.

St. Thomas Aquinas, in his book Summa Theologica, was very specific on the conditions he viewed as necessary for a Just War. There must be a ruler, who has the authority to conduct a war, and a just cause, where Augustine's notion of war to avenge injuries is noted; the final requirement is that the war must be initiated by those who have the right intention, which was for him to achieve good and avoid evil (Aquinas 1988: 64–65).

Aquinas further notes that actions taken in self-defense are only justified if made proportionate to the force being used in the first place, since the action can become illicit and evil (Aquinas 1988: 70; see also Waltzer 1977: 129). The concepts of proportionality, authority, and a just cause will be critical aspects of a system of justice in the cyber domain, as will the concern of non-combatant immunity during these operations—also called discrimination (Waltzer 1977: 138). One cannot harm a civilian in order to protect a civilian since this violates a notion of justice and discrimination of victims during the use of force. The other reason this is important is to limit violence. Proportionality of means is used to prohibit incidents that go beyond what is needed to achieve military goals (Heinze and Steele 2009: 6).

The community of nations is also an important consideration in the system of justice and war. As Potter (1973: 10) notes, "failure to intervene, the refusal to give all possible aid to a beleaguered victim may be viewed as the default of a moral obligation and a disservice to the nascent community of nations." In this instance, the innocents or victims may in fact be the entire community of states in the system. As Heinze and Steele (2009: 11) note, the utility of organizing conflict in its classical sense as between states has little utility in modern-day realities. Actions violating the given norms in the system might infringe on the rights of all, not just one, so a response may be in order to restore the system for the community rather than a particular state.

The Just War tradition has grown through the years, adding clauses and considerations through time. Important for our purposes are the notions of violence in the last resort, clear declarations of causes and aims of war, and the need for a reasonable chance of success for combat operations (Potter 1973: 13–14). Violence must be considered the last resort, when all other options have been explored. This is done in order to forestall violence to meet violence. The goal is to keep the cycle of violence from escalating unchecked. A declaration of the aims of war is important in order for the society under attack to know what factors may lead to the action and how they may right the wrong done. Finally, a violent action must have a reasonable chance of success; otherwise the action is futile and is likely to lead to needless death and suffering (Heinze and Steele 2009: 6).

The tradition can be helpful in uncovering the means and justifying action by states in the foreign policy realm. An obvious deficiency of the tradition is the concept of justice—for whom? Often the victors write the history and are able to restore order in their image. How do we know a wrong being undone is not a right from a different perspective? The insular nature of the Just War perspective must give us pause in its application. The community of states must be the ideal, not just the individual state.

Another problem is that war and violence remain a very unseemly means of restoring order. The question of the means justifying the ends always rears its head in ethics debates. As Potter (1973: 11) interjects, "war is clearly a clumsy, inefficient, unpredictable, wasteful, and hideous form of sanction, a very faulty instrument of enforcement." Can justice ever be done if the tactic to restore order is so reprehensible in the first place?

The Just War tradition is in a state of flux given the use of preemptive war after the 9/11 attacks on the United States. The United States and the British have challenged the legalist Just War perspective advocated by Waltzer (1977) and have pushed for a recast of the tradition in what might be considered a right to war (O'Driscoll 2008: 3). In some ways, all that remains of the tradition is the notion of combat in self-defense (O'Driscoll 2008: 3). Yet this framework is too limiting for our application in the realm of cyber combat.

The questions we ask are the following: Can these limitations be overcome? And can the Just War tradition be applied to the system of cyber conflict? Certainly this tradition offers a much clearer path of guidance than Clausewitz or Sun Tzu. Using these prior frameworks, war and violence will likely harm civilians. Therefore these considerations of justice should be taken into account.

A corresponding and resulting concern is whether violence is even really a consideration in the cyber debate. As Rid (2011) notes, there have been no deaths resulting from actions in cyberspace. Therefore, the analogy with war may have limited value. The problem with this line of logic is that while Rid is correct to note that deaths have not resulted, the cyber discourse remains troubling and violent. Notions of catastrophic violence remain the norm when policymakers speak of the dangers of cyber warfare; as such, cyber security remains in the domain of conflict and aggression. Whether this framework is analytically useful for strategy is a different consideration.

Cook (2010: 412), in responding to Dipert (2010: 401), notes that the concept of Just War can apply to cyber conflict, emphasizing that the problems of uncertainty about effects and attribution problems have been faced by other frameworks applying the Just War ideals. The possibility that physical violence can ensue means that the Just War concepts can be applied to this domain. Although the Just War framework does not provide an easy guide to cyber warfare, it remains the most promising aspect of considering what the rules of cyber action might be, once the parties are in a conflict situation. Given these considerations, it is then useful to examine the theory of restraint in cyber conflict and the current norms in operation.

## RESTRAINT AND TABOOS IN CYBER CONFLICT

As outlined in Chapter 3, the system of cyber operations is conducted under the premise of restraint. States are unlikely to utilize cyber weapons because of the potential for collateral damage, blowback, and replication.[8] States will be restrained from using massive cyber operations because of the potential for civilian harm. The Internet and cyberspace are not the domain of the military, but the domain of all. States also operate under considerations of blowback, since cyber weapons can be unlimited in scope and scale when utilized by state actors. The potential for retaliatory harm is great given the domain of the weapon. Costs are also an important concern in that cyber weapons can be replicated and repurposed. A cyber weapon let out into the wild does not terminate and die off, rendered useless, but it can be reformed to meet new challenges and targets. For these reasons, restraint dominates in the cyber domain.

It seems clear that a taboo has developed around the use of certain weapons due to these notions of restraint. Nuclear weapons (Tannenwald 1999) and chemical weapons (Price 1995) are said to be weapons that are unthinkable to deploy in a modern combat operation. Yet the possibility that these sorts of weapons might be used exists, if there is a significant conflict between two core values or taboos (Dolan 2013). If the devastation confronted during an initial cyber operation is so great as to cause a massive loss of life, the taboo surrounding the use of this weapon in a combat or even civilian context could then be broken since the sacred nature of the taboo was violated in the first instance. Yet, as we have investigated in Chapter 4, this has not happened, and we argue that it is unlikely to happen.

This line of thinking is likely in operation for considerations of the use of drones. The idea would be that deaths to US military personal are more devastating than the loss of life to collateral damage in a drone operation. The taboo against warfare from a distance—with robots so to speak—is violated in the instance when the prime consideration is to prevent the loss of life in the attacking civilization. This promotes the general line of thought that the idea of justice in combat is more a function of moral justification for operations, rather than a set of guidelines for the use of force.

In the instance of drone combat, the consideration is that there is a trade-off between the losses of life to the attacking force given the potential loss of life in the targeted force. As with the Just War tradition in general, the primary value is associated with the referent state, rather than the state against which the operation is being conducted. In order to justify violence, the attacking state presents a scenario in which its citizens are threatened and likely to lose their life, and thus it must be justified to attack.

The problem with this line of thinking is that it presents us with a world made up of worst-case scenarios. By preparing for the worst, we ignore the everyday, the mundane, that makes up cyber operations (or drone operations). Cyber violence presents a similar choice in taboo violation in that infiltrating a secure network or a critical system is justified in order to harm the target society in response to an operation; and the remoteness and authentication issues associated with the tactic make it easier to violate the taboo in the first place.

Talk of a cyber Pearl Harbor is unhelpful and represents the typical straw man argument deployed by those who wish to promote the consideration of extremes. In a system of cyber justice, extreme choices play no realistic guidance for policy. Extremes will be confronted if they occur, but until there is a real danger of their occurrence, it is almost useless to plan for the worst and then act according to these plans. Any system of cyber operations must consider how cyber weapons have been used in the past, the impact of the use of cyber weapons on society in general, and the escalating potential of counter-cyber violence perpetrated by the targeted society.

For some (see Himma 2004 for a review), the Internet and connectivity have become a basic right. Violating this right brings about implications about the ethical lines being crossed in order to take action. These notions of rights and justice must be kept in mind in cyber operations. Protection of the state may be a right, but the higher community ideal of access and information may win out. For these reasons, rules and norms are vital in the cyber world.

## RULES AND NORMS IN CYBER CONFLICT

O'Driscoll (2008: 2) argues that the rules of the use of force were recast after the events of 9/11. A similar process may be ongoing in that the rules of force are being recast in light of technological developments. Drones and cyber combat present challenges to the norms and rules utilized by states to justify the acceptance of conflict in the system. This is the debate we dive into in relation to cyber operations.

Rules and norms can apply in cyberspace. To argue that this domain is so different that it defies normal concepts is a tenuous line of logic, given the constant technological changes that have always forced adaptation in society. Norms are standards of appropriate behavior for international actors. These actors are constrained from behaving outside these normative structures (Finnemore and Sikkink 1998). Rules are a different consideration in that they are considered the specific application of norms to particular situations (Cortell and Davis 1996). Cyber conflict is a particular situation to which existing international norms can be applied; the question is which ones and how they should be applied.

The clear question we have is how might a system of normative restraint and control be applied to the use of cyber combat? It seems evident that restraint is how cyber states are presently interacting in the system (Chapters 4 and 5). The remaining query is if this system will survive and endure as time goes on. As other states start to gain cyber capabilities, will they continue to practice the limited use of cyber tactics due to fears of collateral damage?

Chapter 4 demonstrates that norms are being applied in cyberspace. A way to demonstrate this is by observing the lack of evidence of severe cases found in recent history. There is no cyber conflict between states at war, such as Iraq and the United States. The Russian invasion of Georgia in 2008 was accompanied with a cyber operation, but these incidents were limited to simple defacements and denial of service methods and had no significant impact on the overall military strategy.[9] India and Pakistan are longtime rivals and have been engaged in military skirmishes for decades, yet their disputes in cyberspace have been limited. It seems that no country wants to open the "Pandora's box" of escalating cyber conflict, as fear of retaliation, either in cyberspace or by conventional means, seems to be restraining action.

The danger is that states are now seeking to expand their cyber offensive capabilities given the perceived success of Stuxnet and other operations (Peterson 2013). In the United States, the budget request in early 2013 was to jump from 900 cyber troops to 3,900, including offensive operations teams. The 2014 military personnel cuts, thus far, do not include these cyber troops. Various news organizations have been documenting China's use of offensive malware, and it has been suggested that in Russia recent legal moves to control cyberspace are really just attempts to control hackers and co-opt them for the state.[10]

The goal would then be to institutionalize the perspective that cyber weapons are a prohibited taboo, not to exceed the damage already initiated by states thus far. As Dolan (2013: 37) notes, taboos "are a special breed of socially constructed norms that, once internalized, make first use of these weapons odious and unthinkable." To encourage this perspective, data is useful in order to counter the hype of the current discourse. In the media and policy world, the idea is that cyber weapons are proliferating and escalating. While the use of the tactic is certainly increasing through time, there is no evidence that the practice is being adopted by new actors, that the practice is escalating in damage or capability, or that the escalation is not caused by vulnerabilities in the target rather than the will of the offender.

The way taboos can be institutionalized is if it is made clear that they violate the basic rules of action. The rules of war originate in the chivalrous code and the concepts of mutuality and consent in war (Waltzer 1977: 37). What is unclear is just what the rules of war may be, given the domain of cyber conflict. Certainly the Geneva Conventions are a critical system of governance for warfare, but it is unclear if these rules apply to the cyber community. The Tallinn Manual (Schmitt 2013) applies the current rules of warfare to cyber, but these are just suggestions and not a fact of international law. How can articles of war be enforced when no physical territory is captured, combatants do not meet each other with bullets but rather botnets, and potential prisoners of war will never be captured? In fact, the lack of demonstrated violence in terms of wounds and physical pain might suggest that cyber conflict is a nonviolent method of warfare. This concern extends the notion of nonviolence a bit too far, but it is useful to recognize that technological aides often change the strategic calculations and necessities of states. Examining what normative and rule-based considerations actors invoke when using the practice of cyber conflict might illuminate a system of cyber norms and rules for the entire system.

## THE POLICY DISCOURSE ON JUSTICE AND RESTRAINT IN CYBER CONFLICT: OLYMPIC GAMES AND THE UNITED STATES

For some, Stuxnet was a major cyber incident that represented the dawning of a new era.[11] The goal of the Olympic Games cyber operation was to present a setback to Iranian efforts to enrich uranium so as to forestall the need for direct attack against their nuclear weapons program. As a dispute that included a series of incidents, the Olympic Games demonstrated the complexity of cyber conflict in that the initiator needed to have advanced knowledge of control networks with Iran, to breach an air gap that cut off systems from public access, and to specifically target critical systems while making the operators think the system remained working as normal. It was an immensely complex operation that defied the capabilities of anyone but an advanced nation-state.

The resulting debate revolves around the level of seriousness attributed to the Stuxnet incident. Did it really damage Iranian systems enough to set back the program? We remain a bit skeptical in that the impact of Stuxnet seems minimal at best, as we have discussed in Chapter 6. While Iran had to replace a set of centrifuges, it is by no means clear that this was a serious setback, and evidence suggests they actually increased uranium enrichment. What is really interesting for our purposes is the internal debate in the White House about the nature and implications of the Stuxnet virus. David Sanger (2012) gives some hint of this in his book *Confront and Conceal.*

The original staging of the project was done during the Bush administration; even with its disregard for international norms in its operations in Iraq,

Afghanistan, and Pakistan (Shannon and Keller 2006), administration officials were careful to plan for a limited operation, targeting only nuclear facilities. It was noted that "much of it [time planning] spent with lawyers trying to make sure that the code they were writing did not violate the laws of armed conflict. The cyberattack had to be as accurate as the best guided missile—it couldn't take out hospitals or schools; it had to be focused on Iran's centrifuge plants" (Sanger 2012: 192). From the onset, the Stuxnet operation was a careful surgical strike that might follow the dictates of *jus in bello*.[12]

What is interesting about Stuxnet is how involved both Presidents Bush and Obama were in the operation. While George W. Bush was more concerned with the technical aspects of the program, according to Sanger's recounting, Obama was more focused on the implications of the incident. As Sanger (2012: 201) notes, "it's fair to say there wasn't a major strategic or tactical decision made without him [Obama]." This perspective follows the dictations of proper authority required in a Just War.

This dialogue also highlights an essential difference in application with cyber weapons; the lines between *jus ad bellum* and *jus in bello* are blurred since there is no real dividing line between actions prior to war and actions during war. Since cyber conflict is not a conventional form of warfare, there is no useful way to distinguish between what happens before a cyber operation and what happens during a cyber operation in the country launching the operation.

Sanger (2012) points out that Obama clearly noted the potential for collateral damage resulting from the incident, asking "what type of collateral damage might occur? If a cyberattack focused on compromising the power grid that supplied Natanz, as the Bush administration had contemplated, might it trigger some other, unanticipated harm to civilians?" (202). A corresponding issue was raised about the probability of retaliation through attacks on American troops, Israel, and Saudi oil facilities (Sanger 2012: 202), which might invoke the fear that civilians would eventually be the target if the United States chose to launch this sort of weapon.[13]

The fact that the Stuxnet code did get out into the wild and away from the Natanz plant is what makes cyber weapons so problematic and dangerous. It is difficult to control a weapon that can effectively spread anywhere, even if years of planning go into preventing this from happening. The unintended consequences of war remain a concern, even during the most precise technological versions of combat. The more advanced states can program in termination dates for their operations, but it is by no means a given that all states would do this if given a chance, or that this would even work to limit cyber violence. The unpredictable nature of cyber weapons makes it difficult to argue that they are the tools of ethical states. Stuxnet, for all the planning that went into it, was still an unpredictable operation. As Sanger (2012: 204) notes, "suddenly, the secret worm that the Americans and Israelis had invested millions of dollars and countless hours perfecting was showing up everywhere, where it could be picked apart . . . there was no question it was a fuck-up." Proportionality in combat requires the ability to control the weapons you unleash, at least in cyber operations where the considerations between what happens before a conflict and during the conflict are blurred.

Beyond Stuxnet, it is difficult to find any evidence of concern for proportionality and collateral damage in the cyber debate in the United States. Most of the discourse is focused on worst-case scenarios and the fear associated with cyber incidents rather than how the tactic should be used. The *International Strategy for Cyberspace*, released by the White House, notes that cyber incidents launched against the United States can result in retaliation given a set of conditions. "When warranted, the United States will respond to hostile acts in cyberspace as we would to any other threat to our country. . . . We reserve the right to use all necessary means—diplomatic, informational, military, and economic—as appropriate and consistent with applicable international law, in order to defend our Nation, our allies, our partners, and our interests" (White House 2011: 14). The strategy goes on to note that the state will exhaust all other options first and will only react in a manner consistent with its values. These are measured considerations, but the question is will these constraints be placed on operations?

The Department of State is a bit more specific in noting that the laws of war do apply in cyberspace and these actions must be governed by the concepts of *jus in bello* and *jus ad bellum*. As Harold Koh, legal advisor in the US Department of State notes, "developing common understandings about how these rules apply in the context of cyberactivities in armed conflict will promote stability in this area. That consensus-building work brings me to some questions and answers we have offered to our international partners to explain how both the law of going to war (jus ad bellum) and the laws that apply in the conducting of war (jus in bello) apply to cyberaction."[14]

In contrast to the *International Strategy for Cyberspace*, the Department of State remains a bit more nuanced about the use of cyber weapons. They note, "in the context of an armed conflict, the law of armed conflict applies to regulate the use of cyber tools in hostilities, just as it does other tools. The principles of necessity and proportionality limit uses of force in self-defense and would regulate what may constitute a lawful response under the circumstances."[15] Going further, it is noted that an understanding of the concept of proportionality denies the use of cyber tactics that could cause harm to civilians or civilian networks. "Parties to armed conflict must assess what the expected harm to civilians is likely to be, and weigh the risk of such collateral damage against the importance of the expected military advantage to be gained."[16]

Overall, we can see a concern for the limitation of cyber conflict, civilian harm, and the concept of proportionality in some aspects of the cyber conflict discussion. Others are not so measured and highlight the likelihood of armed responses to cyber action and worst-case scenarios. This discursive battle remains ongoing, and the question is just how much sway the norms of action and the concept of justice have in the cyber rules debate. Because of this, it remains prudent to outline a system of guidance for cyber operations given the dictations of the Just War tradition and prior discussions surrounding cyber actions.

## CONSTRUCTING GUIDELINES FOR CYBER JUSTICE

As with any taboo, a system of cyber justice where the use of the tactic is limited and restrained must be founded upon the notion that the tactic represents a stigma not to be violated (Price 1995). Since cyber conflict in the fifth domain is relatively new, stigmas resulting around the practice have not developed yet. It is only in the protective actions of Estonia and, more recently, statements by the United States and China that we have seen these practices pointed out for their unique nature and application beyond the normal bounds of foreign policy interactions. Even though cyber action is minimal, according to the data, it still remains that anything and everything are acceptable behavior between states and actors in the cyber realm. It has only been through individual countries' restraint that cyber operations have been so limited in impact and scope. Table 8.1 outlines a system of best practices for international cyber actors.

In order to avoid errors in moral and ethical applications, but also to provide an arrangement of rules, it is important to advocate a system of justice in cyber conflict that considers actions that violate the core of the Just War tradition as

*Table 8.1* GUIDELINES FOR CYBER JUSTICE AND AN INTERNATIONAL SYSTEM OF CYBER NORMS

1. Actors should only act in order to restore a right and to prevent further harm.
2. The key consideration for justice in cyber conflict is if a cyber incident was launched in order to forestall harm and with good intention.
3. A right restored should be a community right, not an individual right.
4. Avoiding collateral damage in cyberspace remains the highest condition prior to launching cyber operations.
5. There have been no deaths resulting from cyber actions, and this should remain the standard line by which operations are conducted.
6. The repercussions of the use of cyber tactics should be kept in mind at all times; the leader allowing the action should be held responsible.
7. The concept of proportionality applies not only to the means of the attack, but also to the impact of the attack.
8. The best method to control the escalation and proliferation of cyber technologies is to choose to not utilize them for offensive purposes, and also to choose to not respond to their use with conventional methods.
9. There is a need to move toward creating a global monitoring system to share in collective defense and punishment when cyber violations occur.

"red lines" never to be crossed. While some states might find it imperative to act in the national interest and without consideration of the wider international community, the consequences of such actions could be devastating. More important, when major powers act without consideration of the international community and create new norms of action, the consequences of their actions may come back to haunt them.

Norms are important in action, and are considerably more effective than benchmarks that might be created in the cyber world. Enfranchising a system of cyber norms would be an important step in limiting the worst abuses. A benefit would be the lack of necessary enforcement mechanisms since norms are enforced as shared standards of behavior, rather than through threats and formal reaction forces. Punishment comes from the community rather than individuals. What practices then must be promoted to keep the cyber conflict system from escalating?

According to the evidence presented, the United States is considerate in its use of cyber operations, at least to this point, and it now behooves us to examine what an optimal system of cyber justice might include. In relation to what is now considered the Just War tradition, the United States considers non-harm of civilians, the authority of the sovereign, and the continuation of legal norms in war important characteristics in cyber actions. Alternatively, it does not consider acting with proportionality, in the last resort, or acting preemptively as limitations to action in cyberspace, despite the rhetoric. The United States has acted preemptively, aggressively, and offensively, as have China, Russia, and most recently North Korea. The United States has acted with measured purpose, but not after all other options have been explored.

The consideration of violence as the last resort may not apply to cyber conflict. In some ways, cyber techniques could be the first option pursued since they are seen as less intensive than direct conventional violence. As Fixdal and Smith (1998: 303) note, the last resort criteria are not strictly chronological. A state can conduct actions in cyberspace while it negotiates further. The key point should be that dramatic actions that result in death should only be utilized as a last resort, but lower-level cyber operations could be permitted, if done with the right intentions or to "induce compliance," as the Tallinn Manual seems to imply (Schmitt 2013: 37). This suggests that a new, two-tiered system of combat operations is developing in which kinetic options are differentiated from non-kinetic uses of violence.

Given the consideration for the actual pace and magnitude for cyber operations, it seems critical to limit the worst practices in cyberspace, which are simply highlighted as offensive-preemptive or retaliatory actions, that do not consider the scope of the action and the potential for civilian harm. Other dangerous actions include operations that are not authorized by a responsible sovereign and actions that do not limit harm to civilians, such as the design of weapons that are able to replicate into civilian systems without time-sensitive cut points. Any of these actions could have dangerous repercussions for the state in question and for the international community.[17] The fear is that states will develop automated systems that design and implement cyber operations, and this should be a normative red line that cannot be crossed.[18]

If a cyber operation is conducted, it must be conducted under the consideration of the right intention, or avoidance of evil dictate in the Just War tradition. Actors should only act in order to restore a right, to prevent further harm, and without the goal of achieving any ends beyond the restoration of a right. What should remain clear is that cyber conflict is not akin to humanitarian intervention and the recent turn in the Just War tradition (O'Driscoll 2008: 16). Therefore restoring a right might be a tough condition to meet with a set of cyber rules influenced by the concept of a Just War.

The key condition for applying a Just War framework to cyber conflict is to ask if a cyber incident was launched in order to prevent further harm and with good intentions. An incident such as Stuxnet might be justified if the intention was to limit harm to civilians and individuals by a direct military attack that might have been warranted otherwise. Stuxnet likely remains the best of all the bad options and, as such, it could be said that the incident had positive intentions. There was just intent in the idea to limit actual harm through conventional military attacks. As O'Driscoll (2008: 17) notes, "this new weapons technology holds out the promise that the use of force might now be 'controlled' and 'humane' in its application." The problem, as we document, is that damage cannot be limited to military targets since cyber actions are unpredictable in nature.[19] This issue leads to problems with discrimination in conflict, which is a problem that would be made worse if cyber weapons become automated. There is no such thing as a safe cyber conflict.

The issues of a just cause for action and self-defense remain difficult to apply to cyber actions. As Dipert (2010: 395) notes, "a Just War Theory that abandoned or extensively modified the traditional understanding of casus belli would simply not be Just War Theory as we know it." Therefore, any consideration of Just War in cyberspace is modified and inconsistent with some tenets of the Just War ideal. Yet, there is some pushback to this idea, and we remain supportive of the idea that the conditions of the Just War tradition remain applicable in cyberspace.

Fixdal and Smith (1998: 306) make the case that under the context of humanitarian intervention, it might be unwarranted to view self-defense as the only possible just cause for the use of force. In some ways, cyber actions have the same problems. Eberle (2012) argues that the idea of a just cause for action has limited value in a cyber conflict situation. Supporting this idea is the notion that Heinze and Steele (2009: 8) advance in arguing that the just cause condition was at first used to punish wrongdoers but it "has since been legislated out of existence by positive international law." Yet, perceptions do matter, and a cyber response could be warranted under the just cause framework based on the notion of perceived injustice (Eberle 2012). We should still remain hesitant in using this framework; responding to the perceived slights of a cyber incident with conventional violence is a step too far.

The cyber incident perpetrated by Chinese agents on news organizations in 2012 and 2013 in response to negative stories about the new Chinese leader does not meet these characteristics.[20] Disputes such as the Russian operation on Estonia's Internet and banking systems are actions to deny a right, not restore a right. Therefore they go beyond the bounds of the Just War tradition and should be eliminated. There is no right intention here, no wrong being corrected or a just cause; there is only a wrong being done. Of course, as with the Just War tradition, perceptions of an action depend on the referent actor. If the actor perceives a wrong done, it may act with just purpose, but these insular views of the Just War tradition must be modified to reflect current realities. A right restored should be a community right, not an individual right.

Avoiding collateral damage in cyberspace remains the highest condition in cyber operations. The wider repercussions of cyber actions should limit the practice. Abuses in the domain will generally spread to non-military arenas. If this is even a possibility, the actions should be limited and punished. Civilian harm, in terms of critical systems or even information systems, is not a system of best practices that one would want to enfranchise.

As Rid (2011) notes, there have been no deaths resulting from cyber actions, and this should remain the standard line by which operations are conducted, especially in the realm of civilian harm. The idea that these incidents can impact civilian health services is reprehensible. This is a line no state should cross; yet there is even a debate about this, as the Tallinn Manual seems to suggest that it is permissible to use cyber actions against someone who has a pacemaker (Schmitt 2013: 144).[21] The positive view here is that, while these options might be possible logistically, they remain improbable in application—just as chemical and nuclear war remains beyond the realistic possibility in combat operations.

The concept of the Just War tradition considers the application of the use of force by a sovereign as an important concern. Some consider the need for a sovereign (or legitimate authority, in modern parlance) to be the representation of a constraint on force in a democratic system (Pattison 2008). More accurately, the suggestion that force be limited to the use of a legitimate authority is important in that someone can be held accountable for the use of the tactic and the potential failures if the plan backfires, as noted by President Obama in his consideration of the tactic. The repercussions of the use of cyber tactics need to be kept in mind in the application of the Just War tradition. Who exactly would be responsible if the tactic is used?

As Cook (2010: 416) notes, applications of the Just War framework apply to the effects of a response, not the debated methods of reply. In that way, it is important to consider asymmetries in cyber operations. Some states will utilize the tactic because they cannot hope to compete with material and conventional capabilities of their competitors, so they will attempt to punch above their weight by utilizing cyber tactics. This problem brings forward the notion of proportionality; no matter how small and incapable a state may be in conventional tactics, using disproportionate force in the fifth domain only incentivizes a conventional and massive response by the targeted state. Here, the concept of proportionality does not just apply to the means of the cyber incident or dispute, but also to considerations of the impact of the operation given potential imbalances. Punching above your weight with cyber operations only invites responses that cannot be controlled and likely will be argued as justifiable by the violated state. Given that Chapter 6 and 7 point out that these cyber operations are almost never successful, this frame of seeking to achieve more with limited operations seems even more ill advised.

A problem for future cyber operations is their unpredictability (Eberle 2012). As Fixdal and Smith (1998: 304) argue, proportionality is about the scale of the response. It behooves any state utilizing cyber technologies and seeking to level the playfield to remember that, despite any feeling of satisfaction in utilizing a tactic that is thought benign and in the domain of espionage, the receiving state may not choose to accept these perceptions and may utilize the full force of its arsenal to launch a retaliatory response, whether the scale of the operation was planned or not. The unintended consequences of war remain an apt issue in cyber conflict, as does the fog of cyber war. There is always an inherent unpredictability in conflict, and this seems to be even more the case in cyber conflict.

The best method to control the escalation and proliferation of cyber technologies is to choose to not utilize them for offensive purposes, but also to choose to not respond to their use with conventional methods. In following what have reportedly been Chinese incidents, the United States has not chosen to respond with cyber means (see Chapter 5), but with diplomatic measures—clearly making it known that it recognizes the source and intent of the operations. These actions serve as warnings and ways of preventing further escalation in the arena. Another idea promoted by Brenner (2013) is to respond to cyber incidents with low-level sanctions like denials of visas and financial restrictions to the technology sector. Responding to force with counter-force only brings about more of the same. Incentivizing a system of rules and norms in cyber practice often will mean stepping away from the brink and choosing a different path.

The final question is just who might monitor cyberspace? This is the real dangerous point in the debate since there is currently no one in the system who might take on this job. The United Nations remains stymied by infighting and inaction. Regional organizations like the European Union or NATO remain vested in the interests of the West (despite global outlooks) and incapable of monitoring the entire globe. The architecture of the Internet is fractured and disparate.

We would suggest a new institution that combines the abilities of the International Atomic Energy Agency (IAEA) with the Antarctic Treaty System.

The IAEA has been accused of acting in the interests of the West, but these concerns have been muted by non-Western leadership that has demonstrated real impartiality in action. A similar agency to monitor conflict in cyberspace might be warranted. Likewise, a treaty system like the Antarctic Treaty, signed in 1961, which declared Antarctica the domain of science and off limits to the desires of nations and militaries for abuse, remains the standard by which other treaties limiting action might be built. The Internet and digital communications should be the domain of science, industry, and education—not conflict and war.

To that end, we also need to establish transparency in cyber actions. We cannot protect and constrain if information about the incidents, methods, and perpetrators remains secret. This book has been an effort in transparency, but through our own coding and data collection methods. The best practice would be to set up a monitoring function through some intergovernmental organization that monitors cyber incidents as they happen and produces reports after the event. Healey (2013: 17) calls on the military and intelligence community in the United States to declassify information on cyber conflicts. We need to move toward creating a global monitoring system to share in collective defense and punishment when these violations occur.

## CONCLUSIONS AND FUTURE DIRECTIONS

There is always an inherent contradiction at work when one considers ethics and justice in international affairs. As Bulley (2010: 452) notes, there is morality on both sides of the biblical Abraham's decision: the choice to act under God's orders comes counter to the need to protect the son. In some ways, cyber considerations suffer the same moral dilemma. To act with offensive intent in cyberspace might ensure the protection of the state and citizens, but might it be better to not violate the realm of cyberspace and keep this arena from being further securitized? This is the undesirable question that leaders must face in the consideration of cyber operations, a dilemma which Obama faced and tried to control. Yet, the digital realm tends to defy controls and plans; it replicates and behaves in ways that cannot be predicted. With this to consider, it is best to avoid utilizing cyberspace for foreign policy ends and means. If the goal of the state and actors is to reduce tragedy (Brown 2007), the cyber realm should be held sacred and off limits.

Rather than updating the tradition of what a Just War is in the context of modern conflict, as Pattison (2008) seeks to do, we consider how justice in cyber conflict might be administered in light of how the tactic has and will be used in the future. For some, cyber dependence brings vulnerability (Clarke and Knake 2010). For us, cyber interactions bring new possibilities. The rush to securitize the cyber issue is distressing in that it can cut off avenues of connections and growth that otherwise might be beneficial for society. It is for that reason that a series of guidelines that consider moral and ethical actions needs to be developed.

It seems clear that President Obama did not want to violate the taboo against the use of cyber operations for fear of collateral damage. Continuing developments suggest a push, on one hand, to maintain the legality of all cyber actions, but also, on the other hand, to prepare for offensive cyber actions made with pre-emptive intent.[22] Skirting this line seems nearly impossible; offensive doctrines in cyberspace cannot maintain a standard of justice unless there is a clear and present evidence of a direct imminent incident.

Using evidence and a reflection on how the Just War tradition might be applied to cyber conflict, we have outlined a system of best practices in cyberspace. These include restricting and banning offensive-preemptive actions in cyberspace, as they lack the just cause condition. The highest condition has to be the consideration of discrimination, or non-harm of civilians. Authority of the sovereign is important in that a leader needs to first contemplate the consequences and means of action, but also to claim responsibility when actions trigger unpredictable responses. The state leader must also demand that the means of a cyber incident include non-replication into civilian systems.

If actions are to be taken with the just intention, then the operation must not be about retaliation, but rather about righting a wrong done and avoiding more destructive options. Responses should avoid collateral damage in terms of deaths to non-combatants, but also should restrict collateral damage to civilian infrastructure. The just cause condition can only be satisfied in the most grave and traumatic of attacks. It is therefore unlikely to be seen in cyber actions. If cyber actions are taken, they must be made with the right intent, to prevent future harm. Finally, proportionality needs to be considered in cyber operations. A cyber operation cannot be undertaken if it might exceed the initial slight. Incidents must be proportional to the offense or issue at stake.

The issue, then, is how these ideals can be communicated to others, or cascade in the normative language (Finnemore and Sikkink 1998). A corresponding concern is to recognize that one leader (Obama in this case) may not hold the same values as another leader. Only with the careful consideration of how cyber operations might be conducted, what the intent will be, and the goal of forestalling further violence might they be considered actions with a just intent. These are the cyber rules; they should not be violated under any circumstances because these are community, not individual, rights.

To keep a norm from being violated, there must be an emotional response to that violation (Dolan 2013). There is no doubt that if a cyber operation on critical systems was ever propagated that harmed civilians, the media would cover the violation to no end. The constraints invoked by a globalized Internet media culture could protect the system (the Internet) from ever being violated during conflict situations. Yet, as always, the concern is with who the target is. If the target is seen as a norm violator in the first place, and thus deserving of a just response to its violations, this system of norm governance will break down. It is for these reasons that institutions like the IAEA might be useful and required in a system of just rules for cyberspace. Norms can become the normal, the everyday, but they also remain ripe for violation by the few if there is no repercussion for violations. Since the advent of the idea of cyber war almost 25 years ago, the system has managed to act restrained and, accordingly, the question is dependent on the future.

## CHAPTER 9

# Conclusion

## CONNECTING EVIDENCE WITH REALITY

A continuing theme throughout this investigation of cyber conflict has been the importance of evidence. We need evidence and data in order to counter hype and bluster. Cyber conflict is obviously a developing and important issue for international security dialogue, yet we question the tone of this debate and its foundations. The media speak of cyber conflict as some sort of unknowable, even mystical, threat. Declarations such as this are typical: "cyberspace is now a battlespace. But it's a battlespace you cannot see, and whose engagements are rarely deduced or described publicly until long after the fact, like events in distant galaxies."[1] These shallow perspectives should be a thing of the past, since they are covered in trite inflections meant to scare the reader and to provoke reactions by governments. We can and do know the contours of the cyber battlespace, and the cyber threat can be met with a measured and proportional response that does not provoke overreaction. That should be a goal and a lesson from this research. Cyber conflict is an international issue, but overreactions to the threat the domain poses can serve to escalate the issue further, and cyber war predictions could become a reality. This volume uses theory and evidence to possibly pave a way out of these escalating scenarios.

This volume has demonstrated that the major lines of conventional wisdom are mostly incorrect. Cyber conflict has not changed how states operate, it has not led to a revolution in military affairs, and the fears associated with the tactic are overblown. Instead, we advocate a more measured response to the issue of cyber security. Protection is important, but protection begins at home. Many of the steps needed to prevent cyber conflict can be taken by the state and individuals through simple processes focused on ensuring internal security, basic computer hygiene practices, and logical network security protocols. The resilience-based strategies are also likely a prudent response to cyber threats.

The debate over the vast span of the United States' National Security Agency's data collection program is indicative of problems in this realm when we securitize cyberspace.[2] While many cited the need for oversight or were aghast at the level of internal monitoring the organization committed, few noticed that the main issue might be that the NSA now has a searchable database of American computer usage and phone habits.[3] The danger is not so much in what the NSA is doing, but in how it is collecting information and who might have access to it. The agency perhaps created the biggest national security computer target in history through its efforts to ensure the safety of Americans from terrorist threats. This demonstrates that often, in cyberspace, we are our own worst enemies. Many of the targets that become incentives for international security organizations are low-hanging fruits that foreign governments cannot help but go after. The errors are often located in weaknesses in internal security practices; the initiator can hardly be blamed for finding such obvious targets appealing.

This leads to another issue that we raise throughout this volume: the need for the settlement of the root causes of conflict. Cyber conflicts are not disconnected from the normal international relations policy sphere. International cyber operations are directly connected to the long history of interactions between states. Traditional security rivals extend to cyberspace. Ignoring this process misses the root causes of cyber conflicts and instead commits the error of focusing on the tactic rather than the fundamental issues of disagreement between states.

The good news is that, so far, cyber conflicts have not occurred at the rate the media and policy pundits would have us believe. Evidence for severe operations that would change how international interactions are conducted is lacking at this point. Here, we will review the main terms and themes of this volume, our theory, and our findings, and finally, we will conclude with some policy advice and future considerations for the cyber security debate.

## WHAT IS CYBER CONFLICT, AGAIN?

Key questions asked throughout this volume concern the definition of cyber conflict and the implications of cyber actions in the international realm. For our purposes, cyber conflict is the use of computational technologies in cyberspace for malevolent and destructive purposes in order to impact, change, or modify diplomatic and military interactions between entities. Since this work is focused on the realm of international relations, cyber actions must be state-to-state or state-to-entity interactions in order for our theories and ideas to have leverage over the questions at the heart of this work. The initiator or the target must be state-based for our theories to apply.

Cyber conflict will have the highest probability of occurring among rival states. Instead of analyzing cyber conflict and its possibilities for all states in the international system, we limit our analysis to the most conflict-prone states that are identified as rivals. Rivals are more likely to involve themselves in escalated crises, military skirmishes, and even war (Diehl and Goertz 2000; Thompson 2001). It would be very strange to consider the use of cyber actions in non-rival states. We find that there are no other cases that need to be included beyond the few we that have already added (China-India, Russia-Estonia), since cyber conflict is truly confined to rivals. Therefore, if cyber conflict is to occur, it is most likely to be a tactic for rivals over other pairs of states. Cyber incidents and disputes have been launched by rivals, albeit at a very minimal rate over our 11-year span of investigation. The severity of these incidents is also an important question, and here we have presented evidence that suggests that most cyber incidents are low-level operations.

To be clear about our usage of terms, we have relied on the terms of *cyber incident* and *cyber dispute* to distinguish them from the overused term *cyber attack*. It is unclear what exactly a cyber attack is, since it now seems to mean everything from a Twitter hack to a full-scale government operation. Instead, we use the term *cyber incidents*, which are isolated operations launched against states with a specific purpose and that last a matter of hours, days, or weeks. Cyber incidents usually consist of a specific target or infrastructure of a state. Examples such as Ghost Net and Titan Rain are incidents involved in the ongoing theft operation that China is engaging with the United States, and they are part of an overarching cyber dispute.

Cyber disputes are larger campaigns in cyberspace, launched against states that can contain one or several incidents. Disputes usually have a higher purpose and goal for the initiating state. These can last from a day to months or even years. Cyber disputes, if prolonged, have the ability to escalate tensions among rivals when the response to these actions enters the realm of power politics. China has been in an espionage dispute with the United States for the entire span of our 2001–2011 dataset time period. The Russia-Estonia cyber dispute, on the other hand, in 2007 lasted for only couple of weeks.

There are four basic categories of methods that rival states can use against each other. Methods of cyber conflict utilized by states can be termed *cyber weapons*. Vandalism defaces websites and pages with SQL injection of coding that usually produces a negative view or propagandist message on the target site. Images that degrade the target's moral or national identity usually result from these methods. These are used for propagandist campaigns and are at a very low level of severity. Denial of service methods flood particular websites as hackers control hundreds upon thousands of remotely accessed computers known as "botnets" or "zombies." Websites are effectively inaccessible and are shut down for a matter of hours, days, or weeks due to the flood of information requests, which makes the websites inoperable. These usually have psychological effects and can evoke negative responses from target states and can, surprisingly, escalate tensions between states. Intrusions, more commonly known as Trojans, Trapdoors, or Backdoors, are remotely injected software that are benign at first and then become malicious after intruding upon a network. Theft operations or cyber espionage is usually carried out through intrusion methods. This is the most commonly used method for Chinese hackers. Infiltrations include logic bombs, worms, viruses, packet sniffers, and keystroke logging and can be some of the most sophisticated cyber weapons, which can inflict lasting damage on states. Advanced persistent threats (APTs) are targeted types of malware that can either come in intrusion or infiltration form, and can surgically seek out what they are intended to destroy, steal, or erase. They are the most sophisticated of cyber weapons. These are the methods that can do the most damage and can lead down the road to an actual cyber "war." However, we see restraint being the norm, and escalation seems to be limited in cyber conflict—at least thus far.

## RESTRAINT AND REGIONALISM IN CYBERSPACE

We developed our theory of cyber engagement fully in Chapter 3. The argument considers that cyber restraint is expected to dominate cyber interactions and should be predictive of future cyber operations. States will restrain themselves from crossing the "red lines" of cyber conflict because of the high operational and normative cost associated with these operations. They will not shut down military networks, knock out power grids, or black out Wall Street; the fear of blowback and retaliation not only in cyberspace, but by conventional means as well, is too great. States will also avoid these actions because of fears of collateral damage and infecting the rest of the Internet. Actions taken in cyberspace tend to invade all aspects of cyberspace. Even when states take actions to keep operations in the realm of cyber, the operations tend to spread and proliferate in ways not predicted.

Escalated offensive capabilities will not be used because they could lead directly to war, civilian harm, and economic retaliation, which would then escalate conflict among states. These tactics would spread the conflict from the cyber realm to conventional conflict. Therefore, restraint is what we expect to find when we examine cyber conflict among states. States will do what they believe they can get away with and then will go no further. Restraint is the outcome we expect to see among states, while the process we expect to see at work is what we term *cyber straitjacketing*.

The low level and limited amount of cyber conflict we do observe will mostly be between regional rivals, an unexpected result given the global reach of cyber technologies. Cyber regionalism is the assertion that most rival interactions in cyberspace will have a regional context, usually tied to territorial issues and other traditional issues between regional actors. However, because cyber conflict is restrained, these cyber incidents and disputes will usually take the form of propaganda, vandalism, or inconvenient denial of service methods and will not escalate to militarized conflict solely because of cyber issues. Escalation, especially among regional rivals, has been prevented through restraint thus far. The danger is that if the use of cyber weapons becomes more mundane in the future, then escalation will become the natural reaction to incursions on the cyber front. The corresponding danger is the enfranchisement of offensive cyber weapons, which will escalate cyber arms races.

We also argue that regionalism will characterize many of the cyber disputes that do occur. Despite the ideal of a globalized technology that breaks down the geographical confines of conflict and moves states into cyberspace, regional issues still dominate the agenda for cyber rivals. Issues that start at the local level bleed into cyberspace. Most disputes will be characterized by regional interactions, with the exception of those perpetrated by some global powers that have global concerns.

Espionage is what we expect to find between rival states. Cyber espionage is defined as the use of dangerous and offensive intelligence measures in the cyber sphere of interactions. Conventional spying can be costly, both monetarily and politically. By using cyber weapons, primarily intrusions, states are able to steal sensitive information rather easily, especially if the target state leaves its networks and cyberspace vulnerable and unprotected. In many ways, it is the least a state can do. Espionage via cyber means is therefore to be expected, but the severity of the incidents will be limited.

## WHAT DO WE KNOW ABOUT CYBER OPERATIONS NOW?

### Basic Cyber Dynamics

This book is a project about evidence and facts; our work paints a very different picture when compared to much of the discourse from cyber security companies, the media, and analysts. While there are many who advocate a measured reaction to cyber threats, these voices are clouded out among the noise that is often presented without evidence. Chapter 4 supports our theories of cyber restraint, regionalism, and espionage with empirical analysis. We find that, of 126 pairs of states considered to be active rivals (Diehl and Goertz 2000; Thompson 2001), only 20 engage in cyber conflict. This is a 16 percent rate among the most disputatious pairs of states in the international system. Over the 2001–2011 time period analyzed, we found that only 111 cyber incidents within 45 overall cyber disputes have occurred. This makes cyber incidents and disputes very rare when compared to events such as terrorist attacks or even militarized interstate disputes (MIDs). For the same 20 pairs of states, there have been 590 times more terrorist attacks than cyber incidents and 40 times more MIDs over the same time period of 2001–2011 (Ghosn et al. 2004).[4]

Severity is the next important question: If the rate of cyber conflicts is low, what does this tell us about the impact and reach of such events? Might it not be, as Rid (2013: 29) points out, that most incidents are basically what malware experts term *low-hanging fruit*? This means that the incidents that are exhibited are simple heist-style operations, made possible by the vulnerability of the targets. We find that, out of a severity score of five, with five being the most severe and one being the most benign of cyber operations, the average severity score for all cyber incidents is 1.62 and for cyber disputes is 1.71. All of the above empirics indicate that there is strong evidence for restraint in cyberspace among rival states. States will only do what they think they can get away with, and will escalate no further.

We also find evidence for the contention that cyber conflict between states is not uniform; that is, there are different dynamics of cyber conflict between each pair of states. The incidents between China and the United States are different from those between Russia and Estonia. China's main purpose in initiating cyber incidents with the United States has been to steal information and military secrets. Russia was perplexed at the boldness of the Estonian relocation of a Soviet war memorial and wanted to punish the tiny Baltic country. Not all cyber conflicts are created equal. China is the most active state in cyber conflict and also does most of the initiating with its various rivals. The United States is the second most active state in cyberspace and is the most targeted state. For the most part, the United States, although one of the most offensively capable states in cyberspace, has restrained itself from retaliation and escalation with those that infiltrate its networks. The global hegemon, with its power and influence, has yet to open the cyber "Pandora's box." Even during combat operations, the United States fails to use its cyber capabilities. More perplexing is the restraint given to targeting terrorist banking networks (Clarke and Knake 2010), likely due to the knock-on effects in civilian banking systems.

The most severe cyber disputes we found are those intended to change the foreign policy behavior of the state, infiltrate a critical infrastructure, or compromise the networks of states' military apparatuses. The Olympic Games operation against Iran's nuclear weapons program, the Russian infiltration of the United States' Eastern Seaboard Power Grid, and the Chinese theft operations against the American, Japanese, and Indian militaries are the disputes we found to be the most severe, with the highest probability of escalation. These incidents represent the most states have done to each other in cyberspace and, although worrisome, there has been no escalation in terms of the basic rate at which the tactic has been used, nor have any disputes escalated in 2012 or 2013. In order for this trend to continue, the restraint mechanisms in place need to evolve into a system of norms to which all states will adhere. We are witnessing the birth of a global system of cyber restraint; whether this becomes a stable trend is the remaining question.

Besides the dyads containing the United States, cyber conflict between rivals tends to have a regional tone. East Asia, South Asia, the Middle East, and the post-Soviet space are where we find evidence for cyber regionalism. These are rivals in the regions that have unsettled territorial or policy disputes. Cyberspace is where they vent some of their frustrations and seek to achieve a better position given the regional hierarchy and dyadic considerations. However, cyber conflict usually does not escalate beyond propaganda-type exchanges, or nuisances, disruptive in the regional subsystem. We do not see evidence of cyber incidents or disputes between rivals severe enough to evoke a conventional military or economic response. Therefore, a mode of conflict that can achieve global reach in a matter of seconds is relegated to specific actors, such as the great powers. For now, cyber interactions appear to be dictated by regional considerations.

Cyber espionage is present between rivals. This is hardly surprising because we assert that cyberspace is just the newest forum for one of the oldest professions in the world: spycraft. China is the state that does the most spying in cyberspace, with the United States being its favorite target—not that the United States is guiltless, given the revelations of the NSA's activities.

China is a rising power that cannot challenge the status quo superpower militarily (at least not yet); therefore, it bridges this perceived power gap by gaining the advantage in cyberspace. There is pressure on the state to achieve its economic dream, and one way of achieving this is to utilize cyber tools to steal information. China also engages in cyber espionage with other powers such as Japan and India. Retaliation against China has yet to be exhibited, evoking more confirmation that cyber restraint is at work. During a summit between China and the United States in June 2013, the United States formally raised the issue of Chinese spycraft for the first time; yet the way they couched the issue was that China needs to get its hackers under control. The discourse was not that spycraft was a state-sponsored problem, but that it was a criminal issue in the economic sector. Restraint by China needs to be promoted by the international community, so that China one day does not go too far and open up the entire international community to the dangers of cyber escalation. China needs to be checked by regional and global powers, but as of yet, no one seems willing to cross this threshold, at least formally.

## Cyber Events and Foreign Policy

The next critical question we ask relates to how rival states react, in terms of foreign policy, when their networks are infiltrated. Chapter 5 uncovers the answers to these questions. Due to the restraint mechanisms in place, we expect cyber incidents and disputes launched on target states to have little to no effect on the relations between rivals. The results of our data analysis generally support this assertion. Neither cyber incidents nor disputes have a significant impact on foreign policy interactions between the 20 pairs of states in our sample of active cyber rivals—thereby increasing support for our claim of cyber restraint in the international system of states.

However, there are some cyber weapons or methods used by states that evoke negative and significant foreign policy responses. One such tactic is denial of service (DDoS). This is surprising due to the low level of sophistication used to implement these methods, as well as their insignificance in terms of lasting physical damage to target states. What DDoS methods can do is affect a large portion of a target's population; this makes the execution of such methods high-profile events, even creating psychological effects. Governments are forced to react and to respond to these methods publicly and negatively, with scorn for the initiating state. This process is similar to naming and shaming in the human rights field (Murdie 2011). We find the same dynamics for disputes involving DDoS and vandalism methods. Disputes involving private and non-military government networks as the targets also evoke negative foreign policy responses. This is because most of these targeted incidents involve denial of service methods and are more public, requiring state governments to react for their constituents.

We now know that cyber incidents that are intended to change state behavior also evoke negative and significant foreign policy responses. Attempting to coerce a government to do something it does not want to do will evoke a negative response most of the time. Even in cyberspace, where we find restraint dynamics and low-level incidents, states do not like being told how to conduct their foreign policy.

Our cyber regionalism hypothesis finds further support with a fixed effects panel regression that we ran in relation to weekly events data in Chapter 5. Regional rivals use cyber incidents and disputes to send messages to their adversaries, yet they stop short of escalation to more conventional forms of conflict (military or economic). Another implication of cyber regionalism, especially in East Asia, is that the United States still holds sway over the countries of this region; therefore rivals who may be allied with the Americans have found that cyberspace is the perfect forum to vent frustrations with each other without upsetting the superpower too much. Japan and South Korea are examples of this; they are close allies of the United States yet have much animosity toward each other.

Looking at cyber conflict at the dyadic level in our weekly events investigation, we found that the United States responds with negative and significant foreign policy after it is the victim of a cyber incident or dispute. The one exception is China, against whom the United States does not react. Disputes initiated by Iran, Syria, North Korea, and Russia have a negative effect on their relations with the United States. However, cyber incidents and disputes originating from China and infiltrating American and Japanese cyberspace lead to more cordial and positive foreign policy responses.

## Case Study Evidence

China is the most aggressive user of cyber tactics in the international system; by reacting positively, the status quo powers may be trying to reign China in and appease it into joining a normative system of self-restraint for all states that have cyber capabilities. For example, Japan is a regional rival of China and does not want to escalate tensions with it in the fifth domain. The United States has shown great restraint itself, as it is the most offensively cyber-capable state in the world, and has not, with the exception of Iran, used its power and advantages against China. Instead, it raises its issues diplomatically. It is trying to lead by example in order to get China to cease its more frequent cyber activity.

Diving deeper into the specific implications of our work, Chapter 6 uncovers the dynamics and realities of some of the recent and heavily covered state-based cyber incidents in the international system: the Bronze Soldier, Stuxnet, and Shamoon. These were highly organized malicious incidents that did create chaos within the targeted states, but the severity and long-term impacts of the actions were negligible. Estonia is now a leader in the cyber security policy forum in the West, and far from Moscow's sphere of influence. Iran continued to enrich uranium after Stuxnet infected its networks, undeterred by the setbacks that the worm created. Finally, Saudi Arabia, a staunch supporter of the Iranian oil embargo, continued this support after the Shamoon incident infected its prize corporation, the oil conglomerate Aramco.

Chapter 7 looks at three high-profile cyber actions by non-state actors: Cyber Gaza, incidents perpetrated by the Syrian Electronic Army, and the multi-target espionage campaign, Red October. We found that these non-state actors have used the cyber domain to wreak havoc on their more powerful state-based adversaries. As these actors are no match for the conventional military capabilities of their enemies, they instead lash out in the form of vandalism, DDoS, and intrusive methods, where the primary side effect of their actions is confusion and fear in the target governments and populations. However, as with the incidents covered in Chapter 6, the long-term effects of these actions are few to nonexistent. Israel is still containing Hamas in Gaza, American media firms are still publishing stories on the Syrian civil conflict that paint the Assad regime as inhumane and tyrannical, and states affected by the Red October espionage are still hiding secrets.

### Cyber Norms and Justice

What should states do about the potential threats, realities, and possible blowback of cyber conflict escalation? Chapter 8 presents our framework for a normative system of cyber restraint based on the Just War tradition. Based on the need to protect the innocent, the consideration of proportional response for the cause of self-defense, and setting up rules and norms as to allow the peaceful coexistence of cyber states, we assert that the Just War standards are the most appropriate ones when it comes to the regulation of cyber conflict internationally.

In the future, states should restrain the use of cyber tactics since there is no guarantee that civilians will not be targeted in this domain. Furthermore, it is permissible for a state to utilize cyber tactics if its operation is predicated on pre-empting further violence and not utilizing conventional military tactics that can cause more deaths and destruction. We stress, however, that this should not give states a license to use cyber capabilities. Only a careful, measured, and legal use of the tactic is appropriate in the normative sense.

More important, the cyber domain should continue to maintain a taboo with regard to the militarization of the domain because of the repulsive implications that such militarization holds for a major cyber strike. For now, a massive cyber incident that would destroy civilian systems is beyond the bounds for cyber powers. But what of the future? We worry that when international legal standards can be applied to cyberspace, they will be applied at will and in specific situations, often to justify operations after they happen (Schmitt 2013). Possibly, the only way to overcome this obstacle is to set up international institutions to monitor the use of cyberspace. This has worked in that Antarctica has not been militarized. Space and nuclear weapons seem to be regulated; why can this not happen in cyberspace? This question alone requires its own book-length investigation.

## GRIEVANCES AND ISSUES

Issues are at the heart of international politics (Mansbach and Vasquez 1981; Vasquez 1993). Every international political interaction occurs under the cover of an issue driving the conflict, interaction, and point of contact. Without issues, there is no disagreement, only inertia in world politics. The main failing of the field of cyber security is the tendency to analyze the tactic of cyber operations devoid of its international political contexts. Contexts matter, and they color much of what happens in the cyber world.

One thing we have tried to make clear is that most cyber issues seem to be connected to international rivalries. While we did focus our investigation on rivals, we expanded the analysis a bit to include some cases that did not involve explicit rivals when warranted. Yet, these cases are few and far between. Only the Russia-Estonia and China-India pairs of states qualify. Again, rivals fight over issues at stake (Valeriano 2013; Mitchell and Thies 2012; Vasquez and Leskiw 2001). Cyber rivals interact the same way; all conflicts are driven by specific issues.

If cyber security is a problem for the international agenda, it then is a mistake to analyze this process devoid of the issues that drive cyber relationships. China and the United States interact repeatedly in the cyber realm because they have fundamental disagreements at stake. It is the same with Russia and the post-Soviet states it seeks to manage (Estonia, Ukraine, and Georgia). Most important, Israel and its regional antagonists have many issues at stake, and these issues have led to cyber interactions. In this volume we have predicted, explained, and examined the shape of cyber interactions. The focus in the field of cyber security on tactics rather than the root causes for the use of tactics is misguided. Just as the field of international relations cannot ignore cyber security, cyber security as a field needs the field of international relations in order to understand the complete picture of the domain under analysis.

The same issue of willful ignorance became a problem with nuclear doctrines and nuclear deterrence as a field. With all the efforts to apply an appropriate strategic doctrine to the nuclear question, the field as a whole skipped discussion of the sources of discontent between the Soviets and the Americans in favor of analyzing how to fight or prevent nuclear war through deterrence. By missing this step, we focus more on the tactic and technology than on the real driver of the relationship. Weapons, tactics, and technology have little applicability when removed from the political context. This has been the wisdom of Clausewitz (2007), and it still holds today during the digital era.

As we note here, cyber conflict is largely ineffective in getting states to change behavior. Cyber conflict and cyber espionage do not signal a step-change in the military analysis or international relations field. Some cyber interactions provoke a reaction; by and large, low-level operations are accepted parts of international interactions, but higher-level operations are forbidden. This suggests that cyber operations overall tend to be futile. Cyber operations often do not achieve their desired goals, they are difficult to implement, and they often provoke unintended reactions. Cyber operations often only achieve the desired goals when stealing technology is the primary objective. Yet, simply stealing technology is not an end to itself. The plans need to be developed, put into operation, and repeated on a massive scale. Certain states might rely on cyber espionage to gain a technological advantage, but so far it is unclear if this is actually the result of cyber operations in the long term.

Overall, we have not witnessed a grand change in state-to-state behavior with the coming of cyber conflict. It has not resulted in a revolution in military affairs. It has only led to the use of new technologies, a development that has been constant for humankind. The only difference is the expansion of targets and the speed of interactions. Targets are expanding in that non-physical sources of spoils are now on the table. An enemy can infiltrate a banking sector, personal information, or the basic machinery that controls our daily life. Yet, as we explain here, states will be restrained from doing so because of the nature of the weapon in use and the taboos against the violation of the civilian section in this arena. Cyber operations will be used, but they will generally be low-level operations more akin to propaganda and espionage rather than warfare.

The other change is the speed at which interactions in the diplomatic, military, and public diplomacy realm can occur. This is a new direction for international interactions, but it is not vastly different from the advent of the telegraph, telephone, and more recent digital interactions. Now that the battlefield can shift, some seem to have jumped to the conclusion that it will shift and that this will have enormous implications for the rest of the world. We suggest that this is not the case, and policymakers and the media need to be more restrained in their views on the subject. Some reality needs to be mixed with the excitement that our digital futures bring.

## DETERRENCE, DEFENSE, AND THE OFFENSE

The question we have avoided until now is strategy. What is the best method of cyber protection during the developing era of cyber power? We have skirted this question because it has normative implications that need empirical evaluation before speculation. Now that we have reviewed our findings, it seems appropriate that we examine the strategies and policy options available to states. There are basically three options for cyber-capable states: defense in terms of walls; offense in terms of maximizing cyber capabilities; and deterrence in the form of demonstrated capabilities in order to ward off intrusions.

The basic strategy advice is to avoid putting anything of value in accessible locations. No matter how secure your facility is, it can be breached. The obvious response to this is air gaps and other forms of protection that make it nearly impossible to be breached from external locations. The sole worry here is that intelligence will be compromised from the inside by double agents or wavering employees. Going further than basic protections to establish defensive walls and moats is unwarranted. Walls cut off the natural communications and connections inherent in digital interactions. Walls make it more difficult for operators to collaborate and engage the outside world. Paving over these pathways can limit the options of system makers. Inhibiting research and communications that come with digital connectivity would be a tragic consequence to protecting sensitive materials when there appears to be little risk of what might be called cyber war.

The Russian solution of utilizing typewriters rather than computers is also a step too far.[5] This form of protection is not a moat, but a cliff. Dropping off the digital cliff out of fear is a response that makes little sense given the possibilities opened through digital connections. The Russian option is basically a regression in the hopes of protection.

Offensive actions and preparations are not really the solution to the fear that pervades cyber conflict. These actions only set off the security dilemma. Since the cyber domain is public by policy, the types of strategies that states take in it are often very clear; a state cannot develop an offensive strategy without making it known to all active parties, who can then prepare for their own offense.[6] In the action of preparation, the fear inherent in the security dilemma is activated, pushing the witness side to take extreme actions to protect the state. The state that started building up the military then responds again in kind and escalates its own activities. This results in a series of overlapping security organizations and operations devoted to offensive actions. Their final scope is often far beyond the original intention. Although it can be suggested that cyber actions are simple choices from a cost-benefit standpoint, this ignores the iterative escalation of cyber actions in this context. Here we do not see simple offensive preparations, but offensive spirals that move the acquisition process far beyond the bounds from a cost-maximizing standpoint.

Deterrence is the art of making known what you want done, or not done, and making this option a reality through the threat of force. This is tricky, if not impossible, in the cyber world, as actions taken to demonstrate capabilities also make those capabilities useless and exposed. In cyber conflict, the demonstration of a weapon then makes that weapon open to all. States are also loath to use their cyber capabilities because they might harm civilians or skirt the mandate allowable in international law. So, it is tough to demonstrate capabilities when this process either makes the weapons useless or these weapons cannot be demonstrated because to do so would violate the basic norms and laws that govern state interaction. In the nuclear world, there could be a nuclear test that everyone could witness. This is nearly impossible in the cyber world because the very act of a test would give away your tactics to the entire world; or the test would really be effective against a functioning cyber community, not an abandoned island, and thus would be no longer a test but a real demonstration that requires a reaction.

There is a new and developing frame that might be termed *deception*. As Singer and Friedman (2014: 103) note, "a new debate has emerged in recent years, with some arguing that in lieu of playing a never-ending game of whack-a-mole, trying to track and then shut down all terrorists use of the Internet, it might be to let the groups stay." In this way, the system can watch and track potential initiators, following them back to their bases rather than wiping them out, along with any hope of catching a state red-handed.

The goal really should be resilience (Chittister and Haimes 2011). Defenses can always be breached, even internally, as Stuxnet and Edward Snowden have demonstrated. Offensive capabilities only start the security dilemma inherent in international politics. We have established throughout that deterrence is not in operation in cyberspace given the nature of the weapons. What is left then?

Resilience seems to be the only remaining option. Much like a large chain store that assumes a certain amount of shrinkage of merchandise, there must be some assumption that digital defenses will be breached. The most important and sensitive information needs to be locked away in locations not accessible; other forms of information can sometimes be allowed to be lost in favor of encouraging communications and collaborations. Walls and typewriters are a step too far in terms of protection. Our evidence presented in this volume clearly supports the contention that cyber actions are relatively low-level operations. Rational thinking about the costs and benefits in terms of losses is required here. Stepping back to the Stone Age of communications is not an effective means of dealing with digital threats of a low severity level and in fact exerts more costs than the potential losses to cyber incidents and disputes.

While resilience is advised, it is not exactly evident what constitutes resilience in operation. The EU follows a policy of cyber resilience, but it is less clear how exactly this is put into operation.[7] Rather than building cyber offensives, states would be advised to explore how reliance would work in the cyber world. It is truly the only option that maximizes strategies in the emerging cyber world, yet as of now, it is a process that has not been explored strategically.


## THE CYBER PRESENT

The American response to the cyber security dilemma seems to rely on offensive methods and to follow its conventional military doctrines. Power and force are typical solutions to any problem any Great Power has developed. The recent presidential directive that suggested that the United States "reserved the right to take anticipatory action against imminent threats" is indicative of this process.[8] It is worrying that it will provoke other states to do the same, possibly breaking the current cyber taboo.

In addition, while we have seen little evidence of the United States punishing states it sees as violators in cyberspace, the language it uses is dangerous and has the potential to escalate the conflict. Secretary of Defense Charles Hagel notes, "we were aware that many of these [cyber] attacks are emanating from China, probably the most insidious, dangerous, threat overall to this country, and there are lots of threats."[9] Instead, the state should first take simple steps to protect itself. Basic Internet safety is the watchword, not offensive capabilities. McGraw (2013: 111) makes the point that "cyber war, cyber espionage, and cyber crime all share the same root cause: our dependence on insecurity networked computer systems." Our systems are insecure because we make them this way. Updating browsers, air gapping systems that are critical, monitoring Internet traffic for upticks associated with botnets, and having flexible and dynamic systems that allow for traffic switching when one area becomes a problem are all important steps that need to be taken before there is a rush for the offense. Most important, the user must be trained in positive Internet habits.

The Flambé story brought up in the first chapter is typical of the stories one hears in the backrooms of cyber security gatherings. People do stupid things, such as clicking on links they know they should not, or sharing information in places they know might come back to haunt them. We must first return to the basics before we overreact. Much like a person who sets his wallet out on a table and leaves for an extended time and then cries foul when the wallet is taken, our cyber vulnerabilities are often of our making. When errors like that happen, it is prudent to not overreact and first look within the target for the vulnerabilities for which one is responsible. This is not to suggest that we live in a peaceful world in which a state does not take security seriously, it is only to suggest that security begins at home.

We must also be vigilant toward the cyber industrial complex. An interesting question often develops in the cyber security field: Why do we take the reports, statements, and leanings of Internet security professionals at face value? They are the ones who stand to gain the most from cyber threats. They will be hired to clean systems, develop monitoring programs, and root out worms. Of course, they are going to be the ones to hype the threat the most. Fifty-seven percent of security firm technological experts surveyed by McAfee and the Security and Defense Agenda believe that we are currently engaged in a cyber "arms race."[10] Forty-three percent of these people surveyed also believe that the worst-case scenarios we have been arguing against in this volume are inevitable.[11] Finally, 45 percent believe that cyber security is just as pressing an issue as border security in the United States.[12] Clearly there is money to be made if this threat is real; therefore keeping the hype alive for these firms is of great importance. Before we take the suggestions of a global cyber threat from cyber security professionals, it is first prudent to ask who is hyping this threat and why.

It is also critical that the lessons of Chapter 8 are taken to heart. For now, massive cyber operations that impact the civilian population are not allowed; they are taboo. They violate the sacred core of what we value and hold important—the immunity of non-combatants. Operations that would harm civilians are the red line the cyber community has yet to cross, and for now, seems unlikely to cross. But norms and taboos have to be upheld. The revulsion one feels from this area must hold in order to keep the taboo in operation. If the collective assumption becomes that these things will happen and we must prepare for them, then the norm becomes broken and the violations in cyberspace become part of the everyday, the typical, and the accepted. Institutions might help mitigate this issue, but it is also up to the policymakers, the media, and government officials to be mindful of this process and to be aware that, often, the threat is of their own making.

Finally, it should be clear that we fear what we cannot understand, predict, or control. Cyberspace contains all of these traits, and the fear provoked by this realm is therefore natural. Yet cooperation and trust are also natural in this domain. As Kallberg and Thuraisingham (2013) note, there is a remarkable amount of trust in the Internet. We have moved most banking, communications, and government interactions to the cyber realm with little consequence. Cyber conflict threatens this, but we still trust this system with our banking details, our personal connections, and communications. Every day we trust our computers with our most sacred and most private information. There is no reason to suggest that this process is wrong, provided simple things are done to protect the systems. We call here for a realistic evaluation of threats. A measured and careful study of what we fear, why, and how, is apt in all aspects of the security discourse. By understanding the nature of fear, we can understand the threats that motivate action.

Some call for intense cyber monitoring. This would protect states and corporations by ensuring that cyber actors are known and dealt with. Unfortunately (or fortunately), this approach is impossible. If you try to monitor everyone, you monitor no one. As Dipert (2010: 398) suggests, "defensive cyber security efforts could violate the privacy or other civil rights of innocent non-state parties, or incidentally cause damage to one's own citizens, economy or computer systems." Protecting the state from damage can actually do more harm than good.

There are basic things that states need to do to protect their cyber borders. Extreme reactions in the shape of offensive forces and defense walls will only prevent the natural connections that cyber relations enfranchise. Following the dictates of rivalry, cyber rivals would then seek to harm and restrict the options of enemies. The cyber realm should be held sacred and separate because of the possibilities it contains. Securitizing the domain will only restrict its development and hinder progress overall.

## OUR CYBER FUTURES

We understand our current cyber reality well, but what about the future? Many seem to assume the future will be filled with netwar. If our current reality is directly connected to the Internet, might not our futures be as well?

While the future is likely to include more digital connections between people, systems, and the state, it is not at all clear that these advances will assure a militarized cyber reality. We have other examples of when technology has become militarized and demilitarized. Airspace, for example, became the domain of the military. The fear of aerial bombings and the corresponding horrors of such systems did become a reality, a very vivid reality, during World War II. Yet, since then, outside a few isolated examples, civilian-based aerial bombardments have not become the norm. The Korean and Vietnam conflicts were strangely mostly devoid of bombing of civilian populations. When that did happen in Vietnam and Cambodia, the leadership of the state making that choice was rightly vilified. We now seem to live in an era of smart bombings and immense concern with collateral damage through air campaigns. There are, of course, examples of failures of these doctrines and considerations, but they are the outliers, not the norm. The cyber era will likely exhibit the same pattern. We will see a few instances of cyber conflict, but these conflicts will be outside the norm and will not result in the massive loss of human life.

Possibly the best example would be to consider space technology. While it has been militarized in some senses, by and large this is the domain of international cooperation for the betterment of all. The advent of satellite-hunting spacecraft has not materialized, and it is unlikely to. When space becomes the domain of the military, it is generally for propaganda purposes and not for any real purpose.

This likely will be our cyber future, an area of vast cooperation with a few examples of deviation.

The problem is that even the basic steps are often discarded in favor of the extreme, offensive options. Singer and Friedman (2014: 174) argue that we need a Cyber center for disease control (CDC), a place where all cyber viruses and information are cleared and solutions to threats are offered. Others advocate transparency for all cyber threats of which governments are aware. As of 2014, the Heartbleed vulnerability was discovered, but it is likely that governments knew of this exploit much sooner and chose to say nothing in case it should prove useful for their own ends.

It is tough to predict the future. One does not want to be wrong, to be made to look silly by a prediction that does not come to pass. Yet, in some ways, the purpose of social science is to go out on a ledge and make grand statements based on evidence that others are unable to make. To keep our digital future safe, the main advice would be to avoid making the offensive frame the dominant form of cyber interactions. Resilience is the main strategy that is likely to work; we must seek to avoid militarizing the domain, and when violations do occur, we must be prepared to recover. We must assume that cyber incidents will happen, but to react with offensive intent will only escalate the situation and provoke more of the same. Offensive plans will only make the opposing side consider similar responses and repeat the human pattern of arms races, where one side fears the advances of the other and seeks to one-up them, dooming both sides to a never-ending mechanical process of competition (Richardson 1960).

Assuming the worst is not the way to make policy. Buying into the notion that we will be faced with a future of cyber conflict based on offensive technologies will only make this prophecy come true. Instead, there is a better, nonviolent path in cyberspace. It is not the path of pacifism, but the path of choosing a better way (Howes 2013). The way that it is done is by not escalating threats through tit-for-tat responses, but through dialogue, consideration, and holding the new cyber domain sacred (Axelrod 1986).

## TECHNOLOGY AND CONFLICT

One thing that must be said about the field of cyber security is that the novelty of technology is vastly overstated. This is true for the cyber debate as well as the drone debate—for virtually any debate regarding a new technology that should alter the battlefield and how countries interact. Frequently scholars make the claim that technology has transformed the military strategy debate or the norms of foreign policy. This has not been historically true, nor is it true today. In some ways, the cyber debate is distracting us from asking the real questions about the root cause of an animosity and how we can solve the discord that divides countries or individuals.

One take-away from this work might be that there is no evidence that cyber conflict has changed the dynamics of international relations. States still rely on conventional technologies and often are restrained from using both conventional and unconventional strategies because of concerns about blowback, repercussions, or legal and public relations consequences. Norms matter, and norms proliferate and cascade (Finnemore and Sikkink 1998). This is true no matter what the technology is and how it might be used.

Technology is no solution for international discord. Strategic bombing was largely ineffective during World War II, and during recent conflicts such as the Persian Gulf War and Kosovo; cyber techniques have done little to achieve state goals, whether the state in question is Estonia or Iran (Pape 1996).[13] As Cronin (2013) states, when tactics drive strategy, we are doomed. This, in some ways, is the outcome of the cyber discourse, and we hope to change that by demonstrating that cyber tactics are limited, and that we should therefore question their strategic value.

The debate needs to shift a bit, back toward the reasons for intervention and conflict, not the technology that can be used to make these adventures easy. Conflict is never easy, kinetic or non-kinetic. There might be something evolving that could be called a two-tiered system of war, with one tier being conventional and the other being non-conventional weapons; nevertheless, even this new system still demonstrates that conflicts and threats often fail to achieve the intended designs. From drone attacks that increase Pakistani and Afghani animosity toward the United States to Iran ramping up nuclear production in the face of Stuxnet, to Cheney's stated use of a demonstration effect of invasion failing to deter nuclear weapons proliferation (Danner 2014), there are plentiful examples of new tactics failing to achieve their desired goals. Therefore it is important that we revise our considerations of cyber conflict as a tactic, its potential for future use, and its place in the international relations discourse.

## CONCLUDING REFLECTIONS

We have come to the end of our investigation. At this stage it is useful to review whether our theories and inclinations need reassessment in light of evidence. This is the stage that generally comes at the end of the scientific method. Our main contention is that the hype associated with cyber conflict does not meet reality. The threat is dangerously overstated, and pushing policy and arms acquisitions in a direction that lines up with this threat could be dangerous for the stability of the international system. So far, we have yet to see cyber conflict change the nature of international interactions, and it is unlikely to do so. Yet, if states buy into the cyber hype, arm themselves with phalanxes of hackers, and continue to put up defensive walls that cut off society from the benefits of digitized advancements, there is a great danger that we will all miss out on the positivity inherent in the Internet and will see this realm militarized.

On top of this, there is also the danger that by employing extreme defensive measures, we might make cyberspace less secure internally. By walling off the outside, the inside can become less secure to those already within the system. This is part of the concern and backlash against the NSA controlling cyber defense and setting up a "cyber star wars" system to intercept cyber incidents.[14] Harkening back to the question of who watches the watchmen, if the NSA controls cyberspace within the United States, who then controls the NSA?[15]

As with most social science efforts, there is always the possibility that one can be wrong. The goal should be avoiding the typical process of theory-saving enterprises (Vasquez 1999). One must accept the facts as they are and modify or discard theories as needed. The entirety of this work could quickly be proven wrong by one drastic cyber operation. If a state were to use cyber weapons to destroy, maim, and harm civilians, our analysis would be subject to reinvestigation. Yet, we stand by our statements, theories, and data. As the future shapes up now, the worst-case scenario does not seem to be developing, and isolated examples of cyber extremism do not discount massive amounts of data that suggest a different, more cooperative path.

Instead, we are possibly witnessing the greatest renaissance in human communications in history. Of course, this development is fraught with fear and trepidation. Dependency conjures up images of vulnerability and weakness. We are not so pessimistic. The real danger might be in letting the fears associated with cyber technologies impede the natural progress that interactions in cyberspace might bring. Cyber communications and interactions have the ability to be the greatest force for peace, development, education, and research. Yet, with every new technology that changes our lives, people react with fear. We argue here that this process does not need to develop in relation to cyber interactions; the evidence we have so far suggests that such fear is mainly an aspect of the hype promoted by the media and others who will benefit. This realm should remain peaceful, but also, states should avoid securitizing and militarizing the issue. The true danger is making the fear become a self-fulfilling prophecy through an overreaction to the perceived nature of the threat.

Here we have described the shape of international interactions in cyberspace. There is much less conflict exhibited than one would expect based on the prognostications of experts. Cyberspace is being militarized, but it is not the domain of warfare yet. At the present time, we observe the opposite of cyber conflict. Cyber cooperation dominates. Peaceful digital connections between states and individuals outweigh the negativity in cyberspace. We must remember this as we move further into a cyber future.

This realm will only be as dangerous as we let it. We all will watch the developments that come in cyberspace with bated anticipation, but likely without the fear and hatred that have bled into other domains. This is the reality of the cyber threat. It is of our own making and should be discarded with other ideas that have no basis in evidence. The evidence we present here suggests a digital peace, not cyber war.

# APPENDIX
# Research Methods

Our dataset is composed of 20 rival dyads that have engaged in cyber conflict since 2001. These are the only dyads of a possible 126 rivals that have used cyberspace as a strategic tool during this time period (Klein, Diehl, and Goertz 2006). We delineate these dyads into separate groups, and as the analysis is over a period of time, the most appropriate technique is using panel data regressions. Panel data are used to observe the behavior of different entities across time and can also account for spatial correlations, and we find that accounting for both temporal and spatial correlations is required for this analysis. Our entities are dyads, and we look at the effects of events for these pairs of states to get an overall analysis of foreign policy interactions. For our purposes, we measure the effects of cyber incidents and disputes on the conflict-cooperation scores for all dyads that have chosen to use cyber techniques as a foreign policy tool. There are two models that can be used to uncover these effects using panel data: random effects and fixed effects. Random effects models assume that the variation across our dyads is random and is uncorrelated with the independent variables in our model. Random effects are useful if it is believed that differences across dyads have some influence on the dependent variable. This type of panel regression accounts for spatial correlations. For this analysis, we assume that the differences in the nature of cyber conflict for each dyad will have an influence on our conflict-cooperation scores, since the nature of each rivalry is different. In other words, not all dyadic relationships between states are created equal, and this needs to be corrected. The intensity and relations range for each rival that uses cyber tactics as a foreign policy tool are not the same; therefore the random effects model corrects for this and is appropriate for the analysis. However, we find that running a fixed effects model is also warranted, as with time may come different conflict cooperation dynamics, where the context of a cyber incident or dispute may be different. Rival relationships go through ebbs and flows, and fixed effects account for different temporal correlations.

Fixed effects models are used when the primary interest is analyzing the impact of factors of interest varying over time. This model assumes that each dyad has its own individual characteristics that may influence the independent variables. Something within each dyad may affect either the independent or dependent variables and must be controlled. Another assumption of fixed effects is that each dyad is different, and thus the error term and constant of each dyad should not be correlated with the other dyads. This type of panel regression looks at how each dyad changes over time and controls for this phenomenon. For example, the conflict-cooperation dynamic for the US-China dyad may be different in 2001 than it is in 2008, and fixed effects accounts for this. Thus, the fixed effects approach for panel regression controls for trending and minimizes any unit root issues that might arise. As we are also interested in the separate effects of cyber conflict on conflict and cooperation between states, we also run a fixed effects model that treats each separate dyad as a dummy variable on the others. We therefore run both models for panel data. Random effects are used to get an overall picture of cyber conflict on conflict cooperation on the entire population, and fixed effects are utilized to uncover the individual and unique effects on cyber conflict for each dyad in the dataset. Next we explain the nature of the variables in the datasets.

The unit of analysis for our events data is dyadic week. Our time period analyzed is 2001–2011. Each event for each dyad within a week is given a Goldstein (1992) interval score, and the cumulative score of the conflictual or cooperative relationship for that dyad each week is the dependent variable. Figure 5.1 lists the possible Goldstein scores available for the dependent variables. The more negative the cumulative weekly score, the more conflictual the relationship for the pair of states, and the more positive the cumulative score, the more cooperative the relationship. The Goldstein scale is an appropriate tool for this analysis as the independent variables, cyber incidents and disputes, are rare events. As there are only 111 cyber incidents within 45 overall disputes with over 13,000 data points over an 11-year time span, we assert that the weekly Goldstein scores that are recorded after one of these rare events occurs are a response to the cyber incident or dispute. Concerns for endogeneity, therefore, are controlled due to the sparseness of the recorded cyber events. The dyads are also directed (Bennett and Stam 2000), which means that each dyad has two separate groupings: one where a state in a dyad is the source of conflict or cooperation, another where it is the recipient of the conflict or cooperation. As we are using panel regression techniques, separating pairs of states into directed dyads is crucial to get accurate results of the relationship between cyber conflict and foreign policy interactions. Therefore, there are 40 total separate groups in the panel data.

Our independent variables are compiled from the dataset introduced in the previous chapter. These data cover all cyber incidents and disputes between rivals during the years 2001–2011. Our main explanatory variables are cyber incidents and cyber disputes. These variables, as well as every other independent variable used, are dichotomous, where "1" is coded if cyber conflict is present, "0" if not.

These variables are also directed, therefore, when a country initiates cyber conflict against its rival; it is matched with the opposite directed dependent variable of the target state (Bennett and Stam 2000). The assumption is that a directed cyber incident or dispute against a country initiates a conflict-cooperation dynamic (or a foreign policy response) from the targeted state. The cyber incident or dispute is lagged one week before the conflict-cooperation response. Each independent variable explained below is run separately from the others so as to avoid covariation in the results.

To review, cyber incidents are individual events that target a country for a matter of hours, days, or weeks. To fit the time period of our dependent variable, incidents are coded as one per dyadic week. There are three types of cyber incidents: nuisances, defensive operations, and offensive strikes (see Chapter 2 for more details). We also use the possible targets of a cyber incident as independent variables. Targets are private, government but non-military, or government and military. Finally, we code incidents based on the objective of the initiator: disruptions, theft, and change in behavior (see Chapter 2 for more details).

Cyber disputes are operations containing a number of incidents that are part of an overall cyber campaign. For example, the Olympic Games initiated by the United States and Israel against Iran included the incidents of Stuxnet, Flame, Duqu, and Gauss. The different types of disputes are found in Chapter 4, and each is used as a separate independent variable. Disputes can be combinations of nuisances, defensive operations, and offensive strikes, as well as combinations of private, government non-military, and government military.

We also code cyber incidents and disputes by method. Methods are the ways in which initiators are able to access the networks of their rivals. Remembering Chapter 2, there are four basic methods: vandalism, denial of service, intrusions, and infiltrations. Advanced persistent threats (APTs) are the most sophisticated form of cyber tactics. This specific method can be either an intrusion or an infiltration, and can target specific parts of networks that other methods cannot.

Our last cluster of explanatory variables measures the severity of cyber operations. This scale is ascending, where "1" is the least harmful and "5" is the most severe. Our data collection thus far has found that the most severe incidents to date are only in the "3" severity range.

Our control variables are added to each regression run with each of the explanatory variables in the analysis and attempt to confirm our third and fourth hypotheses. The "Major Power" variable is coded as "1" if there is a major power in the dyad, "0" otherwise. The "Same Region" variable controls for the effects of region; a "1" is coded if the two countries in the dyad also lie in the same region, "0" otherwise. These controls also make our panel regression analyses multivariate. With these controls and the fact that our main independent variables, cyber incidents and disputes in whatever form, are rare events, any colinearity issues are controlled. We suspect that cyber conflict is a tactic used between regional rivals.

Our regions include East Asia, South Asia, the post-Soviet space, the Middle East, Europe, and the Americas. We see small aggressions like cyber incidents as evidence that states may wish to expand their standing in the region, and cyber conflict could be a useful psychological tool. Regional dynamics are therefore an important control for this data analysis.

# NOTES

## CHAPTER 1

1. The term *cyber* is used because it is conventional in the discourse. Whether or not it is an accurate or a useful term to describe Internet communications and conflict is beyond this analysis. We have to work with the terms that have become conventions. In Chapter 2 we will further define, dissect, and examine the terms *cyber war, cyber conflict*, and *cyber power*.

2. Stokes, Bruce. 2014. "Extremists, cyber attacks top Americans' security threat list." *Pew Research Center*, January 2, 2014. Accessed March 2, 2014. Available at http://www.pewresearch.org/fact-tank/2014/01/02/americans-see-extremists-cyber-attacks-as-major-threats-to-the-u-s/.

3. White House. 2014. "Cyber security." White House Website. Accessed March 3, 2014. Available at http://www.whitehouse.gov/issues/foreign-policy/cybersecurity.

4. Parrish, Karen. 2013. "Panetta wars cyber threat growing quickly." *US Department of Defense*, February 6, 2013. Accessed March 5, 2014. Available at http://www.defense.gov/news/newsarticle.aspx?id=119214.

5. Krivobok, Ruslan. 2013. "Russia to create 'cyber troops'—Ministry of Defense." *RT*, August 20, 2013. Accessed March 5, 2014. Available at http://rt.com/news/russia-cyber-troops-defence-753/

6. Richard Clarke and Robert Knake, Jeffrey Carr, Leon Panetta, Mikko Hypponen, the Mandiant Group, and Eugene Kaspersky are among these pundits and prognosticators of cyber hype.

7. Barlow, Thomas. 2013. "China ups ante in cyber warfare." *The Australian*, May 31, 2013. Available at http://www.theaustralian.com.au/national-affairs/opinion/friendly-china-ups-ante-in-cyber-warfare/story-e6frgd0x-1226654075003.

8. "Department of Defense strategy for operating in cyberspace," July 2011. Available at http://www.defense.gov/news/d20110714cyber.pdf.

9. Sanger, David E. 2013. "As Chinese leader's visit nears, US is urged to allow counter-attacks on hackers." *New York Times*, May 21, 2013. Accessed December 20, 2013. Available at http://www.nytimes.com/2013/05/22/world/asia/as-chinese-leaders-visit-nears-us-urged-to-allow-retaliation-forcyberattacks.html?goback=%2Egde_1836487_member_243106963&_r=0.
Dave, Paresh. 2013. "Some companies looking at retaliating against cyber attackers." *Los Angeles Times*, May 31, 2013. Accessed July 7, 2014. Available at http://articles.latimes.com/2013/may/31/business/la-fi-hacking-back-20130531.

10. Sanger 2013.

11. Dave 2013.

12. Shactman, Noah. 2012. "Darpa looks to make cyberwar routine with secret 'Plan X.'" *Wired*. Accessed July 2, 2013. Available at http://www.wired.com/dangerroom/2012/08/plan-x/.

13. Bumiller, Elisabeth, and Thom Shanker. 2012. "Panetta warns of dire threat of cyberattack on US." *New York Times*, October 11, 2012. Accessed March 6, 2013. Available at http://www.nytimes.com/2012/10/12/world/panetta-warns-of-dire-threat-of-cyberattack.html?pagewanted=all&_r=0.

14. We define cyber incidents, which are single targeted cyber operations, and cyber disputes, which are longer-term operations that may hold many separate incidents, in detail in the next chapter.

15. Also defined in detail in Chapter 2, DDoS methods involve the flooding of particular websites or networks with remotely accessed computers, effectively shutting the target down for a matter of hours, days, or weeks.

16. Flame was a virus that infiltrated networks, copied the information, and then erased all of the information stolen from the host network. Its most famous infiltration was of the Iranian nuclear program network.

17. Haquest, Charles, and Emmanuel Paquette. 2012. "NSA: Americans deny responsibility for a cyber attacks against the Elysse Palace in 2012." *The Express*, November 20, 2012. Accessed May 20, 2013. Available at http://lexpansion.lexpress.fr/high-tech/cyberguerre-comment-les-americains-ont-pirate-l-elysee_361225.html.

18. Warstall, Tim. 2013. "The biggest cyber attack ever is slowing down the Internet." *Forbes*, March 27, 2013. Accessed May 31, 2013. Available at http://www.forbes.com/sites/timworstall/2013/03/27/the-biggest-cyber-attack-ever-is-slowing-down-the-internet/.

19. Gross, Doug. 2013. "Massive cyberattack hits Internet users." *CNN.com*. March 29, 2013. Accessed May 31, 2013. Available at http://www.cnn.com/2013/03/27/tech/massive-internet-attack.

20. Ibid.

21. Biddle, Sam. 2013. "That Internet war apocalypse is a lie." *Gizmodo.com*, March 27, 2013. Accessed May 31, 2013. Available at http://gizmodo.com/5992652/that-internet-war-apocalypse-is-a-lie.

22. Media outlets include *CNN*, the *New York Times*, and the *Washington Post*, among many.

23. Weinschenk, Matthew. 2012. "Cyber security's new face: Growing threats and growing profits." *Wall Street Daily*, February 22, 2012. Accessed July 7, 2014. Available at http://www.wallstreetdaily.com/2012/02/22/cyber-security-growing-threats-and-profits/.

24. This does not mean that cyber will not need enforcement per se, only that it will not require enforcement from outside, as states voluntarily bind their hands when adhering to a normative system.

25. The movie *Skyfall* (2012) makes the interesting point that even James Bond cannot protect us from cyber threats. He is just as much part of the problem and the only solution is to bridge the gap between the digital and physical layer by using brute force. Valeriano, Brandon. "Cyberwar and Skyfall: Bond enters the digital age," Duck of Minerva, November 10, 2012. Available at http://www.whiteoliphaunt.com/duckofminerva/2012/11/skyfall-and-cyberwarjames-bond-enters-the-digital-era.html?utm_medium=twitter&utm_source=twitterfeed.

## CHAPTER 2

1. Lee, Melissa (Host). 2011. "Code wars: America's cyber-threat." *CNBC Website*. Accessed August 24, 2011. Available at http://www.cnbc.com/id/42210831.

2. What is meant here is that a defacement of a Georgian website that shows the Georgian president dressed as Hitler is mere propaganda and can be easily protected against, while complex worms such as Stuxnet take years of development and planning. These types of attacks have been categorized together, and the purpose of this book is to dissect and categorize every cyber incident and dispute in order to put them in the proper context.

3. Welch, Chris. 2013. "AP Twitter account hacked, makes false claim of explosions at White House." *The Verge*, April 23, 2013. Accessed March 2, 2014. Available at http://www.theverge.com/2013/4/23/4257392/ap-twitter-hacked-claims-explosions-white-house-president-injured

4. It is rather unfortunate that the term *cyber* has become the prefix for all things digital or conflict based in international interactions. It seemed outdated and antiquated, but terms are what they are, and we have to follow conventions in this regard.

5. "To reach another person on the Internet you have to type an address into a computer—a name or a number. That address must be unique so computers know where to find each other. ICANN coordinates these unique identifiers around the world. Without that coordination, we wouldn't have one global internet." http://www.icann.org/en/about/welcome.

6. We would like to thank the anonymous reviewer for making this trope clear to us. The idea of a fragile Internet is an assumption and has not been backed with facts or evidence. If the Internet is as fragile as many would make us think, then it is strange that we rely on it for so much, from personal communication to business, to even monitoring and locating our children.

7. Reissmann, Ole, and Sebastian Fischer. 2011. "Fighting Internet threats: Germany arms itself for cyber war." *Der Spiegel*, June 16, 2011. Accessed August 14, 2014. Available at http://www.spiegel.de/international/germany/fighting-internet-threats-germany-arms-itself-for-cyber-war-a-768764.html.

8. Murphy, Matt. 2010. "War in the fifth domain." *The Economist*, July 1, 2010. Accessed December 4, 2012. Available at http://www.economist.com/node/16478792.

9. In other research it could include individuals versus states, other individuals, or organizations.

10. Arthur, Charles. 2012. "Cyber attack concerns raised over Boeing 787 chip's 'back door.'" *The Guardian*, May 29, 2012. Accessed December 4, 2012. Available at http://www.guardian.co.uk/technology/2012/may/29/cyber-attack-concerns-boeing-chip.

11. "Department of Defense Strategy for Operating in Cyberspace," July 2011.

12. It is important to note that this typology is not necessarily an ascending scale, as some Trojans can be more potent than worms. This typology is constructed to delineate the types of strategies that cyber attackers are able to employ for exploitative or malicious intent. Table 2.1 constructs the severity scale of cyber disputes and incidents, or level of impact as a result of the dispute.

13. Symantec. 2014. "Advanced persistent threats: How they work." Accessed September 5, 2013. Available at http://www.symantec.com/content/en/us/enterprise/white_papers/b-advanced_persistent_threats_WP_21215957.en-us.pdf.

14. "Nothing in the present Charter shall impair the inherent right of individual or collective self-defence if an armed attack occurs against a Member of the United Nations, until the Security Council has taken measures necessary to maintain international peace and security. Measures taken by Members in the exercise of this right of self-defence shall be immediately reported to the Security Council and shall not in any way affect the authority and responsibility of the Security Council under the present Charter to take at any time such action as it deems necessary in order to maintain or

restore international peace and security." http://www.un.org/en/documents/charter/chapter7.shtml.

15. It might be more prudent to take the perspective of Healy (2013: 23), who notes that although cyber conflicts can be fast, they are by no means conducted "at the speed of light."

16. The bureaucratic battles between the various service branches in the United States and other countries over the domain of cyber could be a book on its own. The internal organizational rivalries continue to battle for access and influence in the cyber world on the contention that this domain will be important in the future and to avoid losing out on controlling the spoils of the technology.

17. At this point, it is unclear just what configuration might be more likely to lead to cyber conflict. It is an open aspect of research.

18. Rumsfeld, Donald. "Department of Defense Website, Press Conference at NATO Headquarters." June 6, 2002. Accessed February 1, 2011. Available at http://www.defense.gov/transcripts/transcript.aspx?transcriptid=3490.

19. Ibid.

20. Sanger, David E., and Thom Shanker, 2014. "NSA devises radio pathway into computers." *New York Times*, January 14, 2014. http://www.nytimes.com/ 2014/01/15/us/nsa-effort-pries-open-computers-not-connected-to-internet.html?ref=davidesanger&_r=0.

## CHAPTER 3

1. Some may disagree with the basic premise of this statement, but we hope to make it clear throughout this book that the cyber threat has been overinflated and that there is little evidence of large-scale cyber operations given how long the tactic has been around (some would say the early 1990s) and the number of ongoing conflicts between cyber capable enemies.

2. For various reasons, we are not proposing a theory of cyber terrorism for individuals. We only attempt to make a connection between cyber espionage and how cyber terrorism may be utilized in reality. There are various reasons a substate actor would resort to terrorism, and these mainly have divergent logics from why a state would launch cyber espionage operations.

3. Mueller, John, and Mark G. Stewart. 2011. "Probability neglect: Why the government massively overestimates the risks of terrorism." Accessed September 8, 2011. Available at http://www.slate.com/id/2303168/.

4. http://www.nytimes.com/2014/03/12/world/europe/nsa-nominee-reports-cyberattacks-on-ukraine-government.html?hp&_r=0

5. Goodman (2010: 108) argues the opposite: less severe options are not an issue since only certainty is needed in cyber deterrence. It is unclear how waiving the condition of severity makes certainty more possible, not less.

6. As we discuss later, this does not mean that low-level cyber operations are off the table. In fact, many states will utilize these options. Our point is that these tactics are minimal, have little impact on the foreign policy process, and generally occur when they are the easiest path to take to express a position.

7. Zetter, Kim 2013. "Stuxnet missing link found, resolves some mysteries around the cyberweapon." *Wired*, February 26, 2013. Accessed May 28, 2013. Available at http://www.wired.com/threatlevel/2013/02/new-stuxnet-variant-found/3/.

8. http://rt.com/usa/kaspersky-russia-nuclear-plants-612/

9.  Markoff, John, and Thom Shanker. 2009. "Halted '03 Iraq plan illustrates U.S. fear of cyberwar risk." *New York Times*, August 1, 2009. Available at http://www.nytimes.com/2009/08/02/us/politics/02cyber.html.

10. Schmitt, Eric, and Thom Shanker. "U.S. debated cyberwarfare in attack plan on Libya." *New York Times*, October 17, 2011.

11. Garamone, Jim. 2013. "Despite hackers, DoD retains faith in weapons systems." *DoD Website*, May 30, 2013. Accessed September 17, 2013. Available at http://www.defense.gov/news/newsarticle.aspx?id=120173.

12. Pellerin, Cheryl. 2010. "Lynn: Cyberspace is the new domain of warfare." *DoD Website*, October 18, 2010. Accessed September 17, 2013. Available at http://www.defense.gov/news/newsarticle.aspx?id=61310.
    White House. 2011. "International strategy for cyberspace: Prosperity, security, and openness in a networked world." May 2011. Available at http://www.whitehouse.gov/sites/default/files/rss_viewer/international_strategy_for_cyberspace.pdf.Kerry, John. 2013. "Remarks at the US-ASEAN Ministerial Meeting." *State.gov*, July 1, 2013. Accessed September 17, 2013. Available at http://www.state.gov/secretary/remarks/2013/07/211377.htm.

13. Maness, Ryan C., and Brandon Valeriano. "Russia's coercive diplomacy against Ukraine: The power politics story." *Duck of Minerva*, March 3, 2014. Available at http://www.whiteoliphaunt.com/duckofminerva/2014/03/russias-coercive-diplomacy-against-ukraine-the-power-politics-story.html.

14. Perlroth, Nicole. 2013. "Hackers in China attacked the Times for last 4 months." *New York Times*, January 30, 2013. Available at http://www.nytimes.com/2013/01/31/technology/chinese-hackers-infiltrate-new-york-times computers.html?pagewanted=all.

15. Mandiant. 2013. "Mandiant releases annual threat report on advanced targeted attacks." *Mandiant*, March 13, 2013. Accessed March 14, 2013. Available at https://www.mandiant.com/news/release/mandiant-releases-annual-threat-report-on-advanced-targeted-attacks1/.

16. Media Note. 2013. "US-China strategic and economic dialogue outcomes of the Strategic Track." *State.gov*, July 12, 2013. Accessed September 17, 2013. Available at http://www.state.gov/r/pa/prs/ps/2013/07/211861.htm.

17. This would suggest that the states do not locate cyber targets in simple locations, that it does not bunch targets together, and it does not expose them to prying eyes. In many ways the fault of Pearl Harbor was that it grouped so many important targets in one place. This sort of process is to be avoided in cyberspace by the construction of reasonable and effective defenses to protect the state from intrusion.

## CHAPTER 4

1.  Markoff, John, and Thom Shanker. 2009. "Halted '03 Iraq plan illustrates U.S. fear of cyberwar risk." *New York Times*, August 1, 2009. Available at http://www.nytimes.com/2009/08/02/us/politics/02cyber.html.

2.  Schmitt, Eric, and Thom Shanker. "U.S. debated cyberwarfare in attack plan on Libya" *New York Times*. October 17, 2011. Available at http://www.nytimes.com/2011/10/18/world/africa/cyber-warfare-against-libya-was-debated-by-us.html?_r=0.

3.  Stuxnet was likely initiated sometime in early 2009, started showing up in state's networks in June 2009, yet was not reported in the media until June 2010.

4.  Lag times are necessary, for example, Stuxnet was likely initiated sometime in early 2009, started showing up in state's networks in June 2009 and was reported in the media by June 2010.

5. It could also be of note that our dataset is biased toward the West since the assumption of media, firm, and institutional openness is a Western assumption. Where possible we translated, either by hand or by machine, foreign language sources.

6. To first locate the relevant news stories of cyber incidents and disputes between rivals, we enter the search query "rival A (e.g., Iran)" AND "rival B (e.g., Israel)" AND "cyber" OR "internet attack" OR "infrastructure attack" OR "government attack." The capitalization of the conjunctions is required in the search query. What we look for in this search is the date and duration of the incident, who initiated the incident, the foreign policy objective of the initiator (disruption, theft, change the target state's behavior), whether or not a third party was involved in the incident, whether or not there was an official government statement by the initiator about the incident (denial acceptance, or no official statement), and the method and severity of the incident (See Tables 4.1–4.4 for more detail). The time period is from January 1, 2001 to December 31, 2011 so that we could get an 11-year sample and also capture the main period of active Internet engagement. In most cases, sources were collaborated by multiple newspaper articles, blogs, and reports (coming from both think tanks and Internet security firms) controlling for source validity and to avoid letting one perspective dictate a data point. Each news story, report, or post utilized is carefully examined to ensure that the proper coding has taken place.

7. It is important to note that this typology is not necessarily an ascending scale, as some Trojans can be more potent than worms. This typology is constructed to delineate the types of strategies cyber-attackers are able to employ for exploitative or malicious intent. Table 4.2 constructs the severity scale of cyber disputes and incidents, or level of impact as a result of the dispute.

8. http://www.symantec.com/content/en/us/enterprise/white_papers/badvanced_persistent_threats_WP_21215957.en-us.pdf.

9. The cases of Iran and Israel plus India and China were added from the Thompson (2001) rivalry data. Estonia and Russia were added due to the notoriety of the case at the request of peer reviewers.

10. Our coding was checked for reliability after the initial data collection effort. The first three coders then switched areas of coverage and checked 10 percent of another person's coding efforts. Finally, two undergraduate students were given the same information and asked to check 10 percent of the dataset for reliability at random.

11. Notable cyber interactions not included in the analysis: Cuckoo's Egg (1988), Morris Worm (1989), the Dutch Hackers incident during Desert Storm (1990), Eligible Receiver (1997), Solar Sunrise (1998), Russian Patriot Hacking, such as during NATO's operation Allied Force (1999), Chinese Patriot Hacking, such as after the NATO bombing of the Chinese Embassy in Belgrade (1999), and Moonlight Maze (1999) because they all took place before the time frame of our analysis; Global War on Terrorism (2001–), Israeli-Palestinian interactions because they are not state to state cyber attacks; espionage into German, French and Canadian ministries (2007–) because no rivalry exists between these states and China; and Unified Protector (2011).

12. Taiwan's international legal sovereignty (lack of international recognition) makes its status as a state questionable. However, as it does have domestic sovereignty (home rule), and is included in Klein et al. dataset, therefore we did not omit it from the analysis.

13. It is frequently noted that the most prominent cyber actors might also correlate with Internet penetration in society. We find the opposite and that there is no correlation between Internet usage and cyber offensive actions. Space precludes our inclusion

of this table, but we find that many of the least active Internet societies also tend to use cyber operations. This may be because these states have little to fear in terms of retribution.

14. The Snowden revelations likely will challenge this finding in the future, but as of now most of these programs seem either to start after 2011 or have no clear target, therefore we do not code them in this iteration of the data. It remains to be seen as to what the NSA was trying to accomplish with the actions revealed in these documents, at least enough to code state-to-state cyber incidents originating from the United States against one of its rivals.

15. Phishing attempts are when hackers use personal pieces of information to acquire and ask for passwords by simple e-mail or other social media interactions. Representatives must be trained at recognizing and avoiding such operations.

16. http://lexpansion.lexpress.fr/high-tech/cyberguerre-comment-les-americains-ont-pirate-l-elysee_361225.html accessed 12/5/2012.

17. Huth and Allee look at outcomes of territorial disputes and we term them *territorial issues*. They look at how the disputes are settled. Ghosn et al. (2004) look at the processes of territorial disputes, where they look at the origins of how the dispute happened in the first place. A show of force first must happen for these disputes to be coded. We use both datasets for scope and breadth.

18. http://defense-update.com/20130628_dempsey_threatens_responding_cyberattack_by_military_action.html

19. Enders, Walter, and Todd Sandler. 2000. "Is transnational terrorism becoming more threatening? A time-series investigation." *Journal of Conflict Resolution* 44(3): 307–332.

20. https://wits.nctc.gov/FederalDiscoverWITS/index.do?N=0.

21. As Rid and McBurney (2012: 6) note, cyber-weapons may require specific target intelligence and major investments of R&D. Therefore these major operations are likely beyond most (but not all) terrorist organizations.

22. At this point we have not coded Red October, since it is unclear who perpetuated the attack. Various groups have their theories, but attribution is tenuous at this time.

## CHAPTER 5

1. The Estonian Parliament actually voted to destroy the statue but President Toomas Hendrik Ilves vetoed the measure, arguing it was unconstitutional. This act probably diffused the situation somewhat; the Russian retaliation could have been worse. https://helda.helsinki.fi/bitstream/handle/10224/4043/bronz_soldier2008.pdf?sequence=1.

2. Rothkopf, David. 2013. "The Cool War." *Foreign Policy*. February 20, 2013. Available at http://www.foreignpolicy.com/articles/2013/02/20/the_cool_war_china_cyberwar?page=full.

3. Directed dyads dropped from the analysis are the Russia-US and Russia-Estonia pairs of states. This is because no cyber incidents were inflicted on Russia from these states, and thus there is no variation in any of the explanatory variables for these two directed dyads.

4. Alperovitch, Dmitri. 2011. "Revealed: Operation Shady RAT." *McAfee White Paper Report*. Accessed May 1, 2013. Available at http://www.mcafee.com/us/resources/white-papers/wp-operation-shady-rat.pdf.

5. McAfee Labs. 2010. "2010 threat predictions." *McAfee Reports*. Accessed May 10, 2013. Available at http://www.mcafee.com/us/resources/reports/rp-threat-predictions-2010.pdf.

6. Shanker, Thom, and Elisabeth Bumiller. 2011. "Hackers gained access to sensitive military files." *New York Times*, July 14, 2011. Accessed May 1, 2013. Available at http://www.nytimes.com/2011/07/15/world/15cyber.html?pagewanted=all&_r=0.

7. Lemos, Robert 2011. "Byzantine hades shows China's cyber chops." *CSO Security and Risk*, April 21, 2011. Accessed May 10, 2013. Available at http://www.csoonline.com/article/680203/-byzantine-hades-shows-china-s-cyber-chops

8. Ibid.

9. Jackson, Kevin L. 2011. "China linked to Lockheed Martin cyber attack." *Forbes*, June 8, 2011. Accessed May 1, 2013. Available at http://www.forbes.com/sites/kevinjackson/2011/06/08/china-linked-to-lockheed-martin-cyber-attack/.

10. http://usnews.nbcnews.com/_news/2013/06/07/.UbPDPDzD3TY.twitter. Accessed June 9, 2013.

11. Department of Justice. 2014. "U.S. charges five Chinese military hackers for cyber espionage against U.S. corporations and a labor organization for commercial advantage." *Justice.gov*, May 19, 2014. Accessed August 4, 2014. Available at http://www.justice.gov/opa/pr/2014/May/14-ag-528.html.

## CHAPTER 6

1. Rid, Thomas. 2013. "Cyber sabotage is easy." *Foreign Policy*, July 23, 2013. Accessed November 22, 2013. Available at http://www.foreignpolicy.com/articles/2013/07/23/cyber_sabotage_is_easy_i_know_i_did_it?page=full.

2. Clapper, James. *Statement for the Record: Worldwide Threat Assessment of the US Intelligence Community*. March 12, 2013. Available at http://www.dni.gov/index.php/newsroom/testimonies/203-congressional-testimonies-2014/1005-statement-for-the-record-worldwide-threat-assessment-of-the-us-intelligence-community.

3. Mite, Valentinas. 2007. "Estonia: Attacks seen as first case of 'cyberwar.'" *Radio Free Europe Radio Liberty*, May 30, 2007. Accessed October 20, 2013. Available at http://www.rferl.org/content/article/1076805.html.

4. A perfect illustration of this hyperbole comes from a *Business Insider* article that starts with, "How did we destroy Iranian nuclear facilities? With a thumb drive." Never mind that nothing was destroyed, at least in the total sense. The implication that thumb drives did all the work, ignoring the application of ground assets, is problematic. Available at http://www.businessinsider.com/the-biggest-threat-to-national-security-is-the-thumb-drive-2013-7?goback=%2Egde_1836487_member_260748420.

5. Anonymous. 2007. "Most Russians refuse to regard dismantling the Bronze Soldier Estonia's internal affair-poll data." *Regnum.com*, March 20, 2007. Accessed November 23, 2013. Available at http://regnum.su/english/cultura/799302.html.

6. Ari. 2007. "Bronze Soldier polls." *A Lamb with No Guiding Light*, May 13, 2007. Accessed March 2, 2014. Available at http://noguidinglight.blogspot.com/2007/05/bronze-soldier-polls.html.

7. Davis, Joshua. 2007. "Hackers take down the most wired country in Europe." *Wired* 15(9). Accessed August 2, 2012. Available at http://www.wired.com/politics/security/magazine/15-09/ff_estonia?currentPage=all.

8. Finn, Peter. 2007. "Cyber assaults on Estonia typify a new battle tactic." *Washington Post*, May 19, 2007. Accessed August 2, 2012. Available at http://www.washingtonpost.com/wp-dyn/content/article/2007/05/18/AR2007051802122.html.

9. Traynor, Ian. 2007. "Russia accused of unleashing cyberwar to disable Estonia." *The Guardian*, May 16, 2007. Accessed October 20, 2013. Available at http://www.theguardian.com/world/2007/may/17/topstories3.russia.

10. Saar Poll. 2013. "Public opinion and national defence." *Ministry of Defence of Estonia,* October 2013. Accessed March 4, 2014. Available at http://www.kaitseministeerium. ee/files/kmin/nodes/13918_Public_Opinion_and_National_Defence_ 2013October.pdf.

11. International Conference on Cyber Conflict Webpage. *NATO Cooperative Cyber Defense Centre for Excellence,* Accessed August 4, 2012. Available at http://www.ccdcoe. org/cycon/.

12. "110th Congress First Session: HR Res. 397." Available at http://www.gpo.gov/fdsys/ pkg/BILLS-110hres397ih/pdf/BILLS-110hres397ih.pdf.

13. Traynor 2007, online edition.

14. Traynor 2007, online edition.

15. State Department. 2002. "A Decade of Deception and Defiance." State Department Website. September 12, 2002. Accessed March 3, 2014. Available at http://2001-2009. state.gov/p/nea/rls/13456.htm.

16. United Nations. 2006. "Security Council Committee established pursuant to resolution 1737. Available at https://www.un.org/sc/committees/1737/.

17. Langner, Ralph. 2010. "The short path from cyber missiles to dirty digital bombs." *Langner,* December 26, 2010. Accessed March 5, 2014. Available at http://www.langner. com/en/2010/12/26/the-short-path-from-cyber-missiles-to-dirty-digital-bombs/.

18. Takahashi, Dean. 2011. "Evidence suggests Stuxnet worm set Iran's nuclear program back." *Venture Beat,* January 15, 2011. Accessed October 20, 2013. Available at http:// venturebeat.com/2011/01/15/evidence-builds-that-stuxnet-worm-was-aimed- at-averting-war-over-irans-nuclear-weapons/.

19. Balustien, Michael. 2013. "Stuxnet virus might have improved Iran's nuclear capabilities: Report," May 16, 2013. Accessed October 20, 2013. Available at http:// nypost.com/2013/05/16/stuxnet-virus-might-have-improved-irans-nuclear- capabilities-report/.

20. Stuxnet was actually thought to have been released into Iran's nuclear program network as early as November 2007, but this was likely the probe/beacon stage; the virus was discovered in June 2010.

21. Harris, Shane. 2014. "Forget China: Iran's hackers are America's newest cyber threat." *Foreign Policy,* February 18, 2014. Accessed February 19, 2014. Available at http:// complex.foreignpolicy.com/posts/2014/02/18/forget_china_iran_s_hackers_ are_america_s_newest_cyber_threat.

22. Sanger, David E. 2014. "Syria War stirs new US debate on cyber attacks." *New York Times,* February 24, 2014. Accessed February 25, 2014. Available at http://www. nytimes.com/2014/02/25/world/middleeast/obama-worried-about-effects-of- waging-cyberwar-in-syria.html?_r=0.

23. We do not code this action in the DCID because the start date is 2012 and the data extend only to 2011.

24. Mount, Mike. 2012. "US officials believe Iran behind recent cyber attacks." *CNN,* October 16, 2012. Accessed February 24, 2014. Available at http://www.cnn. com/2012/10/15/world/iran-cyber/.

    Weitzenkorn, Ben. 2012. "Shamoon worm linked to Saudi oil company attack." *NBC News,* August 23, 2012. Accessed February 24, 2012. Available at http://www. nbcnews.com/id/48766448/ns/technology_and_science-security/t/shamoon- worm-linked-saudi-oil-company-attack/.

    Falk, Jeff. 2013. "Shamoon computer virus attack marked new height in cyber conflict." *Phys.org,* February 13, 2013. Accessed February 24, 2014. Available at http:// phys.org/news/2013-02-shamoon-virus-height-international-cyber.html.

25. Reuters. 2012. "Shamoon virus most destructive yet for private sector, Panetta says." *Reuters*, October 11, 2012. Accessed February 24, 2014. Available at http://www.reuters.com/article/2012/10/12/us-usa-cyber-pentagon-shimoon-idUSBRE89B04Y20121012.

26. Forbes. 2014. "The world's 25 biggest oil companies." *ForbesAccessed*, April 27, 2014. Available at http://www.forbes.com/pictures/mef45ggld/1-saudi-aramco-12-5-million-barrels-per-day/.

27. Clapper, James, p. 2.

28. Jeffery Carr, "Who is responsible for the Saudi Aramco network attack." *Infosec Island*, August 29, 2012. Available at http://jeffreycarr.blogspot.com/2012/08/whos-responsible-for-saudi-aramco.html.

## CHAPTER 7

1. Solomon, Eric. 2014. "Syria's death toll now exceeds 140,000: Activist group." *Reuters*, February 15, 2014. Accessed March 10, 2014. Available at http://www.reuters.com/article/2014/02/15/us-syria-crisis-toll-idUSBREA1E0HS20140215.

2. Anonymous. 2012. "Mass cyber war on Israel over gaza raids." November 19, 2012. Accessed March 14, 2014. Available at http://www.aljazeera.com/news/middleeast/2012/11/2012111973111746137.html.

3. Sanger, David E. 2014. "Syria War stirs new US debate on cyberattacks." *New York Times*, February 24, 2014. Accessed March 3, 2014. Available at http://www.nytimes.com/2014/02/25/world/middleeast/obama-worried-about-effects-of-waging-cyberwar-in-syria.html?_r=0.

4. Ricks, Thomas E. 2014. "The future of war: You better be ready to fight like it's a pre-electronic age." *Foreign Policy*, April 18, 2014. Accessed April 22, 2014. Available at http://ricks.foreignpolicy.com/posts/2014/01/15/the_future_of_war_ii_as_the_nature_of_war_changes_the_familiar_dividing_lines_of_ou.

   Cowell, Alan. 2012. "Cyberwar and Social Media in the Gaza Conflict." *New York Times*, November 19, 2012. Accessed March 24, 2014. Available at http://rendezvous.blogs.nytimes.com/2012/11/19/cyberwar-and-social-media-in-the-gaza-conflict/?_php=true&_type=blogs&_r=0.

5. Editorial. 2013. "President Morsi's repulsive comments." *New York Times*, January 15, 2013. Accessed March 13, 2014. Available at http://www.nytimes.com/2013/01/16/opinion/president-morsis-repulsive-comments-against-jews.html?_r=1&.

6. Pfeffer, Anshel, and Oded Yaron. 2011. "Israeli government, security services websites down in suspected cyber attack." *Haaretz*, November 6, 2011. Accessed March 2, 2014. Available at http://www.haaretz.com/news/diplomacy-defense/israel-government-security-services-websites-down-in-suspected-cyber-attack-1.394042.

7. Ackerman, Gwen, and Saud Abu Ramadan. 2012. "Israel wages cyber war with Hamas as civilians take up computers." *Business Week*, November 19, 2012. Accessed March 13, 2014. Available at http://www.businessweek.com/news/2012-11-19/israel-wages-cyber-war-with-hamas-as-civilians-take-up-computers.

8. Fitzpatrick, Alex. 2012. "Cyber attacks in Israel and Gaza increased after cease fire declared." *Mashable*, December 5, 2012. Accessed March 12, 2013. Available at http://mashable.com/2012/12/05/cyberattacks-gaza-israel/.

9. Anonymous. 2013. "Arab uprising: Country by country—Yemen." *BBC News*, December 16, 2013. Accessed March 12, 2014. Available at http://www.bbc.com/news/world-12482293.

10. Anonymous. 2013. "Arab uprising: Country by country—Libya." *BBC News*, December 16, 2013. Accessed March 12, 2014. Available at http://www.bbc.com/news/world-12482311.

11. Jones, Bryony. 2012. "Timeline: Israel Gaza conflict." *CNN*. Available at http://www.cnn.com/2012/11/20/world/timeline-gaza-israel-conflict/.

12. Ibid.

13. Ibid.

14. Ibid.

15. Anonymous. 2012. "Mass deleted #OpIsrael #GazaUnderAttack." *Pastebin*, November 17, 2012. Accessed April 27, 2014. Available at http://pastebin.com/uLbLTeJs

16. Besant, Alexander. 2012. "Cyber attacks on Israel reach tens of millions." *Global Post*, November 18, 2012. Accessed March 4, 2014. Available at http://www.globalpost.com/dispatch/news/regions/middle-east/israel-and-palestine/121118/cyber-attacks-israel-reach-tens-millio.

17. McGuire, Patrick. 2012. "The Gaza Strip cyber war." *Vice*, November 19, 2012. Accessed March 4, 2014. Available at http://www.vice.com/read/the-gaza-strip-cyber-war.

18. Sanger 2014.

19. Anonymous. 2013. "Security alert: Syrian Electronic Army—Response to Western intervention in Syrian Civil War." *Fishnet Security*. Accessed March 6, 2014. Available at https://www.fishnetsecurity.com/6labs/blog/security-alert-syrian-electronic-army-response-western-intervention-syrian-civil-war

20. Ibid.

21. Ibid.

22. Ibid.

23. Welch, Chris. 2013. "AP Twitter account hacked, makes false claim of explosions at White House." *The Verge*, April 23, 2013. Accessed March 2, 2014. Available at http://www.theverge.com/2013/4/23/4257392/ap-twitter-hacked-claims-explosions-white-house-president-injured.

24. Ibid.

25. Ibid.

26. Kastrenakes, Jacob. 2013. "New York Times website taken down by hack, Syrian Electronic Army involvement suspected." *The Verge*, August 27, 2014. Accessed March 2, 2014. Available at http://www.theverge.com/2013/8/27/4665230/new-york-times-website-taken-down-sea-suspected/in/5114785.

27. Mandiant. 2014. "Mandiant Intelligence Center Report." *Mandiant.com*. Accessed February 25, 2014. Available at http://intelreport.mandiant.com/.

28. Sanger 2014.

29. Islamic Relief USA. Accessed March 2, 2014. Available at https://donate.irusa.org/page.aspx?pid=558&gclid=CKeg4eC-9LwCFcg7MgodoXQAWw.

30. Haughney, Christine, and Nicole Perlroth. 2013. "Times site is disrupted in attack by hackers." *New York Times*, August 27, 2013. Accessed March 14, 2014. Available at http://www.nytimes.com/2013/08/28/business/media/hacking-attack-is-suspected-on-times-web-site.html?_r=0.

31. Brandom, Russell. 2013. "New York Times and Twitter hack traced by to a single spear phishing email." *The Verge*, August 23, 2013. Accessed March 15, 2014. Available at http://www.theverge.com/2013/8/28/4668346/new-york-times-twitter-hack-linked-to-phishing-email-syrian-electronic-army/in/5114785.

32. Sanger 2014.

33. Kaspersky Lab. 2013. "Kaspersky Lab identifies 'Red October,' an advanced cyber-espionage campaign targeting diplomatic and government institutions

world wide." *Kaspersky Lab*, January 14, 2013. Accessed March 2, 2014. Available at http://www.kaspersky.com/about/news/virus/2013/Kaspersky_Lab_Identifies_ Operation_Red_October_an_Advanced_Cyber_Espionage_Campaign_ Targeting_Diplomatic_and_Government_Institutions_Worldwide.

34. Collinson, M. 2013. "'Red October' virus programmers mining state secrets for highest bidder," *Defence Report*, February 9, 2013. Accessed May 30, 2013. Available at http://defencereport.com/red-october-virus-programmers-mining-state-secrets-for-highest-bidder/.

Egan, M. 2013. "'Red October' malware: What you need to know," *PC Advisor*, January 18, 2013. Accessed June 1, 2013. Available at http://www.pcadvisor.co.uk/how-to/security/3421342/red-october-malware-what-you-need-know/#ixzz2UmbZ0ViR.

35. Egan 2013.
36. Egan 2013.
37. Egan 2013.
38. Tselikov, Andrey. 2013. "Russian internet surveillance: Meet the new boss, same as the old boss." *Global Voices Advocacy*, November 1, 2013. Accessed February 23, 2014. Available at http://advocacy.globalvoicesonline.org/2013/11/01/russian-internet-surveillance-meet-the-new-boss-same-as-the-old-boss/.

39. Lardinois, F. 2013. "Eugene Kaspersky and Mikko Hypponen talk Red October and the future of cyber warfare at DLD," *TechCrunch* website, January 21, 2013. Accessed May 30, 2013. Available at [http://techcrunch.com/2013/01/21/eugene-kaspersky-and-mikko-hypponen-talk-red-october-and-the-future-of-cyber-warfare-at-dld/.

40. Kaspersky 2013.
41. Egan 2013.
42. Constantin, L. 2013. "Java exploit used in Red October cyberespionage attacks, researchers say," *PC Advisor*, January 15, 2013. Accessed May 30, 2013. Available at http://www.pcadvisor.co.uk/news/security/3420649/java-exploit-used-in-red-october-cyberespionage-attacks-researchers-say/#ixzz2UmdYhlqp.

43. McAfee. 2012. "57% believe at cyber arms race is currently taking place, reveals McAfee-sponsored cyber defense report." *McAfee*, January 30, 2012. Accessed March 2, 2014. Available at http://www.mcafee.com/us/about/news/2012/q1/20120130-02.aspx.

44. William and Mary. 2014. "Teaching Research, and International Policy (TRIP)." Accessed March 24, 2014. Available at http://irtheoryandpractice.wm.edu/projects/trip/FP-IvoryTower_Survey_2012.pdf.

45. Valeriano, Brandon. 2012. "Mind the cyber gap? Deterrence in cyberspace." *Atlantic Council*, July 11, 2012. Accessed March 4, 2014. Available at http://www.acus.org/new_atlanticist/mind-cyber-gap-deterrence-cyberspace.

## CHAPTER 8

1. Shengnan, Zhao, and Wu Jiao. 2013. "China calls for cyber rules." *China Daily*, October 3, 2013. Accessed March 4, 2014. Available at http://usa.chinadaily.com.cn/china/2013-03/10/content_16295060.htm.

2. Wohlstetter, John C. 2013. "Chinese 'hackers' is a misnomer. They're spies." *Wall Street Journal*, March 12, 2013. Accessed May 30, 2013. Available at http://online.wsj.com/article/SB10001424127887323978104578332020833172726.html?mod=WSJ_Opinion_LEFTTopOpinion&buffer_share=a2781&utm_source=buffer.

3. The two states have accounted for a combined 75 cyber incidents and 41 disputes.

4. Perlroth, Nicole. 2013. "Hackers in China attacked the *Times* for last 4 months." *New York Times*, January 30, 2013. Available at http://www.nytimes.com/

2013/01/31/technology/chinese-hackers-infiltrate-new-york-times-computers. html?pagewanted=all.

5. Mazzetti, Mark, and David E. Sanger. 2013. "Security leader says US would retaliate against cyberattacks." *New York Times*, March 12, 2013. Accessed March 2, 2014. Available at http://www.nytimes.com/2013/03/13/us/intelligence-official-warns-congress-that-cyberattacks-pose-threat-to-us.html?smid=tw-share&_r=0.

6. The recently released Tallinn Manual is an amalgamation of international law and the Just War tradition, used to delineate rules for cyber operations. Much like the issue with the legal tradition in cyber operations, the manual goes to great lengths to justify operations in a legal sense rather than to untangle what practices might be just or ethical in cyber operations.

7. An example of the confused discussion in the Tallinn Manual is on page 37, where the manual seems to imply that it is justified to attack State B's irrigation facilities if State B is attacking a "electrical generating facility at a dam in State A in order to coerce A into increasing the flow of water into a river running through both states." While the action may be proportional in the strictest definition of the term, it is unclear if the retribution by State A is related at all to the attack by State B.

8. Here we are focused on the use of cyber weapons by states rather than individuals. States have ethical constraints under the community of nations, while individuals are not similarly restricted. Fortunately, this issue does not limit the application of our arguments; since cyber operations are so costly and complicated, it is unlikely that an individual can conduct a serious cyber operation without the help of state-based resources.

9. This operation does not reach the level of war since it did not include 1,000 battle deaths under the Correlates of War definition of war.

10. Boulanin, Vincent. 2013. "Arms production goes cyber: A challenge for arms control." *SPIRI*, May 2013. Accessed March 4, 2014. Available at http://www.sipri.org/media/newsletter/essay/Boulanin_May13.

11. Ackerman, Spencer. 2011. "With Stuxnet, did the U.S. and Israel create a new cyberwar era?" *Wired*, January 16, 2011. Accessed May 28, 2013. Available at http://www.wired.com/dangerroom/2011/01/with-stuxnet-did-the-u-s-and-israel-create-a-new-cyberwar-era/.

12. *Jus in bello* refers to the law of the conduct of warfare, while *jus ad bellum* refers to the justification for the war in the first place. http://www.icrc.org/eng/war-and-law/ihl-other-legal-regmies/jus-in-bello-jus-ad-bellum/index.jsp.

13. In fact, many think the Shamoon virus that attacked Saudi Arabian oil control facilities was launched by Iran as retaliation for Stuxnet.

14. Koh, Harold. 2012. "International law in cyberspace." *US Department of State*, September 18, 2012. Accessed March 15, 2013. Available at http://www.state.gov/s/l/releases/remarks/197924.htm.

15. Ibid.

16. Ibid.

17. That these concerns might not limit action by non-state actors or terrorists is beside the point. The laws of war apply to states, not individuals acting beyond the state. We can only analyze, control, and incentive actions by conventional states since these are the actors under the justification of international law and the court of public opinion.

18. Shachtman, Noah. 2013. "This Pentagon project makes cyberwar as easy as angry birds." *Wired*, May 28, 2013. Accessed April 22, 2014. Available at http://www.wired.com/dangerroom/2013/05/pentagon-cyberwar-angry-birds/.

19. The Tallinn Manual (p. 144) suggests that cyber operations that are discriminate in nature are allowed, yet it is impossible to determine if any cyber operation can ever be truly discriminate due to the nature of the domain.

20. For more detailed information about this incident, see Folkenflik, David. 2013. "New York Times the target of chinese cyber attack." *Npr.org*, January 31, 2013. Accessed March 4, 2014. Available at http://www.npr.org/2013/01/31/170787379/ new-york-times-the-target-of-chinese-cyber-attack.

21. The Tallinn Manual seems to suggest it is acceptable to attack someone engaged in cyber warfare if he or she has an Internet-accessible pacemaker, and as long as the operation is meant to terminate the target, not to bring about pain. This is a perverse set of logics and tenuous in that health systems are now justified as targets under certain considerations. We believe that this line violates the core principles of the Just War tradition in its goal to forestall violence. Violence to end violence might be justified, but it should not be acceptable in this context because the violence is perpetrated through what generally is a life-saving device (a pacemaker), not a mode of warfare.

22. Fisher, Max. 2013. "Leaked documents hint at Obama's emerging cyberwar doctrine." *Washington Post*, June 7, 2013. Accessed March 4, 2014. Available at http://www.washingtonpost.com/blogs/worldviews/wp/2013/06/07/leaked-documents-hint-at-obamas-emerging-cyberwar-doctrine/.

## CHAPTER 9

1. Gross, Michael J. 2013. "Silent War." *Vanity Fair*, July 2013. Accessed August 23, 2013. Available at http://www.vanityfair.com/culture/2013/07/new-cyberwar-victims-american business?goback=%2Egde_1836487_member_247473541.

2. Groll, Elias. 2013. "PRISM continues US government of tradition of death by PowerPoint." *Foreign Policy*, June 7, 2013. Accessed June 15, 2013. Available at http:// blog.foreignpolicy.com/posts/2013/06/07/prism_continues_us_government_ tradition_of_death_by_powerpoint.

3. Friedersdorf, Conor. 2013. "What if China hacks the NSA's massive data trove?" *The Atlantic*, June 8, 2013. Accessed July 1, 2013. Available at http://www.theatlantic.com/technology/archive/2013/06/what-if-china-hacks-the-nsas-massive-data-trove/276637/.

4. https://wits.nctc.gov/FederalDiscoverWITS/index.do?N=0.

5. Elder, Miriam. (2013). "Russian guard service reverts to typewriters after NSA leaks." *The Guardian*, July 11, 2013. Accessed October 12, 2013. http://www.theguardian.com/world/2013/jul/11/russia-reverts-paper-nsa-leaks.

6. Valeriano, Brandon. "Cyber hype: Flame, Stuxnet, and Boeing 787's falling from the sky." *Atlantic Council: New Atlanticist, Policy and Analysis Blog*, August 7, 2012. Available at http://www.acus.org/new_atlanticist/cyber-hype-flame-stuxnet-and-boeing-787s-falling-sky.

7. European Commission. 2013. "EU cybersecurity plan to protect open internet and online freedom and opportunity—Cyber security strategy and proposal for directive." July 2, 2013. Accessed April 3, 2014. Available at http://ec.europa.eu/digital-agenda/ en/news/eu-cybersecurity-plan-protect-open-internet-and-online-freedom-and -opportunity-cyber-security.

8. Shanker, Thom, and David E. Sanger. 2013. "US helps allies trying to battle Iranian hackers." *New York Times*, June 8, 2013. Accessed April 3, 2014. Available at http:// www.nytimes.com/2013/06/09/world/middleeast/us-helps-allies-trying-to-battle-iranian-hackers.html?smid=tw-share&_r=1&pagewanted=all&.

9. Simeone, Nick. 2013. "Hagel, Dempsey discuss North Korea, Iran, cyber challenges." *US Department of Defense*, June 11, 2013. Accessed April 4, 2014. Available at http://www.defense.gov/news/newsarticle.aspx?id=120257.

10. Valeriano, Brandon, and Ryan Maness. 2013. "Perceptions and opinions of the cyber threat." *Duck of Minerva*, January 23, 2013. Accessed February 22, 2013. Available at http://www.whiteoliphaunt.com/duckofminerva/2013/01/perceptions-and-opinions-of-the-cyber-threat.html.

11. Ibid.

12. Ibid.

13. Review. 2013. "A damning verdict on the bombing campaign in Europe during the Second World War." *The Economist*, September 19, 2013. Accessed February 2, 2014. Available at http://www.economist.com/news/books-and-arts/21586520-damning-verdict-bombing-campaign-europe-during-second-world-war-costly.

14. Sanger, David E. 2013. "NSA leaks make pan for cyberdefense unlikely." *New York Times*, August 12, 2013. Accessed March 4, 2014. Available at http://www.nytimes.com/2013/08/13/us/nsa-leaks-make-plan-for-cyberdefense-unlikely.html?smid=tw-share&pagewanted=all.

15. Parroting the famous phrase, "Who watches the Watchmen?"

# REFERENCES

Albright, D., P. Brannan, and C. Walrond. 2011. "Stuxnet Malware and Natanz: Update of ISIS December 22, 2010 Report," *Institute for Science and International Security Report*, February 15, 2011. Available at http://isis-online.org/uploads/isisreports/documents/stuxnet_update_15Feb2011.pdf.

Andres, Richard. 2012. "The Emerging Structure of Strategic Cyber Offense, Cyber Defense, and Cyber Deterrence." In *Cyberspace and National Security: Threats, Opportunities, and Power in a Virtual World*, Derek Reveron, Ed. (Washington, DC: Georgetown University Press).

Aquinas, Thomas. 1988. *St. Thomas Aquinas on Politics and Ethics*. Translated and Edited by Paul E. Sigmund (New York: W.W. Norton and Company).

Arquilla, John, and David Ronfeldt. 1993. "Cyberwar Is Coming!" *Comparative Strategy* 12 (2): 141–165.

Arquilla, John, and David Ronfeldt. 1996. "The Advent of Netwar." In *Athena's Camp: Preparing for Conflict in the Information Age*, MR-789-OSD, 1996 (Copyright 1996 RAND): 275–293.

Axelrod, Robert. 1986. "An Evolutionary Approach to Norms." *American Political Science Review* 80 (4): 1095–1111.

Azar, Edward E. 1972. "Conflict Escalation and Conflict Reduction in an International Crisis, Suez 1956." *Journal of Conflict Resolution* 16 (2): 183–201.

Baldwin, David A. 1985. *Economic Statecraft* (Princeton, NJ: Princeton University Press).

Barzashka, Ivanka. 2013. "Are Cyber-Weapons Effective?" *The RUSI Journal* 158 (2): 48–56.

Beardsley, Kyle, and Victor Asal. 2009. "Winning with the Bomb." *Journal of Conflict Resolution* 58 (2): 278–302.

Beckley, Michael. 2012. "China's Century? Why America's Edge Will Endure." *International Security* 36 (3): 41–78.

Bennett, D. Scott, and Allan C. Stam. 2000. "Research Design and Estimator Choices in the Analysis of Interstate Dyads: When Decisions Matter." *Journal of Conflict Resolution* 44 (5): 653–685.

Berger, Peter L., and Thomas Luckmann. 1967. *The Social Construction of Reality: A Treatise on the Sociology of Knowledge* (New York: Anchor Books).

Betts, Richard. 2013. "The Lost Logic of Deterrence." *Foreign Affairs*. March/April.

Betz, David J., and Tim Stevens. 2013. "Analogical Reasoning and Cyber Security." *Security Dialogue* 44 (2): 147–164.

Billow, Charles G., and Welton Chang. 2004. "Cyber Warfare: An Analysis of the Means and Motivations of Selected Nation States." *Institute for Security and Technology Studies at Dartmouth College*. November 2004. http://www.ists.dartmouth.edu/docs/cyberwarfare.pdf.

Bremer, Stuart A. 1992. "Dangerous Dyads: Conditions Affecting the Likelihood of Interstate War 1816–1965." *Journal of Conflict Resolution* 36 (2): 309–341.

Brenner, Joel. 2013. "Grey Matter: How to Fight Chinese Cyber Attacks Without Starting a Cold War." *Foreign Policy*, March 8, 2013. http://www.foreignpolicy.com/articles/2013/03/08/gray_matter#.UUOTPw6Wj4g.email.

Brodie, Bernard, ed. 1946. *The Absolute Weapon: Atomic Power and World Order* (New York: Harcourt Brace).

Bronk, Christopher, and Eneken Tikk-Ringas. 2013. "Hack of Attack? Shamoon and the Evolution of Cyber Conflict." *James A. Baker III Institute for Public Policy Working Paper*.

Brown, Chris. 2007. "Tragedy, 'Tragic Choices' and Contemporary International Political Theory." *International Relations* 21(1): 5–13.

Bueno de Mesquita, Bruce. 1981. *The War Trap* (New Haven, CT, and London: Yale University Press).

Bulley, Dan. 2010. "The Politics of Ethical Foreign Policy: A Responsibility to Protect Whom?" *European Journal of International Relations* 16 (3): 441–461.

Carr, Jeffrey. 2010. *Inside Cyber Warfare* (Sebastopol, CA: O'Reilly Media).

Chansoria, Monika. 2012. "Defying Borders in Future Conflict in East Asia: Chinese Capabilities in the Realm of Information Warfare and Cyber Space." *Journal of East Asian Affairs* 26 (1): http://international.vlex.com/vid/borders-conflict-capabilities-cyber-421050858.

Chenoweth, E., and M. J. Stephan. 2011. *Why Civil Resistance Works: The Strategic Logic of Nonviolent Conflict* (New York: Columbia University Press).

Chittister, Clyde G., and Yacov Y. Haimes. 2011. "The Role of Modeling in the Resilience of Cyberinfrastructure Systems and Preparedness for Cyber Intrusions." *Journal of Homeland Security and Emergency Management* 8 (1): Article 6, 1–18.

Choucri, Nazli. 2012. *Cyberpolitics in International Relations* (Cambridge, MA: MIT Press).

Choucri, Nazli, and Robert C. North. 1975. *Nations in Conflict: National Growth and International Violence* (San Francisco, CA: Freeman).

Christensen, Thomas J. 2006. "Fostering Stability or Creating a Monster? The Rise of China and U.S. Policy Toward East Asia." *International Security* 31 (1): 81–126.

Cioffi-Revilla, Claudio. 2009. "Modelling Deterrence in Cyberia." In *Modelling Cyber Security: Approaches, Methodology, Strategies*, Umberto Gori, Ed. (Amsterdam: IOS Press): 125–131.

Clapper, James R. 2013. "Statement for the Record: Worldwide Threat Assessment of the US Intelligence Community." Senate Select Committee on Intelligence. March 12, 2013.

Clarke, Richard A., and Robert K. Knake. 2010. *Cyber War: The Next Threat to National Security and What to Do About It* (New York: Harper Collins.)

Clausewitz, Carl von. 2007 Reprint. *On War*. Translated by J. J. Graham (New York: BN Publishing).

Colaresi, Michael. 2005. *Scare Tactics: The Politics of International Rivalry* (Syracuse, NY: Syracuse University Press).

Conrad, Justin. 2011. "Interstate Rivalry and Terrorism: An Unprobed Look." *Journal of Conflict Resolution* 55 (4): 529–555.

Cook, James. 2010. "'Cyberation' and Just War Doctrine: A Response to Randall Dipert." *Journal of Military Ethics* 9 (4): 411–423.

Cortell, Andrew, and James Davis. 1996. "How Do International Institutions Matter? The Domestic Impact of International Rules and Norms." *International Studies Quarterly* 40 (4): 451–478.

Crescenzi, Mark J. C. 2007. "Reputation and Interstate Conflict." *American Journal of Political Science* 52 (2): 382–396.

Cronin, Audrey K. 2013. "Why Drones Fail: When Tactics Drive Strategy." *Foreign Affairs*, July/August 2013.

Danner, Mark. 2014. "In the Darkness of Dick Cheney." *The New York Review of Books*, March 6.

Davi, Marco. 2010. "Cyber Security: European Strategies and Prospects for Global Cooperation." Presented at the *European Security and Defense Forum*, November 11, 2010.

Dehlawi, Zakariya, and Norah Abkhodair. 2013. "Saudi Arabia's Response to Cyber Conflict: A Case Study of the Shamoon Malware Incident." *Intelligence and Security Informatics*, 2012 IEEE International Conference, June 4–7, 2013, 73–75.

Demchak, Chris. 2011. *Wars of Disruption and Resilience* (Athens: University of Georgia Press).

Denning, D. E. 2012. "Stuxnet: What Has Changed?" *Future Internet* 4 (3): 672–687.

Devine, Thomas J. 2009. *Accommodation within Middle Eastern Strategic Rivalries: Iranian Policy Towards Saudi Arabia 1988 to 2005*. Doctoral Thesis, McGill University, Montreal, QE. Accessed March 20, 2014. Available at http://digitool.library.mcgill.ca/webclient/StreamGate?folder_id=0&dvs=1395091457520~487.

DeRouen, Karl R., and Jacob Bercovitch 2008. "Enduring Internal Rivalries: A New Framework for the Study of Civil War." *Journal of Peace Research* 45 (1): 55–74.

Diehl, Paul F., and Gary Goertz. 2000. *War and Peace in International Rivalry* (Ann Arbor: University of Michigan Press).

Dipert, Randall. 2010. "The Ethics of Cyberwarfare." *Journal of Military Ethics* 9 (4): 384–410.

Dolan, Thomas. 2013. "Unthinkable and Tragic: The Psychology of Weapons Taboos in War." *International Organization* 67(1): 37–63.

Dugan, Laura, and Erica Chenoweth. 2013. "Moving Beyond Deterrence: The Effectiveness of Raising the Expected Utility of Abstaining from Terrorism in Israel." *American Sociological Review* 77 (4): 597–624.

Dunn-Cavelty, Miriam. 2008. *Cyber-Security and Threat Politics: US Efforts to Secure the Information Age* (New York: Routledge).

Easton, David. 1953. *The Political System: An Inquiry into the State of Political Science* (New York: Alfred A. Knopf).

Eberle, Christopher J. 2012. "Just Cause and Cyber War" (April 30, 2012). Available at SSRN: http://ssrn.com/abstract=2048447.

Eriksson, Johan, and Giampiero Giacomello. 2009. "Who Controls the Internet, and Under What Conditions?" *International Studies Review* 11: 205–230.

Farwell, James P., and Rafal Rohozinski. 2011. "Stuxnet and the Future of Cyber War." *Survival* 53 (1): 23–40.

Fearon, James D. 1995. "Rationalist Explanations for War." *International Organization* 49 (3): 379–414.

Feklyunina, Valentina. 2008. "Battle for Perceptions: Projecting Russia in the West." *Europe Asia Studies* 60 (4): 605–629.

Ferwerda, Jeremy, Nazli Choucri, and Stuart Madnick. 2011. "Institutional Foundations for Cyber Security: Current Responses and New Challenges." *Working Paper CISL # 2011-05*. September 2011.

Fielder, James D. 2013. "Bandwidth Cascades: Escalation and Pathogen Models for Cyber Conflict Diffusion." *Small Wars Journal*, June 19, 2013. Available at http://smallwarsjournal.com/jrnl/art/bandwidth-cascades-escalation-and-pathogen-models-for-cyber-conflict-diffusion.

Finnemore, M., and K. Sikkink. 1998. "International Norm Dynamics and Political Change." *International Organization* 52 (4): 887–917.

Fixdal, Mona, and Dan Smith. 1998. "Humanitarian Intervention and Just War." *Mershon International Studies Review* 42: 283–312.

Gartzke, Erik. 2013. "The Myth of Cyberwar: Bringing War on the Internet Back Down to Earth." *International Security* 38 (2): 41–73.

Gartzke, Erik, and Michael W. Simon. 1999. "Hot Hand: A Critical Analysis of Enduring Rivalries." *Journal of Politics* 61 (3): 777–798.

Geers, Kenneth. 2010. "Cyber Weapons Convention." *Computer Law and Security Review* 26 (5): 547–551.

George, Alexander L., and Andrew Bennett. 2005. *Case Studies and Theory Development in the Social Sciences* (Cambridge, MA: MIT Press).

Ghosn, Faten, Glen Palmer, and Stuart Bremer. 2004. "The MID3 Data Set, 1993–2001: Procedures, Coding Rules, and Description." *Conflict Management and Peace Science* 21: 133–154.

Goldstein, Joshua S. 1992. "A Conflict-Cooperation Scale for WEIS Events Data." *Journal of Conflict Resolution* 36 (2): 369–385.

Goodman, Will. 2010. "Cyber Deterrence: Tougher in Theory Than in Practice?" *Strategic Studies Quarterly*, Fall 2010.

Guinchard, Audrey. 2011. "Between Hype and Understatement: Reassessing Cyber Risks as a Security Strategy." *Journal of Strategic Security* 2: 75–96.

Guitton, Clement. 2013. "Cyber Insecurity as a National Threat: Overreaction from Germany, France, and the UK?" *European Security*. doi: 10.1080/09662839.2012.749864.

Gvodsev, Nicholas K. 2012. "The Bear Goes Digital: Russia and Its Cyber Capabilities." In *Cyberspace and National Security*, Derek Reveron, Ed. (Washington, DC: Georgetown University Press).

Hansen, Lene. 2011. "Theorizing the Image for Security Studies: Visual Securitization and the Muhammad Cartoon Crisis." *European Journal of International Relations* 17 (1): 51–74.

Hansen, Lene, and Helen Nissenbaum. 2009. "Digital Disaster, Cyber Security, and the Copenhagen School." *International Studies Quarterly* 53: 1155–1175.

Healey, Jason. Ed. 2013. *A Fierce Domain: Conflict in Cyberspace 1986–2012* (Washington, DC: Cyber Conflict Studies Association).

Heinze, Eric, and Brent Steele. 2009. "Introduction: Non-state Actors and the Just War Tradition." In *Ethics, Authority, and War: Non-State Actors and the Just War Tradition*, Eric Heinze and Brent Steele, Eds. (New York: Palgrave).

Hensel, Paul R., and Paul F. Diehl 1994. "It Takes Two to Tango: Nonmilitarized Response in Interstate Disputes." *Journal of Conflict Resolution* 38 (3): 479–506.

Hersh, Seymour. 2010. "The Online Threat: Should We Be Worried about Cyber War?" *New Yorker*, November 2010.

Himma, Kenneth. 2004. "The Moral Significance of the Internet in Information: Reflections on a Fundamental Moral Right to Information." *Journal of Information, Communication, and Ethics in Society* 2 (4): 191–201.

Hobbes, Thomas. 2009. *Leviathan*. Original print 1651 (New York: Seven Treasures).

Holsti, Ole R. 1992. "Public Opinion and Foreign Policy: Challenges to the Almond-Lippmann Consensus Mershon Series: Research Programs and Debates." *International Studies Quarterly* 36 (4): 439–436.

Howes, Dustin Ells. 2013. "The Failure of Pacifism and the Success of Nonviolence." *Perspectives on Politics* 11 (2): 427–446.

Huth, Paul K. 2009. *Standing Your Ground: Territorial Disputes and International Conflict* (Ann Arbor: University of Michigan Press).

Inkster, Nigel. 2013. "Chinese Intelligence in the Cyber Age." *Survival: Global Politics and Strategy* 55 (1): 45–66.

Jervis, Robert. 1979. "Deterrence Theory Revisited." *World Politics* 31 (2): 289–324.

Jervis, Robert. 1989. *The Meaning of the Nuclear Revolution: Statecraft and the Prospect of Armageddon* (Ithaca, NY: Cornell University Press).

Kahn, Herman. 1960. *On Thermonuclear War* (Princeton, NJ: Princeton University Press).

Kallberg, Jan, and Bhavani Thuraisingham. 2013. "State Actors Offensive Cyberoperations: The Disruptive Power of Systematic Cyberattacks." *IT Pro* (May/June): 32–35.

Karatzogianni, Athina. 2010a. "The Thorny Triangle: Cyber Conflict, Business, and the Sino-American Relationship in the Global System." *Selected Works* Online Academic Forum, March 2010. Accessed March 28, 2014. Available at http://works.bepress.com/athina_karatzogianni/11.

Karatzogianni, Athina. 2010b. "Blame It on the Russians: Tracking the Portrayal of Russian Hackers during Cyber Conflict Incidents." *Digital Icons: Studies in Russian, Eurasian, and Central European New Media* 4: 127–150.

Kello, Lucas. 2013. "The Meaning of the Cyber Revolution: Perils to Theory and Statecraft." *International Security* 38 (2): 7–40.

Kelsey, Jeffrey T. G. 2008. "Hacking into International Humanitarian Law: The Principles of Distinction and Neutrality in the Age of Cyber Warfare." *Michigan Law Review* 106: 1428–1452.

Kerr, P. K., Rollins, J. and Theohary, C. A. 2010. "The Stuxnet Computer Worm: Harbinger of an Emerging Warfare Capability," *CRS Report for Congress* R41524 (Washington, DC: Congressional Research Service, December 9, 2010). Available at http://www.fas.org/sgp/crs/natsec/R41524.pdf.

King, Gary, and Will Lowe. 2003. "An Automated Information Extraction Tool for International Conflict Data with Performance as Good as Human Coders: A Rare Events Evaluation Design." *International Organization* 57 (3): 617–642.

Klein, James P., Gary Goertz, and Paul F. Diehl. 2006. "The New Rivalry Dataset: Procedures and Patterns." *Journal of Peace Research* 43 (3): 331–348.

Kugler, Richard L. 2009. "Deterrence of Cyber Attacks." In *Cyberpower and National Security*, Franklin D. Kramer, Stuart H. Starr, and Larry K. Wentz, Eds. (Washington, DC: Potomac Books), 309–342.

Lardinois, F. 2013. "Eugene Kaspersky and Mikko Hypponen Talk Red October and the Future of Cyber Warfare at DLD." *TechCrunch* website, January 21, 2013. Accessed May 30, 2013. Available at http://techcrunch.com/2013/01/21/eugene-kaspersky-and-mikko-hypponen-talk-red-october-and-the-future-of-cyber-warfare-at-dld/.

Lawson, Sean. 2012. "Putting the 'War' in Cyberwar: Metaphor, Analogy, and Cybersecurity Discourse in the United States." *First Monday* 17 (7): 1–18.

Leng, Russell. 1993. *Interstate Crisis Behavior, 1816–1980: Realism Versus Reciprocity* (Cambridge: Cambridge University Press).

Leng, Russell J. 2000. "Escalation: Crisis Behavior and War." In *What Do We Know about War*, John A. Vasquez, Ed. (New York: Rowman and Littlefield).

Levy, Jack S., and William R. Thompson. 2010. "Balancing on Land and at Sea: Do States Ally Against the Leading Global Power?" *International Security* 35 (1): 7–43.

Lewis, James A. 2009. "The Korean Cyber Attacks and Their Implications for Cyber Conflict." *Center for Strategic and International Studies*, October 2009. Accessed June 14, 2013. Available at http://csis.org/publication/korean-cyber-attacks-and-their-implications-cyber-conflict.

Lewis, James A. 2010. "The Cyber War Has Not Begun." *Center for Strategic and International Studies*, March 2010. Accessed September 16, 2013. Available at http://csis.org/files/publication/100311_TheCyberWarHasNotBegun.pdf.

Lewis, James A. 2013. "Raising the Bar for Cybersecurity." *Center for Strategic and International Studies* Report, February 12, 2013.

Libicki, Martin C. 2007. *Conquest in Cyberspace* (Cambridge: Cambridge University Press).

Libicki, Martin C. 2009. *Cyberdeterrence and Cyberwar* (Santa Monica, CA: RAND).

Lindsay, Jon R. 2013. "Stuxnet and the Limits of Cyber Warfare." *Security Studies* 22 (3): 365–404.

Lorell, Mark, Julia Lowell, Michael Kennedy, and Hugh Levaux. 2000. *Cheaper, Faster, Better? Commercial Approaches to Weapons Acquisitions* (Washington, DC: RAND Corporation).

Lynch, William J., III. 2010. "Defending a New Domain." *Foreign Affairs* 89 (5): 97–108.

Machiavelli, Niccolo. 2003. *The Prince*, George Bull, Ed. (New York: Penguin Books).

Maness, Ryan C., and Brandon Valeriano. 2015. *Russia's Coercive Diplomacy: Energy, Cyber and Maritime Policy as New Sources of Power* (London: Palgrave Macmillan).

Mansbach, Richard W., and John A. Vasquez. 1981. *In Search of Theory* (New York: Columbia University Press).

Masters, Jonathan. 2012. "Hamas." *Council on Foreign Relations*, November 27, 2012. Accessed March 20, 2012. Available at http://www.cfr.org/israel/hamas/p8968#p1.

McClelland, Charles A. 1983. "Let the User Beware." *International Studies Quarterly* 27 (2): 169–177.

McGraw, Gary. 2013. "Cyber War is Inevitable (Unless We Build Security In)." *Journal of Security Studies* 36 (1): 109–119.

Maoz, Z., and B. San-Akca. 2012. "Rivalry and State Support of Non-State Armed Groups (NAGs), 1946–2011." *International Studies Quarterly* 56 (4): 720–734.

Mitchell, Sarah McLaughlin, and Cameron G. Thies. 2012. "Resource Curse in Reverse: How Civil Wars Influence Natural Resource Production." *International Interactions* 38 (2): 218–242.

Morgenthau, Hans J. 1948. *Politics Among Nations: The Struggle for Power and Peace*, Brief Edition (New York: McGraw-Hill).

Morgenthau, Hans. 1952. "Another 'Great Debate': The National Interest of the United States." *The American Political Science Review* 46 (4): 961–988.

Mueller, J. 2006. *Overblown: How Politicians and the Terrorism Industry Inflate National Security Threats, and Why We Believe Them* (New York: Free Press).

Murdie, Amanda. 2011. "Aiding and Abetting: Human Rights INGOs and Domestic Protest." *Journal of Conflict Resolution* 55 (2): 163.

Nissenbaum, Helen. 2005. "Where Computer Security Meets National Security." *Ethics and Information Technology* 7: 61–73.

Northcutt, Stephen. 2007. "Logic Bombs, Trojan Horses, and Trap Doors." *SANS Technology Institute Security Laboratory*. Accessed June 14, 2013. Available at http://www.sans.edu/research/security-laboratory/article/log-bmb-trp-door.

Nye, Joseph S. 2010. "Cyber Power." *Essay from the Belfer Center for Science and International Affairs, Harvard, Kennedy School*. May 2010.

Nye, Joseph. 2011a. "Nuclear Lessons for Cyber Security?" *Strategic Studies Quarterly* (Winter): 18–38.

Nye, Joseph. 2011b. *The Future of Power* (New York: Public Affairs).

O'Driscoll, Cian. 2008. *Renegotiation of the Just War Tradition and the Right to War in the Twenty-First Century* (New York: Palgrave Macmillan).

Onuf, Nicholas Greenwood. 1989. *World of Our Making: Rules and Rule in Social Theory and International Relations* (Columbia: University of South Carolina Press).

Pape, Robert A. 1996. *Bombing to Win: Air Power and Coercion in War* (Ithaca, NY: Cornell University Press).

Pattison, James. 2008. "Just War Theory and the Privatization of Military Force." *Ethics and International Affairs* 22 (2): 143–162.

Paul, Thaza Varkey, Patrick M. Morgan, and James J. Wirtz, eds. 2009. *Complex Deterrence: Strategy in the Global Age* (Chicago, IL: University of Chicago Press).

Peterson, Dale. 2013. "Offensive Cyber Weapons: Construction, Development, and Employment." *Journal of Strategic Studies* 36 (1): 120–124.

Potter, Ralph B. 1973. "The Moral Logic of War." In *Peace and War*, Charles R. Beitz and Theodore Herman, Eds. (San Francisco: W. H. Freeman and Company), 7–16.

Powell, Robert. 1999. *In the Shadow of Power: States and Strategies in International Politics* (Princeton, NJ: Princeton University Press).

Price, Richard. 1995. "A Genealogy of the Chemical Weapons Taboo." *International Organization* 49 (1): 613–644.

Price, Richard. 2013. "How Chemical Weapons Became Taboo, and Why Syria Won't Overturn the Aversion." *Foreign Affairs* Online. January 22, 2013. Accessed March 10, 2014. Available at http://www.foreignaffairs.com/articles/138771/richard-price/how-chemical-weapons-became-taboo.

Reveron, Derek. 2012a. "An Introduction to National Security and Cyberspace." In *Cyberspace and National Security: Threats, Opportunities, and Power in a Virtual World*, Derek Reveron, Ed. (Washington, DC: Georgetown University Press), 3–20.

Reveron, Derek. 2012b. "Conclusion." In *Cyberspace and National Security: Threats, Opportunities, and Power in a Virtual World*, Derek Reveron, Ed. (Washington, DC: Georgetown University Press), 225–230.

Richardson, Lewis Fry. 1960. *Arms and Insecurity* (Pittsburgh: Boxwood).

Rid, Thomas. 2011. "Cyberwar Will Not Take Place." *Journal of Strategic Studies*. First Article: 1–28.

Rid, Thomas, and Peter McBurney. 2012. "Cyber Weapons." *The RUSI Journal* 157 (1): 6–13.

Rid, Thomas. 2013. *Cyber War Will Not Take Place* (London: Hurst & Company).

Rowe, Neil C. 2008. "Ethics of Cyber War Attacks." In *Cyber Warfare and Cyber Terrorism*, Lech J. Janczewski and Andrew M. Colarik, Eds. (Hershey, PA: Information Science Reference).

Sagan, Scott D., and Kenneth N. Waltz. 1995. "The Spread of Nuclear Weapons: A Debate." *Foreign Affairs*, May/June 1995. Accessed March 20, 2014. Available at http://www.foreignaffairs.com/articles/50846/eliot-a-cohen/the-spread-of-nuclear-weapons-a-debate.

Saltzman, Ilai. 2013. "Cyber Posturing and the Offense-Defense Balance." *Contemporary Security Policy* 34 (1): 40–63.

Sample, Susan G. 1998. "Military Buildups, War, and Realpolitik." *Journal of Conflict Resolution* 42 (2): 156–175.

Sandler, Todd. 2011. "New Frontiers of Terrorism Research: An Introduction." *Journal of Peace Research* 48 (3): 279–286.

Sanger, David E. 2012a. *The Reckoning: How President Obama Has Changed the Force of American Power* (New York: Crown).

Sanger, David E. 2012b. *Confront and Conceal: Obama's Secret Wars and Surprising Use of American Power* (New York: Random House).

Sarkees, Meredith Reid, and Frank Whelon Wayman. 2010. *Resort to War: A Data Guide to Inter-State, Extra-State, Intra-state, and Non-State Wars, 1816–2007* (Washington, DC: CQ Press).

Schelling, T. C. 1966. *Arms and Influence* (New Haven, CT: Yale University Press).

Schmidt, Brain C. 2002. "On the History and the Historiography of International Relations." In *Handbook of International Relations*, Walter Carlsnaes, Thomas Risse, and Beth A. Simmons, Eds. (London: Sage Publications), 3–22.

Schmitt, Michael. 2013. "The Tallinn Manual on the International Law Applicable to Cyber Warfare." *NATO Cooperative Cyber Defence Center for Excellence*. Accessed May 31, 2013. Available at http://www.ccdcoe.org/249.html.

Schrodt, Philip A. 1993. "Event Data in Foreign Policy Analysis." In *Foreign Policy Analysis: Continuity and Change in Its Second Generation*, Laura Neack, Patrick J. Haney and Jeanne A. K. Hey, Eds. (New York: Prentice Hall).

Semjonov, Aleksei. 2007. "Bronze Soldier: April Crisis." *Legal Information Center for Human Rights*, Accessed March 20, 2014. Available at http://www.lichr.ee/main/assets/engbn.pdf

Senese, Paul D., and John A Vasquez. 2008. *The Steps to War: An Empirical Study* (Princeton, NJ: Princeton University Press).

Shannon, Vaughn P. and Jonathan W. Keller. 2006. "Leadership Style and International Norm Violation: The Case of the Iraq War." *Foreign Policy Analysis* 3 (1): 79–104.

Sheldon, John. 2012. "Toward a Theory of Cyber Power: Strategic Purpose in Peace and War." In *Cyberspace and National Security: Threats, Opportunities, and Power in a Virtual World*, Derek Reveron, Ed. (Washington, DC: Georgetown University Press), 207–224.

Singer, J. David. 1972. "The 'Correlates of War' Project: Interim Report and Rationale." *World Politics* 24 (2): 243–270.

Singer, P. W., and Allan Friedman. 2014. *Cybersecurity and Cyberwar: What Everyone Needs to Know* (Oxford: Oxford University Press).

Snidal, Duncan. 1985. "Coordination versus Prisoner's Dilemma: Implications for International Cooperation and Regimes." *American Political Science Review* 79: 923–942.

Stone, John. 2012. "Cyber War Will Take Place!" *Journal of Strategic Studies*. doi: 10.1080/0 1402390.2012.730485.

Tannenwald, Nina. 1999. "The Nuclear Taboo: The United States and the Normative Basic of Nuclear Non-Use." *International Organization* 53(3): 433–468.

Thompson, William. 2001. "Identifying Rivals and Rivalries in World Politics." *International Studies Quarterly* 45: 557–586.

Valeriano, Brandon. 2013. *Becoming Rivals: The Process of Interstate Rivalry Development* (New York: Routledge).

Valeriano, Brandon, and John A. Vasquez. 2011. "Paths to War and Peace in a Post-American World." In *What Lies Ahead? Debating the Prospects for a Post American World*, S. Hogue, S. Clark, and S. Stairs, Eds. (Toronto: University of Toronto Press).

Valeriano, Brandon, and Ryan C. Maness. 2012. "Persistent Enemies and Cybersecurity: The Future of Rivalry in an Age of Information Warfare." In *Cyber Challenges and National Security*, D. Reveron, Ed. (Washington, DC: Georgetown University Press).

Valeriano, Brandon, and Ryan Maness. 2012. "The Fog of Cyberwar: Why the Threat Doesn't Live Up to the Hype." *Foreign Affairs*. Available at http://www.foreignaffairs.com/articles/138443/brandon-valeriano-and-ryan-maness/the-fog-of-cyberwar?page=show#.

Valeriano, Brandon, and Ryan C. Maness. 2014. "The Dynamics of Cyber Conflict Between Rival Antagonists, 2001–2011." *Journal of Peace Research* 51 (3): 347–360.

Vasquez, John A. 1991. "The Deterrence Myth: Nuclear Weapons and the Prevention of Nuclear War." In *The Long Postwar Peace: Contending Explanations and Projections,* Charles W. Kegley, Jr., Ed. (New York: HarperCollins).

Vasquez, John A. 1993. *The War Puzzle* (Cambridge: Cambridge University Press).

Vasquez, John A. 1995. "Why Do Neighbors Fight? Proximity, Interaction, or Territoriality." *Journal of Peace Research* 32 (3): 277–293.

Vasquez, John A. 1999. *The Power of Power Politics: From Classical Realism to Neotraditionalism* (Cambridge: Cambridge University Press).

Vasquez, John, and Marie Henehan. 2001. "Territorial Disputes and the Probability of War, 1816–1992." *Journal of Peace Research* 38(2): 123–138.

Vasquez, John, and Christopher S. Leskiw. 2001. "The Origins and War-proneness of International Rivalries." *Annual Review of Political Science* 4: 295–316.

Vasquez, John A., and Brandon Valeriano. 2010. "Classification of Interstate Wars." *Journal of Politics* 72 (2): 292–309.

Wallensteen, Peter. 1984. "Universalism vs. Particularism: On the Limits of Major Power Order." *Journal of Peace Research* 21 (3): 243–257.

Waltz, Kenneth N. 1979. *Theory of International Politics* (New York: Columbia University Press).

Waltzer, Michael. 1977. *Just and Unjust Wars: A Moral Argument with Historical Illustrations.* 3rd ed. (New York: Basic Books).

Waltzer, Michael. 2006. *Just and Unjust Wars: A Moral Argument with Historical Illustrations.* 4th ed. (New York: Basic Books).

White House. 2011. "International Strategy for Cyberspace: Prosperity, Security, and Openness in a Networked World." May 2011. Press.

Wright, Quincy. 1965. *A Study of War.* 2nd ed. (Chicago, IL: University of Chicago Press).

Yannakogergos, P. A. 2013. "Keep Cyberwar Narrow." *The National Interest* website, May 17, 2013. Accessed June 18, 2013. Available at http://nationalinterest.org/commentary/keep-cyberwar-narrow-8459.

Zagare, Frank C., and D. Marc Kilgour. 2000. *Perfect Deterrence* (Cambridge: Cambridge University Press).

Ziliak, Thomas Z., and Deidre N. McCloskey. 2008. *The Cult of Statistical Significance: How the Standard Error Costs Us Jobs, Justice, and Lives* (Ann Arbor: University of Michigan Press).

# INDEX